A PRIME MINISTER ON PRIME MINISTERS

End papers
A drawing of No. 10 Downing Street seen from the Foreign Office in 1932 by W. Monk.

HAROLD WILSON

A PRIME MINISTER ON PRIME MINISTERS

WEIDENFELD AND NICOLSON
and
MICHAEL JOSEPH

Weidenfeld & Nicolson
11 St John's Hill London SW11

and

Michael Joseph
52 Bedford Square London WC1

ISBN 0 718 11625 9

Made and printed in Great Britain by
Butler and Tanner Ltd, Frome and London

CONTENTS

A nineteenth-century engraving of the interior of the House of Commons.

Introduction:
The First Prime Ministers

This study of Britain's first Prime Ministers begins with Sir Robert Walpole, acclaimed by the common consent of historians as the 'first Prime Minister'.

The phrase was neither new nor complimentary. It carried with it the implication of 'Court favourite'; what was disliked and distrusted was the monopolization of power and royal patronage in the hands of a single minister. It had been derisorily used of Queen Anne's 'Managers', Godolphin and Harley: in their case the insult was based on a comparison with the servile advisers of Louis XIV. But even earlier, in the 1670s, Charles II's principal official, Danby, had been so described.

There had always been 'favoured men of business' going back to Joseph in ancient Egypt. In England there had been Henry VII's Morton, Henry VIII's Wolsey and Cromwell, Elizabeth's Burghley, James I's Cecil and Carr and Charles I's Buckingham and Strafford.

Walpole was at pains to deny that he was a Prime Minister: so did Grenville in the 1760s and Lord North a decade later. More frequently used were the terms 'sole minister' – a description highly unpopular in the Parliament of the day – and 'first minister'. Another phrase used was simply 'minister'. Gouverneur Morris, who played a leading part in the drafting of the Constitution of the United States, explained the provisions relating to the Presidency: 'Our President will be the British Minister' – which, of course, he has never been.

But increasingly the post of First Minister was signified by the tenure of that of First Lord of the Treasury. As Lord Blake has put it: 'It seems best to regard the First Lord of the Treasury as Prime Minister unless there is some palpable reason to the contrary.'

The exception was Pitt the Elder (Chatham) who was never First Lord: he controlled two of his administrations with the nominal title of Secretary of State for the Southern Department. In the third, during which ill health and mental stress overcame him, the Duke of Grafton was the nominal head, with Pitt, until his illness, in real control, holding the post of Lord Privy Seal.

Although the title 'Prime Minister' became more general, it had no legal warrant until comparatively modern times. It was used in an official document for the first time in 1878 when Disraeli signed the final instrument of the Congress of Berlin as 'First Lord of the Treasury and Prime Minister of Her Britannic Majesty'. The Prime Minister did not appear in the Order of Precedence at Buckingham Palace until 1904, when he was accorded precedence after the Archbishop of York. Until then he had to defer in Court terms to quite junior members of his administration, usually Government Whips who held – as they do today – such nominal Court appointments as Vice-Treasurer or Vice-Chamberlain of the Household. The first statutory recognition of the Prime Minister was the Chequers Estates Act, 1917, which provided that Chequers, given to the nation by Lord Lee of Fareham, should be occupied by the 'Crown's First Minister'.

From the late eighteenth century onwards the head of Government always took the title of First Lord. The only exceptions were Salisbury, who appointed Northcote, W.H. Smith and Balfour as First Lord. In that capacity each in turn lived in 10 Downing Street, since No. 10 is reserved not for the Prime Minister but for the First Lord – as witness the plaque on the door. The practice by which Prime Ministers are also First Lord is unlikely to change in the future, since the Ministers of the Crown Act, 1937, and subsequent legislation lay down the salary and pension for the person 'occupying the position of Prime Minister *and First Lord of the Treasury*' (my italics).

If Walpole is taken as the first Prime Minister, then from him to James Callaghan we have a total of fifty in 255 years. Lord Blake in his British Academy Lectures, reprinted as *The Office of the Prime Minister*, sets out a statistical analysis of the first forty-nine. At the age of twenty-four, William Pitt the Younger was by far the *youngest* man to become Prime Minister, the next being Grafton at thirty-three and Rockingham at thirty-five. The only other under-forties were Devonshire and North. The *oldest* on taking office was Palmerston at seventy, followed by Campbell-Bannerman at sixty-nine and Neville Chamberlain and Aberdeen at sixty-eight. The latest age at which anyone has retired from the premiership was Gladstone's eighty-four. The average age of all the Prime Ministers on first appointment was fifty-five and a half, but this figure is as low as it is because of the comparative youth of the Prime Ministers in the first hundred years or so from Walpole's taking office. From Walpole to Grey the average age was forty-seven: since 1830 the mean has been fifty-nine. Only one (myself) has been under fifty in this century; only three – the others being Peel and Rosebery – since the first Reform Act in 1832.

In terms of tenure of office, Walpole himself holds the record with twenty-one years, followed by the younger Pitt with nineteen. The nearest challengers are Liverpool with fourteen, Salisbury just behind him, and Gladstone with a tenure of twelve years. The shortest incumbencies were those of the Earl of Bath, from 10–12 February 1746, and Earl Waldegrave, who lasted twice as long, from 8–12 June 1757. A contemporary satire on the Bath premiership, *A History of the Long Administration*, concluded:

> And thus endeth the second and last part of this astonishing Administration which lasted 48 hours and 3 quarters, seven minutes and eleven seconds; which may truly be called the most honest of all administrations; the minister to the astonishment of all wise men never transacted one rash thing; and, what is more marvellous, left as much money in the Treasury as he found in it.

There has been a very marked change in the social origins of Britain's Prime Ministers. Disraeli is the thirty-first in our list of fifty. Before him, all but three were landed aristocrats or came from aristocratic families. I have listed both the Pitts as well as Walpole as *non*-aristocratic since the elder Pitt became an Earl only in respect of his services as First Minister. Of the nineteen since Disraeli, only six come from an aristocratic background – Salisbury, Rosebery, Balfour, Churchill, Eden and Sir Alec Douglas-Home, who renounced his earldom on his appointment. Six out of the fifty went to what would now be regarded as State primary schools.

Only four can be said to have had a real industrial experience before entering Parliament – here I exclude those of us who after a period as a departmental minister, found themselves in opposition, and took up an appointment in the City or some branch of industry or commerce. Baldwin worked in his father's steel and engineering firm; Bonar Law, a Canadian who emigrated to Scotland, in a Glasgow merchant bank and later in a firm of iron merchants; Neville Chamberlain, after failing through no fault of his own to grow sisal in the Bahamas, became a Birmingham metal fabricator before his election to the House; and Harold Macmillan worked in his family's publishing business.

Even though Walpole took office simply as the King's servant, there were, in Parliamentary terms, advantages both for him and the Sovereign, in that Treasury control over the vast royal patronage was virtually decisive in the winning of elections. In an age of pocket and rotten boroughs with a very small electorate, the palace purse-strings were sufficient to procure a majority for the King's minister in any general election. But his control of patronage within Parliament was not enough to keep a Parliament voting for him, hence the large number of eighteenth-century administrations. Patronage remains a factor of great importance right up to the Reform Act of 1832.

But throughout Walpole's administrations he was never in any sense the Chief Executive. The Chief Executive was the King; the departmental heads derived their authority from him. The Cabinet Council was neither chosen by Walpole nor under his control. This Council, over which George II from time to time presided – as did George III in 1779 and 1781 – included in addition to such ministerial members as the First Lord, the Secretaries of State, the Lord Chancellor and the Lord President, such functionaries as the Archbishop of Canterbury, the Lord Chief Justice, the Lord Chamberlain, the Lord High Steward and the Commander-in-Chief, plus one or two peers and others of high standing. Sir Lewis Namier has described it more as a Council of State than an administration. Against this was the 'efficient Cabinet', the ministers over whom Walpole presided. In the reign of George III, though the Sovereign tried occasionally to play the Council off against the 'efficient Cabinet' (or *conciliabulum*), the wider body virtually ceased to function.

Walpole's role was more that of royal spokesman in Parliament, and his tenure of office was at all times at the King's pleasure. He was in fact Leader of the House on behalf of the Sovereign.

Nevertheless, it was in the Walpole era that accountability to the King, while essential for survival, ceased to be a guarantee of survival. After twenty-one years Walpole went, while still possessing the royal confidence, precisely because he could no longer deliver the confidence of Parliament. As the great historian of the eighteenth century Professor J.H. Plumb has put it: 'Essential though it was to possess the confidence of the King, domination of Parliament proved more important. When at last Walpole failed to do so he went. By then, however, his system was so strong that it made little or no difference. The Whig aristocracy remained in power.'

Walpole's resignation was, in fact, a turning-point in British constitutional and prime ministerial history. He had created for the premiership what Walter Bagehot 125 years later was to attribute to the Cabinet, 'a position of a hyphen which joins, a buckle which fastens, the Legislative part of the State to the Executive part of the State'. From then on, the fiat of the Crown was not enough unless the minister could retain the confidence of Parliament. By 1742 Walpole had failed this test. It was Lord North who made the doctrine articulate in a submission to King George III: 'Your Majesty is well apprised that in this country the Prince on the Throne cannot with prudence oppose the deliberate resolution of the House of Commons.'

Yet the Crown retained its veto for some years. George III dismissed the Fox–North coalition a year after it had replaced the Rockingham administration, and Pitt was more than once within an ace of dismissal if the King's illness had persisted, for had the Prince of Wales (later George IV) secured the regency for long enough, Pitt would have been summarily dismissed in favour of Fox and his friends. This is not to assert a royal power distinct from and superior to that of Parliament. The Prince Regent could have appointed Fox only on the assumption that the new administration could obtain and retain the support of a majority in the House. As late as the reign of William IV in 1834 the monarch was able – for the last time – to dismiss a ministry, that of Lord Melbourne, which still had a majority in the Commons.

What was significant in Lord North's resignation was that the whole administration resigned with him. Even then Thurlow, the Lord Chancellor, insisted on retaining office as a Court appointment. The growth of the practice by which the entire Cabinet disappeared with its chief proved a considerable reinforcement of the First Minister's power, for it greatly reduced the opportunity for mischief-making and the forming of internal cabals based on personal ambition.

Walpole's contribution to the establishment of the office of Prime Minister was more than the recognition that the head of Government had to carry the confidence not only of the Sovereign but also of Parliament, and more than the development of the system of his 'efficient' Cabinet presided over by the First Minister. It was his own success in dominating the House of Commons for the best part of twenty years, and in creating a legend by his successful administration at home and abroad. When, after a generation of peace and growing prosperity, he was manœuvred into the somewhat ludicrous though popular War of Jenkins' Ear, his evident personal distaste for the war, and a run of military reverses, lost him the control of Parliament. But nothing would ever be the same again. Britain had adopted a prime ministerial system, and at least an embryonic form of responsible Cabinet Government.

Walpole, until the war of 1739, was a master of playing the dual role of what has been called 'minister with the King in the House of Commons' and 'minister for the House of Commons in the closet'. As time passed the old division between hard-line Tories and hard-line Whigs, going back to William III's take-over from James II, was becoming blurred. He had the patronage to maintain the 'Court and Treasury Party' in office, but his success lay in attracting the support of ten to fifteen dozen independent back-benchers, mostly from the shires, owing no declared loyalty either to the Court or to the anti-Court faction. He had to face dangerous crises, for example on his Excise Tax proposals and on financial provision for the Prince of Wales, but his success was due to his constant vigilance and his complete understanding of his fellow Parliamentarians. In this he inherited the benefit of the 1716 Septennial Act, with elections only every seven years. In his long premiership he had to fight only three general elections, and here the power of Treasury patronage in constituencies with a tiny electorate was decisive. Moreover the virtual assurance of a succession of seven-year Parliaments strengthened the currency of patronage. Job security for seven years against the shorter period of the Triennial Act cost more; it made the task of the jobber easier, and his return in both political and monetary dividends that much greater.

Britain's first Prime Minister decided from the outset that power lay in the Commons and that he therefore must be a commoner. He refused the peerage

A contemporary print of Walpole (*left*) in the House of Commons. To his right is Arthur Onslow, the Speaker.

offered him in 1723, though he asked that it be conferred upon his son. For twelve years he was the only Cabinet member of the House of Commons, indeed the only commoner in the Cabinet. Yet it was not until two centuries later that, with King George V's rejection of Curzon in favour of Baldwin, it was finally established that the Prime Minister must be in the Commons. Of the thirty-eight Prime Ministers between Walpole and Baldwin, nineteen became Prime Ministers as peers, not counting those, such as Disraeli, who took a peerage during their term of office as Prime Minister, or who succeeded to a peerage between one period of office and another.

Walpole's achievement then was the legacy of political stability, after a century of division and turmoil. But it was more than that. There were his positive achievements both in foreign and domestic affairs. As Geoffrey Holmes has written:

> By the late 1730s Walpole could point to twenty-five years without major war, to substantial though not universal economic prosperity, low taxation, the repair of the social fabric by the reconciliation of the landed and moneyed interests, and a marked lowering of the political temperature – all part of the climate that made stability possible and all traceable, to a greater or lesser degree, to his specific policies.

It would be easy but misleading to speak of the success of his foreign policy. England for many years past had not known a quarter of a century free from war abroad, to say nothing of civil war and the Jacobite rising, but it was not a brilliant or expansive period in foreign policy, comparable for example with the age of Chatham, or even Palmerston. Walpole took pride in the treaties with Spain in 1729 and Austria in 1731. They may even have gone to his head. He was a healer at home rather than an arbiter abroad. His foreign policy, remote and disengaged, while certainly helping Britain to remain in peace and fatten herself on her own pasture, was for the greater part undistinguished and sterile. Britain was largely isolated. Her entente with France, encouraged by Walpole, was of no account by 1735, and he soon succeeded in losing the friendship both of Spain and Austria.

The War of Jenkins' Ear was not of Walpole's seeking: he was losing the support of the King and even of his Cabinet. To the Duke of Newcastle he said: 'It is your war and I wish you joy of it.' Yet the country was ready for war. He could have taken on Spain in the mid-1730s with great advantage in colonial conquest and trade: Spain was able to count on his pacifist approach, and to win new trade opportunities in consequence. The Jenkins War was popular and his reluctant acceptance of his new role as war leader brought about the end of the Walpole era.

But if they achieved nothing for Britain's prestige abroad, Walpole's twenty-five years of peace had been good for internal stability. His economic policies were the basis of his reputation, in his lifetime and since. He restored public confidence and State credit with his unwinding of the crisis caused by the South Sea Bubble. Even earlier he had begun to refund the National Debt at lower rates of interest, and introduced a Sinking Fund for paying off war debt seventy years before the younger Pitt had the same idea. He kept the Budget taut, simplified the customs duties and reformed the administration of the revenue. He risked Parliamentary defeat on his excise scheme in 1733 and had to abandon it to avoid resignation. (It was, in fact, left to Pitt to carry it through to success.) His trade and tariff policy was in the main protectionist: the revolution in fiscal theology had to wait half a century for Adam Smith and his ministerial disciples.

Walpole, hounded from office over the conduct of a war he never sought, and the cause and outbreak of which he resented, remains the longest-serving Prime Minister of all. Still more, he was a not altogether passive witness of the growing power of Parliament: he enunciated the principle of accountability to Parliament as well as to the Throne. Above all, from his time on, Britain could not for very long carry on without a Prime Minister in charge. For the years which followed, years of short-lived administrations and First Ministers of varying quality, he had ensured that Britain would always have a leader, one whose ability to survive and to act would depend uniquely on his acceptability to the elected House of Commons.

This is not a history of the eighteenth century, so I do not propose to include a short summary of the premiership of such of Walpole's immediate successors as Wilmington, Pelham, Bath, Newcastle, Waldegrave, Devonshire, Bute, Grenville and Rockingham. But clearly reference must be made to William Pitt the Elder, who became Earl of Chatham, not only because it is impossible fully to understand Pitt the Younger without so doing, but also because the political history of Britain over the greater part of the second half of the eighteenth century is dominated by the issue of American independence, up to and including the first years of the younger Pitt's first administration. For the same reason, Grafton, North and Shelburne cannot be excluded.

William Pitt, 1st Earl of Chatham painted in 1772 after R. Brompton.

William Pitt, Earl of Chatham, is universally placed high among Britain's Prime Ministers, and is no less deservingly regarded as one of our greatest war leaders, ranking with his son, the younger Pitt, Lloyd George and Winston Churchill. The point has been made that he was never formally Prime Minister, by the acknowledged test of being First Lord of the Treasury. But it is right to acknowledge him as three times Prime Minister, as Lord Blake does in the ordinal list of the Prime Ministers from Walpole onwards, where he puts his first effective administration as that of November 1756 to April 1757, after the retirement of Newcastle and before the appointment of Devonshire. There is no dispute that in all three administrations Pitt, though holding the position of Secretary of State for the Southern Department in the first two and Lord Privy Seal in the third, was the head of the King's Government.

His whole career was dominated by two related ideals, the strengthening of Britain's trade and colonial empire and her military and naval power in the world. 'When trade is at stake ... you must defend it or perish.' His words summarized his first campaign on entering Parliament in the 1730s and they were uttered in support of his demands for war with Spain. European wars, entangling alliances – particularly the idea that English world interests should be sacrificed to interests of Hanover – interested him little. After the Wars of Jenkins' Ear and of the Austrian Succession, Pitt's horizons increasingly encompassed the North and South Atlantic and the Caribbean, the coasts of India and the wider Eastern seas. Only rarely did he temporize: on his appointment as Secretary of State, in 1756, the pro-Hanoverian passages in his draft of the King's Speech were clearly designed to repair past damage and rebuild his position with the King. In 1751 he was content to support a peace with Spain which fell far short of the aims he had pronounced.

With war on the point of breaking out again in 1755, Pitt led a campaign comparable only with that of Churchill in the late 1930s against the Government's incompetence and unpreparedness, the threat to Britain's mastery of the seas, the neglect of America, and the dangers of a lost empire. He condemned the payment of military subsidies 'to buy courage and defence' instead of strengthening America, building up the fleet and creating a national militia. He warned that Britain would lose Minorca. The King fought hard against giving him power, but had to send for him when he refused to help Fox form a Government – and on Pitt's own terms. He listed the Cabinet he wanted, with Devonshire as figurehead and Newcastle out; he demanded and secured an inquiry into the failures of the outgoing ministry.

Pitt lasted only from November 1756 to April 1757, when he was dismissed. He had overplayed his hand, but in less than five months he had sent the German levies home, created a militia, and laid down a major naval shipbuilding programme, with priority for fast frigates. His unpopularity at Court and in the corridors of power was far exceeded by the wave of enthusiasm for him all over the country. Newcastle saw that he had to return, and came to an agreement with him which the King had to accept. A lesson had been learned: Pitt changed his position on Hanover, and came to support the Prussian alliance. His main strategy remained the command of the seas, and the amassing of colonial gains, mainly at the expense of the French, with all this could mean for trade.

1758–9 were the years of the great victories: Prussian successes over the French and Austrians; the capture of Louisburg, opening up the St Lawrence; the capture of Fort Duquesne on the Ohio (renamed Fort Pitt); the French loss of Guadeloupe and their defeat at Minden; the destruction of French ships at Lagos Bay; then in the closing months of 1759 the conquest of Quebec and the control of French Canada (leading to the capture of Montreal in 1760) and Hawke's victory over the Brest fleet at Quiberon Bay.

Then, with George III now on the throne, Pitt began to lose influence. There was a degree of war-weariness, concern about taxes, City worries. Pitt lost support in Cabinet and it was clear that a peace treaty unacceptable to him would soon be negotiated. Eager to smash the Spanish fleet before the Royal Navy reverted to a peace footing, he could not carry the Cabinet and resigned. When the treaty was debated he was gravely ill and had to be carried into the House, where, allowed to speak from his seat, he thundered for three and a half hours against the ignominious peace, with so many hard-earned gains thrown away. For over three years he was an onlooker, and seriously ill much of the time, mental sickness supervening on his physical sufferings. An elder statesman, a legend, he was listened to in the House and more widely. His consistent championing of the Americans, then and more particularly after he finally left office, made him a lonely voice of reason against the tragic and arrogant measures which were driving the colonists beyond the point of any possible return.

In June 1766 Pitt returned for his final period of office, on his own terms. He nominated Grafton, Camden and Shelburne as his closest associates: the others were hand-picked from individual groups, to meet the King's desire to break up party discipline – 'to root out the present method of banding together' was how the King put it. Pitt was now Lord Privy Seal, though the nominal First Lord was the Duke of Grafton, then aged thirty, the youngest of all Prime Ministers except the younger Pitt.

Pitt was too ill to carry the burden of representing the administration in Parliament and he went to the Lords as the Earl of Chatham. As a recent biographer has pointed out, the move not only destroyed his role as the Great Commoner but landed him in a staid debating chamber where his Parliamentary triumphs could no longer be possible. Despite his illness, he set out to assert his position. Written directions were given to the individual ministers. But his main aims, conciliation of the Americans and the heading-off of separatist tendencies, the curbing of the power of the East India Company's nabobs, and the forging of a tripartite alliance between Britain, Russia, and Prussia, made no headway. Soon illness, increasingly mental, took charge. 'Gout in the head' was the current phrase for madness, in his case aggravated by severe physical symptoms, including paralysis. His colleagues continued to act in his name, but he was totally ineffective from March 1767. On 14 October 1768, he formally resigned. In the lucid periods that remained to him in the last ten years of his life he was a violent critic of Grafton's administration and those of his successors, and in particular used what remained of his authority and standing to advise a conciliatory approach to the problems and actions of the North American colonists.

Grafton remained as head of an increasingly unhappy administration until January 1770. For a time he was waiting and hoping for a recovery by Pitt, whose illnesses until then, like George III's later, had been cyclical and marked by unexpected returns to sanity. He was fortunate in the close support and even friendship of the King right up to his resignation.

Grafton had urgent problems to face: riots in 1768, well handled by his close associate Weymouth, and the continuing Wilkes affair. His major problem was the situation in the American colonies, where the Americans were taking up a highly provocative stance, almost encouraged by provocative actions by Whitehall. He retired in January 1770, then aged thirty-four, as Peter Durrant has put it, 'less because he lost his nerve than because he lost heart'. The Rockingham Whigs, a disciplined party, were in full cry over the Wilkes affair, and Chatham was a bitter and sporadically articulate opponent.

The King treated his resignation as an act of 'desertion'. His ministers disdained to follow him: there was a clear successor in Lord North. Grafton in his youthful retirement lent his support to North's American policies, finally breaking with them in 1775 over the issue of coercion against the colonists.

Lord North, the Prime Minister who lost the American colonies. Painted by N. Dance.

If a representative group of people interested in public affairs were invited to take part in a poll to decide the worst Prime Minister Britain has ever had, it is likely that a big majority would select Lord North, give or take a sizeable minority whose vision for recent times is stronger than that for past ages and who would plump for one of the present surviving former Prime Ministers. A century and a half of historical comment has tended to repeat the judgment of successive generations on North. Yet he was an efficient administrator, a skilful Parliamentarian, and a remarkably fine speaker in the House.

It was perhaps the times that were out of joint; it was certainly a cursed spite that he had the job of putting them right. Probably none of his contemporaries could have done so: relations with the colonists were already exacerbated beyond repair, before he took over. None knew this better than he. He has perhaps been somewhat unfairly treated. Clearly the loss of the American colonies was, in the language of *1066 and All That*, 'a Bad Thing'. Certainly it was so regarded by those living at the time of Yorktown, who were entitled to feel that this was the end of all Britain's greatness. In the event, Britain was on the verge of a new industrial and commercial revolution, brought about by the rapid technological change which, though at a high cost in human, social terms, was to make Britain for a century the workshop of the world. Moreover, despite the crass policies and wrong assessments made by the King and his Cabinet, it is by no means certain that even if Pitt and Grafton had been heeded the situation could have been saved at any time after 1770.

When North took over from Grafton, in January 1770, any hope of forming a viable Government seemed gone, thanks to the disarray of Grafton's last years and scenes inside and outside Parliament over the continuing Wilkes affair. Yet by the end of the year North was in control with a strong Parliamentary majority. The stupid actions of London over the Stamp Act and attempts to interfere with the American colonists' trade had almost certainly gone past the point of no return. In 1772 Rhode Island radicals seized the revenue cutter *Gaspee* and burnt it. The authorities were giving one London-appointed governor after another powers almost despotic in character, and elected colonial assemblies were seeking to make their local executive answerable to them. The Boston Tea

Party episode a year later was met by an attempt to put down the colonists with naval and military force. North entirely miscalculated what would be necessary, and in 1774 the separate colonies were seeking joint action through the first Continental Congress.

North, far too late, put forward conciliation proposals in 1775, and actually reduced the naval establishment in the estimates. In 1776 came the Declaration of Independence and the outbreak of fighting. The strategy, controlled over a distance of three thousand miles with the slowest of communications, was to seek to split the colonial opposition by driving a wedge between the New England forces and the rest. In October, Howe captured Philadelphia, symbolic as the seat of Congress and of the Declaration of Independence, but a few weeks later Burgoyne's army was forced to surrender at Saratoga. North recognized the importance of this defeat: 'The consequences of this most fatal event may be very important and serious, and will certainly require some material change of system.'

North now lost heart. Saratoga, it has been said, was to him what Norway was to Chamberlain. He sought to resign, but the King would have none of it. North bombarded him with pathetic letters whining for his release. He was totally unable to do the job. Writing, as was customary, in the third person, he said in January 1778: 'The anxiety of his mind has deprived Lord North of his memory and understanding.' Two months later he said that capital punishment was 'preferable to that constant anguish of mind which he feels from the consideration that his continuance in office is ruining His Majesty's affairs'. 'Let me not go to the grave with the guilt of having been the ruin of my King and country,' he implored. He pleaded with the King to bring Chatham back, but a week later Chatham collapsed in the Lords and died.

North stayed for four more years. Parliamentary opposition became fiercer, with Fox and Burke, then Sheridan and later the younger Pitt leading the onslaught. The Commons passed the famous Dunning motion that the influence of the Crown had increased, was increasing and ought to be diminished.

The surrender of Lord Cornwallis's army at Yorktown in November 1781 was the final blow. In February 1782 Pitt acted as teller in a motion of censure and North's majority slumped to nineteen in a total vote of over 450. In March, Pitt himself made one of the concluding speeches in a further censure motion which was carried. North resigned, taking his entire administration with him – the first time this principle had been followed. No less important in constitutional terms was his declaration to the King: 'Your Majesty is well apprised that in this country the Prince on the Throne cannot with prudence oppose the deliberate resolution of the House of Commons.' He resigned at the age of forty-nine, and made a speech thanking the 'Commons of England', which as a Parliamentarian he had dominated, for the 'very kind, the repeated and essential support he had for so many years, received from them'.

He died ten years later.

The Earl of Shelburne, who was Prime Minister from 3 July 1782 to 24 February 1783, was one of the most superb failures among eighteenth-century statesmen.

He failed because he reached the top at the precise moment when the peace negotiations with the victorious Americans reached the decisive stage – and since the Americans were in a position to dictate the terms and Britain's international standing was the lowest since the time of the Stuarts, no possible agreement stood any chance of being popular. Anything put forward which Parliament could have accepted would have been rejected out of hand by the Americans; anything the Americans could accept would have been defeated by a huge majority in a Parliament which had not begun to realize what the American war and victory had signified. More than one Government concerned with the negotiations would have to be sacrificed before a treaty could be signed, and there could be no lasting Government until a leader emerged with no responsibility for the war. He would have to be very young.

The Duke of Portland's first administration, ('the Fox-North coalition'), lasted from March to December, 1783. He fell foul of the King over a proposal to pay the Prince of Wales an allowance far greater than George III had had as heir to the throne, but it was the controversy over India which enabled the King to get rid of him, and it was the younger Pitt who secured his dismissal.

The India Bill provided for a 'Commission for the Government of India' to be nominated by Parliament, not the King. It was in fact designed as an almost limitless bounty for Fox and his friends. The patronage which would result could keep the Government in office as long as Parliament lasted, and provide an unchallengeable election fund when it was dissolved.

It was Pitt who moved in on the Government. He ensured that the King's name was used in the Lords against the proposal. The Lords rejected it, and the King seized the chance to dismiss the administration in December, 1783. The ministry protested that they had never been told of the King's disapproval of the measure, though one of them voted against it in the Lords when he learnt of the King's view. Fox tried to invoke the principle of the responsibility of ministers and considered the great bulwark of the Constitution threatened. It was simply a case of an aggrieved monarch meeting force with both force and guile.

Opposite The Cabinet Room at No. 10 Downing Street with a portrait of Sir Robert Walpole over the fireplace.

Overleaf William Pitt the Younger painted by Hoppner.

1

The Younger Pitt

WILLIAM PITT, son of the great Earl of Chatham, became Prime Minister on 19 December 1783 at the age of twenty-four. He held the office for almost nineteen years in all, second only to Walpole.

If Walpole was the creator of the office of Prime Minister, Pitt is rightly described by historians as the first to hold the office in a sense in which it could be recognized today. While he could still be summarily dismissed by the King, even though enjoying the confidence of Parliament, he was, in the language of those days, the 'efficient' head of his Cabinet. Subject to some grumbles and queries by the King, its members were chosen by Pitt, and where necessary dismissed at his request. More than that, Pitt's administrations were more coherent than those of any of his predecessors, and the policies he enjoined on them and which they accepted were the policies of them all, and were collectively recommended to Parliament. It has been said of him: 'Pitt began as a Whig. His legacy was the second Tory party – the party of reaction and repression – later the party of Peel.' Peel indeed described himself as a disciple of Pitt, and Peel himself has been generally regarded as the first 'modern' Prime Minister, in the sense that his premiership more closely resembles that of a Prime Minister of the 1930s or 1950s than that of Walpole, whose term of office ended a century before Peel's only real administration began.

Pitt, born in 1759, the year of his father's great victories, was dedicated by his father to the service of the Crown at a very tender age. When he was seven he was asked, not entirely in fun, for his views on some great political issue: he was referred to in his home as 'the philosopher' or 'the young Senator'. He was encouraged to study political questions as well as the classics: there is a story that his father would take him into the park at his home, and set him to orate to the surrounding trees, transformed for the purpose into members of the House of Commons. Educated at home, he was a sickly youth and hardly kept proper terms at Cambridge, from his entry at the age of fourteen, until he was seventeen. He then lost no time in entering Parliament, nominated to the pocket borough of Appleby, in Westmorland, in January 1781 at the age of twenty-one.

The Parliament he entered was dominated by the need to come to terms with the humiliating defeat in North America. The war was lost. The peace had still to be negotiated. North, Rockingham, Shelburne and Portland in turn had lacked the broad back needed to carry the odium of a treaty of surrender. No one with any responsibility for the war could make the peace. Pitt not only had the alibi of youth – he was eighteen when Burgoyne's army surrendered at Saratoga – he was his father's son, and Chatham had warned and raged against the policies that brought the war. More than that, Pitt himself had gone into the attack within days of entering Parliament. He confronted Lord North in the debate on the Address in Reply to the King's Speech opening Parliament. In the first few weeks he made seven speeches denouncing the 'accursed, wicked, barbarous, cruel, unnatural, unjust and diabolical war'.

On 7 February 1782 he acted as teller in the division lobbies on a motion of censure lost by the narrow margin of 217 votes to 236. On 15 March he succeeded in carrying a motion of censure, making one of the concluding anti-Government speeches. North was succeeded by Rockingham, who soon died, and Shelburne was then appointed. Pitt, at twenty-three, became Chancellor of the Exchequer. It was not a position of high prestige; indeed seventy years later Queen Victoria refused to have Disraeli as Home Secretary, but did not

Previous page
Contemporary cartoon of Pitt's dilemma over Catholic Emancipation.

mind his becoming Chancellor. But Pitt was now launched.

His responsibilities ranged beyond finance. He was Shelburne's only effective spokesman in the House of Commons and had to bear the main brunt of the attacks of Lord North and his colleagues, now in opposition, particularly on the approach to peace. While he refused to disclose the proposed terms, he said flatly that the recognition of American independence was unconditional and would not be revoked even if the peace parleys broke down. The King was furious at this declaration but Pitt and the whole administration were committed. A series of Parliamentary defeats on the peace issue now weakened the Cabinet, and Shelburne resigned in February 1783, to be followed by a coalition between North and Charles James Fox under the nominal leadership of Portland. When this fell, following the King's intervention over the East India Bill, Pitt, on 19 December 1783, became First Lord of the Treasury.

An engraving of the Younger Pitt by James Gillray in 1789. By then he had been Prime Minister for over five years – and was still not yet thirty years old.

In an age of gamblers few would have staked much on his prospects. He was the only minister in the Commons, and at the age of twenty-four would have to be in constant attendance and speak on all major debates in the face of the combined force and hostility of the factions and ambitious groups that made up the House. He was greeted with derision when he announced that he had an India Bill ready which looked back to the schemes of Chatham, was tidy and workable, and provided a guarantee against the patronage and corruption that were the hallmark of the Rockingham–Fox–North measure. He met his opponents head on. This was the Bill: he challenged them to produce their alternative. He turned their censure motions and manœuvred them into a position where they would have to deny India any government at all, deny the King the revenue needed for the Government at home and, by refusing to extend the duration of the Mutiny Act, make the King's army illegal. In just three months he had routed the Opposition and become master of the House. More than that, he had laid down a system of government for India that was to last for seventy years.

Two weeks later Parliament was dissolved. Pitt won the election by a landslide. His majority was over a hundred: 160 of those who had voted against him on the India Bill lost their seats. Pitt was able to concentrate above all on the state of the country, which was saddled with the accumulated National Debt caused by the war with America. Trade and industry were stagnant. Government accounts were unviable. Interest on the inflated National Debt of £240 millions, added to the King's Civil List and the still continuing military and naval expenditure, exceeded the Government's revenue by £2 millions. Interest on the debt alone was £8 million a year, half the revenue receipts. The debt itself was a shapeless, unbalanced burden. £14 millions were unfunded and friendless at a discount of some fifteen per cent.

Pitt was the son of his father. He was also the nephew of another Prime Minister, Grenville, his mother's brother. Grenville had a meticulous mind, he was a master of detail, of statistics. Until the outbreak of war in 1793, Pitt was Grenville, the statistician not the warlord. Working as long hours as any Prime Minister in our history, he applied himself to the revenue problem. He was a disciple of Adam Smith, whose *Wealth of Nations* had been published in 1776. Pitt decided to increase the revenue by increasing trade and making the profession of smuggling an unremunerative occupation. He calculated that if he could reduce the excessive import duties at the ports he could, in time, so increase trade that the accounts would be balanced: the lower duties would accrue to the revenue, instead of a situation where the higher duties accrued to the smugglers. But this would take time; for a year or two the reductions in duty would reduce the revenue. He therefore introduced the window tax, a crude impost on property to make good the gap in the revenue while the reform of the customs was creating the dividend.

More than this, he positively sought free trade. He proposed a free trade arrangement with the new American nation as part of the peace settlement, beginning by setting up free ports in the West Indies to provide a free three-cornered trade system. He also sought to establish free trade agreements with European countries, east and west, though he succeeded only with France: the French agreement of 1786 provided for reductions on French wines in return for concessions on British manufactures.

In 1787 Pitt carried three thousand Commons Resolutions through to reform port duties and excise duties, and built up a revenue surplus of nearly £1 million. He introduced a Sinking Fund for debt redemption and reducing the average rate of interest. £1 million was provided year by year to buy up and cancel debt. He sought new direct taxes: one on maidservants led to unseemly comment in the House designed to reflect on Pitt's lack of interest in the opposite sex. He introduced a tax on manservants and then on bachelors. Consumer taxes of the nature of our modern VAT he imposed on hats, perfumes, horses, sporting dogs and clocks. He succeeded, where Walpole had failed – and nearly been driven from office in the attempt – in making wine subject to an internal excise duty instead of using the customs.

It was not only the revenue side. Pitt attacked wasteful expenditure, especially the costly welfare state of patronage enjoyed by well-connected people enjoying a fat sinecure income for doing no work. Here he proceeded slowly, but with great effect. When an office-holder retired or died he was simply not replaced. The work that had to be done was increasingly entrusted to a trained civil service official. Efficiency and professionalism were the order of the day for the new 'economists'. In 1785 he tried to establish a paid, professional police force for the capital – thus anticipating Robert Peel's scheme, though not its success, by more than forty years. But this he failed to get through the House, because of fears of 'Continental tyranny'.

The economy was responding. In the early 1790s, before the French Republic declared war, his measures were working and seen to be working. Trade and production were increasing, the revenue was rising, and the smuggling profession suffered mass redundancy as lower duties and the diversion of military and naval forces to intercept its operations took their toll.

Pitt's Grenville inheritance was showing results. The statistician-clerk, diligently working long hours into the night on the returns, the schedules, the regulations, the enforcement procedures, was in command, increasingly lonely, increasingly successful. The dawning of his day as the son of Chatham, war leader, had still to come.

He had mastered Parliament. He commanded the confidence of the King. But – 'Look to the King.' The monarch was subject to periodic attacks of illness, coming on without warning and always of unpredictable duration. Modern medical comment suggests that his illness was porphyria, not madness but a condition giving rise to symptoms suggestive of madness. These were of course seized on, as madness, by those who wanted to see the Prince of Wales assume supreme power. For had an attack lasted to the point where the Prince of Wales became Regent, Pitt would be thrust from office. The Prince was Fox's friend: enjoying together the pleasures of a dissolute society, and ensuring Fox's preferment when the time came. On the first occasion when the King was struck down, he recovered suddenly and quickly and there was no further problem for a decade; when the attacks recurred, Pitt's tenure of office was not an insurable risk.

Pitt's strength lay in his control of Parliament. With members generally, he was unloved, cold, disdainful. He went to his seat in the House hardly speaking to a soul. One cannot imagine him going to the eighteenth-century equivalent of the smoke-room and the tea-room or Annie's bar, chatting and drinking with back-benchers. His boon companion was Henry Dundas; on one occasion they were classically drunk on the front bench. That he frequented Bellamy's canteen we know from his dying wish for a Bellamy pie, but since he sat long hours on the bench each day this can only have been for sustenance, not companionship.

The timing of the King's bouts of illness, and still more of his recoveries, denies to us the means of speculating whether a Regency-imposed Fox administration could have won and held the support of Parliament. Without that support, the administration would have fallen. But equally Pitt, even at his most popular, could have been dropped at any time by King or Regent. A Prime Minister at the turn of the century had to serve two masters, and retain the confidence of both.

In 1789 the French Revolution was signalled by the taking of the Bastille. The immediate consequence in Britain was the mounting unpopularity of Whig leaders who had supported revolutionaries and fashionable revolutionary doctrines. Fox's political stock was at a sharp discount, and his alliance with Burke was ended by a quarrel. The Whigs were divided. The landed aristocrats almost to a man denounced the revolutionaries: they had reason to consider that they would be the first victims of a similar movement in Britain. Pitt himself was later to make a successful political bid for some of the most powerful aristocratic Whig anti-revolutionaries, even to the point of creating vacancies in his Cabinet to accommodate them. Surveying Europe, he showed less perceptiveness and vision than one might have expected. His first reaction was a feeling of relief that the military power of the French Crown was less dangerous. The Kaiser's Germans might have felt the same about Tsarist Russia.

The league of European monarchs hastened to seek alliances, more perhaps to protect legitimacy than to safeguard frontiers. Pitt stood a little remote. He was more concerned about Russian designs on Turkey. Despite criticism he supported the infidel Turk against Holy Russia, and his reasoning was plainly based on British interests. He was the first Prime Minister to envisage a Russian threat to the Near East, and specifically feared Russia's naval power and dispositions, as well as the infiltration of Russian agents in Asia Minor, and the Isthmus of Suez, where already there was talk of someone, sometime, constructing a canal. In this he anticipated Disraeli. Both feared any threatened interference with the passage to India.

He won Parliamentary approval for strengthening the Navy, reasoning – as his father had done – that if there were to be a war it should be a naval war, not a Continental land campaign with armies marching and counter-marching, alliances forming, breaking and re-forming, vast subsidies going from the Treasury to petty princelings to pay immobile armies. The war aims would not

Overleaf William Pitt addressing the House of Commons in 1793. An engraving from a painting by Carl Anton Hickel.

be to defeat the enemy on the battlefield: they would be the capture of French colonies in the Americas, particularly the Caribbean, and in the seas of the Far East. Colonies meant trade, and the Pitts, father and son, saw trade, particularly if under British suzerainty, as the first aim of domestic and foreign policy. Meanwhile Pitt still hoped for peace, and indeed announced a plan to pay off £25 millions of the National Debt over fifteen years, or even, he hoped, ten.

His principal diplomatic strategy was to keep the Dutch republic on the right side. He was concerned about the narrow seas. He was concerned about finance: the Dutch were big investors in the Funds and in private financial operations in the City. He came to the point where he was sending secret subsidies to the Dutch, in order to resist either an internal revolt or a French invasion which would cut off the flow of Dutch investment funds to the Treasury and the City. His negotiations succeeded, he halted the French agents in their tracks and aroused great enthusiasm by his announcement of the Triple Alliance between Britain, the Dutch Republic and Prussia. Chatham was in charge now; the Grenville era in the saga of the younger Pitt was over.

By this time the Austrians were seeking to involve Britain in an alliance to force a royal restoration on the French. Pitt would have none of it. Then a brash young Emperor succeeded to the Austrian throne and declared war on the French. Pitt made no effort to join in: he was busy insulating Britain against revolutionary inflation, and tightening up the control over subversives in London, the North and Ireland.

In the autumn of 1792, the French Revolution broke into a new wave of violence. The King was guillotined, Belgium was overrun, and the treaties governing control of the Scheldt repudiated. British interests were now threatened, and the sanctity of treaties violated. The French Republic declared war on 1 February 1793. Pitt entered the war with an ill-prepared attempt to attack Dunkirk and a naval campaign to deal with the French cutters which were sinking Allied merchant ships. The campaign was unfortunately entrusted to the Grand Old Duke of York of nursery fame, and by September it was clear that Dunkirk would hold out against him. There was deep distress at home: was Pitt not his father's son after all? At once, the Navy secured a brilliant victory. Toulon, base of the French Mediterranean fleet, surrendered to a British naval force in return for a promise of protection against the revolutionaries.

This was Pitt's chance, and he failed to take it. Toulon could have become, in the phrase of a later war, the 'soft under-belly' of revolutionary France, if speedy action had been taken to send troops. But Pitt's eyes were on the colonial war. The south of France was not invaded until it was too late; the fleet was driven out by a fierce artillery bombardment under the control of a young gunnery officer, Captain Napoleon Bonaparte.

Pitt's popularity disappeared. His concentration on colonial gains won him the reputation if not of an appeaser, at any rate of a complacent isolationist: he would, it was thought, make peace with the *sans-culottes* in return for a sizeable grant of French colonies. The colonial war was going triumphantly: in Europe there was inertia, at high cost to Britain in terms of unrequited subsidies. George III was increasingly restive and critical. George saw the struggle as a holy war to save monarchies everywhere against godless revolutionaries. Pitt's war aims in Europe were much more limited. It was necessary to stop the spread across the Channel of revolutionary doctrines: security had to be strengthened at home, by the suspension of Habeas Corpus, the employment of spies and *agents provocateurs* and the banning of public meetings of over fifty people, except by licence from the magistrates. He was not so concerned to save the French from themselves, or to fight the battles of foreign monarchs against their own people. Nor were Britain's subsidized allies. Resistance in Europe collapsed: Prussia, the Dutch, Spain made peace with France. The Austrian alliance was just kept alive at the expense of a £4 million loan.

Pitt's cherished Sinking Fund was suspended: it was futile to extinguish the debts of previous wars if they were paying an interest rate lower than that needed for new borrowing. Yet Pitt thought that the war would be short. His new Foreign Secretary, the younger Grenville – a future Prime Minister – and George III had no such hope.

But a political bonus for Pitt came from the divisions in the ranks of the Whigs. Fox was isolated and discredited. In a Parliamentary coup Pitt brought leaders of the old guard, particularly the Rockingham Whigs, into the Government. George Canning became an under-secretary.

Pitt was secure in his Parliamentary support, though growing more and more remote and unapproachable. But the other requirement for remaining in office, the confidence of the King, was wearing thin. There were fresh scares through bouts of illness, and the Prince of Wales began to plan his changes. The King himself was planning to replace Pitt by the Speaker, Henry Addington. In a recent biography of Pitt, Derek Jarrett has put it simply: 'The King had no intention of being lumbered with a minister who could make neither war nor peace.'

Reverse followed reverse. In April 1797 the Austrians signed the preliminaries of a peace treaty with France and the Channel fleet mutinied at Spithead, and shortly afterwards the North Sea fleet mutiny followed at the Nore. The French sought to invade Ireland but were forced back by a storm at Bantry Bay: another invasion attempt in South Wales was frustrated. Yet the mood was to change again. It has been suggested that Pitt's own morale was lifted and that public support for him increased when he decided to accept a challenge to a duel from an opposition MP, George Tierney, whose patriotism Pitt had impugned in the House. (No one was hit.) So Pitt was apparently a man, after all, a sportsman and gambler, and had noble instincts. Above all he was a fighter, and the mood of the country changed when George III sent a message to Parliament warning of invasion preparations in France, Flanders and Holland. There were stories of bands of United Englishmen, United Scotsmen, United Irishmen, bent on destroying the established order of society.

By this time Ireland was in a state of rebellion. The United Irishmen, mainly Protestants, tried to seize Dublin. The revolt was countered by the utmost cruelty on the part of the English troops. Pitt wrote an innocent-sounding letter to the Lord Lieutenant, backing him in crushing the revolt, and continuing: 'Cannot crushing the rebellion be followed by an Act appointing commissioners to treat for a Union?' In 1793 he had caused the Irish Parliament to give the vote in Irish county constituencies to Catholics, though they could vote only for Protestants, since the measure did not give Catholics the right to stand for Parliament. In 1795 the new Lord Lieutenant, Lord Fitzwilliam, was authorized to state his support for full Catholic Emancipation. The King intervened and after receiving formal advice from the Archbishop of Canterbury, the Lord Chancellor and the Lord Chief Justice, formally decided that the granting of Emancipation would be a violation of his Coronation Oath. 'The subject' he

told Pitt, 'is beyond the decision of any cabinet of ministers.' Pitt recalled Fitzwilliam, but the statement had been made, and Irishmen have long memories.

The rebellion, aided by a French force, was crushed. The Irish Parliament rejected a union with Westminster and Pitt used an extraordinary phrase in the House of Commons: 'No man can say that in the present state of things, and while Ireland remains a separate Kingdom, full concessions should be made to the Catholics without endangering the state and shaking the constitution of Ireland to its centre.' The key words, '*while Ireland remains a separate Kingdom*', were widely taken as a broad hint that if the Irish accepted union, Catholic Emancipation could and would follow. This palindromic utterance could be read in two ways. The lure for the Catholics, if they so chose to interpret it, was: agree to union and you have a good chance of Emancipation. The Protestants were led to believe that unless they agreed to union the Government might be forced into concessions on the Emancipation issue. Helped by the action of the Chief Secretary, Castlereagh, in promising compensation to those controlling the seats in the boroughs and to office-holders, the Irish Parliament voted for union, and the Act of Union was passed in both Parliaments, taking effect in January 1801.

But events had not been standing still in the war theatres. Napoleon decided to invade Egypt and cut off Britain from her Indian possessions. He captured Malta, then regarded as being under a form of Russian protection. Nelson destroyed the French fleet in a daring attack, the Battle of the Nile. The angry Russians joined a new coalition, including Austria, Britain, the Kingdom of Naples and Turkey. The subsidy bill mounted again, but this time there were results. Thanks to Suvarov's brilliant campaign, the Russians and Austrians drove the French out of Italy. There were successes in the Dutch Republic. Pitt suggested the possibility of peace negotiations, but the King refused, as he did when Bonaparte approached him. Then Bonaparte's victory at Marengo in 1800 strengthened the French position, whether for peace negotiations or the continuance of the war.

Pitt was ill, overworked, unable to sleep, and virtually unable to stop drinking. The country was in uproar about food shortage and high prices. The Russians had switched sides because the British had offended them by capturing Malta. Then the Irish crisis reopened. A month after Union became effective, the King heard reports that the Cabinet was moving towards Catholic Emancipation. There had in fact been no decision, because of divisions between ministers. But Pitt was stuck with his cryptic statement of two years earlier, for the Irish Catholics were entitled to claim that they had voted for the Union they had previously rejected simply because it was their only hope of securing Emancipation. Now they expected Pitt to deliver. He faced an angry King, committed to his Coronation Oath. His Cabinet was divided, and in any case the King had ruled that it was not a matter for them.

Was Pitt to force Emancipation on the King on the ground that his statement was a commitment, thereby having to confess that he had tricked his Sovereign? Or was he to go to the Irish and say that his statement had never involved any commitment, in which case they would be likely to say that he had tricked them? Resignation was the only way out, and because of his illness and insomnia it would be a blessed relief. Yet although the King was ready to accept this and had already been treating with Addington, the House of Commons could hardly believe the rumours. Pitt was so much the leader of the country.

Opposite George III painted by the studio of Allan Ramsay. His commitment to his Coronation Oath barred the way to Catholic Emancipation.

The King was then taken ill again. Pitt was in effect a caretaker Prime Minister, and the Prince of Wales recognized him as such, at any rate until the Regency Bill could go through all its stages in the two Houses of Parliament. Then the King recovered – in fact modern medicine tells us that one usually recovers quite quickly from porphyria, except in old age – and Pitt went ahead with the resignation formalities. And again, at this late stage, he committed another incredible act. Hearing that the King had blamed his illness on Pitt's action in raising the Emancipation issue, he sent a letter to the King giving him a solemn assurance that he would never again raise the question as long as the King lived.

Why? Derek Jarrett's analysis is compelling:

> If emancipation was to be dropped, why resign at all? He might feel that he owed it to the Irish Catholics to do so, but he would do their cause little good by binding himself not to help them in the future. To resign because your advice has not been accepted may be honourable, but to resign even when you agree that it shall never be accepted in the future seems rather less so.

Was the answer, as Derek Jarrett suggests, that there was no harm in giving the assurance since he would succeed in persuading the King; and that since the assurance, apart from an ambiguity relating to abdication, was for the duration of his reign, he would be freed of his obligation in a new reign? Pitt was twenty-one years younger than the King, though in the event he predeceased him by fourteen years. This is convincing, though an equally probable reason is that he was exhausted and ill, badly wanted rest, and his recovery was made the more difficult by his guilt complex about the original statement.

For Addington it was not a problem. He had the kudos of kissing hands as First Minister, and almost immediately he was to have the satisfaction of securing, to his surprise, the King's blessing for the idea of peace negotiations. The Treaty of Amiens was proclaimed from the Royal Exchange in March 1802. It was a humiliating peace, and there were grave doubts whether it would hold with an increasingly megalomaniac Napoleon.

These doubts helped to swell the chorus of praise for Pitt. He was criticized in the House, and as so often happens a wave of sympathy arose, and a motion was voted by an overwhelming majority expressing the gratitude of the House to Pitt for his 'great and important services to his country'. It was at his birthday dinner on 28 May 1802 that he received the title 'The Pilot that Weathered the Storm' in a hymn of praise specially composed by George Canning, who ended his poem by foreshadowing Pitt's recall:

> And Oh! if again the rude whirlwind should rise
> The dawning of peace should fresh darkness deform
> The regrets of the good and the fears of the wise
> Shall turn to the pilot who weathered the storm.

The Addington peace was as unlike a real peace as Chamberlain's Munich pact, and faith in its future diminished daily. Pitt was far removed from the scene, surveying the south coast defences from Walmer Castle, which was his, as Lord Warden of the Cinque Ports, or relaxing by day in the sports of the countryside and drinking to the point of distraction in the evening. By April

Holwood House in Kent, the country home of Pitt the Younger.

1803 there were few who did not consider war inevitable. Pitt himself, alarmed and mobilized again, began to talk of a broad coalition ministry headed by himself and including Fox. The King was angry at his presumption, but even he could not halt the rude whirlwind that Canning foresaw.

Napoleon was intent on invasion, and commissioned flat-bottomed boats, which struck no terror into the hearts of Britain's admirals. At the critical moment the King was incapacitated and the Prince of Wales was considering the Foxite, Addingtonite permutations. In May 1804 Pitt was back in charge and Bonaparte the self-proclaimed Emperor of the French.

Pitt took over a grim situation in Europe, with his own health deteriorating week by week. More subsidies, more defeats. Britain's security against a French invasion was assured by Nelson's glorious victory off Cape Trafalgar, vindicating his faith in the Navy against Continental armies. Britain would never be conquered. Pitt was dying. He knew it. But Trafalgar gave him the confidence he needed for his last, brief, modest speech, at the Lord Mayor's banquet, whose most celebrated passage is incorporated in the memorial to him, a few yards from where he spoke, in Guildhall. The Lord Mayor had toasted him as 'the Saviour of Europe'. Pitt replied: 'I return you many thanks for the honour you have done me. But Europe is not to be saved by any single man. England has saved herself by her exertions, and will, as I trust, save Europe by her example.'

But not yet. Within days the dying Pitt's hopes were darkened by the news of Napoleon's victory at Austerlitz. Napoleon was supreme on the land, as Britain on the seas. Ten more years of struggle by land and sea followed Pitt's death early in 1806, until the rise of a new coalition from the Tagus in Portugal to the Moskva river in Russia, and Napoleon's legendary challenge to the Russian General Kutuzov and the merciless snows of Russia and the Ukraine. Finally Wellington's Guards' unbroken stand on the field of Waterloo ended the tyranny and ushered in forty years of peace.

As happened again 150 years later, the stand had been made when Britain stood alone. Pitt, like Churchill, speaking to and speaking for his country, had proclaimed Britain's resolve to achieve ultimate victory, and called forth her exertions. Each had the right to claim that those exertions had provided the example which brought victory and peace to a wider world.

From War to Peace 1806–1834

In the twenty-eight years between Pitt's death and Peel's first brief administration in 1834–5 there were eight new Prime Ministers, in addition to Portland, who had held office before Pitt's first administration, and Addington who first held the office in the interval between Pitt's two terms.

Of the eight, the Earl of Liverpool (previously Robert Jenkinson, Lord Hawkesbury) served for nearly fifteen years, from June 1812 to February 1827, and was the longest-serving Prime Minister in the nineteenth century. The other eight, excluding Portland's second administration, accounted for some eleven years between them, Melbourne going on to serve a further six and a half years after Peel's first period of office.

They included Spencer Perceval, 'the prime minister who was murdered', a competent administrator, an ally of Wilberforce in the campaign against slavery, and a sound war leader who gave Wellington his head in the Iberian peninsula, all – apart from the war at sea – Britain would do until Napoleon's adventurism perished in the Russian snows and the charges of Kutuzov's cavalry.

The period between Pitt's death and Peel's first administration covered the end of the Napoleonic War, the first impact on British politics of the industrial revolution, and the social unrest which it engendered; it included the final settlement of the Catholic Emancipation issue, opened up by Pitt – dealt with in the next chapter – and the first major advance in Parliamentary and electoral reform.

Professor Norman Gash begins a chapter in *The Prime Ministers* by asking a question which would be a good test in any radio quiz or mastermind contest: 'Who was Prime Minister at the time of the Battle of Waterloo?' Another might be: Who is the longest-serving Prime Minister since William Pitt? The answer to both is the Earl of Liverpool, whose near fifteen years without a break has not been beaten since, and only by Walpole and the younger Pitt before him.

Spencer Perceval, the only British Prime Minister ever to have been assassinated.

The achievements of his administration were great. Napoleon was defeated, and died six years before Liverpool's own stroke in 1827. His ministry began in 1812, the year of Wellington's capture of Badajoz and Ciudad Rodrigo and Napoleon's retreat from Moscow. It ended in 1827, the year of Navarino, which gave independence to Greece as the Turkish fleet was sent to the bottom by an English admiral. The accolade 'Ministry of All the Talents' was much more assuredly earned by his successive administrations than by Grenville's. Six future Prime Ministers served under him – Canning, Goderich, Wellington, Peel and Palmerston as ministers, Aberdeen as special ambassador to Austria.

Elected to a pocket borough before he came of age, he became a member of the India Board three years later, and for thirty-four years was never out of office,

The Earl of Liverpool, the longest serving Prime Minister of the nineteenth century. An engraving by H. Robinson from a portrait by Thomas Lawrence.

except for thirteen months in 1806–7 during the Grenville administration. He himself served under Pitt in 1793; one of his ministers was still Prime Minister in 1865, seventy-two years later. Castlereagh and Canning were his Foreign Ministers.

Liverpool has been execrated in later years for his savage repression. The Luddites, who had begun their frame-smashing under Perceval, were put down with cruel firmness, the Government's actions calling forth a historic maiden speech by Lord Byron in the House of Lords, on 27 February 1812, on the Frame Work Bill.

It was during Liverpool's ministry that Peterloo occurred, and he defended the actions of the yeomanry. The subsequent execration is no doubt justified, particularly with hindsight: later generations know that there was no Jacobin revolution in sight. But Liverpool and Sidmouth (as Addington had now become) were frightened men: all their spies and *agents provocateurs* could not measure the extent of the infiltration of French terrorists and ideologies. The younger Pitt had reacted with great firmness against the first threat of infiltration. Governments have a habit of over-insuring, especially when the extent of the danger is not known. It would be no defence in a troubled Parliament to say: 'The Government calculated the risk at four to one against, so we felt justified in taking a chance. It was unfortunate that we were wrong.' That excuse would not be accepted if the threat were economic or diplomatic: still less could it be put forward when the threat directly involved security.

Moreover, it has been pointed out that the Liverpool administration had two phases, going wider than law and order. There was the period of 'reactionary' Toryism, characterized by Castlereagh, Sidmouth, Eldon and Vansittart; and the later phase of 'liberal' Toryism, when Canning, Peel, Huskisson and Robinson were among the most powerful men in the Cabinet.

In presiding over his administration Liverpool was the strongest Prime Minister since Pitt: stronger than the generation which followed him. It was his Government, and inevitably as year succeeded year his experience and prestige increased. He put his foot down hard on cabals and splits. Disraeli was very wide of the mark when he coined his phrase 'an arch-mediocrity presiding over a Cabinet of mediocrities'.

As wartime leader he followed the right strategy. Only time and the exhaustion of Napoleon's wide-flung forces could bring victory; adventures such as Walcheren would not. Liverpool was certainly right in defending, against strong Whig opposition, Wellington's operations in the Peninsula, which had begun when he was War Secretary.

It was undoubtedly in foreign affairs, particularly after Canning took over from Castlereagh, that the Government's post-war record was most distinguished. Britain moved away from the Congress system and the Holy Alliance of European monarchs. Liverpool overruled Castlereagh when he suggested that the Prince Regent, during the illness of George III, should sign the accession to the Holy Alliance as an 'autographic avowal of sentiment between him and the sovereigns, his allies'. Liverpool's reply was that such an action would be 'inconsistent with all the forms and principles of our Government'.

Inevitably he was in continual economic difficulties. The war had left a staggering debt burden, and Parliament's refusal in 1816 to renew income tax left the Government with a revenue of £12 millions against an expenditure of £30 millions. The most stringent economy, in defence establishments, cutting back the bureaucracy, reducing the Civil List, and a ten per cent reduction in all official salaries in 1817, would only bridge part of the gap.

Liverpool, together with other ministers, was well versed in the new political economy. He believed that laissez faire was the only way to the 'prosperity' that Robinson, who later became Goderich, then Earl of Ripon, his Chancellor, was preaching. For whatever reason, the post-war years and into the early 1820s were a period of prosperous industry and trade. It was his Government which set up the Currency Commission

Opposite Young Viscount Palmerston in 1802 by T. Heaphy.

and restored gold payments. Liverpool was in fact one of the first of the new free traders, and it was a bold thing for a Tory Government to introduce a new and less rigid Corn Law in the face of opposition from the counties.

While refusing to repeal the Test and Corporation Acts, as early as 1812 he had carried a widely welcomed Relief Bill for dissenters. However he was strongly opposed on doctrinal grounds to Catholic Emancipation. In 1825 he said: 'The Protestant gave an entire allegiance to his sovereign; the Catholic gave a divided one.' By 1825 the Cabinet was going through a period of great strain over Emancipation, where Canning was pressing hard. Early in 1827 Liverpool let it be known that he would soon retire, because of strain and ill health. In February of that year he was taken ill in the small waiting-room near the Cabinet room. It turned out to be a severe stroke and he resigned. He died in December 1828.

George Canning, says Elizabeth Longford in a biographical sketch, like Anthony Eden, is a Prime Minister chiefly remembered for having been Foreign Secretary. Despite his brief premiership of exactly a hundred days, from April to August 1827, he has become a legend in his own right with the Tory Party, and the Canning Club stands as a memorial to his name.

After two years in the House as MP for a pocket borough, he became under-secretary at the Foreign Office under Pitt. He had no time for Fox, and refused to serve in the Ministry of All the Talents. He came back as Foreign Secretary, in the Portland administration, quarrelled with Castlereagh over the handling of the Walcheren expedition, and the two fought a duel. He continued to serve under Perceval, but refused to join Liverpool's long-lived Government, considering that Liverpool would not last. He did not become a minister again until 1816, and then only as President of the Board of Control. When Castlereagh committed suicide in 1822, Canning succeeded him at the Foreign Office.

Canning had been a great supporter of the Congress system of European meetings. Like an embryo Palmerston, he decided there was nothing for Britain in the European League of Emperors and mainly autocratic monarchs. He declined to go to the Congress of Verona, where Castlereagh had intended to go. He sent Wellington instead. For him now, it was English interests first. He regarded this as a wholesome state of affairs: 'Every nation for itself and God for us all.' 'For *Europe* I shall be desirous *now and then* to read *England*.' 'For "Alliance" read "England", and you have the clue to my policy.'

Following Pitt's early years, trade, English trade, was nailed to his masthead, particularly with the links now possible with Latin America. He intervened on behalf of the new republics, sent troops to Portugal, humiliated Spain, and told the House triumphantly: 'I called the New World into existence to redeem the balance of the old.'

When Liverpool suffered his stroke in 1827, Canning appeared the obvious successor, though his chances were clouded by his commitment to Catholic Emancipation. Following his master, Pitt, he reckoned that the pledge Pitt had given to George III not to raise the question in his lifetime was a closed issue now that George IV was on the throne. Wellington and Peel were against his choice, but Canning appealed direct to the King and was chosen.

Emancipation was not immediately an issue – it had been narrowly defeated in the House a month before he became Prime Minister. The other of his two 'bugaboos', as he called them, an easement of the Corn Laws, was never to trouble him. His one achievement was in foreign affairs. It was the treaty with France and Russia under which the Sultan of Turkey, unless he agreed to an armistice with the Greeks, was to be forcibly restrained by the armed strength of the three powers. The Battle of Navarino, which destroyed the Turkish fleet and gave the Greeks their freedom, took place after his death.

Frederick John Robinson, Viscount Goderich and later Earl of Ripon, tends to be treated as a figure in the Downing Street joke-book. He is certainly not in the top league of Prime Ministers, but his failure as Prime Minister covered a period when Tory splits, on both personalities and policy – particularly Catholic Emancipation – would have severely tested a far greater statesman.

Goderich came to the premiership with a substantial record at the Board of Trade and Treasury, where he had earned the title 'Prosperity Robinson', in part a tribute to his presiding over the post-war boom and Britain's clear leadership in industry and trade, in part a gibe because he could not stop using the word. The depression of 1825 did nothing for the prosperity image.

He presided over one of the most divided Cabinets in British history, and he was repeatedly humiliated by

Opposite Sir Robert Peel painted by Linnell and Lady Julia Peel by Sir Thomas Lawrence.

King George IV, who sought to dictate his every ministerial appointment.

The story has been told that Goderich, night after night, burst into tears. This is understandable in such circumstances, but there must be a better way. After disagreements over Navarino and the Government's attitude to the Tories, the end came when Herries insisted on the appointment of Althorp as chairman of a committee on finance, and Huskisson said he would resign if Althorp were so appointed.

There was, however, something of a happy sequel for 'Goody Goderich'. He became Colonial Secretary in 1830–4, President of the Board of Trade again under the calmer Peel administration in 1841–3, and President of the Board of Control from 1843 to 1846.

The Duke of Wellington was Prime Minister for nearly three years, from January 1828 to November 1830, and briefly as a stand-in for three weeks in 1834. His historical greatness lies of course in his military campaigns, culminating in Waterloo. In his later years he became the King's loyal servant, the Grand Old Man, the old retainer of the last two Hanoverian Kings. When the maintenance of the King's Government demanded action by him, he was there, either as a maker of Prime Ministers, or in the premiership himself. His standing enabled him to achieve so major a constitutional change as Catholic Emancipation, for none saw him as a radical. He was safe. The problem was that he was completely out of touch with the people, ignorant of matters of industry and trade and the vast social changes which had come about through the Industrial Revolution.

He was anti-coalition – one senses that he would feel that Badajoz had not been stormed by a coalition.

He could change his stance when he felt a case had been made out, no matter by whom. When Russell carried his motion in favour of repealing the Dissenters Disabilities Acts, which he had opposed, he announced that he would support it, even though the removal of the last discrimination against nonconformists weakened the case against Catholic Emancipation.

It is arguable that none but Wellington could have carried Emancipation. The King, the Church, and a substantial proportion of the people had to be persuaded. He was satisfied on the merits of the case: it was not his view that because a Protestant franchise was in the Constitution it therefore must be defended against change. He played with the idea of limiting the consequences by proposing an agreement with Rome that would involve a Government veto on the appointment of Catholic bishops in return for Emancipation. The issue was forced, as will be seen, by O'Connell's fighting the by-election in Clare, though as a Catholic he could not take his seat.

Wellington decided on Emancipation. His problem was not so much the King as the Cabinet, and that meant Peel above all. Wellington persuaded him that it had to be done, and that it could not be done without Peel. Peel would probably have preferred to resign, but, agonized, accepted the situation. He was to pay for it dearly seventeen years later, when it was added to the repeal of the Corn Laws in the charge-sheet of what Disraeli was to call his tergiversations. The Duke of Cumberland came back from the Continent to warn King George IV that this would be contrary to his Coronation Oath, as George III had asserted, but the King's mind was made up.

Wellington's record on electoral reform was less far-sighted. He was totally resistant; he could not change a basic policy twice. Here he ignored the Canningites, who had resigned on a minor issue of reform and were seeking a way back. Grey, the Whig leader, was ready to embrace them.

The rural disturbances which produced the Swing riots stiffened Wellington against Parliamentary reform, and his speech on the opening of Parliament was intransigent. The Government was defeated, and Grey was to be the Prime Minister who saw Parliamentary reform on to the statute-book.

Charles, second Earl Grey, was Prime Minister for just over three and a half years. But they were the years which saw the great Reform Bill pass into law. Outside the Prime Minister's room at the House of Commons today is an engraving of the historic scene in Guildhall at the dinner to celebrate its enactment.

He had been First Lord of the Admiralty in the 'Ministry of All the Talents' in 1806 and on Fox's death had succeeded him as Foreign Secretary, Leader of the House and head of the Foxite Whigs. Nevertheless, as Leader of the Opposition in Liverpool's time he was only intermittently effective.

On Wellington's defeat in November 1830, he became Prime Minister. His Cabinet was a brilliant one, the best of the Whigs plus the Canningites and Radicals. In his first speech as Prime Minister he told the House that he had the King's approval to introduce a Reform Bill. That clarified the situation, but he had to answer the question, what kind of Reform Bill? There were nearly as many contradictory ideas of what such a Bill should contain as there were adherents of reform itself. The existing electoral scene extended from the totally rotten boroughs, where, according to a contemporary report, 154 individuals returned 307 members of Parliament out of 658, to the new expanding cities and boroughs, under-represented or even totally unrepresented.

Grey appointed what we would now call a Cabinet Committee to prepare a Bill, telling them that their report should be based on the holding of property and existing territorial divisions. He took the Bill they prepared to the King, explaining its provisions, and making clear that they were much more cautious than the measure he had vetoed in Cabinet. His strategy was obviously based on persuading the King: accept this or be ready for something worse.

His Bill, by the standards of those days was undoubtedly radical: it scrapped eighty boroughs, proposed the elimination of one of the two members from many more over-represented constituencies, and reallocated the seats so released to new and growing areas, both the expanding new boroughs and areas in the shires, where population was increasing. The Bill secured its second reading by only one vote, 302 to 301. Grey asked for a dissolution, and the new House gave the Bill a second reading by 367 to 331. It went through its further stages without adverse votes but the Lords rejected it. The King asked Grey not to resign but refused to create enough new peers to carry it. Grey in return insisted that he should introduce another Bill

Lord Grey, the Prime Minister who presided over the passing of the Great Reform Bill in 1832.

on the same lines. Grey kept his Cabinet together, though some demanded a weaker Bill, which the Lords could accept, and others insisted on the creation of more peers. Unrest in the country was mounting.

Grey decided to press for more peers. He introduced a further Bill which went through the Commons and carried the Lords on second reading, but a wrecking amendment was carried on Committee. Grey offered the King the choice either of creating peers or accepting his resignation. The King accepted his resignation, Grey being asked to remain in office until a new

Queen Victoria presiding at her first Council meeting, 20 June 1837. Her Prime Minister, Lord Melbourne, is holding the state paper which received the first signature of Her Majesty the Queen.

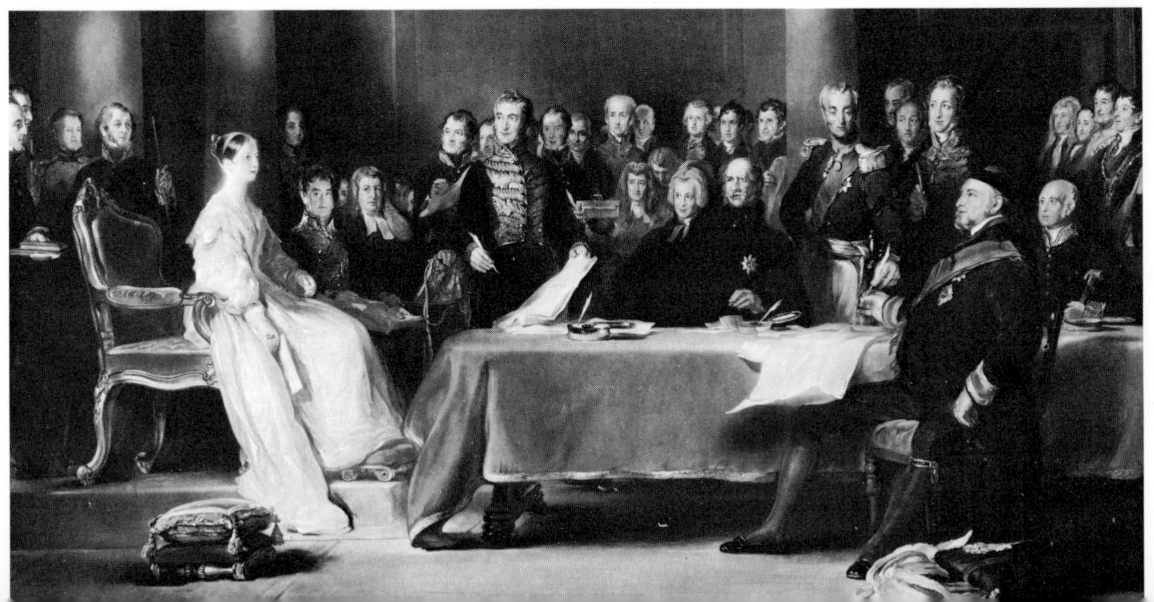

ministry was formed. Wellington failed to create a Government, and the King agreed to create enough peers to carry the Bill. That did the trick: there were sufficient abstentions in the Lords to secure the Bill's passage.

This was the highlight of Grey's brief administration. The foreign scene was quiet, except for the revolution in Belgium, well handled by Grey and Talleyrand. But of even more lasting importance was the measure ending the slave trade. Domestic legislation included Ashley's Factory Act, an Irish Church Bill, a Bank Charter Act, two law reform measures including the establishment of the judicial committees of the Privy Council, and the provision of the first Government grant for education.

The Government fell, in common with so many before it and after it, on an Irish measure, designed to introduce reforms into the Protestant Church of Ireland. The Cabinet was split and Grey resigned, his place in history secured with the 1832 Reform Act.

Viscount Melbourne was a colourful character, his social life not unlike that of Palmerston. He was Prime Minister almost continuously for seven years, years in which a new, young Queen succeeded to the throne and was initiated into the secrets of statecraft by Melbourne, until a new and more intimate adviser, Prince Albert, took over the task. He was also responsible for launching Palmerston into foreign affairs, a field which he was to bestride for the next generation.

Melbourne was a slow developer. Born in 1779 he entered Parliament at twenty-seven, and was forty-six before he first held office as Secretary for Ireland under Canning, and in Goderich's even briefer administration. He returned under Grey at the Home Office, where the great reforms of the criminal law and the creation of the Metropolitan Police had been carried through by Peel. He faced the unrest caused by rural distress and the agitation surrounding the Reform Bill with great severity. He was responsible for transporting the Tolpuddle martyrs. On the credit side he was responsible for the first effective Factory Act and the Poor Law Amendment Act.

After the fall of the Grey administration, William IV, rejecting Russell and Brougham, selected Melbourne as the Whig he disliked least. Melbourne described the offer as a 'great bore', but showed no reluctance about accepting it. He proved a good choice. Taking over a party that no one had succeeded in holding together, he had that indefinable quality of leadership and unification which some Prime Ministers have and others do not. (The Yorkshire saying, 'there's nowt so queer as fowk', attracts a new dimension when the folk are politicians, senior politicians at that, some of them ambitious and ever looking at the Prime Minister's chair in the Cabinet room at No. 10, mentally trying it for size, when they should be concentrating on the problems of the nation.) But after Melbourne's first four months in office he ran into trouble, not with the Cabinet, but with the King. Althorp, Leader of the House, went to the Lords on his father's death; the King would not have Russell as his successor, and peremptorily asked for Melbourne's resignation – the last time that a sovereign sacked a ministry. Peel was sent for, and Wellington held the fort until he arrived.

Peel's minority administration was unviable, and so was his position after an unsuccessful election. Melbourne came back, and remained for over six years. The kindest commentary on those years must be that he survived. His legislative record was minimal. It included the Municipal Government Act and an abortive Irish Poor Law measure.

The accession of the young Queen gave Melbourne a new interest in life. She had been sheltered from the world of politics and society, and he had a considerable educational task to perform. It was in fact rewarding. In constitutional terms she was malleable; she had nothing to unlearn. William IV had created far more problems for a Prime Minister than the new Queen. Melbourne met with her every morning: in the more spacious days of the 1970s the Prime Minister has an audience of the Queen once a week.

During the Bedchamber Crisis, described in the next chapter, Melbourne followed a strict constitutional line. But his Parliamentary position was becoming more vulnerable; he had lost support in the 1837 general election required by the accession of a new Sovereign. His ministry continued, with problems and achievements at a low ebb. Perhaps the most important act of his last three years was the dispatch of his radical colleague Lord Durham to Canada to deal with the problems of the conflict between Upper and Lower Canada. There was trouble in Jamaica, following the freeing of the slaves, and Melbourne's suspension of Jamaica's constitutional ordinance led to a Parliamentary revolt, reducing his majority to four. He resigned – both the Queen and he were near to tears – and in his capacity as father confessor he advised her on the problems of calling in Peel.

2

Sir Robert Peel

IN THE MANNER of ending his active political life, Robert Peel was the most tragic of Britain's Prime Ministers. He was a statesman of consummate ability, one of the few who set Britain on an entirely new course. In a single year he carried Parliament forward, kicking and screaming, a whole generation. By that very act he split his party and, conscious of what he was doing, brought his own career to a premature end.

As the first 'modern Prime Minister' he set the pattern for nearly half a century of British politics. His hero and mentor, the younger Pitt, had created the modern Tory Party. Peel, loyal to what he inherited, nevertheless created the Liberal Party of the second half of the nineteenth century, the party Gladstone was to lead for a quarter of a century. Gladstone himself, described by Macaulay in 1840 as 'the rising hope of those stern and unbending Tories', was a disciple of Peel, a leading figure among his ministers, and accompanied him when he broke away from the Tory majority over the Corn Laws.

A great Prime Minister is usually one who bridges two epochs and carries forward the traditions of his youth into the pattern of the future. This was true of Peel. He was born a year before the outbreak of the French Revolution; he entered Oxford University on the day of Trafalgar; he died, tragically and prematurely, a year before the Great Exhibition of 1851. He spanned and reflected a great social change in politics, the rise of the new men born of the Industrial Revolution which was changing the shape of Britain. His grandfather was a successful calico printer, and his father inherited and expanded the business. Peel shared Pitt's views on the primacy of trade, particularly trade in manufactures, as the principal moving force in politics, but he was born into the industrial world. He knew the social problems the industrial upsurge had created; his father in 1802 had anticipated Ashley, later Shaftesbury, in introducing Bills to deal with the scandalous exploitation of the factory children; Peel himself, though ultimately a disappointment to Ashley, sought to work with him on factory reform. Above all, perhaps without admitting it to himself, he had come under the influence of the new free trade movement, the Anti-Corn Law League of Cobden and Bright, though he shared none of their radical views on electoral reform.

The tragedy of his career lay in his total inability to appreciate a new political phenomenon, the power of party. His belief in the efficacy of argument and the persuasive authority of logic led him to disregard the prejudices of the Tory landed class which was the hard core of his support. But, like Pitt, he was in essence a loner, though more approachable, and also capable of great charm on social occasions. He had a very affectionate family life, and wrote surprisingly tender poems to his wife. Yet he found it hard to come to terms at all easily with his Conservative colleagues. He was shy, awkward and reserved. Never a man to suffer fools gladly, he had no sympathy with party dullards, such as the Tory squirearchy, and had little patience with their inability to recognize self-evident truth, particularly when the truth he was proclaiming was a reversal of what he had recently been instilling into them. As he himself put it:

> To have your own way, and to be for five years the Minister of this country in the House of Commons is quite enough for any man's strength.... But ... to be at the same time the tool of a party – that is to say, to adopt the opinions of men who have not access to your knowledge, and could not profit

Previous page
An engraving of Peel when he was Chief Secretary for Ireland.

Peelfold Farm, Oswaldthistle, Lancashire, the family home of the Peels since George II. Peel's father, the first baronet was born there, Peel himself at Chamber Hall, near Bury.

by it if they had, who spend their time in eating and drinking and hunting, shooting and gambling, horse-racing and so forth – would be an odious servitude, to which I never will submit.

On another occasion he wrote in a private letter to his Chancellor, Goulburn:

> I feel a want of many essential qualifications which are requisite in party leaders, among the rest personal gratification in the game of politics and patience to listen to the sentiments of individuals whom it is equally imprudent to neglect and an intolerable bore to consult.

Peel regarded party as a phenomenon which he would like to have seen go away, as long as the members left their votes behind them. All parties are difficult, some are impossible, but Peel had the unique problem of facing the hostility of a large majority of his own party led at the crucial time – and this proved to be lethal – by Disraeli at his most unscrupulous.

A nineteenth-century view of Harrow. Seven Prime Ministers went to school there.

Like Pitt, Peel's early life was made easy for him. His father was in fact a great deal wealthier, though certainly less extravagant, than the elder Pitt.

He was sent to Harrow, went to Oxford in 1805 and was the first to win a double first in classics and mathematics, after the honours schools were separated. A safe seat was at once found for him at Cashel, Tipperary, in 1809; later he went to Chippenham, before achieving his ambition by becoming the burgess for the University of Oxford.

In the year after his election to Parliament he accepted an offer from Liverpool, the Secretary for War and the Colonies, to become one of his under-secretaries. When Liverpool became Prime Minister in 1812, he gave Peel the much more responsible position of Chief Secretary for Ireland, a post which he held for six years. In 1813 he was concerned in the decision to give a Government grant to Maynooth, a training college for Catholic priests. Maynooth was to cause him trouble as Prime Minister thirty years later when, facing deep trouble in Ireland, he decided to treble the grant and Gladstone resigned his post as President of the Board of Trade.

Peel studied the problems of Ireland systematically, politically, philosophically. He was shocked by the abysmal poverty, the overpopulation and land hunger, and the dependence of the mass of the people on the potato, for the majority the one staple crop.

Ireland was in a state of political ferment. Pitt's statement tying Union to Catholic Emancipation was Peel's inheritance. Peel was more concerned with the condition of Ireland question than Catholic Emancipation which he said 'would not solve the problem of poverty'. This was good Peelite logic, but throughout history empty bellies have frequently rumbled with political demands. Across the Pennines from his home, textile workers had smashed the masters' cropping-frames in the Luddite riots. As Prime Minister he was to face the fury of the Chartists – men with new and revolutionary cries on their lips – but for a century afterwards history students were to be set essays on the proposition that Chartism was a knife and fork question.

Peel left Ireland in 1818, feeling that he had failed. But one achievement he could claim, the creation of the Irish Constabulary. Dr Kitson Clark, in a speech of tribute to Peel in Bury on the centenary of his death, referred to it as 'a body with an unlucky future but probably still one of the best instruments for peace and order that unhappy country had yet known'. Ireland left its mark on him and was later to dictate the two great decisions of his career, Catholic Emancipation and the repeal of the Corn Laws, both of them total reversals of his previous policies.

After eight years in office, six of them in the Irish firing-line, Peel felt he wanted a rest, and experience on the back-benches. His appointment as Chairman of the Commons committee on the resumption of cash payments was his introduction to the subject of finance, of which he was to become one of the great masters. A disciple of the classical economists from Adam Smith to his contemporary Ricardo, he now had a chance to work for sound budgeting, freer trade and the stabilization of the currency based on gold. His committee included such leading ministers as Canning, Castlereagh, Huskisson, Vansittart, and Robinson – two of whom were to become Prime Ministers – and his report was a classical assertion of the new economic orthodoxy. His conclusions, and the training he received, were to lead to his Bank Charter Act in 1844, which regulated the Bank of England's operations and Britain's financial policy for eighty years, apart from three suspensions at times of crisis.

In November 1822, the Prime Minister, Lord Liverpool, offered Peel the Home Office, a post he was to hold until April 1827 and again from January 1828 to November 1830, seven and a quarter years in all. He was undoubtedly the greatest reforming Home Secretary of all time.

His great creation was the Metropolitan Police Force. In March 1823 he moved for a committee to inquire into the question. While this produced useful studies, it recommended against such a force, because the loss of freedom and personal liberty would outweigh anything it might achieve in detecting crime. Pitt's proposals forty years earlier had foundered on the same objection, and Peel now had to contend with the strong popular feelings arising from the use of spies and *agents provocateurs* during the years of repression, aggravated by Peterloo, and by a campaign against the odious Combination Acts, directed against the nascent trade unions and individual groups of workmen.

Peel concentrated for the time on the reform of the criminal law, the most fundamental ever undertaken, before or since. He brought to the morass of existing law all the fervour which Bentham was applying over a wider field. *Cui bono*, everything had to be queried and justified. First he put through a Bill prepared by Sidmouth, his predecessor, dealing with prison reform. Two Acts of his own in 1823 and 1824 continued the process, bringing the more important prisons under the direct control of the Home Office, operating under new general regulations. He cut through the whole system of penalties, beginning with a root-and-branch reform of the list of crimes punishable by death. Five Bills became law in two months, abolishing the death penalty over a wide, previously uncoordinated area, and substituting lesser punishments. These were not always easy to find: transportation was not enough of a deterrent; there was growing opposition to whipping and the treadmill. He rapidly concluded that he must concentrate on an attack on crime and the reduction of the prison population.

By 1826 he had regularized and consolidated the statute law, previously a chaos of arbitrary and unrelated measures going back in some cases to the Middle Ages. He introduced a degree of flexibility in the use of the death penalty by a more systematic use of reprieves, and increased the certainty of punishment. He had amended the legislation controlling the jury system. At the end of the year he was ready to improve the system of detection of crime, and gave notice of a further inquiry into the police of the metropolis. In 1827 he was out of office during Canning's brief ministry – his reaction to Canning's offer of a post and the animosity which grew up between them over Catholic Emancipation was later thrown back at him by Bentinck in the battle over the Corn Laws, Bentinck actually accusing him of having 'chased and hunted Canning to death'. Goderich lasted as Prime Minister only four months, and Peel returned as Home Secretary in Wellington's Cabinet in January 1828. Legislation prepared while he was out of office further consolidated the criminal code: the cumulative achievement of all the measures since 1825 was the repeal of 278 Acts and the consolidation of the rest into eight statutes. In February 1830, just before the Government fell, he gave notice of further Bills to consolidate the law on magistrates, the coinage and forgery, which had they been enacted would have meant that ninety per cent of criminal cases coming before the courts would have been covered by his reform legislation.

But even more urgent was the establishment of the Metropolitan Police. Yet another inquiry was instituted, and this time the committee was in favour. In April, 1829, Peel introduced the Metropolitan Police Improvement Bill, establishing a new police organization in an area roughly covered by a ten-mile radius from central London, financed by a police rate. To the Secretary of State was given the power to establish the force.

Members of the new force paraded in uniform for the first time in September 1829. The old fears quickly died away. The London public came to accept them, joke about them, depend on them, and gave Peel the credit, and the cartoonists material for years, calling them alternately 'Bobbies' and 'Peelers'.

As Home Secretary, Peel also had a special responsibility for Ireland. The campaign for Irish Catholics to be given their democratic 'rights' was growing more active, headed by the Catholic Association. In 1825, Liverpool's Government had passed an Act aimed at suppressing it, but this was allowed to lapse, and Anglesey, the liberal-minded Lord Lieutenant whom Peel had inherited from the Canning administration, reported to London: 'Ireland is . . . in a state of balance.' In the British House of Commons Burdett's motion for Emancipation was carried by six votes, Peel's reply to the debate being almost wholly negative. In this he was not followed by his Prime Minister in a similar debate in the Lords. Though the motion there was lost, Wellington's opposition was muted, related not to principle but to expediency and a demand for safeguards.

Peel's first reaction to the Commons defeat was to resign, but the Cabinet was in danger of breaking up over a wrangle about pocket boroughs, over which Huskisson and the other Canningites had resigned. Had Peel gone now, it would have been likely to have led to the end of the administration and the prospect of an indefinite period of Whig rule. He responded to Wellington's plea to soldier on, but indicated that it could not be for long. He felt that the rearguard action against Emancipation was lost, and he wanted no part in the decision.

The crisis was precipitated by the appointment of Fitzgerald as President of the Board of Trade, which meant his resignation and a by-election. (This barbarous practice continued until the end of World War One; Winston Churchill was one of the victims, losing his seat in 1908 after his own appointment to the Board of Trade.) O'Connell stood against him, and was elected by a massive majority, though as a Catholic he was unable to take his seat.

Wellington called Peel to a series of confidential discussions. On 1 August the Prime Minister minuted the King with a frank statement that he faced a situation in which the only solution was Catholic Emancipation, and asked leave to consult Peel and the Lord Chancellor. Peel's attitude had become more pragmatic: he was still basically hostile to the idea, but set out the arguments as a choice of evils. Wellington's arguments could not be gainsaid: there was a majority in the Commons for Emancipation. If the Government fell, a pro-Catholic majority would take over. Moreover, Ireland faced civil war. Wellington proposed as a positive compromise that the existing law be not repealed, but suspended, a year at a time. Peel's reaction was that any decision should be final, and he clearly saw no alternative to full political equality, with perhaps a bar on Catholics holding such posts as the Woolsack. At the same time he opposed Wellington's proposal that the Irish clergy should be paid out of public funds.

He was prepared to go along with the proposals, though, as Wellington put it, he was not an official party to it. He asked that his reluctant assent should be kept secret. The situation in Ireland deteriorated, with quasi-military organizations arising on both sides. The choice lay between coercion or a 'Catholic' solution.

The King was still unconvinced; the massed ranks of the Anglican bishops were totally opposed. Wellington had convinced Peel that Emancipation could not be carried, nor the pro-Government MPs held together, without him. On 12 January 1829, Peel capitulated. If his resignation, he told the Duke, would make it impossible to carry Emancipation, he would remain in office. From that moment, events moved quickly. The King gave permission to the Cabinet to consider the question, though reserving his position on any advice they might give him. Wellington brought a letter to Peel, saying that he saw no chance of overcoming his difficulties unless Peel remained in office. Peel out, everybody out. Peel replied that he was ready to remain, and bring forward the Government's proposals in the House. If he stayed, as Leader of the House, he could do no other. He was now committed, though this was not public knowledge until on 4 February, at the eve-of-session dinner, he read out to Government

Two Tory Prime Ministers: an early photograph of Peel and the Duke of Wellington.

supporters the text of the King's Speech to be delivered the next day.

Execrated by some of his followers, by Church leaders, by leaders of Oxford University, his constituency; lampooned, cartooned, he tasted the dregs of a Judas. To the end of his days he was to be reminded that he had refused to join the Canning Government because of his objection to Canning as a 'Catholic', i.e. an emancipator. He was to be regarded on other issues as a potential defector if the going got too rough. The virulence of the protectionist reaction against the repeal of the Corn Laws was aggravated by the fact that he had broken faith with his party and his past beliefs once before.

As Rosebery, a great admirer, said in his short biography nearly half a century after Peel's death: 'Granted that he was right in the first transition, he should not have repeated it; the character of public men cannot stand two such shocks ...' Peel offered his resignation as member for the University, and, on receiving no response, resigned. He fought again at the ensuing election and lost. He was almost at once elected for a safe Tory pocket borough. On the lintel of the door leading to Christ Church hall can still be seen the nails hammered into the door, 'NO PEEL'.

In Parliament he made a great speech of four hours, and was warmly cheered, though thirty Government supporters went into the division lobby against him. By the end of March, the Bill was law.

Wellington's Government fell in November 1830. In the spring there had been deep disagreements about Parliamentary reform, concentrated at that time on competing measures to abolish pocket boroughs and provide more seats for some of the new urban areas, as well as certain county constituencies. But the Whigs and Radicals were also running a parallel campaign on fiscal reform, related to the uncomfortably high levels of taxation.

In June George IV died and was succeeded by the Sailor King, William IV. There was some anxiety because the heiress was Princess Victoria, then only eleven, with the unpopular Duke of Cumberland next in line. There was already concern in Parliament about young queens and wicked uncles in Portugal to create an atmosphere of unsettlement. Though the result of the general election was indeterminate, Wellington's Government could not survive for very long and there were manoeuvrings about a coalition, possibly with the Canningites led by Huskisson. Huskisson, however, was killed, knocked down by the *Rocket* at the opening of the Liverpool and Manchester railway as he stepped across to talk to the Duke. Coalition overtures to and by the Whigs broke down over the Whig insistence on Parliamentary reform, which Wellington and Peel resisted.

Unrest in the country caused by the depression came to a head with riots centring on the Lord Mayor's Guildhall banquet. On 15 November the Government was defeated on the King's Civil List: Wellington and his Cabinet resigned. The Whigs returned under Lord Grey.

From that time Parliamentary reform dominated Westminster and spread out into the country. It was essentially a Commons matter, hence Peel rather than Wellington was in the centre of it. He now, at forty-two, had succeeded to his father's baronetcy and to his father's house, Old Drayton Hall near Stafford. From 1831 to 1835 he was occupied in re-building it, greatly enlarging it, and naming it Drayton Manor. He was now in opposition. Until 1830 all but five of his first twenty-one years in Parliament had been spent in office; of the remaining twenty all but five were in opposition. The tide was strongly for reform, as Peel finally conceded: meanwhile he had to lead a party with little stomach for it. He himself was in favour of abolishing the pocket boroughs and transferring their Parliamentary representation to the new areas in the North and elsewhere. But to an extension of the franchise he was strongly opposed, and defended his position on closely argued doctrinal grounds. But he was not going to put forward even his own limited proposals – he had outraged his party once already. 'Peel was for Parliamentary Reform,' Wellington wrote, 'provided it was not carried out by *us* in Office.' On 1 March 1830, Lord John Russell put forward the Government's scheme for a wide redistribution and, by the standards of those days, a massive increase in the electorate: 168 existing seats would be abolished.

Peel, replying, was careful, more so than many of his shellbacks would have wished. He was not against reform in general, but against this particular reform, which was too sweeping and would plunge the country into constitutional crisis. There were criticisms of his tactics – some Tories thought he should have gone for the kill without qualification. They were almost certainly wrong, but they tasted victory when they carried a division against the reduction in the number of English members. The Government withdrew the Bill, and the King descended on the Palace of Westminster in person to dissolve Parliament. The House was in uproar: Peel was called, lost his cool as we might say these days, and shouted and screamed incoherently, to be silenced by the arrival of Black Rod to summon the Commons to the Lords to hear the prorogation read.

The result of the following bitterly fought election was a clear majority for

Apart from Disraeli, Peel was the only Prime Minister to be honoured by a private visit from Queen Victoria. A contemporary print of her arrival at Drayton Manor in 1843.

reform, though not a landslide. Peel virtually withdrew from party and Parliamentary affairs: he knew that the die was cast, and that his more limited scheme had no hope of acceptance. The Bill passed the Commons but was thrown out by the Lords. Riots rocked the country: Peel fortified his home with carbines. The third Bill was introduced. There were attempts to bring members of different views together in order to reduce the temperature by mutual concessions, but the gap was too wide. Peel gave the House and his party his considered advice, to oppose, doomed though he knew it was to failure. The decision was now again with the Lords. On 8 May Grey told the King that the Government would resign unless he agreed to the creation of fifty new peers. The King refused and accepted their resignations. The battle spread from Parliament to the country, with something like a general strike in industrial districts, a run on the banks, and the City fighting back by petitioning Parliament to stop supplies.

The King had Peel sounded out on taking office, but since he understood that this offer was conditional on his introducing a substantial measure of reform he refused. The irrepressible Duke, whose relations with Peel had been cool for some time, tried to put a team together, selecting the Speaker to head it. But this failed, as did an attempt to form a Wellington administration, and the King was told that there was no Tory alternative Government in sight. He therefore had no choice but to agree to concede the demand for additional peers, and the Lords accepted the inevitable.

Peel, vastly relieved at having escaped the odium of a further reversal of policy, now faced an election, where his party lost heavily. He doggedly set out to rebuild it, clear in his own mind that there was no hope of an early return to office, but equally that it would be futile to hope to reverse the Reform Act. He concentrated on his party, which he himself rechristened Conservative. Gloomy though he was about the state of the country, and the likely trend of Whig measures, he pronounced, in his opening speech of the new Parliament, his own attitude to Reform: '. . . that question is finally and irrevocably disposed of. He was now determined to look forward to the future alone, and considering the constitution as it existed, to take his stand on main and essential matters.'

Peel, now *de facto* leader of the Conservatives, concentrated on welding his party into a more united team and turning towards the post-Reform era. Two dangerous and divisive campaigns were over. The yet more dangerous divide over free trade and protection was more than a decade away. Meanwhile he could relax and study the troubles of the Government party.

The new Government were badly split on Irish tithes and the Irish Church Bill. Stanley, later a Tory Prime Minister, was near to resignation, but held his hand; he resigned the following year, as did Graham, and Ripon (formerly Goderich). With Althorp also threatening to go, Grey himself resigned and Melbourne took over, in July 1834. There was talk of Peel being sent for. Peel, it has been said, thought this premature: he would have preferred to see the troubles continue. Neither he nor anyone else could have foreseen that in a little over four months the King would be sending for the Tories.

It was the Coercion Bill which forced the issue. Some of the more rigorous clauses of its predecessor were removed, and it went to the Lords. The Tory peers were persuaded by Wellington to let it through, but they then rejected the Tithes Bill by a large majority. Peel, who was going through one of his periods of coolness to the Duke – this time because of his pique at Wellington's

There are who strangely love to roam
And find in wildest haunts their home.
and some in halls of lordly state,
who yet are homeless, desolate.
The sailor's home is on the main
the warriors, on the tented plain,
the maiden's, in her bower of rest,
the infant's, on his mother's breast;
but where thou art, is home to me,
and home without thee cannot be

Robert Peel

In public Peel was reserved and often appeared a cold man. In private he enjoyed an exceptionally happy marriage. This love poem was written to his wife Julia.

election as Chancellor of Oxford University – went off with his family to Italy.

At home, Althorp's father died, and his move to the Lords meant a reshuffle of the Cabinet. Melbourne chose Russell as Leader of the House and this revived all the old splits. The King, fearing a reversion by the Government to the policies of the previous year, dismissed the Cabinet. When Wellington was sent for on 17 November he said that the Prime Minister must be in the Commons, and the only possible choice was Peel. (This recommendation did not create a precedent. Peers were Prime Ministers until the beginning of the twentieth century, and it was only in 1923 that membership of the Upper House was given as one reason for rejecting the Marquess of Curzon, though his personality was sufficient to constitute a deterrent.)

The choice of Peel produced something approaching a comedy. Peel was in Rome. The electric cable had not been invented and even when he could be found it would take many days, in the pre-railway age, to get back. The messenger in fact took eleven days to reach him and was rebuked by Peel for not saving a day by taking a different route. Peel himself took thirteen days to return. To ensure that the King's Government was carried on, Wellington was sworn as First Lord and Secretary of State and Lyndhurst was sworn as Lord Chancellor.

Peel's surprise was first followed by doubts, but he had plenty of time to resolve them. Since the King's Government had been held up for three and a half weeks due to his absence, he could hardly refuse. Equally he had no hope of a Parliamentary majority; therefore he must insist on a dissolution. He became Prime Minister on 10 December 1834, and succeeded in forming a Cabinet, but the country had the right to expect some statement of the new Government's policy, above all on the Reform Act. On taking office he had to resign his seat and fight Tamworth again. This gave him a chance to publish an election manifesto to his constituents, which would of course receive national circulation. It was read to the Cabinet and published. An era in British politics ended when he declared, following his statement in Parliament two years earlier, that he regarded the Reform Act as 'a final and irrevocable settlement of a great Constitutional question'.

Parliament was dissolved, but the result was indeterminate. The decision would be decided by the first Commons votes in the new Parliament. Peel was defeated by a Whig–Radical combination, which was supported by O'Connell's Irishmen, on the selection of the Speaker, and by seven votes on an Opposition amendment – regretting the dissolution of Parliament – to the Address in Reply to the King's Speech. He struggled on for a few weeks, losing vote after vote, the House itself becoming a bear-garden. He was defeated on Irish Titles, though significantly Stanley supported him. On 8 April he announced the resignation of the Government and Melbourne returned. But 'the Hundred Days' had revived interest in the Conservatives. They had healed their divisions sufficiently to look like a Government and produce an agreed policy. They had a clearly acknowledged leader. There would be no harking back to the arguments about the Reform Bill. The new Conservative Party could look to the Forties and beyond.

In 1839 another opportunity seemed to present itself. In a debate on the suspension of the Jamaican constitution, the Whigs had a humiliatingly small majority of five. Peel's chance of becoming Prime Minister was wrecked by the 'Bedchamber Question'. The Queen was surrounded by Whig ladies, and Peel, fearing their influence, pressed on the Palace a substantial programme of replacement. The Queen refused. By 1841, when the collapse of the Whig Government brought Peel back to office, soon to be fortified with an election victory, the problem had been solved. The Prince Consort had used his mediatory powers, and worked out a programme, subsequently agreed with Peel, of selective replacement, leaving the Queen with her favourite Court ladies.

The Whig Government perished in 1841. It had run out of steam. The keen, manufacturing, free trade radicals were more and more seeking to become the tail wagging the dog. As a last demonstration the Government staged a minor free trade demonstration in the Budget, with sharp reduction in the timber, sugar and corn duties. The Whigs took it because it helped to bridge the deficit, the radicals saw it as an omen of the forthcoming free trade Jerusalem. Peel was not one to be trapped. He attacked not the trade reforms, but the Budget deficit and the whole record of Whig finance. His critical motion was carried by thirty-six votes. The Government hung on for another month trying to needle Peel to commit himself on the Corn Laws. The inevitable general election gave the Conservatives a majority of seventy-six.

With Goulburn as Chancellor, Peel immediately addressed himself to the public accounts. He decided that only bold measures could cover the deficit he had inherited, and at the same time finance the great sweep to free trade which, as Pitt's disciple, he sought. He secured Cabinet approval to the reintroduction of income tax, introduced by Pitt as a specifically war tax, its duration limited to that of the war – indeed it had been specifically laid down that all records were to be destroyed with the peace, though the Treasury obligingly filed one or two copies away for the historians.

Peel was in a strong position, as are most Prime Ministers after a successful election which dismisses a Government seen to be in an advanced state of rigor mortis. That strength was reinforced by linking his proposal to the free trade programme which he saw as the only means of relieving industrial stagnation and the distress and unrest in the factory districts. There was, too, the political advantage of driving a handy wedge between the country Whigs and the radicals of the new capitalism.

When the new session began, Peel announced the income tax, not as an act of financial desperation but as a means to a wider policy. Parliaments of all generations will survive and accept a fiscal shock if, first, they are left breathless, and second, the shock is presented as part of a considered strategy giving hope for the future: he was less circumscribed than many Prime Ministers and Chancellors of the present age.

Estimating the yield of the income tax as £4·3 millions, he budgeted for a surplus of £1·8 millions in place of the Whig deficit he had so savagely denounced in the dying days of the previous Parliament. He would use part but not all of the surplus to make the most sweeping changes in the tariff complex since the early days of Pitt. The general rule was to be a five per cent tariff (or less) on raw materials and a maximum of twenty per cent on manufactured goods. At the same time he announced a review of the existing Corn Laws 'relaxing the amount of protection where it might safely be relaxed, and attempting to reconcile all just protection for agriculture with greater steadiness in trade'. Peel was a great one for 'reviews', as was shown by his handling of the Metropolitan Police question. He had a keen sense of timing, realizing as Home Secretary that he could not move at once. On the Corn Laws it was even more clear that he would have to move slowly in order to carry first his Cabinet with him, and then his party; it seemed wise to let events and public debate do part of the work for him.

Financial reform was followed by structural reform, such as the Bank Charter Act of 1844, already mentioned, and the Companies Act which was the first serious response to the realization that Britain's economy was being increasingly dominated by public companies, some of them quite small, with obligations to shareholders as well as the public interest. The urgency of companies legislation was brought home by the floating of hundreds of companies to build railways, some duplicating routes, some floated or projected with no idea of construction at all, but hoping to exact blackmail settlements from other companies already covering or hoping to cover the same tract of territory.

One of the most important and far-sighted measures was the Railways Regulations Act, 1844. This was the work of Gladstone, Vice-President of the Board of Trade, nominally under the direction of Ripon (for Goody Goderich had surfaced again, for his final public performance). Gladstone worked direct to Peel both on railways and on the intricate, laborious work of rewriting the customs tariff. Railways presented an entirely new, almost philosophical challenge to the legislators. Except in agriculture, the prevailing philosophy exalted competition. Railways were seen as the successors to turnpikes and canals, where the proprietors constructed the 'road' and levied tolls on the individual users, stagecoach, wagon or barge operators. One or two early railways were planned on that principle, but it soon became clear that the only result of having competitive operators with lethal machines capable of 30 mph or more would be a daily toll of accidents. In separately enacting each Bill for a railway, Parliament was therefore creating a local or perhaps even a long-distance monopoly which must of necessity be subject to conrol, not only on safety matters, but on services, and above all on fares and rates for goods traffic.

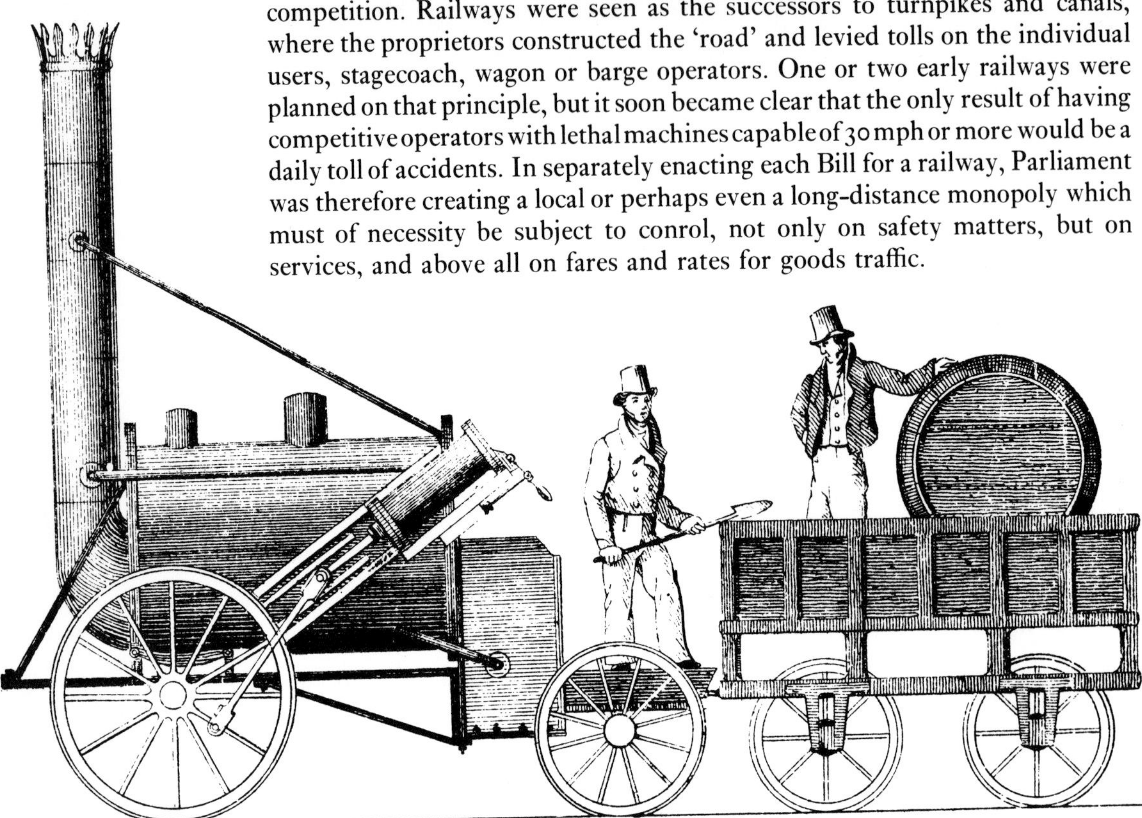

The Rocket – symbol and pioneer of the new Railway Age.

Gladstone set up a Select Committee under his own chairmanship, which took evidence, and produced as an annex to its report the agreed text of a Bill. The resulting Act instituted the Parliamentary trains, one in each direction each day at a penny a mile, the subject of W.S. Gilbert's reference to the discomfort of Parliamentary trains in *The Mikado*. On charges it aimed at a general level of ten per cent profit, but reserved the right – since Parliament was looking ahead in an unknown field – to take the railways into public ownership after twenty-one years, or provide tighter control over charges. There could thus be no breach of faith if the State in the Sixties were to use these powers, after a long period of experience, to facilitate national routes. Further legislation in 1845 laid down a standard gauge for all new construction.

Peel's foreign policy was strong, purposive and unsensational. His Foreign Secretary, Aberdeen, was loyal but rather ineffectual, as his record as Prime Minister during the Crimean War was to confirm. Peel was in charge. Aberdeen had none of the freedom that Palmerston had enjoyed under Melbourne.

It was not a happy international scene when Peel took over. Britain was at war with China and Afghanistan, there was a dispute with the United States over the Canadian boundary with Oregon and with Maine, at the extreme ends of the continent. War fever had been stirred up there on the latitudinal cry of 'Fifty-Four Forty or Fight'. There was trouble with France over the Spanish marriage, where it was feared that French influence over Spain would increase if the young Queen married Louis Philippe's son. Agreement was in fact reached, and an 'Entente Cordiale' proclaimed, the phrase being invented by Aberdeen. It did not last; there was trouble over the arrest of a British missionary and the British consul during a French armed incursion into Tahiti, and over French designs on Morocco and Tangiers following the annexation of Algiers. A war scare, exploited by Parliament, forced Peel to strengthen the Channel coast defences.

By the end of Peel's administration, the foreign scene was much quieter, and his last act as Prime Minister, following his decision to resign over the Corn Laws, was to announce the settlement of the boundary disputes with the United States.

'It was rotten potatoes did it all ... it was that that put Peel into his damned fright.' That was Wellington's judgment on the repeal of the Corn Laws, which ended Peel's career. Certainly the failure of the Irish potato crop was decisive in driving him to repeal then and there: indeed the Corn Law question is inseparable from that of developments in Ireland during the Peel administration.

In the last days of the Whig administration the attempt to force Peel to declare himself on the question of the protectionist duties on foreign corn had led him simply to refer to the social distress in the country and say: '... if I could be induced to believe that an alteration in the Corn Laws would be an effective remedy for those distresses ... I would earnestly advise a relaxation, an alteration, nay, if necessary, a repeal of the Corn Laws.' On taking office, he combined limited changes in the Corn Laws in his sweeping tariff changes. From 1815 there had been a 'sliding scale' of duties varying inversely with the internal price level. When a good harvest at home produced a glut and low prices, import duties were raised to prevent the price to the farmer falling through the floor; when the crop failed, and prices rose, the duties were relaxed. The aim was to establish the steadiest possible price which would give the farmer a reasonable return on his crop and not bring hardship to the consumer. In 1828 the rates of the sliding scale were amended, and in 1842 Peel, as a result of Gladstone's work, introduced new provisions based on 56s. a quarter as a fair intermediate price, and 45s. as the minimum price at which foreign wheat could be imported in any quantity. The duty was fixed at the nominal figure of a shilling when the price was 73s., 16s. when it was 56s., and 20s. when it was 50s.

In the early years of Peel's ministry the Irish situation was growing worse. Poverty was acute and rioting endemic, and the political scene was dominated by O'Connell's Repeal Association, demanding the dissolution of the Union of Ireland with England, mainly because, although Catholic Emancipation had been finally conceded, Catholics had too little a share in the offices of profit under the Crown on both sides of the water, particularly in Ireland itself. Law and order were increasingly threatened, until in October 1843 O'Connell and a number of his followers were arrested. Ireland was once again at the centre of British politics. Peel would not grant the main Irish demands, but trebled the Catholic Maynooth grant, leading to Gladstone's troubled but somewhat illogical resignation from the Board of Trade.

In 1845 potato blight, a fungus disease, struck the Irish crop: large parts of Europe were hit, but for Ireland it meant famine. Two scientists were sent over to assess the situation, and reported that the crop would be half the normal – or three-eighths if seed potatoes were deducted – and warned that if the soil were infected there could be a similar failure in the following year. Peel was now convinced that starvation could be averted only by freeing grain imports.

He had to take his decision in the face of growing pressure from the Anti-Corn Law League for free trade in grain. Peel saw that if he did so it would make their entire case, which they sought to extend to the whole field of tariff policy, that duties mean high prices.

The Cabinet were sharply divided; Peel handled them gently and gave them time. A relief programme was proposed, but the necessary funds would have to be granted by Parliament, which might respond by carrying repeal. Peel told them that it would be dangerous for the Government 'to resist with all its energies any material modification of the Corn Law'. Some of the Cabinet were unhappy, and Graham sent the Prime Minister a warning letter. Peel proposed to open the ports to foreign grain at a low rate, call Parliament and announce the Government's intention to introduce a new Corn Law, unspecified. Only three ministers supported him. The Lord Lieutenant of Ireland was demanding emergency powers. Peel told the Cabinet that he could not agree to the issue of the necessary instructions to the Lord Lieutenant 'and undertake to maintain the existing Corn Law'.

Lord John Russell had just published his *Edinburgh Letter* demanding repeal. Peel still could not get a majority of ministers to support him, let alone a united ministry. He proposed a Bill to phase out the corn duties over eight years. More ministers supported him, but Stanley and Buccleuch indicated that they would resign. Peel now reported to the Queen (and Albert) and it was agreed that Russell should be asked to form a Government. Peel went so far as to write a letter to show Russell, indicating his *personal* support for the proposals in the *Edinburgh Letter*: he could not promise party, or even official front-bench support. He was greatly relieved when he heard that Russell had agreed to form a Government, but Russell then withdrew. In these circumstances Peel would have to tell the Queen he would stay on. He told the Cabinet the choice was not for or against grain duties, but who would head the Government: Peel or Grey or Cobden? Stanley resigned, but Peel got Cabinet support.

Now he had to face his party, and Parliament. On 27 January he announced reductions on a long list of imports, including soap, timber, tobacco. On the Corn Laws, there would be a progressive reduction to 1849, then abolition. The cheers came almost wholly from the Whigs, amid a sullen silence on the Conservative side. Lord George Bentinck, with Disraeli as his brains-trust and hatchet-man, took over the leadership of the protectionist majority on the Tory benches.

The next four months saw one of the most bitter successions of debates in the history of Parliament. Bitter because of the party division on the Tory side, with the majority sitting behind those whom they saw as guilty of defection and betrayal. Bitter because they could sense that the party was not only committed to years of Opposition, but certain to be divided for years ahead, with the only accomplished leaders in the minority faction. Bitter, too, because the angry Tories remembered a previous 'betrayal', on Catholic Emancipation, and there were many strong opponents of Parliamentary reform who also were ready to throw Peel's final acceptance of the Reform Act at Tamworth into the scales against him.

Bitter, finally, because in the most acrid nights of debate the attack was led by Disraeli, with a venom and destructive effectiveness seldom seen in Parliament before or since. Peel could not have expected Disraeli to go to such lengths; probably he did not think he had the ability. But before his conversion to repeal was known, only suspected, he listened to Cobden's attack on the Corn Laws during a debate initiated by Cobden, and was so shattered that he handed his brief to Sidney Herbert, saying: 'You must answer this, for I cannot.' Disraeli picked up an infelicitous phrase by Herbert about agriculturists 'whining for help' and launched his venomous attack on the two ministers in which he excoriated Peel for putting up 'his valet' to reply.

On the second reading of his repeal Bill, with Whig and Radical support, the Bill was carried by 97 votes. Of the Conservatives who were present, 112 voted with Peel, 231 against. Peel knew that this was the end. An unpredictable number of his former followers would shortly exact their revenge, when the House had to decide on the Irish coercion bill to which Peel was committed, and join with the hostile Opposition in the lobby.

On the third reading, furious at Disraeli's charge that his whole life had been one of political larceny, Peel challenged his tormentor – why then had he been 'ready as I think he was, to unite his fortunes with mine in office'? Disraeli insisted on the right to make a personal statement and denied that he had ever 'solicited office'. Peel, it is generally thought, had the most damning evidence of Disraeli's letter of 5 September 1841, in his pocket, but disdained to use it. One must ask why. Perhaps it was that Peel would have felt it degrading to get into the ring with Disraeli, or that the standards of his upbringing forbade him to quote a private letter. More likely it was that he already knew that he could not survive: his decision after Russell's refusal to stand by the Queen had been not only final but terminal; perhaps the death-wish was there, but certainly the death-call was at hand. He had nearly broken down at the beginning of his speech, but managed to carry on with a great fighting performance, and the Bill secured its third reading. Maybe it was that Peel felt as Asquith did later: coming across a phrase of Bolingbroke, 'I never wrestle with a chimney-sweep', he said it was a 'good saying which I sometimes call to mind when I am confronting Bonar Law.'

Meanwhile the Irish Crimes Bill was before the Commons. On second reading Bentinck made his charge that Peel had 'chased and hunted' Canning to death. He claimed that since Peel had admitted being already a convert to Emancipation, he stood convicted of 'base and dishonourable conduct'. An outraged Peel decided to challenge him to a duel, and asked Lord Lincoln to act as second. Lincoln the next day was able to talk him out of it, and persuaded Peel instead to make a reasoned defence of his relations with Canning.

The day after the repeal Bill passed the Lords, Peel was defeated on the second reading of the Irish Crimes Bill. Seventy-four of the Bentinck–Disraeli Tories voted with the Opposition. The following Monday, Peel announced the resignation of the Government. He never held office again, though he remained a member of Parliament and intervened majestically on major subjects, such as Ireland and free trade.

He made his last speech in the House a few days before his death, in the debate on the Don Pacifico incident. With his record of sober and considered policies in foreign affairs, he criticized Palmerston's turbulent and adventurous foreign policy, and warned against intervention in the internal affairs of other countries. That night he voted with a united Conservative Opposition.

The following day, 29 June 1850, he was thrown from his horse and seriously

An engraving of Peel arriving at the House of Commons in 1846 and being greeted by a 'Peeler'.

injured. As the news spread round London, the people flocked in thousands to pay silent and affectionate tribute to him: not so much the men and women of fashion, or the actors on the Westminster stage: it was the costers and porters and waggoners and dockers who maintained the silent vigil until his death.

He had dominated the Parliament of his times: he had done more to carry his country, its institutions and policies into the world of the second half of the nineteenth century than any other statesman; he had, without so intending, though not living long enough to realize it, created a new party of new men, the Liberals of the future.

He left his own epitaph, which was inscribed on statues even in towns with which he had no connection, and political leaders of today can recall seeing them – learning them by heart – as boys. They were the words of his final speech as Prime Minister:

> I shall leave a name execrated by every monopolist who ... clamours for protection because it accrues to his individual benefit; but it may be that I shall leave a name sometimes remembered with expressions of goodwill in the abodes of those whose lot it is to labour, and to earn their daily bread by the sweat of their brow, when they shall recruit their exhausted strength with abundant and untaxed food, the sweeter because it is no longer leavened by a sense of injustice.

Politics in Transition 1846–1854

Lord John Russell – Earl Russell from 1861 – was Prime Minister in the Commons from 1846 to 1852 and in the Lords for less than a year in 1865–6.

Following Peel's resignation in 1846, he tried to pursue a new line. Where Peel had been destroyed because he took too little account of his party, Russell set out to show that party government worked – he would give his party its head. He was the first exponent of open government, a most improbable Anthony Wedgwood Benn of the mid-nineteenth century. (More than a century before Tony Benn, he invented 'life peers', but his first choice as a noble guinea-pig finally refused to accept nomination.)

Russell was not an easy character to work with: William IV had broken a Government over him. He would not drive his Cabinet, or seek to stamp his personality on them: he would preside over them and seek to distil their individual views into a collective decision. It was an idea, and he survived for six years. In fact, true prime ministership lies somewhere between Peel and Russell: you cannot ignore your party, or the particular views of individual ministers, but equally you cannot put the Prime Minister's position into commission.

He would have liked to be different from his predecessors, especially after the election which followed Peel's resignation gave him 330 seats, but the circumstances of the time forced him into hard decisions. The Irish famine of 1846 and its consequences, the financial crisis of 1847, the revival of a more militant Chartism in 1848 – with revolutions all over Europe – forced him to become the defender of law and order. With an open Cabinet facing a determinedly independent House of Commons, he had either to act or to leave Parliament to decide. On an Irish challenge he left the Irish MPs to choose whether their bankrupt Poor Law Unions should be supported by an income tax or a rate in aid. On free trade, not only he but his back-benchers, reinforced by the Peelites, were able to act together to make free trade work. He offered the Peelites posts in his

Lord John Russell.

ministry, which they were not ready to take, but at all times he worked with them.

Inevitably, Russell was preoccupied with the Irish famine and he instituted a massive and costly system of public works, and emergency food supplies, including soup kitchens. The financial crisis of 1847 forced him to cut aid to Ireland. But he had to trim on his measure to sell up insolvent Protestant landlords and transfer their estates to wealthy Catholics.

He was an obsessive free trader and followed Peel's liberalization by reducing the duties on sugar. But his legislative programme, too, was constructive – the English Poor Law Act, the extension of aid for education, his support of the Ten Hour Bill for the factories, the Health of Towns Bills – these amounted to a not inconsiderable programme of reform. His legislation in 1850 to establish a virtually self-governing dominion in Australia, and the Bill to repeal the Navigation Acts, were forward-looking.

But there was no central direction. Even his most cherished measures were subject to amendment by any Parliamentary faction. This was open government, but the emphasis was more on 'open' than on government. He was becoming more like a Speaker than a Prime Minister. Brougham expressed a widespread view: 'A strong Government, which was not to be much liked on the whole, to be preferred to a weak one ... Any Ministry was better than a Ministry without power ...'

Russell sought refuge in a foray with Parliamentary reform, for which Parliament was not ready. In twenty years' time perhaps, but the country was more concerned to have a Government. He suggested life peers, but his party was not interested, and the country, or the more articulate part of it, was bored. He was in fact brought down by Palmerston, a practical man who had to deal with *real-politik* in Europe, and who had no time for theory. John Prest, in his biography, has said that Palmerston's acts of insubordination were not approved of by Russell's colleagues, nor were they regretted. Derby's brief administration followed, and Aberdeen and Palmerston were to occupy No. 10 for the next thirteen years. Graver issues were taking charge, including the war with Russia.

The prime ministership, after Aberdeen, became a man's job. Not until Palmerston's death was there any competition for the post, and such competition as there was led to the recall of Earl Russell for a brief sunset period. At seventy-three he raised the reform question again, supported by Gladstone. But his party was apathetic and the Palmerston group hostile. After eight months he resigned. His inspiration was right, but his timing was wrong. What he had done was to put Parliamentary reform on the agenda. It would be a question whether Disraeli or Gladstone, each seeking party advantage, would carry off the prize. Only two years later, Disraeli, acting not by principle but by instinct, carried through the House a reform Bill going far beyond anything that Russell had dared to introduce.

Edward Stanley, fourteenth Earl of Derby, who succeeded Russell with a minority Government, formed three administrations. The first, from February to December 1852, did little more than prove that the Tory rump following the split over the Corn Laws was capable of forming a Government. In the twenty-eight years which followed the disaster of 1846, the Tories were in office for a little over four and a half years, of which Disraeli, Derby's successor, accounted for ten months. It was not a brilliant period for the Tory Party. History had passed them by. Derby's achievement was to put them on the map, and in so doing he paved the way for Disraeli's spectacular premiership from 1874 to 1880.

He was Earl Grey's Chief Secretary for Ireland, and in total antagonism to Daniel O'Connell. Grey moved him to the Colonial and War Offices. He was the minister ultimately responsible for freeing the slaves in the Empire, but resigned over an Irish Church measure. He refused Peel's offer of a post in the 1834 administration, but finally threw in his lot with Peel in 1841, again for the War and Colonies. He went to the Lords, which meant that in the controversy over the Corn Laws it was Disraeli who led the fight in the Commons. He played no part in the Disraeli–Bentinck attacks on Peel, and still hoped that the Peelites and Conservative rump would one day unite.

He tried to form an administration when Russell was out in 1851, and in 1852 in fact became Prime Minister. This was Wellington's 'Who? Who?' ministry, as the deaf Duke had all the names of the new administration shouted into his ear. Disraeli was Chancellor, his Budget running into ridicule when it became clear that he had got his tax schedules wrong. The Tories were out for eighteen years, though a chance occurred in 1855, when Derby was one of the front-runners to succeed Aberdeen. Lord Ellenborough warned him, when he went to the Palace: 'Don't leave the room without kissing hands', but this is exactly what he did. The country was determined on Palmerston, and Derby failed to present a convincing alternative.

The fourteenth Earl of Derby.

Another chance came when Palmerston's Conspiracy to Murder Bill led to the fall of the Whigs. Derby's second ministry, formed in February 1858, negotiated a satisfactory settlement with the French over the conspiracy issue, carried the repeal of Jewish civil disabilities, and failed on a Parliamentary reform measure. Reform had become fashionable again, and from then until Disraeli's measure of 1868, competition between the parties to carry a reform measure dominated the political scene. He called an election, but despite twenty-five gains he was still in a minority.

The next few years carried nothing of advantage for him, and more and more he was spending his time in Knowsley, combining sport with a new translation of the *Iliad*. On his return to office in 1866, the issue was again Parliamentary reform, where Disraeli in the Commons – not Derby in the Lords – wrong-footed the Liberals and carried the Bill through the House. Six months later, Derby stood down for Disraeli. Even his resignation was humiliating: before he could officially go to the Queen to present his resignation, she was treating with Disraeli over the succession.

All that has been written about Derby presents a story of failure. We must await Lord Blake's forthcoming biography before anyone can pronounce with authority on the premiership of the fourteenth Earl. The fifteenth Earl, as we shall see, is a different story.

George Hamilton Gordon, Fourth Earl of Aberdeen, was Prime Minister of a coalition Cabinet from 19 December 1852 to 1 February 1855. He had succeeded his grandfather when he was in his teens, so, unlike Derby who preceded him, and Palmerston his successor, he never had an apprenticeship in the House of Commons. In the later war years he undertook mainly diplomatic tasks, and did not return to Parliamentary work until 1828, when he joined Wellington's Cabinet as Chancellor of the Duchy of Lancaster. When the Canningites resigned over the rotten boroughs issue he became Foreign Secretary, where his main involvement was the creation of the independent kingdom of Greece. In Peel's short first administration he was Secretary for War and the Colonies for four months, returning as Foreign Secretary when Peel formed his majority Government in 1841. He was therefore involved in the settlement of the war with China, and the negotiations with the United States on the two boundary questions, north-east and north-west. He improved relations, temporarily, with France, and was the author of the phrase 'Entente Cordiale'.

He gave Peel his full support on the repeal of the Corn Laws, and went into the Peelite camp when the Government fell. On Peel's death he became the recognized leader of the Peelite group. At a time of great political fluidity, it was becoming clear that the only type of Government holding out any hope of survival would have to be a coalition, and Aberdeen began to be talked of as a potential coalition leader. In 1852 he became Prime Minister with six Peelites, six Whigs and a Radical. Had the phrase still been in fashion it could well have been called 'Ministry of All the Talents', containing as it did Gladstone, Graham, Russell and Palmerston. It was the third Government to hold office in 1852, but rapidly settled down. Gladstone's 1853

Budget was one of its triumphs, and the same year Palmerston as Home Secretary carried through an important advance in factory legislation. But the war clouds were gathering in the Near East, and Britain and France declared war on Russia in March 1854.

The events which led to Palmerston's brief resignation – nominally over Parliamentary reform but really over Aberdeen's handling of the war – and Aberdeen's fall are set out in the following chapter. Aberdeen was not created to be head of an administration at war. He was an Asquith rather than a Lloyd George. Indeed, it is arguable that his ineffective war leadership was not the only charge that can be made against him. A number of commentators have stated their belief that the war itself could have been prevented if Aberdeen had made clear from the outset that Britain and France meant what they said when they threatened war. Contemporaries and historians have felt that Lord Palmerston's call to office was the result of strong public clamour. Britain had fought no serious war for nearly forty years, and the stories of incompetence and neglect filed by the journalists aroused the whole country. One can do no more than speculate about how Aberdeen would have stood the test if there had been no war. There is every reason to think that he and his impressive team would have been one of the most efficient and successful in mid-nineteenth-century history.

George Hamilton Gordon, fourth Earl of Aberdeen.

3

Viscount Palmerston

PALMERSTON, OF ALL PRIME MINISTERS, became a legendary figure in his own time, and has been a legend ever since. He was the darling of the crowd, of the salons, and countless ladies, including Lady Jersey, Lady Cowper, Lord Melbourne's sister, and – almost certainly – the wife of the Russian Ambassador to London (later Paris), Countess Dorothea von Beckendorff, Madame de Lieven. On one occasion in the late 1830s, when the Foreign Secretary was staying at Windsor Castle, where one of his mistresses was also staying, he entered late at night the wrong bedroom. The occupant, who was a lady-in-waiting, screamed the house down and woke the Queen – who was later told the reason, misunderstood what had happened and was convinced that Palmerston had only narrowly been prevented from committing rape.

A tough record as War Minister earned him the title 'Lord Pumicestone'; next, his extra-mural activities that of 'Lord Cupid'; and finally his irrepressible personality that of 'Pam', portrayed by the cartoonists as a sprightly figure, always with a straw in his mouth. There is probably no truth in the story that at the age of seventy-eight he was about to be cited as co-respondent in a divorce suit, but the rumour put his political opponents in consternation, fearing that he would gain an electoral landslide as a result.

His ministerial career accounted for forty-eight of his fifty-eight years as an MP. At a time of shifting parties and party groups, he was not so much a piece of flotsam on the waves, he was riding them. He switched parties at exactly the right moment. From his entry into the House in 1807 the Tories (Pitt's party) were 'the natural party of Government'. From 1830 to 1865 the Whigs were. Palmerston timed his crossing of the great but shifting divide with precision. A devoted Canningite, he moved with the radical, free-trade-minded Tories to what became the mid-century Liberal Party, to be joined by the Peelite secession from the Tories.

Henry John Temple, Harry to his family, was born in 1784, son of an Irish peer, ineligible to sit in the Lords. Palmerston entered Parliament for a pocket borough in the Isle of Wight, on condition that he never set foot in the constituency, even at election times, for the proprietor feared that Palmerston might wrest the control of the voters from him. He had already been nominated as Junior Lord of the Admiralty. For six months he remained silent in the Commons, and then had to make a major three-hour speech defending the fleet's bombardment of Copenhagen to prevent the Danish fleet joining Napoleon. In that speech he laid down what he was still asserting half a century later: right, and the law of nations, should be observed in international relations as long as they did not interfere with vital British interests.

But he was then, by his own decision, condemned for some nineteen years to a dead-end job. Spencer Perceval, now Prime Minister, offered him the Treasury. Palmerston, just on twenty-five, refused: he felt that he was an indifferent speaker and that this would be unacceptable in the Chancellor but would matter less in a Secretary-at-War, which he became. Perceval proposed that though the post did not normally carry Cabinet rank, he should join the Cabinet. Palmerston modestly excused himself.

He was Secretary-at-War for nearly nineteen years, years mostly of drudgery, passionately defending the punishment of flogging in the Army, though, later, on grounds of humanity, suggesting a limitation to 200 lashes. Yet he strongly resisted a proposal that a soldier whose punishment had been suspended because of his condition should not be subject to the rest of the

Previous page Lord Palmerston, an early photograph from the Mountbatten Papers.

sentence when his wounds had healed. His positive contribution to the Army was his concern for the education of Army orphans, and he established Sandhurst – until then, officers had been sent to foreign military academies to learn their trade. He also maintained a running battle, or demarcation dispute, with the Commander-in-Chief, on one occasion penning a 30,000-word memorandum in support of his claims. He served through the Liverpool administration, and joined that of Canning. He was offered the Treasury again, but as appointment to a new office of profit meant a by-election this was deferred until Parliament went into recess, Palmerston continuing as Secretary-at-War. In the end, Canning withdrew the Treasury offer, partly because of the opposition of George IV, but Palmerston finally joined the Cabinet.

In May 1828 he resigned from Wellington's Government after he and Huskisson had opposed their own side on the East Retford pocket borough issue. As a back-bencher Canningite, he moved away from his party, drawing close to the Whigs. At the same time, he was making a successful speech on foreign affairs denouncing the Portuguese Queen's wicked uncle Miguel in Portugal; he was soon afterwards opposing Louis Philippe's coup in France, and speaking more and more of the rights of small nations and liberal minorities.

The 1830 general election which automatically followed the death of King George IV improved the position of the Whigs, and placed Wellington's Tory Government in danger. Palmerston refused to join a Tory Government alone and demanded that the Whigs, Lord Grey and Lansdowne, should also be invited. He made it clear that he supported Parliamentary reform and by so doing made himself finally unacceptable to the Tories. His intimate, Princess Lieven, a very close friend of Grey, brought these two together. When Grey came to form a Government, Palmerston became Foreign Secretary. It was a post he was to hold for fifteen and three-quarters of the following twenty-one years, by far the longest tenure in Britain's history, after which he was Prime Minister for nine and a half years. No major war broke out during his period at the Foreign Office, or at Downing Street.

It was the age of Britain's greatness. Her Navy was unchallenged and Palmerston did not hesitate to use it, or the threat of it, in pursuit of individual policies and initiatives in one part of the world after another. He was no less averse to using his own qualities of initiative and calculated adventurism, or the indiscreet pronouncement in pursuit of his policy, which was usually the pursuit of British interests, and the humbling of over-proud foreign potentates. This was 'gunboat diplomacy' it is true, and his language was jingoistic, but he was not a warmonger. He had a passionate desire for peace, and his provocative initiatives, often carrying great risks, were designed to avert threats to peace. There is every reason to think that had he been Foreign Secretary in 1853–4, the Crimean War could have been averted. He hated immobilism, he wanted to stir things up. The most undiplomatic Foreign Secretary of all time, in the conventional sense of the word, he relied on clarity of expression and action to let any potential aggressor know exactly where he stood. Had any of his risky actions gone wrong he could have *forced* Britain into war, but while he was around there was no danger that Britain would *drift* into war.

He stated his philosophy in 1848. The furtherance of British interests should be the only objective of a British Foreign Secretary. It was in Britain's interest to preserve the balance of power in international affairs – for him, Britain had no permanent friends or permanent enemies. 'Constitutional States' were however the natural allies of Britain, and it was therefore Britain's interest to maintain constitutional Governments throughout the world.

Dismissed by the Queen (and the Prince Consort) in 1851 for defying the Queen's instruction supported by Russell to submit all important telegrams and announcements to her when he welcomed Louis Napoleon's becoming Emperor, he was nevertheless brought back into the Cabinet by Aberdeen, after the abortive Derby–Disraeli administration of 1852. But he returned as Home Secretary, because of the Queen's firm refusal to authorize his appointment to the Foreign Office. In years of mounting danger it was as ludicrous a situation as if Neville Chamberlain had brought Winston Churchill into his Cabinet in 1937 and made him President of the Board of Trade. But the whole period showed the interest of the Queen and the Prince Consort in all aspects of foreign affairs. Yet only three years and three months after his dismissal as Foreign Secretary he was kissing hands on his appointment as Prime Minister, to take charge of operations in a war he might well have averted.

The record of his Foreign Secretaryship virtually throughout the 1830s and from 1846 to 1851 has become a classic. Under Grey, Melbourne and Russell he seemed almost to hold the whole wide world in his hands.

There was the Belgian crisis of 1830–1. The son of Louis Philippe had been narrowly elected by the Belgians to their throne. Palmerston was not going to stand for any Franco–Belgian Anschluss. Using a technique he made his own, he issued a warning to the French Court by sending a dispatch to HM Ambassador, Paris, via the French Embassy in London, unsealed. He knew it would be opened, read, and communicated to the French Government. When the French, already climbing down, complained of Britain's interference, he sent another letter through the same channel complaining of the intemperance of the French Foreign Minister's language.

On the crisis in Portugal, he had before coming to office expressed support for the young Queen: 'The civilized world rings with execrations upon Miguel.' As Foreign Secretary, while not intervening directly, he was on the watch for any interference with British shipping, no doubt hoping that some provocative action in that direction would enable him to act more vigorously. When Don Pedro, Maria's father, ruler in Brazil, fitted out a fleet in the Azores to attack Miguel, Palmerston ordered strict neutrality, but when he heard that twenty thousand Spanish troops were on the Spanish border with Portugal ready to support Miguel, he warned Spain that if they interfered in Portugal Britain would support Pedro. He took up every affront to British property, and instructed Admiral Parker, anchored with his fleet just outside the three-mile limit, to protect British vessels against interference. When, a year later, storms forced Parker's force to enter Tagus harbour, Palmerston warned Miguel not to interfere: 'Any insult offered to His Majesty's flag, however small the vessel which bears it, would be resented and avenged by all the means which Great Britain can command ... any hindrance opposed to the execution of these orders will be considered an act of hostility.'

Another wicked uncle story was later to develop in Spain when, on her father's death, the Princess Isabella, aged three, became Queen. On her Uncle Carlos joining with Miguel, Palmerston formed the Quadruple Alliance with Talleyrand and the Governments of the two Queens, to act together in the Peninsula. ('I should like to see Metternich's face when he reads our treaty.')

Opposite Lady Palmerston painted by Sir Thomas Lawrence.

Carlos and Miguel surrendered to the British admiral. Carlos sought asylum in England, but escaped and another bloody civil war followed.

By 1834 Palmerston was intervening on behalf of the Poles. Jasper Ridley, in his biography says:

> Palmerston had now emerged, without really intending it, as the champion of liberalism in Europe. Both Englishmen and foreigners came in time to think of Palmerston as the very personification of John Bull; but he was a John Bull with the most polished manners, who spoke perfect French and was always at home in the cosmopolitan milieu of the international aristocracy, where personal friendships were not unduly affected by political and national disagreements.

After the brief Peel administration in 1834–5, Palmerston was back, stopping the proposed marriage between Maria and a French prince, and taking the lead in using the Navy to interfere with slave traders. After trouble with the Portuguese, he introduced a Bill to direct HM ships to stop and search Portuguese ships on the high seas, and impound any carrying slaves. Later, in 1844, in opposition, he was to make the greatest speech of his life, a three-hour speech against the slave traders. From then on there was no compromise wherever the Navy might operate. On the Opium War with China, he was less of a moralist, intervening on the side of the opium smugglers, who were doing well out of it, simply because they were British.

Back in office in 1846, after the fall of Peel's administration he resumed the liberal offensive. He no longer had the Princess Lieven to help him. Her husband was Ambassador in Paris, she had become the mistress of Guizot, and from then on she became Britain's and Palmerston's implacable enemy.

In the European revolutions of 1848, Palmerston was in his element. It was then that a German reactionary composed the lines:

Hat der Teufel einen Sohn,
So ist er sicher Palmerston.

His old enemies Guizot in France and Metternich in Austria were swept from power. Louis Napoleon came to power.

Meanwhile Palmerston was becoming the arbiter of a wider and wider area of Europe. He came out strongly against Austria in the war between the Austrian Empire and Sardinia. The aged Radetzky commanded the Austrian forces against Charles Albert of the little Sardinian kingdom, and finally crushed him. Palmerston proposed Anglo-French mediation, finally agreeing to submit the issue to a conference at Brussels. The Queen and Albert were against him in his Italian policy, nor was it yet a question of Italian unity. Palmerston's attack on the Austrians almost led to a break in diplomatic relations, worsened as they were by Radetzky's cruel follow-up of his victory, and Haynau's and Windischgrätz's crushing of the rebels. But the Austrians had to face a revolt from the Hungarians, led by their national hero Kossuth, who in their turn were receiving moral support from Palmerston. The Austrians now asked Russia for assistance and the Hungarians and Poles were defeated, Hungary in particular being then subjected to the most brutal reprisals by the Austrian forces.

It was a bad year for national movements. The people of Schleswig-Holstein revolted against Denmark – Palmerston offered to mediate. With Austria supporting Denmark and Prussia mobilized against them, he feared a major European war, and strove to prevent it. In this alone he succeeded. He had failed in some of his major objectives, but he had done as much as anyone to preserve peace.

In 1849–50 came the most characteristic Palmerston action, in support of Don Pacifico, a Spaniard, born in Gibraltar (thus a British citizen by birth) but who later took Portuguese citizenship and became Portuguese Consul in Athens. Don Pacifico lost his property in a riot, made a claim for compensation – almost certainly inflating the figure – against the civil authorities in Greece and was backed by the Foreign Office. The fleet was in the Mediterranean, first reading the riot act to the Austrians over their treatment of the Hungarians, then proceeding to threaten Turkey. On their reaching the Dardanelles Palmerston thought it appropriate to take action against the Greeks too. Greece was blockaded until its Government agreed to compensate Pacifico. This led on 25 June 1850 to an outraged debate in Parliament, when Palmerston defended his extremely dubious action in the most successful and assertive speech of his career: 'As the Roman, in days of old, held himself free from indignity when he could say *Civis Romanus sum*; so also a British subject, in whatever land he may be, shall feel England will protect him against injustice and wrong.'

He had, whether he deserved it or not, one of the most triumphant ovations in the history of Parliament. Enthusiasm for him swept the country, at any rate from those who read the report in the papers.

Eighteen months later, Palmerston was out of office, brusquely dismissed by the Queen's command.

The Palace had not approved of Palmerston's European interventions: too often they had the savour of intervening on behalf of rebellious minorities against the lawful, if in most cases autocratic, sovereign rulers. The Queen, still more Prince Albert, resented what they regarded as his high-handed and independent style of conducting foreign relations. It was still an age where the Foreign Secretary, above all ministers, was the instrument – indeed the direct spokesman – if not of regal power, at any rate of regal authority and regal status. Victoria repeatedly represented to the Prime Minister that she could not tolerate Palmerston's habit of sending dispatches to *her* ambassadors all round the globe, which had not been submitted to her for approval. Russell was warned that if this occurred again she would insist on the Foreign Secretary's resignation.

On the first representations, Palmerston grovelled, both in his submission to the Queen and in a personal conversation with the Prince Consort. It was General Haynau's visit to London which immeasurably worsened the situation. In this case, Palmerston was procedurally wrong but completely in tune with popular feeling, which he shared.

General Haynau was detested in Britain for his brutal atrocities after he had put down the risings in Italy and Hungary. Londoners christened him 'General Hyena'. Visiting Barclay's brewery he was beaten up by the workmen, and had to take refuge in a public house until the police arrived. The Queen demanded that an apology be sent to Vienna. Palmerston concurred, though he shared the general support of Haynau's treatment, but his apology was qualified. Expressing his regret for the attack, he said how badly advised it had been for the General to come to England at all. The Queen saw the draft, was furious at the language, and insisted that Palmerston should send an unqualified apology, with no criticism of Haynau's visit. Palmerston then had to tell her that her amendments were too late: the dispatch was on its way to Vienna. He was instructed to send another dispatch, cancelling the original and following her instructions. Palmerston refused, and told Russell that he would resign: in the event, he complied with the Queen's wish that the earlier dispatch be cancelled.

Another incident involved Kossuth, the Hungarian patriot, who visited London and was hailed everywhere as a hero. The Queen read in the *Morning Post* that Palmerston was to receive him, a rebel against the Austrian Emperor, and sent a peremptory instruction to Lord Russell. Palmerston refused to cancel the invitation and the question was raised in Cabinet; Palmerston accepted the majority view that he should not see Kossuth. But two days later he was glorying in a message from two radical London boroughs congratulating him on his support of the Hungarian. This was worse in the Queen's eyes than receiving Kossuth. But Palmerston could not be ousted on so popular an issue.

A month later came Louis Napoleon's coup. Though the Cabinet decided on a neutral line, Palmerston had already told the French Ambassador, Waleski, that he warmly approved of Louis Napoleon's action. HM Ambassador in Paris had been told to maintain a neutral line, but when he queried Palmerston's comment to Waleski, Palmerston's reply said he had been expressing a personal opinion. The Queen, on seeing the draft of the message, asked for a correction to be made, and was then told it was too late, it had been transmitted. She demanded Palmerston's dismissal, and Russell asked for his resignation. Whether Palmerston was being careless, nonchalant or deliberately provocative is not clear, but this, unlike the Haynau affair, was not an action likely to be popular in the country: he had to go. Strangely, the press began a campaign against his dismissal, and a great deal of the odium fell on Prince Albert. Palmerston was still so angry that he hired a journalist to write a pamphlet attacking Albert, but was prevailed upon to suppress the document and pay off its author. Despite the press, despite a debate in Parliament where the radicals attacked his sacking, he remained silent. His own radicalism had reached the limit, and he was not going to be pressured into attacking the Palace.

Two months later, the Government were defeated on the Militia Bill, to which Palmerston had moved an amendment, to create a national force, centrally controlled. This was the event which went down to history in Palmerston's phrase 'my tit-for-tat with Johnny Russell'. A brief Conservative administration under Lord Derby intervened, with Disraeli as Chancellor of the Exchequer. There were rumours that Palmerston would join Derby, who did in fact make unofficial approaches to him. At one point he seemed to have told them he would accept, but the free trade issue stood in the way. The Government went to the country, and gained over a hundred seats. The Conservatives now accepted that protection was dead, and Palmerston saved them from the official Opposition motion by an amendment welcoming their conversion to free trade. On the Budget, Derby's Government fell, and Aberdeen formed a coalition of Whigs and Peelites. Palmerston was invited to join. The Queen vetoed any return to the Foreign Office, and Palmerston became Home Secretary.

Though his heart was not really in the job, he recorded a creditable performance. Working closely with Shaftesbury (formerly Ashley, Palmerston's son-in-law) he carried through Parliament a further instalment of Factories Act reform, disappointing Shaftesbury on the working hours of women and of boys under eighteen, which remained at sixty a week, but removing loopholes from earlier legislation, and banning all labour by young workers between 6 pm and 6 am. He introduced a trade union Bill, confirming the right of unions to combine for peaceful purposes, but not legalizing peaceful picketing – this had to await a further Act in 1859: in any event Palmerston's Bill was withdrawn in the Lords.

But he succeeded with the Truck Act, removing a grievance felt by miners and others. The Act required employers to pay wages in coins of the realm, instead of allowing them to insist on their employees spending their wages in the company store. He was one of the first to attack pollution, with his Smoke Abatement Bill. He had a fight to carry his Bill through prohibiting burials inside churches, and he also carried a Bill to regulate the drink trade. He liberalized the prison code, especially on solitary confinement, ended the system of transportation for a wide range of offences, liberalized the treatment of young offenders and introduced reformatory schools.

But, as a member of the Cabinet, he was all the time closely watching developments in Eastern Europe. Public opinion, led by press campaigns, was hardening against Russia. Napoleon was making claims to be the protector of Catholics in Turkey, as the Russians claimed the right to protect Orthodox Christians there. The Tsar was roughing it up with the Turks, and claiming further rights of intervention which would have meant the effective control of Turkey's internal administration; 'Turkey', he asserted, 'is the sick man of Europe.' Turkey was indeed in a desperately weak situation, almost ungovernable, divided – with open revolt in her outlying provinces.

There was a growing feeling, fomented by the *Morning Post*, a pro-Palmerston paper, that Aberdeen was too weak, and that the country needed Palmerston. His experience might well have enabled him to hold back both Napoleon and the Tsar from hasty action, and he had experience in securing a Russian withdrawal from Moldavia and Wallachia, the 'Principalities', the origin of modern Romania. Now they were there again. Palmerston started minuting Aberdeen from the Home Office with highly expert memoranda on the Eastern Question.

He urged peace, and felt that if Russia had been solemnly told that an invasion of the principalities would lead to the British and French navies entering the Bosphorus or the Black Sea, Russia would not have invaded. Public opinion, aided by the press, was aroused against Russian atrocities. Palmerston was not innocent so far as briefing of the press was concerned, particularly the *Morning Post*. In Cabinet he was demanding action; on 7 October he proposed that the Navy should be sent into the Black Sea with orders to seize every Russian ship they could find and bring them into Turkish ports, agreeing to release them only when the Russian Army withdrew from the principalities. But the Turks moved first and declared war, clearly forcing Britain's hand. Palmerston pressed for full support, but Aberdeen was congealed in his own passivity.

Palmerston was also fighting a battle against Russell's proposals for a further instalment of Parliamentary reform, which a majority of the Cabinet was disposed to accept, and was minuting Aberdeen both on that and the Eastern Question. Prince Albert pressed Aberdeen to use Palmerston's opposition to Parliamentary reform to force Palmerston's resignation: as so often Albert was totally out of touch with opinion in the country, where the demand for Palmerston was growing. Aberdeen wrote to Palmerston taking his reply as his resignation and, since he could not meet the Home Secretary on reform, accepting it.

NOW FOR IT!

A Set-to between "Pam, the Downing Street Pet," and "The Russian Spider."

This was another example of Aberdeen's unfitness for the premiership, which was to become still more clear when war began. He was anxious to see Palmerston go – Palmerston was a nuisance on the war crisis, as well as on Parliamentary reform. So politically innocent was Aberdeen that he probably felt that Palmerston would be reviled for his reactionary views on reform. On the contrary many would judge that the real reason for Palmerston's resignation would be on the major issue, the issue on which Palmerston had most experience, and felt most strongly. Only a foolish Prime Minister would have been a party to setting Palmerston loose on the back-benches. There can be little doubt what Palmerston's real motive was: his discontent with the handling of the war situation.

He could not have lost sleep over the press handling. Aberdeen was condemned, the Prince Consort attacked, since it was widely believed that Palmerston's resignation had been forced by a conspiracy between Prince Albert and Aberdeen, perhaps not an untrue reading of the situation. Within eight days Palmerston was back, but those eight days meant that at every worsening in the situation more and more people would turn to Palmerston.

On 27 February 1854, Britain and France sent an ultimatum to Russia demanding withdrawal from the principalities within a month. No reply came, and on 28 March Britain and France declared war on Russia.

It was the first major war since Waterloo, and at first, particularly with Aberdeen as leader – anxious to minimize hostilities and get down to peace terms – the British war effort seemed to suggest that nothing had changed in military thinking over the past fifty years. No one knew where to attack; there was apparently no war-book. Palmerston supported an attack on the Crimea and the capture of the fortress of Sevastopol; his proposal for invasions through Turkey to the Caucasus was left to the Turks. A naval expedition was to be sent to Kronstadt, St Petersburg's naval fortress.

The attack on the Crimea was botched from the start. Totally inadequate commanders, complete lack of planning, inaccurate intelligence about where Sevastopol's defences were weakest, no strategy and worse tactics, a rudimentary supplies organization, and no preparations for the cholera outbreak which decimated the British and French armies – these contributed to the failure to break through in Russia and to the disillusion at home. This was the first war to be reported by an accredited war correspondent. The reports of *The Times* reporter W.H. Russell soon led to a public outcry and Florence Nightingale's embarkation to the Crimea. Of 30,000 troops, 6000 were killed in action, and 8000 were in sick bay suffering from wounds or cholera. More troops were needed, the Navy was in the wrong place; in the end Cunard offered to transport them. Reports of intense cold, and inadequate protection against it, and of the Sevastopol army losing men at the rate of a regiment a day, together with the anger over the Charge of the Light Brigade, were undermining Aberdeen's leadership. Russell, the Foreign Secretary, resigned over the conduct of the war, demanding that Palmerston should go to the War Office. Roebuck put his crucial motion of censure in the House, which was carried by very nearly two to one, and the Government resigned. Palmerston's speech loyally defending the Government has been likened to that of Churchill in the Norway debate in May 1940. The House voted against his arguments to make him Prime Minister.

The country was united for Palmerston. Derby, as Leader of the Opposition,

Opposite A *Punch* cartoon of Palmerston at the time of the Crimean War.

was invited to form a Government and he went so far as to ask Palmerston if he would take the War Office. Palmerston accepted, on condition that Clarendon remained Foreign Secretary, knowing Clarendon would not be seen dead with Derby.

When every conceivable alternative had been tried and failed, the Queen sent for Palmerston, who became Prime Minister on 6 February 1855. His Cabinet was impressive: Clarendon was Foreign Secretary, Gladstone Chancellor, Graham at the Admiralty, and Panmure, a former Whig War Minister, was given the War Office, the ancient post of Secretary-at-War being finally abolished. Yet, as soon as the House met, he lost Gladstone, Herbert and Graham. Roebuck had insisted on pushing his demand for an inquiry into the conduct of the war, and Palmerston, who had resisted, gave way. The three Peelites resigned in protest. Palmerston rapidly replaced them; he was now unchallengeable and told his brother: 'I am, for the moment, *l'inèvitable.*'

Fresh vigour coursed through the tired arteries of the administration – on supplies, transport, the raising of troops. Only Disraeli was unimpressed. In a letter he wrote that Palmerston

> seems now the inevitable man; and though he is really an imposter [*sic*], utterly exhausted, and at the best only ginger-beer and not champagne, and now an old painted pantaloon, very deaf, very blind, and with false teeth which would fall out of his mouth when speaking if he did not hesitate and halt so in his talk, here is a man which the country resolves to associate with energy, wisdom and eloquence, and will until he has tried and failed.

By the spring of 1855 Palmerston was thinking of possible peace negotiations and went over the ground with Napoleon III on his state visit to London. Now the death of Nicholas I and the succession of the reportedly liberal Alexander II opened up new possibilities. The Austrians had undertaken to send a massive army to occupy the two principalities, and the Russians now made clear their willingness to withdraw, one of the key Allied conditions for peace. Confident of his strong position, Palmerston, unlike Napoleon, toughened his terms – the Russians should not only clear out of the Black Sea but hand over the Crimea to Turkey. Meanwhile the war continued; there were fresh gains in the Crimea, Sevastopol fell, the Russian Black Sea fleet was destroyed. The Russians feared a spring offensive in the north, invading Finland, capturing Kronstadt and threatening St Petersburg itself. Austria issued an ultimatum. Negotiations began in Paris and an armistice was agreed the following day. Although Palmerston still pressed for his maximum terms, not only his Cabinet but the French were for a softer peace. But the Black Sea was demilitarized: the two principalities were merged as the new State of Romania, under the nominal sovereignty of the Sultan of Turkey, but for all practical purposes independent.

Palmerston's peacetime premiership was relatively uneventful, although he survived another nine and a half years. He took over at a time of shifting party allegiances, when Parliament was supreme in making and destroying ministries. Until the Reform Act of 1832, great swings in party loyalties operated in terms of, comparatively speaking, geological time. Pitt created a Tory Party which lasted for a generation. After the Reform Act of 1867 the grip on parties exercised by Disraeli and Gladstone and their respective legacies was tightened, until Chamberlain split the Liberals in the Eighties over Home Rule, and the

Tories in the early years of the twentieth century over tariff reform. But between the two Reform Acts, groupings based on policy or personal loyalties flowed and eddied like a frozen river in the melting season. It was the heyday of Parliamentary power in the sense that it was, as Walter Bagehot emphasized, the elected body which made and unmade Cabinets. Lord Blake in his British Academy Lectures pointed out that each of the six Parliaments elected between 1841 and 1865 brought down at least one administration, and sometimes two, before its dissolution.

It was at this fluid period of our history that an ageing Palmerston held office for over nine years in all, with a break of sixteen months in 1858–9. This was due not only to his mastery of Parliament, and the absence of pure ideological divisions, it was due to his hold over the people. After the 1857 election Lord Shaftesbury said: 'There seems to be no measure, no principle, no cry, to influence men's minds and determine elections; it is simply, "were you or were you not? Are you, or are you not, for Palmerston?"'

Despite the shifting sands of Parliamentary support, Palmerston remained remarkably equable. He was even criticized for being too light-hearted and uncaring about the Indian Mutiny, not least by the Queen, who told him that if she had been an MP she would have denounced him in the House for incompetence.

In 1858 he made a rare misjudgment. Following the Orsini plot to kill Napoleon III and the Empress Eugénie on the way to the Opera, and conscious that Orsini had not only been connected with Italian refugees in London but had obtained his explosives from England, Palmerston introduced a Conspiracy to Murder Bill, in response to an insistent French demand. On second reading, the Government were defeated, thanks to Disraeli's marauding tactics. Only a few months after his election victory Palmerston resigned and Derby became Prime Minister, with Disraeli as Chancellor.

The Derby administration was very much a Government on sufferance, and it did well to survive for sixteen months, which included a somewhat indecisive general election. Disraeli invited Palmerston to join the Government; even if he were not Foreign Secretary, it was suggested, he would dominate the foreign policy of the ministry. Palmerston and Russell, up to then living a cat and dog existence, had discussions. On 6 June the Parliamentary Liberal Party met at 'Willis's Room', formerly Palmerston's haunt, Almack's. There, it has been said, the Liberal Party was born. It signalled the end of the Whigs, but who would lead the new grouping, Russell or Palmerston? The Queen sent for Granville, who rapidly realized that he could not form a credible administration. It had to be Palmerston, and when Derby was defeated on a vote of confidence, Palmerston returned. His new Government was broadly based: Whigs, Radicals and Peelites. Gladstone became Chancellor.

Palmerston was soon in trouble with churchmen who asked him to call a national day of prayer because of the cholera epidemic in Scotland. He briskly replied that it was better to improve sanitation in Edinburgh. He nonchalantly ran into further trouble when he said that all children were born good and were led into crime by bad education and bad associates; he was forced to retract until he made it clear that he had not meant to impugn the doctrine of original sin. Some churchmen complained that he treated Heaven 'like a foreign power', which was exactly what he was doing.

He interested himself in the rebuilding of the Parliament building after its

Broadlands in Hampshire, Palmerston's country house that was handed down through the female line to the late Countess Mountbatten and is today the home of Lord Mountbatten.

destruction by fire. He rejected Scott's plan for the Foreign Office as a 'hideous Gothic structure' and persuaded him to produce a new design on Palmerston lines, the original plan being offered to the directors of the Midland Railway and becoming St Pancras station hotel.

He continued to appeal to the country over the heads of Parliament; in the language of today he 'went walkabout', and it paid off. His biographer, Jasper Ridley, has noted that his image was changing, the cartoon not so much now projecting the old straw-in-mouth image, but 'the old sentinel', manning a gun on the turret of a fortress.

His biggest problem was how to handle Gladstone. A brilliant administrator, creator of the most imaginative Budgets since the days of Peel and Pitt, Gladstone had an obsessive tendency to pontificate in a manner that would be embarrassing to any Prime Minister. Parliamentary reform was moving towards the top of the Parliamentary agenda, and limited schemes were being put forward for extending this or that electoral qualification. The issue was highly controversial and delicate. In May 1864 Gladstone, without warning and without consultation, made a speech in which he said that he saw no reason, in principle, why every man who was not mentally incapacitated should not have the vote. Palmerston, who was already having doubts about Gladstone's mental stability, was alarmed – on this argument, what about women too? The Queen expostulated. The Prime Minister regarded it as an invitation to working-class movements to agitate not for a measured reform but for manhood enfranchisement. Gladstone received a magisterial rebuke, for, Palmerston said, this would put the country into the hands of the trade unions.

Shaftesbury memorialized that there were only two men Palmerston hated: Bright, who was 'boorish', and Gladstone. To Shaftesbury Palmerston said: 'Gladstone has never behaved to me as a colleague in such a way as to demand from me any consideration.' He went further. He had this to say to Shaftesbury about the man he had brought in out of the Peelite wilderness: 'Gladstone will soon have it all his own way and whenever he gets my place we shall have strange doings.' In another comment, he said that he thought Gladstone would wreck the Liberal Party 'and end up in a madhouse'.

Foreign affairs were a major issue in the election which ejected Derby and brought back Palmerston. After years in which he had, generally, supported the rights of established States against resurgent minorities, he was being forced by Russell more and more in favour of Italian unity. Sardinia, the expansionist leader of the Italian revolution, under Cavour's revolution was involved in war against Austria. Russell was committed to Italian unity, France supported the Risorgimento.

Palmerston, at first strongly committed to the existing order, ended – largely through the influence of Russell – with the reputation of being one of the architects of Italian unity. The real creator of the Italian state was France. Though France played the Garibaldi invasion cautiously, supported by Britain, the events in Italy were already moving towards a unity which Palmerston did not live to see. Relations with France were bad through most of his premiership, to the point where, as in the days of Pitt, there were real fears, which Palmerston accepted, of a French invasion. One of his most serious estrangements with Gladstone was over financial provision to strengthen the Channel defences.

He was involved in the Middle East, strengthening the Turks against the

Lebanese Maronite independence movement and actively intriguing to seek – unsuccessfully – to prevent the French project to dig the Suez Canal: his concern with the passage to India mirrored the anxieties of Pitt and was reflected in Disraeli's purchase of a share in the ownership of the Canal when it was dug.

In strong contrast to his liberal ideals elsewhere and indefensible in the light of history was Palmerston's almost blatant support, under the guise of neutrality, of the Confederate states in the American Civil War. As early as 1 January 1861, he referred in a submission to the Queen, to the 'approaching and virtually accomplished Dissolution in America of the great Northern Confederation'. In this he was, unusually, out of touch with feeling in the North, even in Lancashire, where there was heavy unemployment and suffering with the cutting off of supplies of raw cotton. The Lancashire textile workers sent their famous 'memorial' to Abraham Lincoln, saying that whatever their sufferings as a result, they fully supported his fight for human freedom.

Though London society was almost unanimous in support of the South, Palmerston was less partisan and the Queen was still more balanced. Palmerston's own record on fighting slavery was sullied by his unhappiness at Lincoln's emancipation of the slaves. He was certainly in the wrong in his reaction to the removal by a Federal warship of the Confederate envoys Mason and Slidell from the *Trent*, both in Russell's dispatch to Washington demanding an apology and in his provocative action in sending three thousand troops to Canada. Britain was close to war with Lincoln: Ambassador Adam's son later wrote that if the Atlantic telegraph had been already in operation, Britain would have been at war with the United States.

Carelessness rather than policy was responsible for letting the *Alabama* slip out of a Birkenhead dockyard, at great subsequent cost to Union merchant shipping. It was, however, to Gladstone's credit that as Prime Minister he agreed to submit the American claim for compensation to international arbitration – at a heavy cost to the taxpayer when the award was announced.

Before the final act of the American war at Appomattox Courthouse, and Lincoln's assassination, Palmerston, now eighty, was deteriorating. He was ill, he suffered from mental lapses, he tended to fall asleep both in Parliament and Cabinet. Greville, clerk to the Privy Council, recorded, 'He is always asleep, both in the Cabinet and in the House of Commons where he endeavours to conceal it by wearing his hat over his eyes.' Yet in 1865 he dissolved Parliament and increased his majority. Gladstone lost his seat at Oxford, and provoked Palmerston to yet another pithy comment. Three months later Palmerston died.

Undoubtedly the greatest 'character' Downing Street has seen, he was the idol of a great mass of the people, going far beyond the then electorate, to whom none of his contemporaries could appeal. No Foreign Secretary – and this is also true of his premiership until very near the end – exercised such command in the chancelleries of Europe and the wider world. He had established the Liberal Party, at the meeting in the former Almack's club, where half a century earlier he had been a debonair charmer of women's hearts – three, at least, of the seven of Almack's ruling 'Lady Patronesses' being among his mistresses.

Contemporaries and historians have vied for a short summing-up. 'A Conservative at home and a Liberal abroad' is an oversimplification. Disraeli described him as 'the Tory chief of a Radical Cabinet'. Lord Salisbury was nearer the truth when he said that Palmerston 'wanted Radical votes, Whig placemen

Two photographs of 'Lady P' and 'Lord P' in old age from the Mountbatten Papers.

and Tory policy'. But even that is too simple. His policy on many issues was not Tory. An early convert to free trade – which was one of the keys to his foreign policy – a lifetime crusader against slavery, no laggard on Parliamentary reform, his approach on most other issues was essentially pragmatic, not least in his policy on emerging nationalism, where – for example on Italy, and even on some aspects of Near Eastern policy – he covered a good 180 degrees before he finally came through.

Perhaps more important even than policy was his style, his zest and vigour; it was felt in the change in the conduct of the Crimean War when he replaced Aberdeen, it was felt in many aspects of foreign policy. Palmerston wanted to see Britain top nation, and to keep her there. Not all Prime Ministers enjoy the job; few enjoyed it more than Palmerston.

4

Benjamin Disraeli

DISRAELI, EARL OF BEACONSFIELD, was the first Prime Minister to be so described in an official document. This recognition came in the signing of the Treaty of Berlin, 1878, which he signed as, Beaconsfield, *First Lord of the Treasury and Prime Minister of Her Britannic Majesty.*

Very much a man of his time – though one who, more than most, moulded his time to embrace him – he had a unique quality of timelessness. Lord Blake, writer of the most distinguished biography of Disraeli, makes a significant judgment about him. Pointing out that it is hard to imagine Gladstone living in any other period, he says: '... it is quite easy to envisage Disraeli living either today or in the age of Lord North.'

More than any of his predecessors, and most of his successors, Disraeli owed his climb to the top, his survival and his lasting reputation to his utter domination of the House of Commons. Although he made the most disastrous maiden speech in history, he learned his lesson and his coruscating debating style utterly destroyed his leader, Robert Peel, after the latter's 'tergiversation' on the Corn Laws. When he himself for the first and only time commanded a safe majority after 1874, he could, until he went to the Lords, do almost anything he liked with the House. His domination of Parliament was clearly in large part due to his mastery over words, his power through a short phrase to illuminate his theme, be it inventive or philosophic. The Second Edition of the *Oxford Book of Quotations* devotes five columns, two and a half pages, to memorable quotations from his speeches in the House and the country, and from his writings – more than all Britain's prime ministers together, if Wellington is excluded.

Beginning from a complete and almost proverbial lack of political principle, often acting by instinct, he came to master the politician's art of retrospective rationalization, explaining what had been a deft, instinctive uncalculated step in terms of strategy and even deep philosophy. What Britain has most to fear is a Prime Minister, if such there should be, whose first instinctive reaction is wrong, and who is incapable of such rationalization.

Most of all, he came to rationalize his own and later his party's appeal in terms which a later age would have called 'class politics', but in far wider terms than the majority of his own party in Parliament would claim to embrace.

The classical economists of his age listed the three 'factors of production' in terms of land, capital and labour, the first two broadly the privileged, the third largely the underprivileged sectors of the community. Up to a point British politics in these years represented a battle, not always consciously fought, to form alliances between two of these three forces. The aristocratic Shaftesbury, together with Oastler and a number of Tories, joined with 'labour' to force through the Factory Acts, ending the exploitation of child labour in mills and mines. The radical free trade Liberal employers for their part identified the interests of the workers with those of the manufacturers in their fight for the repeal of the Corn Laws and a world of free trade. Disraeli, who began his political life as a committed radical, wove for himself a golden web of philosophy by which he justified the political alliance he sought between labour and land, a mystical link between the age-old traditions of rural Britain with the factory classes, against the political forces identified with the capitalists and the dark Satanic mills. His politically most significant novel, *Sybil – or The Two*

Previous page Disraeli with Queen Victoria.

Nations, describing a realm divided between rich and poor, was dominated by the story and the marriage of the Chartist factory inspector's daughter and the 'Young England' landed aristocrat, Egremont. As he threw off his radical cloak, and became involved with power, he was one of the first in his adopted party to identify with the new urban householders, small men in substance, for the most part, solid and moderate in their views, who were enfranchised by the 1867 Reform Act which he manoeuvred through a House of Commons where he and his supporters were heavily outnumbered.

There was another area in which the more mature Disraeli came to terms with the political world around him; the recognition of the power of party. Fighting a Peel who, as we have seen, had no time or temperament for wooing his supporters, Disraeli first exploited party, and then became a convinced party man. Indeed, his gift for justification led him to identify party as the essential ingredient in democracy: 'I believe that without Party, Parliamentary government is impossible.'

In analysing Disraeli's contribution to British history, especially his position at one of the crossroads in that history, one fundamental trait in his character, especially in his earlier years, enables us to examine his development, and ultimately his contribution both to the political history and the philosophy of his times. Put simply, Disraeli was – until he reached an age quite advanced by the political standards of his times – utterly unprincipled except in terms of his immediate personal advantage. His objectives were clear, first in his earlier years, to enter Parliament, almost careless as to the banner under which he would fight; second, once that was achieved, to emerge from the ruck of back-benchers to the front bench and leadership. Disraeli was old compared with most of his rivals and contemporaries in getting a start in political life. Peel, Gladstone, Palmerston and several others entered Parliament, usually for a rotten borough, at the age of twenty-one or so, and won office within a year or two. Disraeli did not enter the House until his thirty-eighth year. Disappointed in his hopes of office when Peel formed his main administration, he did not become a minister until he was forty-seven. His first post, in 1852, which lasted for less than a year, was Chancellor of the Exchequer, in which position he succeeded only in getting his tax schedules wrong.

But he had arrived. It was only a question of time, and one feels that he often thought of himself in third-person terms, with an inevitability of success even more striking than that he conferred on some of the heroes of his novels. In his early years of office, 1852, 1858–9, and 1866–8, he seemed to have no fixed guiding star of policy, varying rather from shifting expedients to the brilliant Parliamentary adaptability, innocent of all principle, which enabled him to wrong-foot the more stolid Gladstone over reform, and get in first to put the 1867 Reform Act which he manoeuvred through a House of Commons where were of minor importance compared with the discomfiture of his opponents and the enactment of a Bill, regardless of its terms.

Then, finally, in 1874 came the total change in the mature statesman of nearly seventy, when he received a massive electoral victory, a party majority, assuring him of six or seven years' occupation of the Treasury Bench. This gave him not only security but the confidence and ability to analyse how he intended to use that majority, which had come to him as a total surprise. It was in those years that his discursive and ever-exploring mind came to seize on a greater and broader philosophy, his new concept of Britain's role in the world, his success in stopping Russian expansionism, his preoccupation with India, Suez, the vision of Empire.

Despite some legends, Disraeli was not nurtured in poverty. His father, Isaac D'Israeli, was rich enough to be an independent man of letters. Though Disraeli did not go to a public school, his two brothers went to Winchester. Born and bred in London, spending his early life in Holborn and Bloomsbury, he was at first brought up as a Jew, and received lessons in Hebrew. He was baptized into the Church of England when he was twelve. He left school at fifteen, for no very obvious reason, though he studied for some time at home, joining a solicitor's office for three years then deciding that the law was not for him. At twenty, therefore, he was trained for nothing, had no prospects, but was simply a very ambitious and conceited young individualist.

Somehow he inveigled a distinguished publisher to finance him in launching a newspaper aimed at rivalling *The Times* and *Spectator*. This collapsed, and a cocky but brilliant anonymous novel satirizing his publisher–sponsor caused some stir; unfortunately, his responsibility for it became known. By twenty-one he had ventured on an abortive commodity speculation which went wrong, saddling him with debts which dogged him even throughout his premiership, forcing him into renewed borrowing – sometimes short-term at penal rates. He had a nervous breakdown, and when he was twenty-five his family moved out to Buckinghamshire for him to recover – he was unemployed, an invalid, unwanted. In 1830–1 he went on an extended tour of the Mediterranean and Near East, which transformed his life, informed his novels, and instilled a romanticism – for example, about Turkey and Asia Minor – which never left him.

He returned, cured, educated, and in possession of even more bizarre items of dress than he had worn before. He started on the social circuit, took to himself a mistress, not very outstanding in her profession, and got himself mixed up in somewhat far-out radical politics. In 1834 he became linked with Lord Lyndhurst, briefly Lord Chancellor. A new and politically influential mistress, Henrietta Sykes, wife of a baronet, opened up wider political horizons, particularly after he generously agreed to share her with Lyndhurst.

His main concern was to get into Parliament, and he cared relatively little how it was to be brought about. As Lord Blake has said; 'It is very hard to discern any consistent purpose in his political activities from 1832 to 1846, indeed beyond, save an unrelenting though by no means unerring determination to get to the top.' He could not have made his task more difficult. His garish appearance was made the more extraordinary by his hairstyle and outlandish dress. Poseur, charlatan, adventurer, a man with a rapier wit and a wounding pen – all this, combined with his record as a failed speculator, made it harder for him to be received into the political establishment. Even his novel-writing, much of it political, with undisguised caricatures of leading political figures, was an embarrassment.

He had no view of party, still less of political principle, until he was well into his forties, and even that was stimulated by throwing in his lot with the small group of Young England aristocrats, most of them just fresh out of college. These he idealized, and they found reflection in his novels.

His ardent search for a seat in the Thirties was based on no party allegiance and few influential friends, apart from a limited contact with radicalism, before that cause became articulate with the Bright and Cobden Manchester School.

High Wycombe was a convenient and nearby seat, but under what colours should he run?

He had certain Tory leanings, or at any rate he disliked the Whigs, particularly over reform: on the other hand the tide seemed to be setting in against the Tories. He began to nurse the seat as a radical (he later claimed to have been offered but rejected a Tory seat, but no evidence has ever turned up to support this). He assumed that the election would be on the new, somewhat more representative register created by the Reform Act. 'I stand' he announced 'in the radical interest.' Then one of the two Whig members died, and he was forced into an election on the old register, with a minuscule electorate. His friend Bulwer, later Lord Lytton, tried but failed to get him nomination as a Whig, which he would no doubt have accepted. As a radical, with no Tory candidate, but against a Whig, he was beaten by twenty votes to twelve. Six months later there was a general election, on the new register. He stood as an independent, putting forward a programme which delicately intertwined strands from the Whig and Tory philosophies, attacking both but appealing for Tory votes in the hope of keeping out one of the Whigs. He finished bottom of the poll, with 119 votes, against 140 for the second-ranking Whig.

He then tried to stand for the county of Buckinghamshire on a more distinctive Tory policy, but withdrew when the Tories adopted an official candidate. Soon afterwards he was seeking nomination for Marylebone, this time on a distinctively radical platform. He approached the left-wing Liberal, Lord Durham, for support, but was most politely rebuffed. In 1834 he stood as an independent for Wycombe: there was no Tory candidate and Disraeli was not above taking a contribution of £500 from the Tory managers who wanted to dish one of the Whigs. This grant towards his expenses was organized by Lord Lyndhurst, arising no doubt from the camaraderie flowing from the *ménage à trois*, and Lyndhurst's dislike of Peel. After another, narrower defeat, he gave up the radical cause and sought the Tory nomination at King's Lynn, but failed to get it. He then wrote to the Tory leader, put his name down for the Tory Carlton Club, and became the official Tory candidate for Taunton, where he was again defeated – and with no further election in sight.

In those days the death of a monarch precipitated a general election. William IV died in 1837 – an event of which Disraeli made much in *Sybil* – and he was nominated for Maidstone, where he was at last elected. He was later to marry the widow of his Tory running-mate, Wyndham Lewis, who died in 1838.

That Disraeli exercised a frugal economy in matters of principle in his arduous campaign to be elected was instanced by his defence of his vote-catching devices during the 1834 Wycombe election: 'The people have their passions and it is even the duty of public men occasionally to adopt sentiments with which they do not agree, because the people must have leaders.' In modern terms his attitude could well be the last refuge of the political scoundrel who mouths racialist slogans with which in his heart he cannot agree.

His record in the early Forties is not much more edifying. When Peel formed his administration in 1841, Disraeli was not offered even the most humble post. Disraeli, for whom the years were passing, wrote a most bitter and importunate letter to the Prime Minister. This was perhaps excusable, though in modern times it would be a comparatively rare event. But more reprehensible was the sequel five years later, on the third reading of the Corn Law repeal Bill, when, as we have seen, Disraeli alleged that Peel's whole political life had been one

Disraeli's nomination at Aylesbury at the 1868 General Election.

of 'political larceny', and Peel was nettled into asking him why he had been ready 'to unite his political fortunes with mine in office'. Disraeli's denial that he had made such an approach, unless it was based on a total lapse of memory, was not only dishonest; he was taking a tremendous risk that Peel, then or subsequently, would read out the letter.

After Peel's resignation, the Tory protectionist rump was of little Parliamentary account. Its leaders were Stanley, later fourteenth Earl of Derby; Lord George Bentinck, whom Disraeli idolized and needed; Granby and Disraeli. They seemed to be condemned to years in fruitless opposition. In 1849 Disraeli became effective leader in the Commons, the position being formally ratified when Granby succeeded his father in the Lords. The party was in the ferment which afflicts impotent Oppositions. Disraeli told Derby that his task was 'to uphold the aristocratic settlement of the country. That is the only question at stake however manifold may be the forms which it assumes.' No doubt to rally his troops, he attacked the anti-Corn Law forces in one of his most cauterizing speeches, but he knew that he was stirring up dead ashes. Less than three years after repeal, Disraeli himself said, with the utmost cynical realism: 'Protection is not only dead but damned.' For his lifetime and beyond he was right. Joseph Chamberlain split the Conservative Party more than half a century later in trying to revive protectionism, and Baldwin lost his first general election on a limited protectionist campaign nearly three-quarters of a century later.

It is very difficult, especially after his repudiation of protection, to acquit Disraeli of cynical opportunism. He would not have accepted such a charge: he was already rationalizing his views with a wider philosophy idealizing the land, the market towns and the abiding values of our rural society. It was not for many years that he was able to advance from his new rural fortress and embrace the sturdy qualities of the urban householders, by this time the city equivalent of the yeomen of England. But this was again to produce a philosophy to justify decisions he had taken with great success in order to outwit Gladstone in the debates which led to the second Reform Act.

Disraeli did not have to wait as long as he had expected for office, brief though it proved. Russell, by this time Liberal Prime Minister, resigned over his measure, resisted by Palmerston and other members of his Cabinet, for a further instalment of Parliamentary reform. Derby formed an administration and Disraeli became Chancellor of the Exchequer, his first ministerial post. He was forty-seven.

It would be an act of kindness to draw a veil over his Budget, designed mainly to compensate the landed interests for the permanent repudiation of protection. As a Budget it did not add up, and Disraeli, ever more literate than numerate, got his fiscal detail wrong. The Budget was blown out of the water by Gladstone. Furthermore the Opposition had succeeded in patching up its differences: there was a new alliance between the Whigs and the Peelites and the provisional Tory administration was sent packing after ten months. They were out of office for nearly thirteen and a half years, apart from a sixteen-month administration in 1858–9, but they were not to know this. They were counting on a break-up of the Whig–Peelite Government in 1854, when they were baulked by the Crimean War. It was that and the durability of Palmerston, whose premiership was made inevitable by Aberdeen's conduct of the war, which kept them out of office.

For Disraeli the war was a hindrance to the progress, as he saw it, of British

Opposite Palmerston in 1865 by Barraud.

Overleaf A nineteenth-century painting of Windsor Castle where Queen Victoria summoned her Prime Ministers for weekends.

A. E. Chalon R.A.

politics, in other words the political advancement of Benjamin Disraeli, now in his fifties. 'Disraeli is furious with the war, which he thinks keeps Government in,' wrote his colleague Malmesbury.

After the Crimean War, there was, in fact, little to do. Disraeli used the dull years to strengthen his position with the established Church. Nonconformists had been active in attacking the Church of England over church rates and other matters. His other preoccupation was with Parliamentary reform. This was not easy for the Conservatives: they could hardly hope to compete with the more spirited of the Liberals. As a precaution Derby and Disraeli had drawn up a Tory Reform Bill ready to put into play if the need arose. In the Sixties the Tories remained in a state of readiness. There would be considerable political advantage to the party which actually put a reform measure on the statute-book. None, certainly not Disraeli himself, could have foreseen how the race was to be won. It was his tactics which succeeded in killing Russell's Bill of 1866, and ensuring the return of the Conservatives and Disraeli's entry at last into No. 10; as he was to put it, 'the top of the greasy pole'.

The Tories had little in the way of a strategy on reform. Disraeli had no intention of introducing a Bill, no Cabinet authority to do so, and no draft measure to hand which stood any chance of being legislated. Derby, the Prime Minister, was determined to proceed slowly – resolutions in Parliament, followed by a Bill in the next session. Plural voting must be retained, with a minimal extension of suffrage; household suffrage was anathema. In the debate on the resolutions, Disraeli hardly distinguished himself. Contrary to the Government decision, he suddenly promised an immediate Bill, tried to produce one with no preparation, got the statistical estimates of its consequences wrong, dropped one proposal after another, substituted new ones and split the Cabinet, which led to the resignation of Cranborne, later Lord Salisbury.

Yet in the end he won. He wrong-footed the Liberals, and carried a much more fundamental measure than either Derby or he himself had ever contemplated, based on household suffrage. This he never intended. It was like a mad game of musical chairs, with Disraeli's footwork confusing Gladstone, while at the same time he changed the rules – when the music stopped he was in the chair, with the Bill in his hands and through the House. At no point had he the slightest intention of introducing household suffrage – that was simply, to change the metaphor, a case of deft over-trumping.

Afterwards, rationalizing, he sought to claim that in all this he was 'educating his party'. He was rightly able to claim a significant democratic advance, but not to claim that he had planned it. The Tory MPs celebrating in the Carlton Club after the vote had it right. By some chance, Disraeli looked in and received an ovation. The toast they drank was: 'Here's to the man who rode the race, who took the time, who kept the time, and did the trick.' Disraeli, who could hardly ride at all and who, on visits to country houses, could not wait for the moment to arrive after dinner, when they sat down with the ladies, had arrived.

Derby was seriously ill. It was only a matter of time before he must resign, and he asked Disraeli if he was ready to take over, probably the most otiose question in political history. Unknown to him, the Queen, through her secretary, had already sounded out Disraeli, who knew that he was the chosen successor. She had in fact acted unconstitutionally, for Derby had not formally tendered his resignation: in fact she treated Derby with scant consideration. He had hoped to follow the usual practice of delivering his seals of office in

Opposite above Mary Ann Disraeli,
below Hughenden, Disraeli's country house.

person to the Queen. She simply asked him to resign at once. Disraeli was now her 'man risen from the people', as she wrote to her daughter. (A few years earlier she would have written very differently: some man, some people.) Two days after he had kissed hands she wrote again: 'He is full of poetry, romance and chivalry. When he knelt down to kiss my hand he took it in both his – he said "In loving loyalty and faith".' His own letters to her from that time forward were larded with devotion and flattery. He himself is said to have admitted that he laid it on 'with a trowel'.

It had not been ever thus. In 1851 she had blamed him over the abortive attempt to form a Tory administration under Stanley, as he then was. In the negotiations for the 1852 administration, Derby had put forward Disraeli's name for Home Secretary. The Queen, on protocol grounds – for example on the swearing in of bishops and on other occasion – had to have the Home Secretary in frequent attendance. 'I do not approve of Mr D ...' she told Derby, 'I do not approve of his conduct to Sir Robert Peel'. Finally she accepted him as Chancellor of the Exchequer, but she warned Derby: 'All I can hope is that having attained this great position he will be temperate. I accept Mr Disraeli on your guarantee.'

In fact Disraeli in the intervening years had been working his passage with great assiduity. She approved of his efforts to keep the Whigs in power, though his reasons were not hers. He and his wife were actually received at Windsor in 1861. His elegant tribute on the death of the Prince Consort, published and well received by the public, greatly moved her, and he was invited to the wedding of the Prince of Wales, later Edward VII. Disraeli's own note of his visit to Windsor was a sign of things to come. Quoting from it, Lord Blake puts it beautifully: 'Disraeli is investing the Queen with some strange magical quality. She *appears*. She *vanishes*. The myth of "The Faery" is being born.'

Disraeli took great trouble with his party. He commanded the House of Commons for the greater part of his time there. But above all he cultivated the Queen. The pinnacle of the relationship, itself reflecting the flowering of his world, Eastern and Empire policy, was to be the decision during his second premiership to introduce the Royal Titles Bill in 1876. The Queen had set her heart on it. 'The Empress–Queen demands her Imperial Crown' he told his Lord Chancellor. Two previous Prime Ministers had failed to gratify her wishes. Not so Disraeli, though he was disturbed by the timing. But he had to decide for or against before the 1876 session began, because it would have to be announced in the Queen's Speech opening the session. (Throughout history, policy, not only legislative policy, has been forced through, or dropped for a year – perhaps longer – because of the exigencies of the Gracious Speech, though modern Governments now have the safeguard of the customary last sentence of the speech: 'Other measures will be laid before you.') In fact Disraeli added unnecessarily to his difficulties by failing to inform the Leader of the Opposition of its inclusion, which was then and is now the correct procedure for measures of major constitutional import.

Disraeli's first premiership did not last long. He called an election, but the Praetorian Guard – the new household suffrage vote – deserted him. Already sixty-four, he had to face the probability of a further six or seven years in opposition. Immediately he faced the problem which can be, but is not invariably, the fate of a party leader who has lost an election. The Conservative Party throughout history has been more ruthless in seeking to dispatch its defeated

Opposite 'The Top of the Greasy Pole!' Disraeli's own words to describe his succession to premiership in March 1868.

leaders than, for example, the Labour Party or the Liberals – not even Gladstone in his eighties. The knives were out for him. He only narrowly survived a *putsch* which culminated in a meeting at Burghley House, where he was described by one back-bencher as 'that hellish Jew'. Many of his senior colleagues took the view that he should go, some pressing that the new Lord Derby, the fifteenth Earl, should take the leadership. He was saved, in fact, by the lack of agreement on any convincing successor, by his continued mastery of Parliament, and by two speeches made in the country at a most critical time – in Manchester and at the Crystal Palace.

Disraeli did not expect a general election until 1875, though he had Gladstone reeling in 1873. Indeed he had the chance to take office but declined. He was waiting for disillusion and by-elections to take their toll – an early version of 'Fill up the cup'. Considering his age, and the natural impatience of all Leaders of the Opposition, this was masterly self-restraint. And it paid off.

The election was in 1874, not 1875. In January, Gladstone was in trouble with his Cabinet, and faced other difficulties. He decided to risk all on a snap election. The result far exceeded Disraeli's expectations. This side of the Irish Sea the swing was not spectacular, but in Ireland, Home Rulers had a landslide at the expense of previous Liberal members, and for the first time Disraeli had an unchallengeable working majority – in fact the first majority of any kind for an incoming Conservative Prime Minister since 1841.

His majority was invulnerable, his leadership beyond challenge. Top of the greasy pole again, but there secure. He was free for the first time to take a long-term view, and to create for himself a philosophy of Britain and the world which would be distinctively his own. In so far as that proved to be a new conception of Britain's role in the world it is more than probable that it was not yet at all clearly formulated in his own mind.

When one considers the authority a modern Prime Minister exercises over his Cabinet, especially on coming into office, a modern reader of Disraeli's experiences is somewhat surprised how much he had to concede, how much he had to manoeuvre in his own Cabinet. This was to some extent due to the balance-of-power considerations in an administration which included strong personalities, scions of aristocratic houses, Parliamentarians conscious of their own dignity leading to inevitable divisions on policies and philosophies and social standing. Until Disraeli took the lead on the world stage he had to cajole and manoeuvre every inch of the way – he was, in Morley's terms a quarter of a century later, *primus inter pares*. Even in world affairs he tolerated – no doubt felt he had to tolerate – opposition to his fundamental views on the Eastern Question and the Russian problem from his own Foreign Secretary, the younger Derby: opposition which reached the level of disloyalty and even political treason in Derby's attempts to sabotage his Eastern policy through direct contacts with the Russian Court, virtually enjoining the Tsar to take no account of Disraeli's views and demands. In a modern Cabinet, Derby would have gone or been demoted without even knowing what had hit him: Disraeli allowed the dangerous farce to continue for nearly two years before he acted. Then it was, and only then, that – to paraphrase Canning – he called Lord Salisbury into existence to redress the balance of the Knowsley connection.

Disraeli did, however, in addition to his distinctive stance on foreign affairs, put his stamp on one significant sector of home affairs – the social question. If, in foreign affairs, every schoolboy and girl has to learn the phrase 'Peace with Honour', no less in domestic affairs do we recount Disraeli's phase 'Sanitas sanitatum, omnia sanitas'. Decades of cholera outbreaks and scares, polluted rivers and widespread disease had illuminated an intolerable danger to health. One of Britain's greatest civil service administrators, Sclater Booth, the Local Government Board chief, rivalled only by Morant and Beveridge in the next seventy-five years, helped to pioneer our health and pollution legislation, while Cross at the Home Office introduced far-reaching labour legislation: the Employers and Workmen Act, which superseded the old Master and Servant Act, taking breaches of contract outside the realm of criminal prosecution; the Conspiracy and Protection of Property Act, which changed the law of conspiracy in favour of the trade unions and legalized peaceful picketing – a reform which lasted until the unexpected Taff Vale judgment thirty years later. In labour legislation Disraeli toughly backed Cross against the rest of the Cabinet in going far beyond the tepid recommendations of the report of the Royal Commission, 1874. There was housing legislation, too – artisans' dwellings, the Agricultural Holdings Act defending tenants' rights against the landlord, and the 1876 Education Act.

When Disraeli left Downing Street after the election defeat of 1880 he had the right to claim a greater advance in social legislation than that of any of his predecessors, almost more than all of them put together. It would not have been an unfitting Parliamentary epitaph for the author of *Sybil* and the great propagandist of the 'condition of Britain' question.

The conventional personalizing confrontations of schoolday history have led generations to gain the impression that the last third or so of the political history of the nineteenth century was marked by a Westminster in which Disraeli and Gladstone glowered and thundered at each other from the two front-bench dispatch boxes in the House of Commons. In fact, Gladstone and Disraeli faced one another in the House as leaders of their respective parties for only eight years, though there had of course been a continuing exchange of mutual discourtesies during their respective tenures of the Exchequer.

An important part of their confrontation took place after Disraeli's 1874 victory, though in fact Gladstone resigned the leadership of his party in 1875. But his Midlothian campaign in the late Seventies, culminating in the Liberal victory of 1880, was a direct attack on Disraeli and his policies, and it so established Gladstone's *de facto* leadership of his party that the Queen was obliged to send for him when, to her totally unconcealed chagrin, the Liberals won.

In the 1870s the battleground between Disraeli and Gladstone was almost exclusively over foreign policy. Reference has been made to Disraeli's difficulties over relations with Russia, and the behaviour of Derby. But Disraeli was becoming increasingly clear about his objectives. The 1874 victory gave him the confidence and the security of a virtually certain six-year administration which enabled him to extrovert his gifts into the wider world. In his novel *Endymion* one of his characters calls attention to 'Lord Roehampton': 'He is the man. He does not care a rush whether the revenue increases or declines. He is thinking of real politics; foreign affairs, maintaining our power in Europe.' His ministerial career had been devoted to the revenue, but his six years as Leader of the Opposition, from 1868 to 1874 'Shadow Prime Minister', had immersed him in 'real politics'. He started from no preconceived notions, as Gladstone did, and succeeded in formulating an approach which struck a chord

SUEZ CANAL
THE KEY OF INDIA
SWAIN SC

with public opinion. More, he was capable of working out his strategic objectives, and then bringing to their fulfilment the same qualities of deft footwork which had enabled him to master the House of Commons.

In his approach to the Near East question he had a majority of his Cabinet, including for a time some of its most powerful members, against him, until a succession of resignations left him in control. For a time, too, the Queen had prejudices on the Russo–Turkish problem almost diametrically opposed to his, but with her increasing captivation with her Prime Minister she came to accept his views and turn her not inconsiderable capacity for venom against Derby, playing her full part in ousting him from the Cabinet.

Turkey, the corrupt, archaic, cruel Ottoman Empire, was crumbling, crumbling internally against the rise of nationalist movements in what is now Bulgaria, Romania and Yugoslavia; virtually excluded from its nominal fief of Egypt; insecure in its control of what we now call the Arab and Israeli States of what was then known as 'Asia Minor'. Britain's traditional attitude had been not so much one of showing up this effete absolutism as seeking to ensure that its demise and carve-up should not lead to the aggrandizement of powerful neighbours, particularly Russia and the Austro–Hungarian Empire. Disraeli approached the exploding problem with no preconceived ideas. His aims were nearer home – to diminish the power of the Dreikaiserbund, the alliance of the three Emperors of Prussia, Austria–Hungary and Russia, at a time when the French power and influence had been smashed for a time by the Franco–Prussian war. He wanted to see Turkey move forward from her medieval anarchy, both in the homeland and the wider area she controlled. Increasingly he was concerned about the route to India. The opening of the Suez Canal in 1869 had shortened the route to India for the Army, the administrators and businessmen by several weeks and thousands of miles. The Indian Mutiny had underlined the need for speed of reinforcement. His Lord Chancellor, Cairns, following Disraeli's success in buying a minority of the Canal shares, wrote: 'It is now the *Canal* and *India*; there is now no such thing as India alone. India is any number of cyphers; but the Canal is the unit that makes these cyphers possible.'

Trouble began with the rebellion in Herzegovina, at the north-western tip of the Turkish Empire: the Sultan had been wasting his substance in riotous railway-building, regardless of cost or return. The City, which held a third of his virtually worthless debt, had a real interest in seeing reform carried out in Turkey. Disraeli was determined that the Tsar should not profit by Turkish dismemberment. The Canal was vital; four-fifths of its traffic was British. He was concerned, too, by Russian expansionism in the region of the Caspian Sea, following the Russian takeover in the 1860s of ancient Asian kingdoms, getting closer and closer to the northern approaches to India. His geography – and this is true of other Prime Ministers – was not his strongest point. At one point he thought of the Caspian as open water; his fear that a Russian capture of Constantinople would immediately threaten the Canal ignored the thousand miles between the two.

Crisis after crisis occurred: the murder of the French and German consuls at Salonika, followed by threatening noises from Berlin; the Bulgarian atrocities, which Disraeli was guilty of playing down because of wrong information from Sir Henry Elliott, Britain's man at The Porte. While Gladstone fulminated in his Midlothian campaign about the oppression of small nations, and

Opposite A *Punch* cartoon of 1875, the year Disraeli acquired shares in the Suez Canal, or 'The Key of India!'

by implication favoured Russian intervention, Disraeli was concerned with the statecraft of the world stage, with the relations between nations, the balance of power – as always he regarded Gladstone's righteous sermons as sanctimonious humbug.

Even so, he had not yet taken any firm line. He was, so far, easy-going in his relations with the Russian Ambassador Shuvalov. He was not yet committed to the integrity of the Turkish Empire, still less to a hostile confrontation with St Petersburg. He was ill, his Cabinet was sharply divided. While Gladstone was orating, Disraeli was dreaming – of the Queen, of Empire, India. The country was divided: you were either pro-Turk or pro-Russian, rather like the division over the Common Market a hundred years later, until it was settled by the referendum. The Queen was still pro-Turk: it was Gladstone's bitter outbursts more than Disraeli's arguments which moved her. Every statesman should remember his power to evoke a reaction–coefficient greater than unity. As Lord Blake has said, Gladstone engaged in a moral crusade, the Queen and Disraeli engaged more and more in *real-politik*. 'The more Turcophobic Gladstone became, the more Russophobic was Disraeli.'

Serbia had declared war. Her Majesty's Government did not take sides. Derby was working for an armistice, and proposed a conference of the six major powers; significantly, Britain was represented by the still uncommitted Salisbury. Events were moving fast, and public opinion building up at home. Russia was becoming impatient and threatening. Disraeli had to address the Lord Mayor's banquet. He rattled the sabre. Britain's resources, should she be involved in a 'righteous war', were 'inexhaustible . . . She is not a country that when she enters a campaign has to ask herself whether she can support a second or third campaign. She enters into a campaign which she will not terminate until right is done.'

The Tsar made clear that if the conference failed, Russia would act alone to bring Turkey to heel and enforce reform: 'May God help us to fulfil our sacred mission.' Disraeli had to react, while at the same time weakening the alliance of the three Emperors. But it was vital that Turkey should move quickly to reform. Partly because of a pro-Turk British Ambassador, whom Disraeli should have withdrawn, the Turks did not respond to Lord Salisbury's tough demands for reform. Disraeli, ill, with a disloyal Foreign Secretary, was not in command. His hopes of detaching Austria from supporting Russia made no progress. Britain wanted to see devolution and reform in the nationalist provinces of the Turkish Empire; Russia wanted to see them hived off and made independent – and then to infiltrate them.

The Russians, invading European Turkey, in July, were halted and for a time forced back at Plevna. Disraeli warned the Tsar that if war continued, by the wish of either side, Britain would intervene. But in December the Russians took Plevna. War fever reached new heights in London: it was the day when 'Jingoism' was created – 'We don't want to fight, but by Jingo, if we do, we've got the ships, we've got the men, we've got the money too.' With Salisbury moving to his side, and angered by Derby's leaks to Russia of Government policy, he secured Cabinet approval to renewing negotiations with Austria, making public the decision to ask Parliament for a war credit of £6 millions, and to send the new ironclads through the Dardanelles. Derby resigned on the third of these – but came back when it became clear that there had been a ciphering error about Russia's intentions. The Queen was furious at his return.

Lord Beaconsfield in his library at Hughenden.

An armistice followed, but when stories, probably untrue, reached London that the Russians were cheating on the armistice and crossing the demarcation lines, the Cabinet decided to send the fleet through to Constantinople. War was near. It would certainly have broken out had the Russians entered the Turkish capital. The Cabinet toughened their stance, and moved Indian troops from London to the Mediterranean. Parliament voted to call out the reserves. At this Derby finally resigned, later to leave the party and campaign for Gladstone in the 1880 election.

The Treaty of San Stefano imposed on the Turks was rejected by London, which disliked both the carving of the 'big Bulgaria' out of Turkey and the Russian takeover in Asia Minor and along the Black Sea, involving the vital caravan route to the East. But the Russians accepted their obligation under earlier treaties to consult the main European powers and Disraeli, ageing, ill, had his greatest triumph at the Congress of Berlin, which lasted from 4 June to 4 July 1878. He won all his objectives, the 'small' Bulgaria, and a secure frontier for Asian Turkey. He conceded a limited Russian expansion in the Black Sea area, gaining in return the island of Cyprus, a sure base for Britain should it become necessary for the Navy or the Army at any time to hold a watching brief on any further Russian activities – he had caught up with his geography homework. He dominated the Congress, evoking Bismarck's compliment: '*Der alter Jude, das ist der Mann.*' His claim to have returned bringing 'Peace with Honour' was endorsed by a majority of 143 in the House of Commons, every Tory member voting for the Treaty.

His remaining years were undistinguished. He had run out of legislative steam, and at the same time had run into trouble with the Zulu War and the revolt in the Transvaal. A British mission sent to clear up a dangerous situation in Kabul, where a Russian mission had been expelled by Roberts, was murdered, and Roberts had to invade Afghanistan again, but the Russians caused no trouble.

In 1880 Disraeli went to the country, confident of victory. Instead he suffered a major reverse. The Queen was devastated, and wrote tearfully to her daughter. His health deteriorated; just a year later, on 19 April 1881, he died of bronchitis, at the age of seventy-six.

Flags flew at half mast, cathedral bells were muffled and the blinds were reverently drawn over the windows of the London clubs. Gladstone as Prime Minister decided on a public funeral in Westminster Abbey, but Disraeli's will gave instructions for a simple burial in the churchyard at Hughenden in the same vault as his wife, Mary Anne. Whenever in the century since his death, his speeches and letters have been read, he has come to life again, rising up out of every page, with a vitality and humour that outlive the years.

He once wrote, 'the British people being subject to fogs and possessing a powerful middle class, require grave statesmen.' Whatever else he may have been called he was never grave, except during the Middle Eastern crisis. What he did was to make the aristocratic establishment laugh, first at him and then with him; and finally they took him to themselves.

5

William Ewart Gladstone

GLADSTONE WAS A MASSIVE CHARACTER, yet one of the most psychologically complicated personalities in the whole history of Britain's fifty Prime Ministers.

Some historians tend to regard Prime Ministers as two-dimensional figures, rely upon what they have written or read, marked by footnotes and quotations, and as having little more life than a printed page. They tend to ignore that Prime Ministers are real people, neither subhuman nor superhuman, with very human frailties and anxieties, with family problems, frequently financial problems, which can erupt when their mind, according to the history books, should have been, and probably was, concentrated on some domestic or international crisis.

Gladstone was dominated by religion, some would say religiosity. As a young man he was torn between entering the Church or entering politics. After a triumphant debating success at the Oxford Union, his friend, the son of the Duke of Newcastle, recommended him to his father, who controlled the votes of the Newark constituency. He was in deep torment about the career he should follow: Church or State. In the end, he decided to accept nomination – a high Tory sponsored by a high Tory Duke. But at every crisis of his life he returned to religion, dashing off 20,000-word theses, for example on Pope Pius IX's assertion of papal infallibility.

In his private life, setting on one side his enthusiastic midnight excursions to save fallen women from their sin, there was his concern, at critical moments in his career, about his alcoholic and apostate sister, living abroad, who embraced Catholicism. His repeated visits to the Continent to try and save her soul created tensions which entered into his own.

He was by far the best Chancellor of the Exchequer of the century, setting a new pattern in analysis, planning and exposition. In the Pitt–Peel tradition he had, deservedly, a Parliamentary triumph with his 1853 Budget, which was repeated in 1860 but not in 1863, when he tried unsuccessfully to tax charities, many of which were a tax-dodging racket. The strength of his feelings about the rights of small nations, which was the inspiration of his brilliant Midlothian campaign, began with Italy. On a visit there he attended the trial of a Liberal minister, Carlo Poerio, and heard him sentenced to twenty-four years in chains under the tyrannous rule of King Ferdinand of Naples; this led him to embark on a campaign as dedicated as that of the left-wing Labour MPs of this generation on oppression in Chile. This was all to his credit, and he goes down to history as one of the founders of Italian freedom and unity, a cause made the more precious to him by his lifelong studies and writings on classical Latin literature and history.

This concern with the rights of small nations and nationalities was the basis of his confrontation with Disraeli in the 1870s. It played a great part in the major obsession of his life, Ireland. Charity begins at home, and if he was to challenge the autocrats of Europe on the rights of Italian and Slav minorities, he was compelled equally to campaign for the independence of the Irish nation. In this campaign there was probably another motivation: his preoccupation with the rights and duties of the Anglican Establishment led him to seek the purge from the United Kingdom of a country mainly dedicated to Catholicism, moreover a country prone to elect to the House of Commons eighty members who, election after election, held the balance in the House, and who were not backward in throwing their weight behind one party or another to secure their objective.

Previous page Young Gladstone – 'the rising hope of those stern and unbending Tories'.

In the Irish cause he became totally involved, and insisted on remaining in office, at the expense of a fatal split in his party, to achieve his objective of Irish Home Rule. His obsession dominated his party, as he clung to the leadership throughout his seventies and into his eighties. An increasingly rebellious party simply did not dare to get rid of him.

In my Oxford final examination, I found at the top of the history paper the question: 'The Liberal Party was a party without a mission after the death of Gladstone: discuss this statement.' The answer given to the question was a rejection of the statement: it was Gladstone's obsession with Ireland which held the Liberal Party back from what had become the principal desire of its younger members, social reform, which Lloyd George, in the Asquith administration, was to force through. There is no reason to change that view.

The younger Liberals were transfixed. No one would bell the cat. It is a not unfamiliar problem. Winston Churchill held on, as his disloyal physician made clear in his memoirs, when his grip on affairs made government increasingly difficult, and there was in the end a greatly daring *putsch* to get rid of him, on which the facts have not been published. A dominant leader, and fortunately they are becoming a rarer species, can compel fear not only in his declining years but after his death. One gets the impression that M. Pompidou felt insecure for weeks after his election, lest General de Gaulle should insist on a second coming, with a time-scale transcending the hallowed three-day limit. The same fear clearly operated in Express Newspapers, that Lord Beaverbrook would return and continue to make his minions' lives a misery: at the dinner to celebrate the fiftieth anniversary of the *Sunday Express* the ornate menu carried an Osbert Lancaster cartoon showing an archangel Beaverbrook telephoning from above the clouds angrily querying the circulation figures.

One of Gladstone's greatest periods, eighteen or so years before his retirement, was when, having surrendered the leadership of his party, he embarked on the Midlothian campaign, mainly directed to the sufferings of small nations. His greeting wherever he went, with massed bands and cheering crowds, has not been equalled for any other statesman. Nor probably has his power of oratory, and the effect of that oratory. It was that campaign above all which led the Queen, against her most passionate objections, to concede that whoever might be the titular leader of the party, she had no alternative to sending for Gladstone when the 1880 election consigned Disraeli to the shades.

William Ewart Gladstone was born in 1809. Not Gladstone but Gladstones, his family name was changed by deed poll in 1837, by which time he had already been a minister. His father, who lived in what is now the Huyton constituency, had extensive plantation interests and was a considerable slave-owner. In 1838, having already been Under-Secretary of the Colonies under Peel, Gladstone made a two-hour speech defending the former West Indian slave owners, and opposed a motion to reduce by two years the 'apprenticeship' which was until August of that year a euphemism to describe the transitional status of the former slaves.

Educated at Eton and Christ Church, he entered the House of Commons in 1832, and in 1834 he became a Junior Lord of the Treasury, before going to the Colonial Office. He spent much of his Opposition years from 1835 to 1841 travelling, studying, mainly religion, and meeting foreign churchmen, as well as writing on religious matters. His famous but wrong-headed tract of 1838, which he later regretted having written, *The State in its Relations with the*

Church, had a poor reception and was the occasion of Macaulay's often-quoted description of Gladstone as 'the rising hope of those stern and unbending Tories'.

When in 1841 Peel formed his majority administration Gladstone hoped for a Cabinet post. To his intense disappointment he was made Vice-President of the Board of Trade. Peel tried to reassure him by saying that since the President was to be the ageing Earl of Ripon (Goderich surfacing again), all the serious work would fall to Gladstone, who would be operating closely with the Prime Minister. Still disgruntled, he told Peel that he was 'really not fit for it, I have no general knowledge of trade whatever'. To his diary, he confided: 'It has always been my hope to avoid this class of employment. On this account I have not endeavoured to train myself for them. The place is very distasteful to me. . . . The science of politics deals with the government of men, but I am set to govern packages.'

In fact Ripon was useless. Gladstone wrote that although at the start his own mind had been like 'a sheet of white paper', he knew 'more about the business' than Lord Ripon within a month. In due course, when a vacancy occurred in the Presidency of the Board of Control in 1843, Ripon was moved there and Gladstone came into the Cabinet as President of the Board of Trade. Meanwhile he was working directly to the Prime Minister, on Peel's major revision of the tariff, the Budget, and matters of wider Government policy. He was working on these highly detailed trade matters for twelve hours a day, and sometimes fourteen, or even sixteen; he spoke over 120 times in the House, mainly on the fiscal changes, in a single session, to say nothing of handling countless deputations from trade and industry. He was to say later that he regarded the second great tariff revision of 1845, on top of that of 1842, as the most momentous legislative achievements of his career, though before the Budget embodying the changes he had resigned over the Maynooth grant.

Peel knew what he was doing. Gladstone had come to regard economic administration as something entirely congenial, and his leader was clearly grooming him to be a future Chancellor of the Exchequer, thus paving the way for the great Budgets of the Fifties. What Peel did for Gladstone, and Gladstone's early resistance to taking the job, is something that is mirrored in every administration, sometimes several times. Great reputations have been made in departments by ministers who have almost had to have their arms twisted to accept the post offered. When the Labour Government was formed in 1964, two new ministers met outside the Cabinet room, exchanged jobs, and came back to tell the Prime Minister, who told them to go to the departments to which they had been allocated. Within a week both were saying how glad they were to be where they had been sent.

Gladstone was one of those natural committed resigners, still with us today. He was unhappy about Peel's revival of income tax, and pressed hard for a house-tax, but not to the point of resignation. In 1842, still a junior minister, he wanted to reduce the corn duty by more than Peel and other senior ministers felt politically wise. He told Peel he was ready to resign if his views did not prevail. Peel was, Gladstone said, 'much annoyed and displeased', and after a night's consultation with his wife, and no doubt many hours of prayer, Gladstone wrote a letter of retraction and apology. He noted privately that: 'There was no such background of difference between my views and his as to justify the step I had taken. Severances upon narrow grounds would go far to render Government impossible.'

His resignation over Maynooth was more concerned with consistency than with current conviction. In *Church and State* he had attacked the grant, then at £9000 a year, an attack he had never withdrawn. Peel increased it to £30,000, to make a small reduction in the great gap in the provision of finance between the minority Anglican Church Establishments and the majority Catholics. Peel, Graham and others tried to dissuade Gladstone from going, and simply did not understand what the fuss was about. On 3 February he formally resigned, remaining on good terms with the Government, of which he was a strong back-bench supporter. He was later to say that he regretted a decision 'fitter for a dreamer, or a schoolman, than for the active purposes of public life in a busy and moving age'. In the event he voted for the Maynooth Bill.

At the height of the Corn Law crisis, in December 1845, Peel magnanimously invited Gladstone back into the Cabinet as Colonial Secretary in Stanley's place. Under the then rules he had to resign his Newark seat and seek re-election, but the Duke of Newcastle, a hard-line protectionist, threw his influence against his readoption. Gladstone tried hard to find an alternative but failed. He was out of Parliament for twenty months, till his return from Oxford University in 1847, and so was unable to defend his chief in the critical Corn Law debates against Disraeli and Bentinck and the sullen majority of the Tory Party.

With the fall of the Peel administration, Gladstone handed the seals of office to the Queen. He and his fellow Peelites became a group of unhappy displaced persons, voting *ad hoc* on particular issues, drawn sometimes to supporting the Whig administration, particularly on free trade, at other times joining their former colleagues in the division lobby.

1851 was the year when he saw the Poerio trial, and collected the evidence about the tyranny of the Kingdom of the Two Sicilies which produced one of the two or three greatest moral explosions of his life. Sir Philip Magnus in his great and readable biography refers to his torrid memorandum to Aberdeen, the Foreign Secretary, and adds: 'Gladstone had, in fact, erupted suddenly, and violently, like Vesuvius. He adduced many supporting details, and he returned to London . . . seething with indignation.' Magnus describes his being met at the station by an emissary of Lord Stanley (later the fourteenth Earl of Derby), who was seeking to form a minority administration and was sounding out Gladstone about the Foreign Office. Gladstone was not concerned to listen, but poured out invective about Italy to the emissary, Phillimore. It was the beginning of Gladstone's identification with the rights of small nations, struggling to be free from cruel and authoritarian régimes. He almost absent-mindedly agreed to see Stanley, who in the event failed to form a ministry, and Russell's Government briefly continued. Aberdeen studied the evidence and asked Schwarzenberg, the Austrian Chancellor, to make private representations to the Neapolitan Court. All he got were representations about Britain's treatment of political offenders in Ireland, the Ionian Islands and Ceylon.

Gladstone was becoming a Liberal. A free trader he already was, now there was a foreign dimension. But there was the problem of party allegiance. He had condemned Palmerston in the Don Pacifico debate. He was deterred from joining the Whigs by the dominance of Palmerston, and from joining the Tory rump by his distaste for what he regarded as Disraeli's cynical political morality – not forgetting his destruction of Peel.

Russell's effort to unite his wide-ranging party had failed, and Stanley became Prime Minister, with Disraeli as Chancellor. A general election produced a stalemate between Whigs and Tories, leaving the Peelites holding the balance. Disraeli's Budget was a disaster ('disgusting and repulsive' Gladstone remarked to his wife), and when the Chancellor succeeded in getting his tax schedules wrong Gladstone excoriated him in one of the greatest and most successful fiscal destruction jobs in Parliamentary history. It was his first confrontation with Disraeli: neither was yet Prime Minister, nor would be for fifteen years more. The Budget described by Gladstone as the 'fraudulent chimaeras of enchanters and magicians' was rejected by the House, and a new Government was formed under Aberdeen, a coalition of Whigs and Peelites, with Russell as Foreign Secretary, Palmerston now Home Secretary, Gladstone as Chancellor and Graham First Lord. Moving into No. 11 Gladstone was involved in a dispute with Disraeli, who insisted on holding on to the Chancellor's robes of office.

His Budget of 1853 was regarded as one of the greatest of the century. Income tax was to be abolished over seven years: 7d. in the pound for two years, 6d. for two years, 3d. for three years, and abolition in 1860. It was being retained at a reducing scale to enable him to cut customs duties; on 133 articles it was abolished, on 133 more reduced. Every Budget is supposed to have a theme, be it encouragement of savings (Macmillan), social reform (Lloyd George and Churchill), or investment in productive industry (a whole succession of post-Second World War Chancellors). Gladstone's was dedicated to ruthless economy: he defended in strong terms the need to count candle-ends, and his aim was to let money hitherto commandeered by the State 'fructify in the pockets of the people'.

His hopes of abolishing income tax were destroyed by the outbreak of the war between Russia and Turkey. Gladstone was anti-Turkish, as he was still more dramatically twenty-five years later. He resented seeing his Budget strategy disrupted, and increased income tax from 7d. to 1s. 2d., telling the House: 'The expenses of a war are a moral check, which it has pleased the Almighty to impose upon the ambition and lust of conquest that are inherent in so many nations.' Those words were quoted by me as Shadow Chancellor against Harold Macmillan in the debate on the economic consequences of the invasion of Suez.

In the words of Gladstone's biographer, 'loathing everything that concerned the war in the Crimea, Gladstone sought solace by throwing himself into the causes of university and civil service reforms.' Both reforms were historic and in certain respects still dominate those areas today. He helped to prepare the Bill on the reform of his own university, he did everything he could in the face of considerable resistance to throw open civil service entry to widen competition. The Queen was worried – where would this stop? It was a continuous process, virtually completed in 1870 when he was Prime Minister: entrance to all major branches of the civil service was thrown open, as that to the Indian Civil Service had been in the earlier operation. Only the Foreign Office was left under the old system.

The Crimean mismanagement, failures, and deaths through ill-led military operations and by disease, which characterized the Crimean War, led to Roebuck's motion for a Committee of Inquiry in 1855 into the conduct of the war being carried. The Government resigned; Derby refused to form an administration. The Conservatives paid for this by being out of office for the best part of the next twenty years. Russell was called, and failed. Aberdeen met with the Peelites and demanded that they serve under Palmerston. Hence the administration which lasted, as we have seen, with one brief interval, for the next eleven years. Gladstone accepted nomination to the Cabinet, but resigned after two weeks over a relatively trivial procedural question. For this he paid a price: he had run away, and in wartime. He became still more unpopular when, a lone voice, he began to call for a negotiated peace. When Palmerston was defeated over the Orsini plot, Gladstone refused to serve under Derby. Disraeli appealed to him – 'I almost went down on my knees to him' he told Derby. He was on the outside now, and gladly accepted an invitation to go out as Commissioner to the Ionian Islands, where the issue of union with Greece was at stake.

On his return, there was another election after a Government defeat on a minor reform Bill. Derby resigned. Gladstone urged a Derby–Palmerston coalition, with Disraeli in cold storage. When this idea foundered, Gladstone accepted Palmerston's offer of any post he cared to claim: he was back as Chancellor. The reason, he explained privately, was to be found in one word, 'Italy'. The Risorgimento was in full flood, and 1859 is imperishably recorded in the annals of the history of a united Italy.

Always a difficult colleague, except when he proceeded from the difficult to the impossible, Gladstone more than once was near breaking-point with Palmerston, but the bonds held. Though ill with bronchitis he produced his second great Budget:

> Our old friend, Protection, who used formerly to dwell in the Palaces and High Places of the land, and who was dislodged from them some ten or fifteen years ago, has since that period still found pretty uncomfortable shelter and good living in holes and corners; and you are invited ... to see whether you cannot likewise expel him from those holes and corners.

To pay for tariff concessions, the new naval programme to provide ironclads, and the cost of the Chinese military expedition (which he opposed), he raised income tax to 10d. and reduced more duties. His proposals were widely acclaimed – even Napoleon III cabled his congratulations. When he had trouble with the Lords over his paper duty reductions, designed to help the press, he rejected their claimed right to interfere with fiscal legislation and later beat them by consolidating the paper duties with other tax legislation, challenging them, in effect, to throw out the Budget. His victory set the stage for another confrontation fifty years later, when a Lords rejection of the Finance Bill led to the Parliament Act.

He set up the Public Accounts Committee of the House which for 115 years has struck terror into bureaucrats, and ensured that not a penny is spent on any function other than that authorized by Parliament. In a decade where we have seen a proliferation of Select Committees and sub-Committes thereof, the PAC remains the doyen of them all. To serve on it, still more to chair it, is still the aim of some of the most ambitious young members.

Gladstone still had his head down in his Treasury files. On foreign affairs his Italian concerns were doing well, and he felt he had an apt pupil in the new liberal Palmerston. But with the outbreak of the American Civil War he suddenly went berserk. It is too crude an interpretation to say that because his father had owned slaves he supported the South. The institution of slavery he did not support, the South he did. Another small nation striving to be free? Perhaps, but he was totally out of touch with feeling in the North of his own

Hawarden Castle, the ancestral home of the Glynne family which Katherine Gladstone inherited.

country which he should have been able to measure. In 1865, defeated in Oxford on doctrinal questions, he was to run simultaneously for South-West Lancashire, which he won. His pro-Confederate views were not supported in the north of England; one of the most noble gestures in history was the 'memorial' to Abraham Lincoln of the starving Lancashire cotton-workers, unemployed through the denial of Southern raw cotton, expressing their support.

While the Government's posture, immoral though it was, remained nominally neutral between Lincoln and Jefferson Davis, Gladstone, for no apparent reason, exploded at Newcastle: 'There is no doubt that Jefferson Davis, and other leaders of the South have made an Army. They are making, it seems, a Navy. And they have made – what is more than either – they have made a Nation.' As Sir Philip Magnus has said: 'That statement reverberated round the world', giving the impression that Palmerston's Government supported the Confederacy. It was a blot on Gladstone's record which he never erased: it was one of the reasons – the attitude of some of his colleagues provided others

Mr and Mrs Gladstone's bedroom at Hawarden.

– why successive Presidents and Congresses were cool towards Britain, even at critical times for world peace, for generations to come.

Whether Gladstone was seeking a liberation from Treasury schedules, or just failing to find release from his personal problems by saving London's fallen women, he was certainly going through a period of irresponsible pronouncements. As we have seen, in 1864 he exploded about Parliamentary reform although there was not even the beginning of agreement in his party on the next stage of enfranchisement. With no Cabinet authority whatsoever, in a Parliamentary debate on a private member's Bill on reform Gladstone said: 'I venture to say that every man who is not presumably incapacitated by some consideration of personal unfitness or of political danger, is morally entitled to come within the pale of the Constitution.' He then outlined a few exceptions which made the confusion arising from his statement all the greater. But he could not explain away his assertion that the qualities needed for the franchise were, 'self-command, self-control, respect for order, patience under suffering, confidence in the law, regard for superiors'.

Disraeli fulminated about the revolutionary Tom Paine; the Queen told the Prime Minister that she was 'deeply grieved at this strange, independent act of Mr Gladstone's'. Palmerston ticked him off with language he was by this time usually reserving for some obscure European autocrat: 'You lay down broadly the Doctrine of Universal Suffrage, which I can never accept. I entirely deny that every sane and not disqualified man has a moral right to vote ... your speech may win Lancashire for you, though that is doubtful, but I fear it will lose England for you.' He asked pointedly, if every sane man, why not every sane woman? He further rebuked Gladstone for encouraging a trade union deputation to bring pressure on Parliament.

Gladstone's speech, unless one regards him as prone to psychopathy, was inexplicable. As Leader of the Opposition three years later he took a moderate line on reform, and was outflanked by Disraeli.

Palmerston's death in 1865, and the last Russell administration, led to a more ragged Parliamentary situation. Derby's brief administration from 1866 to 1868 was followed by the still briefer one of Disraeli: it was Disraeli under Derby who carried the second Reform Act against Gladstone. But Disraeli's administration was rejected by the electorate, and in December 1868 Gladstone became Prime Minister. The Parliament elected in 1868 lasted for six years. There was nothing Disraeli could do.

Despite Gladstone's speech, there was no further progress on Parliamentary reform. Marx may have made the right assessment:

> In England prolonged prosperity has demoralized the workers... The ultimate aim of this most bourgeois of lands would seem to be the establishment of a bourgeois aristocracy and a bourgeois proletariat, side by side with the bourgeoisie ... The revolutionary energy of the British workers has oozed away ...

Gladstone's assumption of the premiership led to his first absorption in the Irish problem. He had already, before becoming Prime Minister, proposed the disestablishment of the Irish Church. As Prime Minister he was minuting the Queen about Irish reforms. He carried through the Irish Land Act, and three years later he introduced the Irish University Bill, whose rejection Disraeli took care of.

His first administration was quietly effective. One notable achievement was the reference of the US claims over the *Alabama* incident to international arbitration. The award, and the bill which the taxpayer had to meet, were formidable: but his action was significant in establishing the rule of arbitration in disputes between nation-states.

His reforms were to a considerable extent in institutions – including opening up the Civil Service to competition; the abolition of Army commissions by purchase, and War Secretary Cardwell's other important Army reforms; reforms of the judicial system; Irish Church disestablishment; the abolition of University religious tests; the secret ballot, and Forster's epoch-making Education Act, which made elementary education compulsory but not free until 1891.

In February 1874 he was rejected by the electorate. In 1875 he resigned the leadership of the Liberal party, and went into the wilderness. But not for long, for he countered Disraeli's Eastern policy with the Midlothian campaign on behalf of the rights of emergent nationalities.

This was the period of his greatness, transcending everything that had gone before and certainly everything that followed, those tragic years of the Irish obsession which dominated British politics for fifteen years. No statesman – and Gladstone was not even leader of his party – has been greeted by such mass popular demonstrations as accompanied his progress throughout Scotland, at railway stations, on the road, and in the halls where he spoke, where men fought for a seat. No statesman before or since has had so great a triumph, and when Disraeli, to his own surprise and the Queen's mortification, was defeated in 1880, she had no alternative to sending for Gladstone: no one else in the Liberal party, regardless of nominal status or elected position, could even touch the hem of his cloak.

He combined with the premiership the post of Chancellor of the Exchequer. But there was no longer the fire of his earlier Budgets, or even the inspiration and dedication of his earlier period at the Board of Trade, forty years before. He was in his seventies; while the official Conservative leadership was moribund he had to meet the piratical attacks of the so-called 'Fourth Party', – the predominantly aristocratic action group of the Conservative backbenchers – and suffered humiliations no Prime Minister should have to endure. Parliament was distracted by the Bradlaugh case, where an atheist refused to take the oath on being seated.

The Irish Question would have paralyzed any Prime Minister. His imaginative Irish Land Act did not stem the tide of Irish demands, led by Parnell. He was forced into yet another Coercion Bill. Parnell's support was coming to equal that of O'Connell forty years earlier. But Gladstone was not to be challenged. With the words 'the resources of civilization are not exhausted' he put Parnell in Kilmainham jail, and then proceeded to negotiate with him the political terms of his release.

Abroad, his administration was ill-starred. When Disraeli bestrode Europe, Gladstone might have considered Disraeli's policies and posturings meretricious. But foreign policy is measured by success, and Gladstone was unlucky, in part because of his inheritance. His attacks on Disraeli had committed him to some degree of decolonization. He withdrew the British garrison from Kandahar, in Afghanistan. He had condemned the annexation of the Transvaal. Now he faced revolt there, and also in Egypt, the key point of Disraeli's Near Eastern strategy.

It was not Gladstone's fault that the Transvaal was in revolt, and also the Sudan. Both produced disaster for him. The Boers defeated the British at Majuba, killing Colley, the Governor of Natal. Jingoism revived, fed by the Opposition, leading newspapers, and, no less than these, the Queen. The Convention of Pretoria, restoring independence to the Transvaal, provided for British supervision of its foreign relations, except those with the Orange Free State. The Transvaal recognized the Queen's suzerainty, but that was abandoned three years later. Public opinion in Britain was outraged.

Gladstone had to face a new European competition in colonial and potential colonial territories. At the very heyday of imperialism, which Disraeli had so well represented, he had to meet problems where others had embarked on expansion, in the New Hebrides, in New Guinea, and along the vulnerable coasts in East and West Africa. 'I would welcome the Germans as our neighbours in South Africa,' he said, 'and even as neighbours in the Transvaal.' From Disraeli there would have been no such welcome, but if he had been

TAKING THE (IRISH) BULL BY THE HORNS.

A cartoon from *Punch* of February 1870 satirizing Gladstone's assault on the Irish Question.

forced to accept them as facts he would have found a triumphant formula for accepting them.

Totally out of character, Gladstone ordered an attack on Egypt, where Arabi Pasha had revolted in 1882 and murdered foreigners in an attack on Alexandria, in which the British consul was injured. Gladstone would have preferred a European approach, but the Council of Europe, particularly Bismarck, preferred to avert their eyes. Gladstone when he acted, as became clear in his statements in the House of Commons, seemed as much affronted by Arabi's repudiation of debts to the Western world as by the murderous attack on Alexandria. The rising was crushed by Sir Garnet Wolseley's victory at Tel-el-Kebir, at the news of which Gladstone ordered salutes of guns to be fired in Hyde Park. The pacific John Bright resigned from the Cabinet, asserting that Gladstone was worse than Disraeli.

But more and worse trouble was to come next door to Egypt, in the Sudan. The revolting Mahdi, a religious fanatic with great military ability, had taken his army across the territory. In November 1883, an Egyptian army of ten thousand under British command challenged the Mahdi, who annihilated his opponents leaving virtually no survivors. The Mahdi was now master of the Sudan. The Queen virtually ordered Gladstone to avenge the outrage, but her Prime Minister thought that the thin red line was already too far extended.

All he felt was right was to help the Egyptian Government in withdrawing the scattered Egyptian garrisons. Politicians were divided. The Tory Lord Randolph Churchill, now of the so-called Fourth Party, felt that Britain should not be in Egypt, still less the Sudan. Ministers, in Gladstone's absence, resting at Hawarden, decided to send General Gordon, 'Chinese Gordon', a folk hero, to the Sudan. Gladstone somewhat unthinkingly acquiesced.

Of all the prancing proconsuls, none has exceeded Gordon. Disregarding his orders, which were to evacuate, this notorious extrovert decided to write his own, believing in his own mind that he could appeal to the British people over any Government's head. In this he was right, but their support proved of little post mortem comfort to him. Gladstone had no control, and soon realized this. He even cut out and kept a *Punch* cartoon portraying his dependence on whatever decisions, regardless of orders, Gordon might take.

Installed in Khartoum, Gordon ignored his instructions and began to demand from London the military means of crushing the Mahdi. In his diary he confessed to 'having been insubordinate to Her Majesty's Government and its officials, but it is in my nature and I cannot help it'. He went on to say, 'I know if *I* was chief, I would never employ myself, for I am incorrigible.' As the Mahdi's force pressed in on Khartoum he found it difficult to communicate with the outside world. Downing Street, on the information available, believed that evacuation was possible. Gordon, however, was following *Boys' Own Paper* tactics, although using a well-known slave trader to organize his political campaign. This did not help with Liberal ministers who were revolted by the slavery connection.

The Cabinet wanted Gordon recalled, in accordance with his original instructions. Hartington, Secretary for War, proposed a relief expedition, but Gladstone was not seeking a war. Public clamour persisted, and the Government's majority against a jingoist motion in Parliament fell to a humiliating figure. Nevertheless an expeditionary force was mobilized, under Wolseley, to rescue the man who had refused to withdraw in accordance with his instructions when an escape route was open. Meanwhile Gordon was sitting in his Palace, laughing at Gladstone's dilemma.

Wolseley won through to Khartoum, which had fallen two days earlier. Gordon was dead. The Queen, who had been imperiously attacking Gladstone throughout the crisis, sent a savage, if somewhat ungrammatical, telegram to him, which by her orders was not enciphered but sent on an open line through the Post Office, venomously critical of Gladstone's failure to act earlier. Gladstone for his part, perhaps because he was nettled, perhaps because the very surroundings of Downing Street create a siege psychology under attack, was guilty of an act of supreme insensitivity on the night the news was received. He went to the theatre, later excusing himself with the argument that the report had not been confirmed. I can imagine no twentieth-century Prime Minister so acting, except possibly Asquith.

Gladstone's administration of 1880 to 1885 therefore had little to show in terms of legislation, nothing at all in terms of the 'condition of England' question. Overseas it was a record of inactivity and failure – a striking contrast to that of Disraeli before him.

The Cabinet was already divided over Irish policy, particularly the question of removing the Coercion Act on its expiry. The Cabinet split, Joseph Chamberlain and Dilke were on the verge of resignation. The Government were beaten on the Budget, but could not go to the country because new electoral registers made necessary by the Reform Act of 1884, increasing the county vote, were not ready. Salisbury formed an interim Tory Government. The Queen, still quarrelling with Gladstone, nevertheless still offered him an earldom. That might well have been her instinctive but gracious way of ensuring that he never came back.

Salisbury ran his minority Government without pressing Parliament too much. But Gladstone, now in opposition, was taking vital decisions. As early as the end of 1884 he had become personally converted to the idea of Irish Home Rule. In 1885 he decided that this would be his next fight, but the Parliamentary situation was not such as to encourage him to begin that fight.

Now, defeated, he decided to stay on for one purpose, the Old Man's battle to see Home Rule through. As a believer in the rights of small nations he could not resist Ireland's claim to self-determination. Britain was Anglican and nonconformist. Ireland was Catholic apart from Ulster. But now it would be a dedicated Prime Minister with an obsession. At seventy-six he would stay on for that one cause only, Irish Home Rule. But there was still an election to be fought. The result was, not for the first time, dominated by the Irish connection: there were 335 Liberals, 249 Conservatives and 86 Irish Nationalists. If the Irish went with the Conservatives, there would be a dead-heat. Gladstone hoped that Salisbury would call the Liberals and Irish into a constitutional get-together, to take the issue out of Westminster politics. For him there was only one issue: Rosebery told Hamilton, after a visit to Hawarden, that the Old Man had Ireland on the brain. So he had, otherwise he would have precipitated a vote on a domestic issue in the hope of breaking down the Tories' fragile majority. But Gladstone was now totally single-minded. He drove to a Tory house party at Eaton Hall, Chester, and commissioned Balfour, Salisbury's nephew, to represent that nothing but Home Rule would save Ireland and that this should be taken out of party politics. Salisbury's Cabinet rejected the idea out of hand.

Some Conservatives thought Gladstone was trying to split the Conservative Party, but the Old Man was beyond party tactics. The danger of a split was in his own party, where Chamberlain was waiting in the wings, ready to defect, a practice he was to repeat when a leading member of a Tory Cabinet eighteen years later. Others besides Chamberlain were becoming bored with the issue. The surprising thing is that since Gladstone's conversion was being announced to them for the first time, they did not insist on a change of leader. Such was the magnetic power of the Old Man that a new generation was impotent to point the way to new horizons for their party.

When Parliament met, the Salisbury Government announced their rejection of Home Rule and their decision to introduce a new Coercion Act. Gladstone rose and announced that his party would fight them all the way. Without Hartington or Chamberlain? asked the Tories. Gladstone said: 'Yes... I am prepared to go forward without anybody.' The Liberals fought with Irish support on a calculated motion on land reform, 'Three Acres and a Cow', and the Tories were defeated. Gladstone became Prime Minister for the third time. But the Liberals were split, some of them convinced that it was time for a change. The new Liberal Unionists were hiving off. Gladstone could have held them on any issue other than Ireland. His Home Rule Bill went down in the Commons

Opposite William Gladstone by Sir John Millais.

on second reading by 343 to 313, defeated by the defection of Chamberlain and his followers. A defiant Gladstone sat on the front bench, writing his report to the Queen. Next morning he was trying to convince a disheartened Cabinet that he should ask for a dissolution.

The Queen consented. The election which followed was bitter, Lord Randolph Churchill striking the winning note by describing Gladstone as 'an old man in a hurry'. The said Old Man was touring the hustings with the vigour of his Midlothian days, but when the votes were counted there were 316 Conservatives and 79 Liberal Unionists against 191 Gladstonian Liberals and 85 Irish Nationalists. The majority against Home Rule was 118, in an election which was virtually a referendum for or against Home Rule.

Then was the time for Gladstone to go, since he had the virtual certainty of six years' Opposition before him. But the Old Man, despite Churchill, was in no hurry. It is incredible that the party made no attempt to get rid of him. Twentieth-century parties are not capable of such tolerance. That they did not tell him 'Enough is enough', and subscribe for a massive silver salver to express their respect, meant that in a fatalist mood they accepted a certain six years in opposition, with an election under the same leader, who would then be eighty-two or eighty-three, on the same vote-losing subject, a subject boring to them and manifestly boring to the country, carrying with it the likelihood of a further defeat. Younger party members usually look forward to a majority, and the sweets of office. Yet Gladstone survived.

By this time, Parnell was in trouble over a series of 'disclosures' in *The Times*, quoting him as explaining away his denunciation of the murders of Lord Frederick Cavendish, Chief Secretary for Ireland, and T. B. Burke, his private secretary as follows: 'To denounce the murders was the only course open to us . . . But . . . though I regret the accident of Lord F. Cavendish's death, I cannot refuse to admit that Burke got no more than his deserts.' *The Times* challenged him to bring an action if he dared. A Commission was established, which was noteworthy for Asquith's rise to fame as the advocate who destroyed the manager of *The Times* with a devastating cross-examination. The letters were proved to be forgeries, and their author, Pigott, committed suicide when facing arrest.

But Parnell soon created worse trouble for Gladstone. The divorce suit brought by a party colleague, Captain O'Shea, naming him as co-respondent, was an affront to Liberal nonconformist England, and indeed to a wider section of the electorate. Parnell refused to resign, though Gladstone sent a message via Morley pressing him to go. The Irish party split, twenty-six supporting Parnell, forty-four breaking away.

Meanwhile Gladstone was pursuing a negative, even disruptive role in Parliament. Telling the Yorkshire Liberals that until the Irish problem was settled it would be impossible for any useful business to be transacted in Parliament, he introduced wrecking tactics, though he devoted himself mainly to the Irish question. A conversation recorded by Sir Henry Ponsonby, the Queen's private secretary, includes language which can be interpreted as casting doubt on his mental stability.

His party was getting increasingly restive because Gladstone gave no lead on social questions which for a growing number of his colleagues, especially the younger ones, were becoming a far higher priority than Ireland. There were unemployment riots in London in 1886 and 1887, and the great London dock

Opposite Benjamin Disraeli by Millais.

strike of 1889, when Cardinal Manning had stirred the conscience of the nation. Very many of Gladstone's party agreed with Joseph Chamberlain's thrust at him when he asked: 'Why should thirty millions be denied urgently needed social reform just because three millions are disloyal?' Gladstone was actually induced to speak on the condition of England question at Newcastle, but he spoke without conviction or interest. The so-called 'Newcastle Programme' was forgotten as soon as it was launched.

As was now his custom in opposition, he went off at Christmas 1891 for two and a half months' foreign holiday, even though there were strong rumours of a dissolution, which came in June 1892. (Most modern Opposition Leaders are lucky to get three days off at Christmas.) Until the Parnell scandal the Liberals could have counted on a big swing to them, as the Tories had put up a dismal record. Even so, the Liberals were counting on a 100 majority. In the event the Liberals had 273; with 81 Irish Nationalists and one Labour MP they had a majority of 40 over the 269 Conservatives and 46 Liberal Unionists. Salisbury's Government was defeated in the House on 11 August on a motion of no confidence moved by Asquith. Gladstone received through the Queen's secretary a commission to form his fourth administration. Vainly hoping to persuade the Queen of the rightness of his mission, he asked Ponsonby to tell her that Home Rule was a profoundly conservative measure: it would bring peace and content to Ireland, and would turn the Irish into loyalists, and possibly even into Tories.

The second reading of the Home Rule Bill was carried on the night of 21/22 April 1893 by 347 to 304. The Prime Minister then took personal charge of the Committee stage, speaking on nearly every amendment. Despite the introduction of the guillotine (or 'gag' to use the phrase of every Opposition) to cut short debate, the Bill occupied Parliament throughout the summer, with Gladstone in constant attendance. On the night of 1/2 September, the third reading was carried by 307 to 267. Hartington, who in opposition had refused to enter into any parleys with Gladstone over any party programme which could include Home Rule, was now in the Lords as the Duke of Devonshire, and it was he who moved the rejection of the Bill, to which their Lordships agreed by a more than ten to one majority. Sir Philip Magnus describes the reaction in the country to the Bill's defeat: 'It is said that not a dog barked from John O'Groats to Land's End. The country was bored; the subject was exhausted; many of Gladstone's colleagues were secretly relieved.'

The Old Man would not give in. He asked Cabinet to back him in seeking a dissolution, and fight the election on the issue 'The Peer versus The People'. The Cabinet refused to support him.

Twenty-five years earlier, when Gladstone first was told of the Queen's commission, he had continued to chop down his tree, paused, wiped his brow, and said: 'My mission is to pacify Ireland.' He had not succeeded, nor have his successors over more than a hundred years.

There was now nothing to justify his remaining in office. His Irish dream was gone. He could not fight the battle over again on the Peers v. People issue. His Cabinet would not let him 'fill up the cup' with one rejected Home Rule Bill after another. He knew this. The extraordinary thing is that he took so unconscionable a time to go. He even announced in Edinburgh his decision to introduce a new Bill in the forthcoming session.

Then came a clash on an entirely different issue, the Government's reaction

Charles Stuart Parnell.

to an Opposition motion calling for increased expenditure on the Navy. Gladstone regarded the motion as unconstitutional. On his argument, every Opposition motion before or since on improved housing, agriculture or education would have been out of order, and Parliamentary opposition would have been crippled. He was probably confusing two things – one, a declaratory motion, and, two, an amendment to the annual estimates on the Finance Bill, which is out of order under Parliamentary rules if it proposes an increase either in expenditure or taxation. But Gladstone was also fighting on the merits of the motion, objecting to the increased expenditure, and for a period his colleagues feared he might go, not on Ireland, but on an issue of public finance. On 9 January 1894 he addressed Cabinet for nearly an hour, but had no support except that of the First Commissioner for Works when he opposed the various means of raising the money.

But increasingly Gladstone's arguments and language were becoming incomprehensible and senile. He suddenly departed to France. The Cabinet sent an emissary across the Channel to see him and find out what he had decided. He was in the middle of a furious telegraphic argument with the Queen on the appropriate honour for the retiring Viceroy of India. On the issue of the Navy, he refused to send any message to the Cabinet – his mind was made up. He exploded: 'The plan is mad! And who are they who propose it? Men who were not born when I had been in public life for years.' When a Prime Minister or Opposition Leader even begins to think in those terms, it is time to go. He penned a long and excitable screed, but left it in the pocket of an overcoat, and it had to be posted on. Its text was uncompromising.

All this time he was totally opposed to resigning. He had come to believe in a doctrine of Divine Right of Prime Ministers. The trouble was that his Cabinet was so mesmerized that they were beginning to believe in it too. The emissary, Sir Algernon West, was sent back to Biarritz: was he really insisting? Gladstone caused a diversion by again proposing a dissolution, as further Bills had been rejected or mauled by the Lords. This time the Cabinet plucked up courage and sent him a unanimous telegram: 'Your suggestion is impossible.' Gladstone returned to London and went on fighting. He called a Cabinet dinner, where his colleagues confidently expected the announcement of his resignation. The atmosphere was tense, Gladstone was hostile and virtually challenged them to bell the cat. Press rumours were denied in a telegram he drafted saying that resignation was 'wholly unknown in Downing Street and without foundation'.

He finally announced his resignation at a Cabinet on 1 March, nearly two months after the argument began. Prepared and unprepared speeches ended with one minister after another bursting into tears, and Gladstone was wont afterwards to refer to 'that blubbering Cabinet'.

The Queen treated him with exceptional charm, but ominously did not ask him, as was more usual in those days than now, whom he would recommend as his successor. He would have suggested Lord Spencer, to keep out Harcourt. She chose Rosebery.

His remaining years, spent mostly at Hawarden, were devoted mainly to religion, including a great deal of writing on religious subjects, and to the creation of the St Deiniol's Library at Hawarden. But he came out of retirement in 1895 to address mass meetings protesting against the massacres in Armenia. There was a breath of Midlothian again: at the Liverpool meeting Gladstone, who was eighty-four, spoke for eighty minutes. Rosebery, by this time Leader of the Opposition, having thrown in the Cabinet's hand, resigned the leadership on hearing of Gladstone's Armenian initiative, and actually went so far as to refer to him as 'our leader'. A takeover of that kind had happened with Midlothian twenty years earlier, but sixty-four is not eighty-four.

On 19 May 1898 Gladstone died at Hawarden. On a motion moved in the two Houses by Salisbury and Balfour, he was buried in Westminster Abbey.

In political terms his life, like Peel's, ended in tragedy. Peel's trouble lay in his relations with his party. Gladstone, despite his Tory origins, had created the Liberal Party of his age. More than that, he *was* the party. They had no life save that which he breathed into them. Though in some ways he was growing out of date, yet he was more radical, in a revolutionary sense, at eighty-two, wanting to dissolve, to take on the Lords and solve the Irish question at the same time.

Mr and Mrs Gladstone at Hawarden with one of their grandchildren.

But there was a deeper reality. They were politicians; he was not. He had a contempt for political manoeuvrings. For him politics was the secular – and not all that secular – realization of the theological imperatives which were revealed to him from a Source with whom they were not in communion. It was only by a hairsbreadth that he had not chosen Church rather than State, but he never quite felt that he had so chosen. He was pursuing the Divine dictates but in different pathways. With that consciousness, he felt he should not have to argue for his convictions in a Cabinet, for it was in the wider assembly of Parliament that he had not only the right but the duty to preach.

Had he retired eight years earlier would his standing in history have been different? In one sense, no, for he achieved nothing of significance after 1886, and he would not have become so boring and tedious to his colleagues. But in a different sense, his sheer longevity, authority, cussedness perhaps, created a memory, for with his own party he, as much as Disraeli with the Conservatives, became a legend. Through the distinguished peacetime administration of Asquith, Home Secretary in his fourth administration, through and past Lloyd George, he remained the Grand Old Man of his Party. I can recall that up to the time I went to college, in my small bedroom at home was a reproduction of Millais' life-sized portrait – even though that had been a Labour home since 1906 – and a family heirloom was a Gladstone tablecloth embroidered in black to commemorate his funeral.

That Gladstone is no longer a legend today, as Disraeli is with the Conservatives, simply reflects the change in political power, with the Liberal Party now only a shadow of its former self, and a new political generation on the left no longer dedicated to the principles of the party he led.

Towards the Modern Age 1885–1908

Robert Arthur Talbot Gascoyne-Cecil, Third Marquess of Salisbury, came from a long line of State servants going back to Burghley in the reign of Queen Elizabeth I.

In June 1966, after careful inquiries to ensure that despite his wife's death, Clement Attlee, who had loved Chequers, would welcome an invitation to return for a weekend, I invited him there. His stroke had made him even more laconic than in his great days, and the conversation had to be in terms of careful questions designed to elicit a reply confined to a single word. The following exchange was recorded:

'Clem, yourself excluded, and politics apart, who of all the Prime Ministers Britain has had since you became old enough to take an interest do you consider the best, as Prime Minister?' 'Salisbury', he replied.

Sickly at school and college, as Pitt had been, Salisbury was restored to health by a sea voyage round the world. He visited the principal countries of the Empire, and returned, briefed as none of his contemporaries were, on the clashes developing in South Africa and the gold rush in Australia. South Africa was, in his later years in Parliament, to dominate public debate. Whatever views his contemporaries or later historians took of his policies in relation to the South African war, at least he knew the terrain.

Despite his cloistered background, he was a professional before he entered politics. Money was short for the style of life he had to maintain, and he was writing professionally for the *Quarterly Review* on political and imperial questions.

As Prime Minister for just under fourteen years, he served longer than any since Liverpool, and not even Gladstone equalled his tenure of office. No Prime Minister appointed since his time has even reached double figures. Of all the Prime Ministers he became a patriarch in his time.

He had served in the India Office under Derby, later resigning over Derby's – or, rather, Disraeli's – proposals for Parliamentary reform. Despite what he called the 'nightmare' of serving under Disraeli, a cad by his standards, he went back to the India Office in 1874 and replaced the fifteenth Earl of Derby as Foreign Secretary, in which capacity he accompanied his chief to the Congress of Berlin.

When Gladstone was defeated in 1885, it was to Salisbury that the Queen turned. For seven months he headed a minority Government. Gladstone returned for five months, but Salisbury won the ensuing election, and was Prime Minister for the six years up to 1892. No Marquess has made himself more accessible to the people, with his long succession of speeches in the country. Salisbury is noteworthy as the only Prime Minister since the eighteenth century who did not take the title of First Lord of the Treasury. This was given successively to Northcote, W.H. Smith and Balfour, each of whom, as First Lord, lived in Downing Street.

In his Cabinet he had a maverick, Lord Randolph Churchill, whose ill-considered resignation Salisbury survived with no more effort than if he had been brushing a fly off a brief he was reading.

In 1892 the general election returned Gladstone for a further year and a half. He was succeeded by Rosebery, whose extraordinary resignation brought Salisbury back to power, strongly reinforced by the 1895 election. Because of Gladstone's obsession, and the reality of Irish revolt behind that obsession, Salisbury had to spend a great deal of time on that still unresolved question. Despite jokes about the Hotel Cecil, he appointed his nephew Balfour as Chief Secretary, and that elegant soul, who might have had a leading part in Gilbert and Sullivan's *Patience*, became the hammer of the intransigent Irish Catholics, earning the soubriquet of 'bloody Balfour'.

Salisbury was an imperialist: during his premiership Britain acquired Kenya, Uganda, Nigeria and Rhodesia, and established control over the upper waters of the Nile. But it was not the white man's burden he sought, it was a strong coastal line, with the hinterland the preserve of chartered companies.

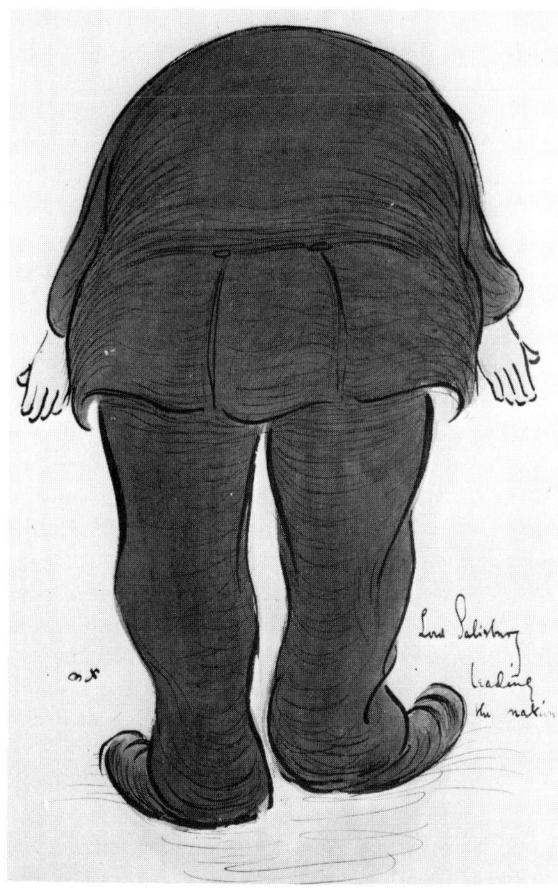

A cartoon of Lord Salisbury by Max Beerbohm, in the possession of the author.

He was Foreign Secretary for eleven years of his premiership, but took more interest in Africa than in Europe. In foreign, as opposed to African, affairs he remained distant and uncommitted: there was in fact no grouping in Europe worthy of his underwriting. The phrase 'splendid isolation' was his, though used more as a gibe against Joseph Chamberlain than against Europe. On one occasion he addressed a Disraeli-ite communication to the European powers, leading not to a grandiose Congress of Europe but to an ambassadorial conference in Constantinople. He broke off talks with Russia when he feared – rightly as it soon proved – Russian expansion into China.

It was in Africa that he was vigilant above all. In the struggle for Egypt he was determined to exclude French claims, and it was under Salisbury that Kitchener stood firm against the French at Fashoda. Once again the Channel defences were reinforced against a possible French invasion. But in Africa his prejudices of fifty years earlier dominated his thinking. He had always distrusted the Boers, and failed to control Chamberlain's scheming in South Africa, despite the baleful effects of the Jameson Raid. It was no accident that Salisbury presided over the events which led to the South African war, which in private he christened 'Joe's war'.

In 1900, at seventy, he was losing his grip. The 'Khaki Election' was Chamberlain's, not his. In July 1902 he retired, having ensured, through the miraculous workings of the establishment of his time, that his successor would be Balfour.

Archibald Philip Primrose, fifth Earl of Rosebery, was Queen Victoria's personal choice from competing claimants when Gladstone resigned. Of all Britain's Prime Ministers, few have presented a more interesting psychological case for analysis. As a young man his confidence rivalled that of Disraeli, though he was more happily stationed in life than his distinguished predecessor. At an age when Disraeli was still trying to seek entry into society, Rosebery had declared his three ambitions in life: to marry an heiress, to win the Derby, and to become Prime Minister. All three he accomplished. He married a Rothschild, though he was on occasion a little rude to his in-laws – when he wanted to go to bed, and they were dilatory, he brusquely ordered them: 'To your tents, O Israel.' His Derby ambitions were achieved during his premiership; not once but twice in successive years his horses finished first at Epsom.

Yet he was no dilettante, but a serious political figure. Following the local government reforms which created the London County Council, his standing was such that he became its first chairman. His oratorical power over a mass, predominantly working-class audience can be compared only with that of Aneurin Bevan half a century later.

When Gladstone resigned, as we have seen, the Queen did not ask him to recommend a successor. If the choice might have appeared to lie between Spencer – whom Gladstone would have chosen – and Harcourt, she chose Rosebery.

Robert Rhodes James has written of his 'charisma'. There can be no doubt of it. He had great charm, backed by the solid currency of a profound study of history and politics. He had organized and financed Gladstone's Midlothian campaign, but his scruples were such that he refused an invitation to serve in the 1880 ministry, as this might have been regarded as a

Archibald Philip Primrose, fifth Earl of Rosebery.

reward. In the end he became an under-secretary in the Home Office, with a special responsibility for Scottish affairs. He nearly resigned over Irish affairs, but the murder of Lord Frederick Cavendish caused him to hold his hand. Nevertheless he was to resign the premiership, on perhaps the most trivial cause of ministerial resignation in history. He went on tour, and his visits to the Dominions confirmed his incipient imperialism.

He returned as Foreign Secretary in the short administration of 1886, in particular handling a crisis in the Balkans with great skill. In 1890, when he was out of office, the death of his wife Hannah plunged him into a deep psychological depression, from which he never fully recovered. Already an insomniac, he found it harder and harder to sleep, a problem which was to end his effective political career.

In 1892 he again became Gladstone's Foreign Secretary, and over the Uganda issue again showed his mettle and imagination. When Gladstone resigned, he became Prime Minister of a Government which for nearly twenty years had been bereft of a philosophy because of Gladstone's Irish obsession. If Rosebery had shown a deep interest in the 'condition of Britain' question, he could perhaps have bridged the twenty years and led his party into the future. But he could not escape the Irish albatross. In his first speech he showed his concern by saying that there could be no Home Rule unless there was an English majority for it. This was a repudiation of Gladstone, who would have been happy to carry Home Rule with the help of eighty Irish MPs, to say nothing of the Scots and Welsh, presumably also excluded by Rosebery. If there is one rule for Prime Ministers, it is this: don't have a subconscious, but if you do have one, don't parade it.

His aristocratic tendencies caused him to quarrel with Harcourt, himself fatally preoccupied with his rejection as Gladstone's successor, over the death duties Budget. 'We are all Socialists now' said Harcourt, endearing himself even less to the laird of Dalmeny. He was beginning to appear frivolous – the Queen, who was clearly not amused, rebuked him. Winning the Derby won him no nonconformist support. Plagued by insomnia, he withdrew into himself, an increasingly lonely figure. No one should attempt the role of Prime Minister who cannot fall asleep the moment he is in bed, the cares and worries of the day behind him. In this essential requisite, Rosebery failed.

He threw his hand in, in the most unaccountable manner. In a debate on Supply there was a snap vote on the amount of cordite in Army depots and the Government was defeated. A Prime Minister in control of himself would have had a number of options. One would have been to reverse the vote, if necessary on a motion of confidence: there would have been little doubt about the result. Another – if he was over the edge through insomnia – would have been his own resignation. The one he took was to announce the resignation of his entire Government, thus letting the Tories in, with a legitimate claim for a general election. The Conservatives (like the Liberals ten years later) stood as a Government; the Liberals fought the election as quitters and went out for ten years.

Rosebery remained the titular leader of his party in opposition. Even then his obsession with Gladstone, as has been seen, led him to greet the ageing statesman's campaign against the Armenian atrocities with a statement that he was relinquishing the leadership to Gladstone – a decision for the party to take, not its increasingly withdrawn leader. There was nothing left for him now but his extremist position over the South African war, his increasing withdrawal in the new century from support of the party he had led, and, fortunately, his historical writings, notably his monograph on Peel.

When Rosebery began, he had everything – talents, negotiating ability, the power to command a mass audience. He failed because he lacked the stability and resilience which leadership demands, because he lacked the power to switch off and become a human being, above all because he lacked the ability to sleep.

Arthur James Balfour, later Earl of Balfour, was Salisbury's nephew. He was a strange blend of tough statesman, as witness his 'bloody Balfour' period as Chief Secretary for Ireland, and academic, as seen in his *Defence of Philosophic Doubt*, *The Foundations of Belief* and his Gifford Lectures on *Theism and Humanism*. Philosophic doubt undeniably inspired a great part of his political career. He was not of the character of which Prime Ministers were made. His Cabinet, it has been said, was a seminar.

His premiership was really longer than the three and a half years after he kissed hands until his resignation in 1905, for he was effectively head of the Government in the last years of Salisbury. His incubus was the same as Gladstone's in his own last years, Joseph Chamberlain, who having destroyed Liberal rule was, with his protectionist obsession, to end the ten years of Unionist rule which followed the election of 1895. A Liberal Opposition split over South Africa meant no hope of Liberal revival until Chamberlain split his party on imperial preference. From then the end of Balfour's Government was only a question of time.

Balfour was a reformer. He established the Committee of Imperial Defence, including Dominion Prime Ministers. He reorganized the War Office, and authorized defence programmes to meet the new challenge of the Kaiser's Germany. He was responsible for Britain's reconciliation with France, culminating in the Anglo–French convention of 1904. In the Russo–Japanese war he was vigilant, and Austen Chamberlain was later to say of him:

> No Prime Minister ever took a closer interest or ... more active part in the conduct of foreign policy ... It does not detract from Lansdowne's services as Foreign Secretary to say that his chief accomplishments would never have been achieved but for the constructive mind of Balfour and the constant support he gave him, not only in executing his foreign policy, but in conceiving and shaping it.

Austen Chamberlain was one who was so devoted to every Prime Minister he served that he probably had those words copied for use again and again. But in so far as they are true, they should be true equally of every Prime Minister in his relations with his Foreign Secretary. Only in the case of Neville Chamberlain, when Anthony Eden was at the Foreign Office, would they have had a hollow ring.

In some ways Balfour's services to the nation were greater after he left office. Though he had resigned the leadership of his party in 1911, Lloyd George was to place far more reliance on Balfour than on his successor Bonar Law in the wartime administration, and, incredibly, on Carson at the same time. Asquith, too, had relied on his advice, not least because Balfour was a permanent member, even in opposition, of the newly created Committee of Imperial Defence. And Balfour played a crucial role in the historic events of 1916, when Asquith was squeezed out in favour of Lloyd George.

Arthur James Balfour.

By one Middle Eastern nation, and the Jewish community throughout the world, Balfour's name is still held in reverence. It was the Balfour Declaration of 1917 which designated Palestine as 'a national home for the Jews'. His successors as Foreign Secretary and Prime Minister, right up to this day, have been invited to Israel to make the annual speech at the Balfour Declaration commemoration dinner. When he signed the declaration – and some attributed it to Dr Chaim Weizmann's contribution to the war effort in relation to the production of acetone – he might have thought of it as no more than the signature of a Foreign Office draft, though his friendship with Weizmann went back over many years. Nevertheless, after he ceased to be an active politician, he looked back on the declaration as one of the most important events of his career.

Sir Henry Campbell-Bannerman.

When the Liberals came back in 1905, their assumption of office being crowned by their landslide victory in 1906, the Prime Minister was Henry Campbell-Bannerman. He had followed Rosebery as Liberal leader, and his steadfast courage and forbearance during the Liberal split over the Boer War had earned him the premiership. More than that his forthright condemnation of the concentration camp methods in 1901–2 as 'methods of barbarism' brought, as Botha was to say, peace and reconciliation in South Africa. Yet the Liberal imperialist reaction to those three words came within an ace of driving Asquith and the Liberal League into putting their own candidates up against those who supported Campbell-Bannerman.

Campbell-Bannerman's contribution to his party in bringing it into the twentieth century after Gladstone's monumental holding operation has not always been fully appreciated, but the Hon. John Wilson's highly readable account – in my opinion, one of the best political biographies of this century – may have brought the relevant facts to a new political generation. The Liberal activists of the 1906 era needed no reminding – one future Prime Minister, on a tour of Scotland at a very early age, spent a night in Stirling where I was taken on a tour of obeisance to see Campbell-Bannerman's statue, and asked for elucidation. My father, who had worked for Churchill in the 1908 election, set Campbell-Bannerman's rule in perspective. A generation not only of Liberals but of those who voted for the Labour Representation Committee candidates in 1906 would have paid a similar tribute.

He had the imagination to send Asquith to the Treasury and Lloyd George to the Board of Trade, clearly grooming both for the posts to which they were to succeed. It is arguable that if Campbell-Bannerman had not died when he did – the only Prime Minister in modern times to die in No. 10 – he might well have recorded greater achievements than Asquith. But he was the Prime Minister who presided over the initiation of the long-overdue social revolution of the early years of the century, of which Asquith in a minor and Lloyd George in a major degree were the instruments.

Campbell-Bannerman was a Scot, and represented Stirling Burghs throughout his period in the House. He had ten years in business before entering Parliament at the age of thirty-two, after which he was quickly promoted to a series of junior ministerial appointments, becoming Chief Secretary for Ireland under Gladstone in 1884–5, and War Secretary in 1886 and 1892–5. His next ministerial office was in 1905 as Prime Minister, having succeeded Rosebery as leader of the Liberals in 1899. Perhaps no one but Campbell-Bannerman could have kept his party in a state of even nominal unity through the Boer War, and the strains of that period persisted right up to and after the Liberal landslide of 1905. When Balfour resigned, there was a determined manoeuvre by Asquith and the other Liberal imperialists to keep Campbell-Bannerman out of the premiership, and even the King tried to persuade him on their urging to take the premiership in the Lords. Campbell-Bannerman's reaction to all this would probably have been the same as it was in Parliament to a supercilious speech by Balfour, who had found his way back to the House after his defeat in Manchester. Campbell-Bannerman crushed him with four words: 'Enough of this foolery.' Not until Attlee would a Prime Minister achieve so much with so few words.

He led the most talented Government of this century until, some would argue, the 1960s and 1970s. It was a Government which included intellectuals like Haldane, Birrell and Bryce, as well as a significant defector from the Conservatives, Winston Churchill. More than that, he created the basis of a Liberal–Labour alliance which made possible the adhesion of Labour and the trade unions to the wartime Governments of Asquith and Lloyd George.

He was already nearly seventy when he became Prime Minister, and his health deteriorated. He resigned on 3 April 1908, and died in No. 10 on 22 April.

Herbert Henry Asquith – 'Herbert', in his early years, 'Henry' from the time he met his second wife Margot Tennant – was born in Morley, near Leeds, on 12 September 1852. He was born two days before the death of the Duke of Wellington, and died in 1928 when Baldwin was Prime Minister, and Margaret Thatcher and Anthony Wedgwood Benn were three years old.

He was Home Secretary in Gladstone's last administration, and together with Peel must rank as the best Home Secretary in the nineteenth century. He was Prime Minister, in peace and in war for eight years and eight months, the longest so far in the twentieth century, beating Winston Churchill by three days.

Asquith's peace-time premiership was one of the most distinguished in our history. He presided over the greatest period of social reform Britain knew until Clement Attlee's period of office. He fought the last major battle over the House of Lords, when they asserted the right to reject a major Finance Bill, and is entitled to a chapter in Britain's constitutional history on that alone. He led Britain into the Great War, and was politically destroyed by that war, being temperamentally and in other ways unfitted for war leadership, with Lloyd George at first closely co-operating and then breathing down his neck.

Following the early death of his father, young Asquith lived with his uncle at Mirfield, a few miles away. He had his early education in Huddersfield and at the Moravian School of Fulneck. Following his uncle's death, he moved to London to another relative, and went to the City of London School, later becoming one of the most brilliant products of Jowett's Balliol.

He read for the Bar, but briefs were hard to come by, and he supplemented his income by regular writing assignments for the *Spectator* and *Economist*. His breakthrough as a barrister occurred in his ruthless examination of the manager of *The Times* before the Parnell Commission of Enquiry, when he succeeded in utterly breaking him down over the Pigott forgeries.

He was elected to Parliament in 1886 as MP for East Fife, and in 1892 he was appointed Home Secretary by Gladstone, a remarkable promotion since Gladstone had until then always insisted that a colleague should prove himself as a junior minister before being invited to join the Cabinet.

After the Lords' rejection of the Home Rule Bill in 1894, and the collapse of the Rosebery administration in 1895, he devoted more time to his legal practice: following his marriage to Margot Tennant he was living a more expansive and costly social life, and he needed the money.

The dominating issue in the Liberals' ten years in opposition was the South African war, where Asquith, with Rosebery, Grey and Haldane, were in the 'imperialist' camp, supporting the war. With Campbell-Bannerman and Lloyd George leading the 'pro-Boer' faction, the Liberal party was gravely split, at one time it seemed irretrievably. The end of the war provided little healing, and neither did the Liberal opposition to the controversial 1902 Education Act, regarded by them as a provocation to their non-conformist following; nor was the 1902 Budget imposing a small tax on imported corn a unifying factor.

Joseph Chamberlain, who had already split the Liberals under Gladstone, now performed the same service for the Unionists. In May 1903, hearing that Ritchie, the Conservative Chancellor, was going to repeal the corn duty, Chamberlain publicly dissociated himself from the Chancellor and the Prime Minister, announcing that the future of the Empire depended on tariff preferences.

Asquith came into his wife's bedroom, she records, waving a copy of *The Times*, 'Wonderful news today, and it is only a question of time when we shall sweep the country.'

The time of which he spoke was just thirty-one months; happy months for the Liberals.

When it came, no one threw himself into the campaign with more vigour than Asquith, and he and his colleagues were speaking for a party inebriated with the exuberance of a long-absent party unity. Some Chamberlainites, who had defected from the Liberals over Ireland, returned. Winston Churchill, the Conservative member for Oldham, crossed the floor of the House and took a leading part in the public debate. Glorious in that dawn to be alive, but to be young was very heaven, and by political standards Asquith was young.

But the Liberal imperialists were out for blood. On the very eve of the 1906 election, they happened to be holidaying in close proximity, and early in September, Asquith, Grey and Haldane agreed on the 'Relugas compact', named after the place where Grey 'had a fishing'. Campbell-Bannerman as Prime Minister was to take a peerage and Asquith was to be leader in the Commons. King Edward was to be given appropriate instructions. But before the conspirators could try to fix the King, there were cold feet and second thoughts. They feared a party revolt, and so were content to propose to the King a series of names for particular Cabinet jobs. Asquith was deputed to bell the cat and see Campbell-Bannerman, who shrewdly began by asking what job Asquith would like – the Treasury, or the Woolsack. They ended their meeting with the party still in opposition, and as every Opposition will, disposing in advance of every post, with the possible exception of the First Commissionership of Works.

Asquith was due to go to Egypt with a legal brief for the ex-Khedive, worth 10,000 guineas. He never went. Balfour followed Rosebery's stupid example and resigned, leaving the Liberals this time clothed in the trappings of office and, to the country, looking like a Government. There was a last-minute manoeuvre, including pressure on the King, to get Campbell-Bannerman to the Lords, and indeed the King sounded Campbell-Bannerman out on that proposition when he went to kiss hands. But where was Asquith that night? At a festivity at Hatfield, with the Marquess of Salisbury, and such was his social compunction and political nonchalance that he returned there again while the Government was being formed.

In the 1960s and 1970s the practice was that all potential candidates, even for the most junior posts, did not stir more than four feet from a telephone.

Herbert Henry Asquith.

Asquith went to the Treasury, where as Chancellor he was to introduce three Budgets. The second differentiated between earned and unearned income, the third provided the finance for old age pensions later introduced by Asquith as Prime Minister. Free trade was reasserted; a Commonwealth Conference was held where dominion pressures for imperial preference met with rigid opposition from His Majesty's Government – 'banged, bolted and barred', against preference was Churchill's description.

In 1907, Campbell-Bannerman suffered a heart attack, and on 3 April 1908 resigned, shortly afterwards dying in No. 10.

The King had gone off to Biarritz. It was to Biarritz that Asquith was summoned on 8 April to accept the royal commission to form a Government. He kissed hands in the Hotel du Palais on 8 April.

The King had earlier vetoed the appointment of Churchill to Cabinet rank while he was still Under Secretary for the Colonies. Now, at Biarritz, the King approved Asquith's offer to Churchill of a more senior post, and he was offered the Board of Trade, together with the salary and status of a Secretary of State, becoming the first of five holders of this post to become Prime Minister in this century so far.

Asquith had already received from Churchill the outline of a substantial social reform programme based upon 'a Minimum Standard' of working conditions and wages, a programme in which unemployment insurance, infirmity insurance, State afforestation, State control of railways and compulsory education until the age of seventeen would all be a part of a package which would, on Poor Law matters alone, go beyond even the recommendations of the minority report of the Poor Law Commission written by the Webbs.

Asquith had the political courage to accept this wide-ranging reform programme, and he gave Churchill his full political backing when, with Beveridge as his assistant, Churchill introduced the system of Labour Exchanges and the first approach to unemployment insurance. Lloyd George was appointed Chancellor, and the social revolution began.

But by 1908 the financing of that revolution was leading to a crisis with the Lords. The country was fortunate to be led by a man with an acute legal brain combined with an acute political mind and a devastating Parliamentary style. The Finance Bill embodying Lloyd George's Budget was thrown out by the Lords, and a constitutional crisis followed. Asquith was at his superb, legal best. He carried a resolution in the Commons rejecting the action of the peers as unconstitutional and was granted a dissolution of Parliament, which left the Liberals in command, but only with Irish and Labour support. King Edward VII died, and his successor, George V, would not agree to the creation of enough new peers to carry the Finance Bill.

After a second election, again won by Asquith, he was authorized to announce that the necessary peers (Asquith prepared a list of 250) would be created. The Lords capitulated and the Finance Bill became law.

This period saw Asquith's utter primacy, and though he faced grave problems in Ireland – including gun-running and violence sponsored by Carson, a leading Tory – as well as the first impact of serious industrial strikes in our history, together with the 'civil disobedience' campaign of the suffragettes, his leadership remained unchallenged. Lloyd George, as Chancellor, with Churchill's help, carried through the greatest social revolution in history up to that time.

On 4 August 1914, Britain and France were at war with Germany. Two legends which subsequently grew up about Asquith must be discounted. He was not taken by surprise. Since 1911 he had been alerted to the danger, and had taken Germany's naval rearmament particularly seriously: hence his decision to move Churchill from the Home Office to the Admiralty, and see the Anglo–French naval agreement through in 1913, whereby the British would rely upon French power in the Mediterranean and France upon the Royal Navy in the North Sea. It was preparation for war which led Churchill to take a 51 per cent stake in the Anglo–Persian Oil Company, to ensure oil supplies in time of war. A 'War Book' was in readiness and opened on 29 July 1914. All in all, it can be argued that Asquith had brought Britain to a greater state of readiness than Chamberlain in 1939.

The second legend, that he was a lazy and fainéant war Prime Minister is equally false. He was fully mobilized, examining with Churchill every conceivable strategic option, as an alternative to the disastrous stalemate in France: in a letter to his regular correspondent Venetia Stanley he set out four possibilities:

> (1) Schleswig (Winston); (2) Salonika or Dalmatia (Lloyd George); ... (3) Gallipoli and Constantinople (Kitchener); (4) Smyrna and Ephesus (FE and others – I rather like this).

It was Gallipoli which was adopted. Churchill was let down by Kitchener's refusal to send enough troops at the right time; Churchill was disgraced and had to resign. Asquith's biggest blunder had been the appointment of Kitchener. From then on, Britain was committed for over three years to the bloody massacres in France, Ypres, the Somme, Passchendaele.

It was national and Parliamentary disillusionment over the tragic stalemate in France which brought his premiership to an end. The French fighting caused a shell shortage. A coalition was set up under Asquith, and Lloyd George left the Treasury for the new Ministry of Munitions: later he became War Secretary. The battles of the Somme led to new groupings and loyalties. Lloyd George was in league with the Conservative leaders. Lord Northcliffe, proprietor of both *The Times* and the *Daily Mail* ran a venomous campaign, fed, particularly in the later stages, by leaks from Lloyd George.

On a visit to Paris, Lloyd George hinted at resignation, then with powerful Tory support he demanded that a full-time War Council with plenary powers be set up, to take control of military operations – Asquith being included. Lloyd George recruited Max Aitken (later Lord Beaverbrook) to his cause, hoping that his fellow-Canadian Bonar Law, hitherto loyal to Asquith, could be won over. The four weeks ending on 5 December 1916 saw a record of Byzantine intrigues and manoeuvres probably without parallel in British history. Law was equivocal, saying one thing to Lloyd George and elliptic in his discussions with Asquith. The press campaign reached unprecedented heights. A brief tactical resignation from Lloyd George, and Asquith was out, the Tory leaders refusing to serve under a re-constituted Asquith Government, but indicating their willingness to serve under Lloyd George.

Asquith never surfaced again as a national leader. While no official coalition candidate ran against him, the Lloyd George 'coupon election' of 1918, smashed the Asquithian Liberals. Yet he was to make history.

The result of the December 1923 election was a stalemate. The Conservatives were the biggest single party, but the combination of Liberals and Labour outnumbered them. This gave Asquith his last opportunity to influence the future political history of Britain, and his decision has in fact changed the course of that history. He decided that Labour should be given a chance to show what they could do. There should be no ganging-up of the two older parties to deny the youngster his chance. And that opportunity was being taken in ideal conditions for a lifelong constitutionalist: Labour, who some in the older parties feared would bring red revolution, would govern on sufferance. Excesses in domestic or international policies could be curbed, and if the new Labour Government were to put forth extremist policies, they could be quickly despatched.

The old statesman controlled the situation, until a red threat emerged, or appeared to emerge. After his experiences, Asquith was not going to support a quarrelling coalition with the Tories, he was not going over those 1916 negotiations again. Labour was to be recognized as at least a potential party of Government, but in the safest possible conditions. It can be said, therefore, that he created a political balance of forces which has lasted well over fifty years, with more to come, in this sense a more stable position than either the eighteenth or the nineteenth century ever knew. But it was achieved at the expense of his own party.

In the 1924 election, when Ramsay MacDonald's party crashed over the Campbell case, and the almost certainly forged Zinoviev letter, Asquith lost his seat in Paisley. He was seventy-two, and he lost in a straight fight with Labour.

There was no road back. In 1925 he became Earl of Oxford and Asquith. He died in 1928.

6

David Lloyd George

IN A RECENT BIOGRAPHY, Kenneth Morgan has described Lloyd George as the rogue elephant among British Prime Ministers'. Lord Beaverbrook said, comparing the two war leaders of the twentieth century, that 'Churchill was perhaps the greater man, but George was more fun.'

He was a politician's politician, with a politician's abilities and some of their deeper failings, larger than life, in glorious technicolour. He understood people, he came from them, and worked among them as a country solicitor. Up to that time it could be said that no Prime Minister had come from humbler origins. Ramsay MacDonald was still to come. Lloyd George spoke for those he regarded as his people, above all for many years his own Welsh people, for example in his epic battles with his arch-enemy, later his friend, the Bishop of St Asaph, over Church rates, Church education, and the disestablishment of the Welsh Church. In a barnstorming campaign, replying night after night to the Bishop, a well-known story is recorded, set out here exactly as printed in Frank Owen's biography, *Tempestuous Journey*:

> 'And now', said the chairman, 'I haff to present to you the Member for Caernarvon boroughs. He hass come here to reply to what the Bishop of St Asaph said the other night about Welsh Disestablishment. In my opinion, ladies and gentlemen, the Bishop of St Asaph iss one of the biggest liars in Creeashion! But, thank God, yess, we haff in Mr Lloyd George a match for him tonight.'

Lloyd George campaigned for Welsh Home Rule before and after his entry into Parliament; then when he turned his superb talents of oratory and debate to wider causes, he seemed to neglect the people from whom he was sprung, and it is said stuffed their letters unanswered into his Commons locker. But his fight was against privilege; it is arguable how far his campaigns, and the revolutionary programme of social reform he carried through as Chancellor of the Exchequer, were more anti-privilege than pro-welfare. Did he, one wonders, perhaps get more satisfaction out of taxing the rich than out of the improvement of the social condition of the people on whom the tax-revenue was spent? Deep down, he was for the people, he was one of those who would agree with Chamberlain's remark about 'the denial of much-needed social reform', and by the time he introduced his reform Budget, nearly a quarter of a century had been lost by an old man's obsession. But he enjoyed the battle and his heart leapt at the opportunity it gave to his dissatisfied country, 'A duke is more dangerous than a Dreadnought and just as expensive.'

He was undeniably the greatest natural orator in the long list of British Prime Ministers, and local and national newspaper accounts record the most enthusiastic receptions to his speeches all over the country, and a remarkable degree of enthusiasm for his maiden speech in Parliament. It seemed that he could very nearly, in the phrase used of him, 'charm a bird off a tree', but that was a gift he enjoyed in private argument as much as on the rostrum. His record in Parliamentary in-fighting, as well as his ability to crush hecklers outside, is just as great: and the very nature of his remarks makes clear that they could not have been prepared with midnight oil, they were an instant reply to a statement or a challenge no one could have foreseen.

Previous page Lloyd George as a young man.

Opposite Stanley Baldwin by Oswald Birley

This ability remained with him to the end, years after he had lost power and the hope of regaining power. In the 1930s, when he was in his seventies, he was listening to a debate on unemployment assistance regulations, in which

Sir William Jowitt, the Attorney-General, was leading for the Government. Jowitt had been elected Liberal MP for Preston, but was immediately lured into the Government by Ramsay MacDonald. He accepted the appointment, joined the Labour Party, stood again and was elected. He was one of the 'National Labour' participants in the Conservative-dominated coalition headed by MacDonald, later Baldwin. The Government in the 1931 'sacrifices' had cut the already inadequate dole, introduced the family means test which drove young girls who could get jobs out of their families, and legislated at a time of record unemployment that no unemployed man could draw dole unless he could prove that he had walked day after day in search of work at factories near and far festooned with notices proclaiming 'No Vacancies' – with a further penalty in terms of boot leather. Jowitt was commending the 'genuinely seeking work' regulations, and Lloyd George, with withering scorn and that incomparable voice, stood and pointed at the Attorney, snarling out with slow emphasis on each word: 'No one could ever accuse the Right Honourable and Learned Gentleman of not genuinely seeking work.' The words have to be repeated by a hearer to get their full effect. On another occasion his old enemy, Sir John Simon, was the target for Lloyd George's supreme contempt. Simon, another National Liberal defector, was sneering at his old colleagues. Lloyd George sent him down by remarking that the Rt Hon. and Learned Gentleman had twice crossed the floor of the House, each time leaving behind him a trail of slime – the last word seemed to hearers to need seconds to deliver it.

Lloyd George taught a generation and more of Parliamentary apprentices the elements of oratory. Harold Macmillan not long ago told the present writer, with magnificent physical gestures, how Lloyd George had taught him to use his arms; not wrists, not hands, not ineffective posturing, but the whole of the arms and shoulders, even the back in a total integration of body into the words.

Lloyd George, the architect of social reform and hammer of the Lords, was the man of action the parties and the country turned to as the war casualties mounted, and Asquith lost control. The drive he had shown as Munitions Minister and War Secretary was turned to the war effort, with the introduction of the convoy system and every step needed for the total mobilization of Britain and her people. But in the last years, especially after the Khaki election of 1918, he appeared increasingly frivolous, more concerned with politicking and scoring cheap points off his opponents, instead of attacking the problems of rising unemployment, building the houses, and creating, as he had promised, 'a Britain fit for heroes to live in'. It was this which led to his fall. The line he took over the Chanak crisis, which nearly led to an outbreak of war, put him for the first time in a minority. He had come almost to believe, like Gladstone before him, in his divine right to rule from No. 10; he had almost, it seemed, forgotten the first requisite of survival, a majority. And the majority whose support he enjoyed was not his to command. The 'coupon' he had given the preponderant Conservative component in the 1918 election was a coupon for a coalition: should they at any time decide against him, or against coalition, he could not claim a debt due on call as having been the price of that coupon.

But when he retired after seventeen years in office, nearly eight as Prime Minister, he could claim a few major achievements. He was the father of social reform. He had led Britain to victory in the war. Third, he had played a leading

Opposite Lady Baldwin by de Laszlo

HARGREAVES ST

part in the Versailles settlement, much criticized by Keynes and others for the penal reparation clauses, but one which lasted longer than many forecast, and which might have been proof against any wrecker other than a Hitler. Fourth, he had succeeded where Gladstone had failed, he had produced a solution to the Irish problem which lasted for a generation; Attlee carried it to its logical conclusion twenty-five years later by the treaty creating a new and independent Irish Republic, both Lloyd George's solution and his excluding the six counties of Ulster.

Yet it was Ireland which brought him down. A powerful and unforgiving section of the coalition Conservative back-benchers could not forgive him, even though their anger was directed far more at Conservative coalition ministers who supported him – Austen Chamberlain, Birkenhead and Balfour – than at him. His dismissal over Chanak was the occasion of his going, but Ireland was the cause. He was in a long line of distinguished Prime Ministers who crashed over Ireland; Pitt in 1801, Peel with the rotten potatoes, and Gladstone. Winston Churchill, in a still wider sweep of history, has put it this way, in *The World Crisis: The Aftermath*, the sequel to his four-volume history of the First World War.

> Yet in so far as Mr Lloyd George can link his political misfortunes with this Irish story, he may be content. In falling through Irish difficulties he may fall with Essex and with Strafford, with Pitt and with Gladstone; and with a line of sovereigns and statesmen, great or small, spread across the English history books of seven hundred years.

David Lloyd George, of ancient Welsh ancestry, was born in Manchester, on 17 January 1863. His life spanned the period from Palmerston's last ministry to very near the end of Churchill's war-time Government. He was only eighteen months old when his father, a schoolmaster from Pembrokeshire, died, and the family went to live with his mother's brother, Richard Lloyd at Llanystumduwy near Criccieth. A brother was born there after they moved. It was a humble home, though never insecure. Richard Lloyd was a shoemaker, a radical, a lay-preacher, and very soon accepted the missive of training the mind and attitudes of young David. In 1877 he was articled to a law firm in Porturados, worked hard on his legal education – helped by his uncle – and passed his examination in London in 1884, setting up practice on his own at Criccieth.

He became a hero as the result of a story which provides the opening for Frank Owen's biography. The Rector of Llangrothen refused to allow the burial on consecrated ground of an old quarryman, a dissenter, in the grave of his child. An 1880 Act had effectively forbidden discrimination, but there were complications about the terms on which the land had been conveyed. The Rector stopped the digging, and ordered the earth to be restored. The quarrymen went to Lloyd George, who told them to carry on, which they did by dead of night. The Rector went to court, and won his case, but Lloyd George took it to appeal. The County Court Judge ruled for the Rector, but Lloyd George demanded leave to appeal. At the High Court of Justice in London, Lord Chief Justice Coleridge gave his judgment for the quarrymen. Lloyd George had invoked the Law Courts for his people. He was soon to use the High Court of Parliament on behalf of their grievances and those of Wales as a nation.

He won Caernarvon Boroughs by the narrowest of majorities, 18, in a total poll of nearly 4000, and in 1890 took his seat in Parliament. He was not in

Opposite Lloyd George's birthplace in Manchester.

a hurry to speak, but when he did so it was on a Bill to compensate publicans who lost their licences, the Welsh members, including Lloyd George, claiming that the money should go in aid of Welsh education. His speech had a good reception, but he had already in the weeks before begun to create an English reputation to match his Welsh one, by speeches in different parts of the country, mainly but not exclusively to expatriate Welshmen. Gladstone had no time for him, too fiery and the fire wrongly directed. For six years Lloyd George's many speeches were mainly on the grievances of the principality. He nearly lost his seat in 1895; he was named in a paternity case in 1896, before being 'cleared' many months later. Increasingly he was working in and through the Liberal Party as a whole, first linking Welsh claims with English problems, and then spear-heading attacks on Salisbury's Government, for example on a hand-out to landowners – the Lords – on an agricultural measure. He was learning the procedures of the House, he began to take an interest in overseas issues – Uganda, the Fashoda incident, still more the Jameson raid, and his growing criticism of Joseph Chamberlain's Southern African policies, culminating in the Boer War.

In the great Liberal split Lloyd George was passionately opposed to the imperialist wing, totally opposed to the war. His great oratory gained a new dimension as he went round the country addressing great crowds denouncing the war, and on many occasions almost as great counter-demonstrations attacking and mauling the 'pro-Boers'. His escape from the hysterical Birmingham meeting, disguised as a somewhat under-sized policeman, is legendary, but it is clear that then, as on other occasions, he undoubtedly risked his life.

For him, as for the Liberal League, it was the Treaty of Vereeniging and Joseph Chamberlain's embracing of Tariff Reform which brought the divided legions under one flag, and when Campbell-Bannerman formed his government in December 1905 Lloyd George became President of the Board of Trade.

On Campbell-Bannerman's death in April 1908, Asquith succeeded, and Lloyd George became Chancellor. Against a background of new Irish troubles and the spectacular impact of the suffragettes on Westminster – and two successful libel actions reflecting on his love life – Lloyd George was preparing the people's Budget. To prepare for it he was assailing the Army's appropriation, and trying vainly to withstand the Navy's demand for the new Dreadnought programme, a demand sustained by the cry 'We want Eight, and We won't wait'. Lloyd George, backed by Churchill, lost the fight. Churchill summarized the outcome: 'A curious and characteristic solution was reached. The Admiralty had demanded six ships; the economists offered four; and we finally compromised on eight.'

Morley commented that if Churchill ever does go to the Admiralty, 'it will be *sixteen* we need, not eight.' But Lloyd George enjoyed the fight. In the long public expenditure struggle – and these, right up to the present, are fought with great intensity and take an inordinate toll of time and temper – he told Charles Masterman, 'I would dearly like a rest, but I would rather have a fight', the hallmark of Chancellors throughout the ages.

It was the level on which Lloyd George was conducting the struggle with the Lords, not only on finance, that raised the political temperature. He cited the actions of Lord Lansdowne, Leader of the Tory peers on the eve of the Licensing Bill, amending the terms of the Conservative Government's 'Brewers' Charter'. Lansdowne had summoned the Tory peers, comprising

The solicitor's office where Lloyd George practised.

more than 80 per cent of the effective strength of the Lords, to Lansdowne House, where it was agreed to reject the Bill.

'In two hours,' Lloyd George said, 'this nobleman arrogated to himself a position no King in England has claimed since the ominous days of Charles the First.'

When a Conservative back-bencher claimed that the Peers were the 'watch-dog of the constitution', Lloyd George picked up the canine reference, 'You mean it is Mr Balfour's poodle! It fetches and carries for him, it barks for him, it bites anybody that he sets it onto.' He told a Scottish audience, even before the Budget was opened,

> We have heard a great deal about self government for Ireland. We want self government for England – and Scotland too! We are not allowed to govern ourselves. There are five or six hundred gentlemen – I beg your pardon, NOBLEMEN – in another House who have got there owing to fortuitous circumstances. From the North, from the South, from the East, from the West, without anyone in particular summoning them they arrive there and begin to decree what legislation the nation shall be allowed to enact for itself. What do they represent? They do not represent Wealth as a whole, not capital, not one-tenth of it. They represent the landowners....

Master Gwilym Miss Mair Master Richard Miss Olwen
Mrs. Lloyd George Miss Megan

MRS. D. LLOYD GEORGE AND FAMILY

It was the greatest fight since the 1832 Reform Bill, a fight that was carried through with the same vigour outside the House. The most famous speech was that of Lloyd George at Limehouse, indeed 'Limehousing' became a Tory epithet for rabble-rousing. Local marsh land made valuable by port development had risen from a rent of £2 or £3 per acre, and was selling at £2,000, £3,000, £6,000, £8,000 an acre.

It is impossible to list all the provocative passages. Let one suffice:

> Who created the increment? Who made that golden swamp? Was it the *Landlord*? Was it *his* energy? Was it *his* brains, his forethought? It was not! It was the combined efforts of all the people engaged in the trade and commerce of that part of London – the trader, the merchant, the shipowner, the dock labourer, the workmen – of everybody *except* the Landlord.

He compared this increment with the remuneration of a doctor and their respective contributions to human welfare; the life of an absentee landlord with that of a miner – he had just been down a pit – and drew a haunting picture of a colliery disaster.

The Times condemned him. The King complained to the Prime Minister in unusually strong language, which led to correspondence between the Chancellor and the Palace. But the language was no more restrained in his speech on the Third Reading, with his clear warning to the Lords. He asked by what authority they claimed those powers. 'Let them realize what they are doing. They are forcing a Revolution. The Peers may decree a Revolution, but the People will direct it. If they begin, issues will be raised that they little dream of. Questions will be asked which are whispered now in humble voice, and answers will be demanded with authority.'

He set the questions out. They went right to the heart of the Lords' qualification for being there at all, still more the right by which they could set aside the judgment of the people in industry who make the wealth of the country.

> These are questions that will be asked. The answers are charged with peril for the order of things the Peers represent. But they are fraught with rare and refreshing fruit for the parched lips of the multitude, who have been marching along the dusty road which the People have marked through the Dark Ages, that are now emerging into the light.

The Lords as we have seen, threw out the Budget, and it took two elections, and the decision of the new King to undertake the creation of new peers, which led to its ultimate passage.

The new reign saw the emergence of new problems, such as the threats to peace in the Mediterranean and the risk of militant trade unions, and the resurgence of old ones, the Kaiser's arms build-up, fresh trouble nearing to civil war in Ireland. For Lloyd George it included the National Insurance Bill, and another pleasurable fight with privilege, as duchesses said, or were quoted as saying, that they would not lick stamps for housemaids, the insurance stamps which Lloyd George was selling at 'ninepence for fourpence'. For Lloyd George there was his first scandal, the Marconi affair, where he and Rufus Isaacs had been improvident in a speculation in the shares of the American Marconi Company, not in fact the British company to whom the Government had given, and the Treasury financed, an important wireless telegraphy concession. But it left a nasty taste. *Mr Punch* summarized the outcome of the

Opposite Lloyd George's wife Margaret with their children.

committee inquiry in a cartoon showing John Bull dismissing Lloyd George and Isaacs with the words, 'My boys, you leave the court without a stain – except, perhaps, for the whitewash.'

In 1913 Lloyd George embarked on a campaign for the taxation of site values, which made little impact in a country which had been set alight by the 1909 campaign. His 1914 Budget, more radical than 1909, and including 'supertax', fell foul of the Speaker's ruling; it was held that it was not a 'money bill' within the criteria of the 1911 Parliamentary Act, and so could not be upheld against a Lords' rejection. They were not the good years for Lloyd George.

But Asquith was using him more. He settled a serious railway strike. He was sent to Ireland to try and bring the warring factions together. With his plans for suspending for a period of years the application of Irish Home Rule to the six counties of the north, at one point he came surprisingly near to an agreement. But by the summer of 1914, it seemed that all was set for avid war over the Amending Bill to exclude Ulster. When the Sarajevo assassination erupted into European war, and day by day Britain was being brought nearer and nearer to European conflict, there was a spectacular change. On 3 August, Balfour proposed that the Ulster Bill be postponed, and then John Redmond, the Irish leader, in one of the most moving and courageous interventions ever made in Parliament, pledged the ending of the current troubles and an Irish attitude which would enable Britain to withdraw troops who might shortly need to be deployed elsewhere.

Lloyd George was galvanized by the outbreak of war. He had a financial crisis to deal with. Peel's 1844 Act was invoked and gold payments suspended. Within a week the situation was under control, and one pound and ten shilling notes were issued.

He was now a national minister. His emergency War Budget could not be faulted on political grounds. He made a rousing re-arming speech to London Welshmen, and extended this to a recruiting tour. Within months he had negotiated a dilution agreement with ordnance factory and other unions concerned with the production of munitions, to allow skilled work to be done by semi-skilled or unskilled men – or women. His stock with the radicals, a minority of whom leaned to pacifism, was falling. With the Conservatives his stock was rising.

On the last day of 1914, in a masterly three-thousand-word State Paper, he set out for Asquith the war alternatives as he saw them: 'stalemate' on the Western Front and the prospect of 'appalling loss of life' whenever Britain were to go on the offensive, and the need to win 'a decisive victory' in some other part of the world. Lloyd George proposed two independent military operations. One was to land a joint force of a million men – British, Serbian, Romanian and Greek – on the Adriatic coast of Austria–Hungary, forcing the Germans to pull troops away fron the Western Front in order to aid their threatened ally, and encouraging Italy to join the war in return for the lure of Austrian territory. Lloyd George's second proposal was a direct military attack on Turkey, which would give Britain 'the chance of winning a dramatic victory'. His plan was to land 100,000 British troops on the coast of Syria, to 'wipe out' the 80,000 Turkish troops there, to relieve Russia of the Turkish military pressure in the Caucasus – so that Russian troops could concentrate on the war against Germany – and to win Palestine for Britain.

Lloyd George warned Asquith that if his proposals were rejected, and the

Government allowed things 'to drift', Britain's morale would suffer, for once the public recognized 'defeat which is unmistakable' on the Western Front, there would be growing resentment at the severe economic distress which must come. It was essential, Lloyd George concluded, to press for a decision 'without delay', and when the War Council met to discuss alternative war zones, he reiterated his proposals for action in the Adriatic and in Syria. The War Council agreed to seek a new point of attack: but chose the Dardanelles as its first objective. Henceforth, Lloyd George supported the Dardanelles campaign, but, together with Churchill, was critical of the attitudes – especially of Kitchener and the War Office – which meant that it was not pushed through to success. Lloyd George did not hesitate to express his criticism forcefully in Council and, in a private letter, Churchill wrote 'LG has more true insight and courage than anyone else. He really sticks at nothing – no measure is too far reaching, no expedient too novel.'

A photograph of Lloyd George, the proud possessor of a motorcar, in 1910.

'Sticks at nothing' was an apt description. In March 1915, Asquith reported to Venetia Stanley that Lloyd George even favoured the imprisonment of men who refused to work in wartime. He was one of the first ministers to argue that Britain should take over the Holy Places of Bethlehem and Jerusalem from the Turks. He opposed – *four* years before the Versailles Treaty – any harsh breaking up of Germany once the war was won, arguing that a weak Germany would give Russia too great a predominance in Europe. Above all – and he was close to the scene through his trade union negotiations – he condemned the reasons for the shell shortage and sought to end the monopoly still enjoyed by existing contractors and the Royal Ordnance Factories. Kitchener's appointment had hardly led to inspiring leadership in the armed forces; it was largely responsible for the *laissez-faire* attitude to the production of munitions.

He introduced a curious measure. There were allegations that workers at a munitions factory near Carlisle were drinking too much and that production was suffering. Lloyd George unveiled the 'Carlisle experiment' and took the brewers and their linked public houses into public ownership. There they remained until Edward Heath's administration 'de-nationalized' them in the early 1970s, in the face of some local criticism – it was good beer.

Lloyd George was at the very centre of the move towards the coalition of May 1915. It was to Lloyd George that Bonar Law, the Conservative Leader, had gone on the morning of 17 May to demand that the shell shortage be remedied and that Churchill leave the Admiralty. Asking Bonar Law to wait for a few minutes at No. 11, Lloyd George went straight to Asquith at No. 10 and, as he later explained, 'put the circumstances quite plainly before him'. Lloyd George told Asquith bluntly that the only way to forestall a damaging Conservative onslaught in Parliament was to offer them an immediate coalition. Asquith bowed to the force of Lloyd George's appeal. That afternoon, when Churchill urged Lloyd George to postpone the formation of a coalition, Lloyd George insisted that there could be no further delay. His arguments that day were a decisive turning point in the conduct of the war. A coalition was formed, and he himself was appointed Minister of Munitions. 'The only thing I care about now', he told Churchill, 'is that we win in this war.' It was in every way good for him. He showed his ability to create out of nothing a powerful ministry, and to make it – always important in Whitehall – a prestigious and assertive ministry, exercising a primacy in the inter-departmental hierarchy which owed more to its minister than to its history.

With both the trade unions and the new contracts with firms who had never previously produced munitions, he was establishing a new relationship, shared by no other minister, with what would now be called 'the two sides of industry', and it was not the traditional Board of Trade distant relationship based on a combination of *laissez-faire* and distrustful statutory regulation. He grew further from Asquith, from his Liberal ministerial colleagues – themselves less distinguished than the new Tories – men who looked increasingly as though they had been left over from the previous peace. Moreover some had been in office for over seven years and showing signs of strain – Asquith included – resulting almost as much from the social obligations of an Edwardian Cabinet as from departmental work.

He was increasingly critical of Asquith, and began to put the heat on, choosing first the need to send British troops to the Greek port of Salonica in order not to allow Serbia to be defeated, and then the issue of conscription. On both issues he spoke forcefully in council. In October 1915, he gave Asquith and Kitchener a fierce warning of the dangers of abandoning an ally to its fate. If Britain abandoned Serbia, he declared, 'the whole of the East would point to the way she abandoned her friends, and that Germany was the country to be followed'. Lloyd George added: 'we have always been two or three weeks late for everything', and he repeated this theme in Parliament two months later in a speech which marked in effect a denunciation of Asquith's war methods, and of the lethargies and failure both of management and men in the war industries:

> Too late in moving here! Too late in arriving there! Too late in coming to this decision! Too late in starting with enterprises! Too late in preparing! In this war the footsteps of the Allies have been dogged by the mocking spectre of 'Too Late', and unless we quicken our movements, damnation will fall on the sacred cause for which so much gallant blood has flowed.
>
> I beg employers and workmen not to have 'Too Late' inscribed upon the portals of their workshops!

These exhortations were not always successful. A week later, on Christmas Eve, Lloyd George was howled down by munition workers in the Clyde when he urged them to speed up the delivery of guns for the front.

Lloyd George's demands for conscription likewise took political courage. Not only did they distance him more from the Liberals than from his new Unionist colleagues, but the trade unions were afraid both of the dilution of labour which conscription might cause, and of the extension of military conscription to industrial conscription. Yet Lloyd George fought on. 'He has been on the true trail', Churchill wrote to his wife, 'more than anyone else in this war.'

Over conscription, the Cabinet was consistently split, almost to the end of Asquith's régime. Finally, Asquith sided with 'compulsion' but it was already near the end.

I have already referred to the involved events which led to Asquith's resignation. Lloyd George took over, and completely changed the higher direction of the war. He set up a War Cabinet of only five – the War Committee of earlier negotiations, writ large and with supreme power. It was backed with a War Cabinet secretariat, based on that of the old Committee of Imperial Defence, but with a stronger team, and more power to force information out of departments and to stimulate as well as co-ordinate action. Alongside it he set up his private secretariat, the 'Garden Suburb' housed in temporary buildings in No. 10's garden. This caused resentment in Whitehall, such developments always do: to some extent Winston Churchill's private secretariat under the not always popular Professor Lindemann stimulated similar reactions.

Lloyd George brought his experience both of the Ministry of Munitions and the War Office to his new task. First, he had to tackle the Navy, and overcome their resistance to convoys. Historians will argue whether Lloyd George was the man who won the war – the claim in the 1918 coupon election. There can be no doubt that his forceful decisions ensured that Britain won the U-boat war, and had that not been won there would have been no victory. Nor was there any sign that it would or could have been won until he acted.

On 1 February 1917, before Lloyd George had been in charge for two months, the Imperial German Command gave orders to its submarine command to sink on sight every merchant ship proceeding from or bound to Allied ports. Starting from a figure of 160,000 tons a week in 1916, their plan was to sink 600,000 tons per month, which would, they calculated, bring Britain to her knees in four months. In February their score was 311,000, in March 351,000 and in April 526,000: in that month the total losses of British, Allied and neutral shipping was 867,000 tons. The Admiralty had resisted convoys all along. They had irrefutable statistics showing that it would be impossible to convoy the 2500 merchantmen who made harbour each week. Until Lloyd George took charge no one had queried the figures. A high proportion of the 'merchantmen' were phantom vessels – fishing vessels returning with their catches, or ferries – for example those plying to the Isle of Wight. In any case a humble commander had successfully convoyed 4000 coal barges to Brest, Cherbourg and Le Havre, with no support but armed trawlers: only nine had been lost. Lloyd George ordered the adoption of convoys, the arming of merchantmen, new killing methods for U-boats (including the mystery Q-ships), the building of new ships and, longer-term, the saving of cargo space by qualitative controls over imports and a grow-more-food campaign. By midsummer the U-boat menace was overcome. From that time to the Armistice in November 1918, less than one per cent of the vessels heading for or leaving UK ports were lost.

Space forbids any treatment of other aspects of the new drive now overtaking the war effort, though none could have been more decisive. Unfortunately nothing Lloyd George seemed able to do could galvanize the military effort on the Continent. He set out with a tougher attitude than Asquith's to the Western Front generals, but his success was little greater.

Whatever the arguments about the Dardenelles, the Allies had failed to open up the war on the enemy from directions other than France. Until October 1917 the Germans had to keep a substantial force on the Eastern Front to hold the Tsarist Russians. Their transport of Lenin in a sealed rail coach through Germany to his rendezvous with the Russian Bolsheviks removed the Russian threat, and made possible a full concentration on the Western Front, where casualties were higher than ever before, where the power of defence against attack meant certain death to any attempt to force a way through minefields and mud, and where a hundred thousand men would die in pushing back the enemy's front a few hundred yards.

Lloyd George lost no time in speeding to the Front. Students of what he found there have asked, after the Somme, why did he sanction Passchendaele? This is not the place to rehearse those arguments. But in the Passchendaele offensive 300,000 were lost, and for this we captured an area of land about equal to the size of Green Park in London. Lloyd George had been assured that an offensive would be a limited operation to create a diversion in advance of the main French attack. Lloyd George was misled; in no time it was a major and continued attack, doomed to failure, and to a mortality ratio heavily in favour of the Germans.

A study of the papers now available of what Haig thought of Lloyd George (almost a political if not class study) and what Lloyd George thought of him is bitterly revealing. Why did Lloyd George not sack him? The answer we are given is that he feared that Robertson, for whom he had more respect, would go too. The manoeuvres of the generals, even the defection of Russia, are a study in classical tragedy, as are the negotiations for an Allied Commander-in-Chief. The dangers became the more acute with Russia and Romania out of the war. The balance of effective military forces and of reserves was changed for the worse, but even before that, was not anything like sufficient to justify the Allied generals' hopes of victory through attrition, where the balance of casualties so favoured the defence.

Opposite Lloyd George the orator.

Equally futile was the use of the tank, which could have changed the land war as decisively as the submarine nearly changed the balance of the war on the seas. In the first attack at Cambrai, they smashed through, but the advantage was lost because the generals failed to send in the infantry to consolidate. In ten days, the Germans had re-captured the lost ground. The church bells had sounded in London on the first breakthrough: the reverse was not even reported to the War Cabinet for several days. Passchendaele had failed; we had lost the possible strategic advantage of the first use of the tanks. 1918 dawned with little hope that it would see the end of the war. But the Germans destroyed their own army in their own over-desperate attempt to break through.

The German offensive of March 1918 drove back the British and French forces further than any of the Allied offensives had ever driven back the Germans. Both Paris and the Channel ports seemed threatened. In London, the War Cabinet was reported to be 'in a panic'. A grave shortage of reserves made the future seem bleak, and there was talk of withdrawal from France altogether. But Lloyd George fought against all talk of withdrawal. While Bonar Law was described by the Chief of the General Staff as 'most depressing', Lloyd George was 'buoyant'. He moved with speed and determination. First he persuaded the Americans to accelerate the despatch of troops and at the same time to commit their as yet incomplete army to the danger points. Then he travelled to France in order to place Sir Douglas Haig *under* the command of the French General, Foch. These decisions were effective, and by May the tide of battle had turned. Six months later, in November, with the Kaiser abdicating and fleeing to Holland, an armistice was signed on the total capitulation of the German armed forces.

Lloyd George was the man, as it proved, who had won the war and called a successful if unscrupulous and short-sighted election to ratify his claim. It was not an arrogant one: victory in the U-boat campaign was enough to justify it, the munitions drive and the mobilization of industry, above all his steady nerve in the crucial months of the German drive for victory in 1918 enable him with honour to rank among Britain's four great war leaders.

Increasingly in the post-war era he leaned on his Conservative colleagues and the businessmen he had brought into the war, including the new breed of newspaper proprietors. Two of the press triumvirate, Northcliffe, Rothermere and Beaverbrook, became senior ministers, the third a senior diplomat and general utility man. As a Liberal Prime Minister's Government it passed comprehension. Where he lost his touch was in his faith that his closest Unionist colleagues, Austen Chamberlain, Carson, Curzon and F.E. Smith, guaranteed his security. The two men he underrated were Bonar Law and Stanley Baldwin.

His four years from the Armistice to his fall were characterized by his failure to mobilize Britain for peace as he had mobilized it for war, widespread discontent over demobilization – and military intervention – and yet his record was not all negative. He gave full authority to one of his Liberal ministers, Edwin Montagu, to inaugurate the first important stages towards Indian self-government – the Montague-Chelmsford reforms of 1919 – and to condemn the use of armed men in firing on a crowd of Indian demonstrators at Amritsar. He supported another Liberal colleague, Churchill, in two major schemes, the first to demobilize the armies on a specially devised equitable basis, whereby on average 10,000 men were demobilized every day for eleven months, and then to reduce Britain's Middle East military commitments and expenditures to a minimum. Strongly supported by a third Liberal Cabinet minister, the President of the Board of Education, H.A.L. Fisher, Lloyd George took the revolutionary step of halting the British military intervention in Russia and opening direct negotiations in London with the Bolsheviks – negotiations that resulted in Britain's first trade agreement with Soviet Russia. Yet when the Bolsheviks invaded Poland in 1920, and threatened Warsaw, Lloyd George was prepared to deliver an ultimatum to Russia, telling the House of Commons: 'nothing justifies a retaliation or a reprisal or a punishment which goes to the extent of wiping out national existence'.

Lloyd George's major triumphs in those years were the Versailles peace treaty, his backing for Woodrow Wilson's concept of the League of Nations – even though that concept was rejected by a hostile Congress – and his settlement with Ireland.

Other achievements abounded, which the historians' belittling of Lloyd George for later 'scandals' should not allow us to overlook. In 1919 he set up a Ministry of Health and a Ministry of Transport. A Forestry Commission was established to begin the replanting of the many forests depleted by war-time needs. An Electricity Supply Act ensured the complete national reorganization of the supply of electric power. By the Acquisition of Land Act 1919, Lloyd George ensured that local authorities purchased land on fair terms; a parallel measure, the Profiteering Act, gave power to the Board of Trade to prosecute against people who made excessive profits out of articles in common use. The Unemployed Workers' Dependents Fund paid allowances to the wives and children of the unemployed, and in the last year of Lloyd George's premiership unemployment was halved.

His predominantly Conservative majority called themselves Unionists. They adopted the title, it has been suggested, as an adjunct to their traditional surname, rather as a bridegroom may attach his wife's maiden name, with a hyphen, to his own. It was when the terms of the Irish settlement were known that the Conservatives became uxorious: their Unionist title meant more to them than their temporary enchantment with Lloyd George. That enchantment had been to some extent forced; because of the balance of forces in Parliament as the result of the 1910 elections, they were in a minority. They could not dictate terms, and Lloyd George was in any case the only possible Liberal Prime Minister for winning the war: at the crucial test Bonar Law could not form a Government. But from 1918 onwards, thanks to Lloyd George's short-sighted selective issue of coupons, they held an unassailable Parliamentary majority. The Conservative hostages in Lloyd George's Government were, in the last resort, expendable – indeed those who proved faithful to him when the testing-time came, so proved for a considerable time to come; there was also concern about the Gregory honours scandal.

Chanak provided the occasion.

For two years, Lloyd George had supported the Greeks against the Turks, despite repeated warnings from Churchill and Montagu that this policy would lead to disaster. The Chanak crisis itself began with reports of Turkish atrocities in Armenia, as Mustapha Kemal advanced towards his objectives in European Turkey. Greece asked the permission of the Allies to enter Constantinople. Troops were sent to Thrace on the European shore. The Allies rejected the Greek proposal, and French, British and Italian troops were sent in to keep the peace. Mustapha Kemal decided to strike and in a brilliant operation he broke through the Greek lines. The Turks sacked Smyrna and burnt it to the ground, then turned their heads towards Constantinople. The British detachment standing in their way comprised only two battalions, under General Harington, and he faced a determined Turkish army with their tails up. It was of paramount importance that the Allies on the spot should remain united: Harington wanted 'three flags', not one. But the French and Italian troops were ordered to withdraw, and Harington was isolated.

The Cabinet met to discuss the crisis on 7 September. Lloyd George was emphatic about what should be done. 'In no circumstances' he told his colleagues, 'could we allow the Gallipoli Peninsula to be occupied by the Turks. It was the most important strategic position in the world and the closing of the Straits (in 1915) had prolonged the war by two years. It was inconceivable that we should allow the Turks to gain possession of the Gallipoli Peninsula, and we should fight to prevent their doing so.' Lloyd George advised his colleagues to agree to strengthen British naval forces at the Dardanelles, and to warn the Turks that if they tried to cross the Bosphorus, 'the British Fleet should certainly fire on them'.

For the next month, Lloyd George's firm view – some might say bellicose view – dominated the decisions of his Cabinet. Lloyd George was also confident of public support. On 15 September he informed his Foreign Secretary, Lord Curzon, that 'The country would be behind us in any steps we took to keep the Turk out of Europe', and at a Cabinet later that day he told his colleagues that 'Mustapha Kemal ought to know that if he crossed the Straits with 60,000 rifles he would be met by 60,000 – to say nothing of the British Fleet'. The time had come, he added, 'to do something concrete'. Lloyd George was supported by a majority of his ministers. Hamar Greenwood advised asking New Zealand and Australia to cooperate, and he was supported in this suggestion by the War Minister, Worthington Evans, and by Churchill, who was asked by the Cabinet to draft a press statement making clear that Britain would take military action to block the Turkish advance, and calling upon the Dominions to send troops, 'in defence of interest for which they have already made enormous sacrifices and of a sort which is hallowed by immortal memories of the Anzacs'.

C'était magnifique but unfortunately it was flashed to the press of the world before the telegram could reach the Dominion Prime Ministers. Canada and Australia reacted angrily. Although the Statute of Westminster was not signed until 1926, the self-governing dominions were taking their own decisions in world affairs, and were independent members of the League of Nations. Mackenzie King sent a furious message through the Governor-General, followed by a further message saying that the Canadian Parliament would decide. Churchill pressed for a declaration of support, nevertheless: 'Presumably it is not necessary for you to summon Parliament.'

Australia's highly idiosyncratic Billy Hughes was no more forthcoming. He complained that the Australian people knew what was afoot through the press communiqué before their Government had been approached: this precluded that full and judicial consideration 'which was a clear right of a national government'. It was totally wrong to be stampeded by newspaper disclosures. They had not been kept in the picture over the preceding weeks: now – after the press disclosures, the Australian Government were being invited, not to decide between peace and war, but to join Britain in a war on which Britain had decided: 'I feel that I ought to speak quite frankly, and say that the unity of the Empire is gravely imperilled by such action.'

These were strong words, and not in any sense mitigated by a more forthcoming response from New Zealand and Newfoundland. Politicians in a hole always welcome comfort, and tend to ignore, or write off, or explain away – perhaps by personal criticism of the personalities involved – the adverse reaction of perhaps more important people, as Canada and Australia undoubtedly were. But General Smuts of South Africa was no more forthcoming than his colleagues from Ottawa and Canberra. The King, in Balmoral, was anxious and had ordered his special train to be in waiting at Ballater. In so far as British policy was concerned he was subject to advice from Downing Street, but he was also King of the dominions beyond the seas. His letter to Lloyd George was full of warnings.

Poincaré was totally hostile, and Britain was virtually isolated, but not as isolated as Harington, who with his small force daily awaited the Turkish hordes under Mustapha Kemal.

As if there were not enough trouble, the ubiquitous Beaverbrook entered the scene and set off for Constantinople. He had been staying at Deauville with the Aga Khan, who feared the consequences of Chanak for the whole Moslem world.

Yet Lloyd George was still determined to check the Turkish advance, and to show Britain's military might. Above all, he believed that 'if it was seen that we were taking immediate action to reinforce our troops', Kemal would be deterred from making an attack. It was his firm belief, he told the Cabinet on 18 September, 'that by a show of force and firmness ... fighting might be prevented', and two days later he urged the despatch to Gallipoli of reinforcements from Egypt, and informed General Harington that if he were to be attacked 'we shall take that as a definite challenge to the power of the British Empire'. When Churchill warned Lloyd George on 27 September that Britain did not have sufficient forces to hold both Chanak and Gallipoli, Lloyd George was insistent that both areas should be held. The evacuation of Chanak, he declared 'would be the greatest loss of prestige which could possibly be inflicted on the British Empire': scuttle would mean that 'our credit would entirely disappear'. As Lloyd George wished, the British troops were therefore reinforced, and remained in their positions with orders not to withdraw.

Meanwhile, Harington in Chanak was facing great pressure. The Turks were approaching in overwhelming numbers. Intelligence reports intimated a Turkish attack on 30 September. Harington, with more sense of diplomacy than his political masters, kept them talking, day after day, bereft of any meaningful instructions. On 11 October, the Pact of Mudania was signed – on the previous day he had been given an unreal authority, on his own decision, to begin action against the Turks if he thought fit.

Mudania averted a war on the wrong issue, in the wrong place and with a totally disparate balance of forces.

But *The Times*, itself bloodthirsty, contained a letter from Tory MPs demanding the recall of Parliament. Eighty, it was now said, were demanding the break-up of the coalition.

The military confrontation at Chanak now gave way to the political confrontation at Westminster.

Overleaf The meeting of Conservative MPs at the Carlton Club.

It began with Bonar Law, whom Lloyd George had tended in wartime to neglect in favour of other Conservatives, though Bonar Law was the Conservative leader. He simply asked, what next? His analysis was devastating, though not a condemnation of Lloyd George. But Beaverbrook was to describe it as a 'root and branch condemnation of the Chanak policy'. Strangely, the *Daily Express* took the same line. He himself wrote that a 'new potential Premier had taken the field, and that an alternative Administration had at last become possible'. The target was now neither the Turks nor the Greeks, it was Lloyd George. The battleground would not be Chanak, but the Carlton Club.

Austen Chamberlain, who was in danger of becoming a tool of Lloyd George, proposed a dissolution, which Lloyd George was seeing as his way out. One member of the Cabinet, the hitherto silent Stanley Baldwin, the silent member for most of his short period in the higher ranks of the administration, acted.

He proved to be the key to the situation. His disillusionment with Lloyd George was total. He had come late into the Cabinet after a sound but undistinguished period as Financial Secretary to the Treasury. A little naïve, he had been shocked when he listened to Lloyd George talking to his Cabinet cronies, at the apparently cynical tone of the conversation. This, surely, was not what we had all entered politics to achieve. Where were the ideals, the objectives for which we had been called into public life? His simplicity was a little unfair: Lloyd George and his colleagues had long been committed to those objectives, and did not feel it necessary to repeat them as a preamble to every tactical discussion.

But when the Carlton Club meeting was called, Baldwin was there. Salisbury had declared his opposition to the continuance of the coalition. Leo Amery – and Baldwin too.

And Bonar Law? He knew that Lloyd George was seeking an election: he probably did not know that the King was resistant. Another key figure was the aristocratic Curzon, who perhaps was harbouring ambitions for the leadership. (Certainly they were there when Bonar Law died in May 1923.) One potential critic of the coalition was hanging back, asking where Curzon stood: he was told that Curzon was for the end of the coalition. The movement was encouraged by the result of the Newport by-election, where an independent Tory was contesting a seat previously held by a coalition Liberal, and romped home, with Labour second and the Liberal a bad third.

The Conservatives were called to the Carlton Club on 19 October 1922, only a few hours after the Newport result was known. Beaverbrook went to see Bonar Law, who showed him two letters; one to his constituency announced his forthcoming retirement from the House, the other his refusal to attend the Carlton Club meeting. Beaverbrook persuaded him to destroy them. Beaverbrook informed all newspapers that Bonar Law would attend the meeting.

Chamberlain vainly addressed it, claiming that there was no difference between the two wings of the coalition. Some disbelieved him, others felt that if there were no differences there ought to be, with cries of 'Ireland'. The decisive speech was that of the unimpassioned stolid Baldwin. Simply he said that the Prime Minister was a 'great dynamic force'. A force which had already destroyed the Liberal Party and, if care were not taken, would destroy the Conservatives.

Opposite The resignation of Lloyd George.

The issue hinged on whether Baldwin would be supported by a more senior Tory. The Conservative Chief Whip, Sir Leslie Wilson, had already let it be

GEORGE
RESIGNS
EVENING
STANDARD

known that he would rather see the Conservatives go to the poll as an independent party, with their own leader, than continue to be tied to the coalition. Now the former Leader of the Party, Bonar Law, made the intervention that Beaverbrook had pressed upon him. It was more important, he said, to keep the Conservatives united, than to win the next election in coalition colours. His argument turned the tide, despite a final plea from Balfour – himself a former Conservative Prime Minister – that the coalition should be preserved.

By a majority of 187 to 87, the meeting resolved that the party should withdraw from the coalition Government.

Lloyd George asked for an audience and tendered his resignation. The King's comment was, 'I am sorry he is going, but some day he will be Prime Minister again.'

The King was wrong.

Lloyd George did not take easily to a life of political impotence. Still less did he relish the election which Bonar Law successfully sought from the King. The Tories had a majority of 77 over all parties. The Labour Party became the official Opposition. The Liberals, who fought the election, with a poster bearing the portraits of Lloyd George and Asquith, were divided, 60 Asquithians, and 55 followers of Lloyd George. Stanley Baldwin became Chancellor of the Exchequer. Churchill lost his deat by a large majority in Dundee. Nothing would ever be the same again. Lloyd George was fifty-nine; he was destined to be a voice in British politics, but not again a force, for more than twenty years.

In the political stalemate which followed the 1923 General Election, Asquith took the decisive and historic step which put the Labour Party in office. Lloyd George would have none of it, and relations worsened again. For years unity was impossible because Lloyd George would not merge his notorious fighting fund with that of the official party.

In 1929 he gave fighting leadership to his old party with Lloyd George's New Deal, an imaginative economic programme largely drawn up by Keynes and other economists, and closely following the lines of President Roosevelt's New Deal in the United States; as with Roosevelt the Liberal programme placed a great stress on agriculture. But the Liberals held only fifty-nine seats, and when MacDonald formed the 'National Government' with overwhelming Tory backing, he refused to lend his support. But his party split three ways, the Samuelites and Simonites joining the coalition. He held his seat in 1931 and 1935.

When Churchill became Prime Minister he had Lloyd George sounded out, by Beaverbrook, about becoming Minister of Agriculture. Correspondence ensued between them, and while Lloyd George suggested taking charge of food supplies, he was, on the whole, allergic to taking any post at all, partly through hostility to Chamberlain, who he rightly felt was against his inclusion.

His last years showed both physical decline and a weakening of his judgment. He was greatly reviled for his visit to Hitler and the encouragement he gave.

In 1943 he married Frances Stevenson and at the beginning of 1945 became Earl Lloyd George of Dwyfor and Viscount Gwynnedd. In March he died.

After the memories of his later years had faded, there was a growing and more favourable reappraisal of his record, especially his leadership in the First War.

The writing of this chapter is based less on books than on a close friendship with two members of his family, Gwilym, with whom I worked for three years in the Second World War, and Megan. Though Gwilym had to some extent distanced himself from the old man by joining the National Government, they never lost contact, particularly when Gwilym had his own ministerial command from 1942. Megan idolized him to the end, and was a rich provider of Lloyd George stories and analysis of her father's decisions and the reasons for them.

Lloyd George had imagination – Celtic imagination – and drive. His solicitor's training ensured that he tied up every loose end, or saw that someone else did. His failure, which was not fatal to Britain, but almost certainly fatal to hundreds of thousands of young lives, was his inability, or lack of resolve, to tackle the problem of the generals, when his judgment as well as his heart must have told him he should act ruthlessly.

Perhaps only a minority of Britain's Prime Ministers had a highly developed sense of imagination, and none more than Lloyd George. But he allowed the inspirations from that imagination to beat themselves out like waves on a hostile shore. Their potentiality for war, despite his mistakes, led to victory. Their potentiality in peace-time perished in over-confidence and willingness to be diverted to politicking in place of policy. And, strangest of all, in the end he failed as a politician in that he was unable to maintain a dependable majority. It seemed that he almost failed to see the need to maintain one. The hubris which called forth the 1918 election produced a tactical, short-term victory; his immediate supporters had won by a landslide, but his sense of political strategy had deserted him. His increasingly autocratic rule made that inevitable. His Irish settlement provided the disenchantment, and Chanak the occasion. The old praetorian guard to which he might have appealed, the Liberal Party, had been destroyed as a political force by his own action, and for short-term advantages. Not as a Prime Minister, not as a social reformer, not as a war leader had he failed; he had simply forgotten, or ignored, the rules that govern the profession of politics.

Interlude: The Unknown Prime Minister

When Andrew Bonar Law was buried in Westminster Abbey, Asquith is said to have suggested how appropriate it was that 'The Unknown Prime Minister' should have been buried close to the Unknown Warrior. His phrase was taken up by Lord Blake in his authoritative biography, *The Unknown Prime Minister*.

A Canadian by birth, Bonar Law had come to Scotland as a boy, and completed his education there. He worked in a merchant bank and a metal importer's firm, and entered Parliament in 1900 at the age of forty-two. He lost his Glasgow seat in 1906, but speedily returned for Dulwich. On losing that seat in 1910, he was elected for Bootle. He had been a junior minister at the Board of Trade under Salisbury and Balfour.

When Balfour resigned the leadership of his party in 1911, Bonar Law was elected leader, though Lloyd George, heading the coalition Cabinet from 1916, made more use of Balfour than of Law, possibly one of his cardinal errors, as increasingly Lloyd George chose his team from Conservatives and miscellaneous businessmen instead of considering the Parliamentary realities which should govern the composition of any coalition. The Carlton Club meeting of October 1922 ended the Lloyd George régime once and for all, and Bonar Law became Prime Minister. He headed the new Conservative Government for only seven months before cancer forced his retirement. He died in October 1923.

As leader of his party he had leaned heavily on the Ulster side. He was a professional, and while Asquith as Prime Minister was dining out nearly every night, Law was attending to his Parliamentary and party duties. He withdrew from active leadership on health grounds in 1921, but it was to him that his party turned when the Conservatives withdrew from the Lloyd George Government. The story is told in the previous chapter.

He had one great difficulty in forming his administration. He could not, yet at least, invite Austen Chamberlain, a doyen of the Conservative Party, to join him; still less could he invite Churchill, nominally a Liberal and much involved in the Chanak affair. That would be a task for Baldwin, who was to succeed him as Conservative leader. Other prominent Conservatives had stayed with Lloyd George: attendance at the Carlton Club, whither Bonar Law himself had been almost physically shanghaied by Beaverbrook, was the qualification for the new Conservative 'coupon'. But it was not a 'Who? Who?' ministry: it included Leo Amery, Wood (later Lord Halifax), Hogg (later the elder Hailsham), Sir Samuel Hoare – and Neville Chamberlain. Baldwin, a decisive influence in the break-up of the Lloyd George administration, became Chancellor, and this was to lead, as we shall see, to a memorable crisis between him and Bonar Law, almost leading to the Prime Minister's resignation. But his main task was to ensure the cohesion of the newly united party: 'I must follow them, I am their leader.'

Bonar Law had the right to seek an election, and it produced an undeniable majority (one which Baldwin was to throw away in his quixotically called election of 1923). Six months after forming the Government he was advised on health grounds to go on a sea voyage. But what he was suffering from was cancer of the throat, and in May he resigned.

He made no formal representations to the King about his successor, but the King was in no doubt that he would have recommended Baldwin. Baldwin would in any case have been the King's choice; there was no need to consult a dying man. Besides, J.C.C. Davidson, later Lord Davidson, who was in the confidence of all those concerned, had made it clear to the Palace that the widespread call for Baldwin represented also the view of the dying Premier.

Andrew Bonar Law.

7

Stanley Baldwin

THE IMAGE HAS GROWN UP of Stanley Baldwin as a rather lazy country squire, scratching the backs of his pigs with his walking stick, prone to lecturing the Classical Association on the glory that was Greece and the grandeur that was Rome; and as a politician the man who underestimated Hitler, misled the electorate on rearmament, and proved a laggard in its achievement, one who presided over the early stages of appeasement, and finally put up a fight in wartime to preserve his iron gates when they were needed for the munitions drive. What has been called the Baldwin age, the title of a symposium, is regarded as a synonym for a generation of wasted years. Some will award him a few bonus marks for his handling of a constitutional crisis which led to the abdication of Edward VIII.

It is time for a reappraisal. There have been reassessments which have swung far in Baldwin's favour, even on the rearmament question. The image of the lazy, classical amateur has been rejected by Winston Churchill. He was the only former ministerial colleague of Baldwin's to speak at the poorly attended ceremony for the unveiling of the Baldwin memorial near his home in Worcestershire in 1949. His judgment? 'He was the most formidable politician I have ever known in public life.'

Churchill's public life, up to the time he spoke, already embraced forty-four years since his first election to Parliament; forty-one years earlier he had been a Cabinet minister. He had served in Cabinets under Asquith, Lloyd George, Baldwin and Chamberlain, as well as his own. In more than forty years of Cabinet-making and Cabinet-breaking, of leaders made and unmade, of cliques and cabals, he had intimately known characters as ruthless as Lloyd George, Birkenhead, Curzon and Carson, not to mention the press lords, Northcliffe, Rothermere and Beaverbrook.

In saying this Churchill clearly based himself on two very different phases, when – in the second Baldwin Government – they were working closely together and Baldwin's formidable powers were deployed on defending and supporting Churchill, and also in the period of political – never personal – antagonism, such as the argument over India, still more over rearmament. They remained friends throughout, but Churchill, wrong most people would feel over India, right on rearmament and the Hitler threat, had cause to register and record Baldwin's formidable powers of self-defence and counter-attack.

When Baldwin handed over to Chamberlain in 1937, he was universally praised as few retiring Prime Ministers have been. When he died, ten years later, there was no one to sponsor the memorial service in Westminster Abbey, and the Board of Trade had to play a part.

Baldwin deserves to go down to history as a healer, one who sought to build bridges, especially in the always potentially explosive area of industrial relations. He became Prime Minister at a particularly difficult time. Less than five years after the end of the war, the tensions with which Asquith had had to cope on the eve of that war had become more dangerous. Post-war unemployment, the increased power of workshop democracy as a result of the wartime concentration on munitions production, a new generation of industrial leaders, particularly at local level, and the new dimension created by the Soviet Revolution, meant a far worse situation than Asquith had faced.

Baldwin has rightly been portrayed as a 'healer' in the coal dispute of 1926, and sometimes contrasted with the allegedly unbalanced and provocative attacks made on the miners by Churchill in the Government paper, *The British*

Opposite Mr and Mrs Baldwin at Chequers during their first weekend after the 1924 General Election.

Gazette. In fact they were working closely together. In the period before the General Strike, Baldwin put Churchill in charge of the efforts to bring peace in the industry. The vast subsidy which the Government provided to bridge the period while the Royal Commission under Samuel was reporting on the economics of the industry and the coal-owners' demand for a reduction in pay and an increase in hours, was Churchill's proposal – not an easy one for a Chancellor to volunteer – endorsed by Baldwin.

Both were vehement in condemning, on constitutional grounds, the TUC's General Strike, especially as they had knowledge of Russian funds entering the country to sustain it. *The British Gazette* was the product of joint management: it carried all Baldwin's speeches and statements, including those made in Parliament – there was no other press medium functioning. Some of his statements were in fact prepared, sometimes as a joint effort, specifically for headline treatment in the *Gazette*.

When the General Strike was over, Baldwin went to France, and Churchill was in sole charge of the attempts to get a settlement in coal. The Chancellor reported to Baldwin that he tended to side with the Miners' Federation against the owners, and used language of characteristic Churchillian denunciation against the owners. It was Churchill, with Baldwin's support, who angrily pressed the mine-owners to agree to national, as opposed to district, negotiation, which the owners wanted as a means of setting district against district, and local union against local union. In the end both Baldwin and Churchill gave way on the issue: it is noteworthy that Harold Laski, not an easy man to please, after accompanying the miners' leaders to Downing Street praised Churchill as 'bigger and more skilful', Baldwin as 'blundering uncouthly'.

In the end both were equally responsible for the sellout to the owners. In the aftermath of the strike, when Conservative members were out to shock trade union power, Baldwin succeeded in killing a private member's Bill aimed at forcing contracting-in as against contracting-out as the way to get individual subscriptions to trade unions, but contracting-in was later included in the Government's own Trade Dispute Acts. (It was repealed by the Attlee Government in 1947, and was the occasion for Sir Hartley Shawcross's famous utterance: 'We are the masters now'.) But, although it was unknown at the time, it was Baldwin who set up the Mond–Turner talks between a leading ICI industrialist and a wool textile union leader, aiming at a new system of industrial relationships.

A healer, of course, does not usually get a good press. Fleet Street thrives on confrontation. The same applied to a Prime Minister's control of his Cabinet. If he uses his political skills to keep the Cabinet together in pursuit of a common aim and common policies, he is condemned as devious; if he forces splits and public recriminations then, as long as he takes the right side in the division, he is a hero. But his Cabinet disintegrates. A formula worked out and painstakingly negotiated with those in dispute in industry, or in a divided party, is attacked as a 'gimmick', or even a 'sellout'. A statement which exacerbates the situation, in industry or in a party setting, is acclaimed as statesmanlike, though there is some difference between the treatment of a Conservative leader and that of a leader of a Labour Government.

Opposite Young Stanley Baldwin with his mother.

Stanley Baldwin was born on 3 August 1867. His life spanned the premierships from Derby to Attlee. His father worked in the family foundry at Stourport,

Harrow: Baldwin is seated second left.

and at a forge at Wilden, close to the family home, producing wrought iron. Just before Baldwin's birth, the family interests were divided, and his father ran the forge before a merger with other interests to form Baldwins Ltd in 1902, later absorbed into a firm which was well known in our time until nationalization, Richard Thomas and Baldwin. He also became chairman of the Great Western Railway and had banking interests. The family firm was prosperous and Baldwin never wanted for money.

After going to Harrow and Cambridge, where he was a somewhat lazy but accomplished classical student, he went into the business, one of only five Prime Ministers with such experience. He was assiduous in learning the technical side, worked normal hours, and knew all the workmen personally. The fact that it was a family business perhaps gave him romantic ideas about employer–worker relations.

His father was Conservative MP for West Worcestershire, later the Bewdley division. In 1904 he himself was adopted for Kidderminster, but was defeated in the 1906 Liberal landslide. Baldwin was nearly forty, and in those days of seven-year Parliaments there was no guarantee of another general election before 1913. But his father died in 1908 and he inherited the seat. He made little impact right up to the war, though he supported the tariff reform cause, and criticized the Lloyd George Budget. Preferring the smoke-room, where he sat puffing his briar-root, to the Chamber, he seemed to have become the quintessential back-bencher, and there is no evidence to suggest that he had any other ambitions.

The wave of strikes, unprecedented in scale and motivation, in the years just before the war led him to speak from his own experience on these matters. These were not his people; there had never been any hint of a strike at Baldwins, and he claimed – rightly – to see new and unwelcome developments undermining half a century of collective bargaining in industry. He drew a sharp distinction between the new syndicalists and the traditional unionists; this was a view which always impelled him to an understanding, even encouragement, of the solid centre of the Labour Party and its reinforcement against infiltration by those he saw propagating alien doctrines.

The outbreak of the war left him frustrated, the more so as he was devastated by the loss of so many near to him. He was critical of the lack of urgency on munitions, welcomed the coalition and, after some misgivings about Lloyd George, supported the disappearance of Asquith. He became Bonar Law's PPS, but with the unusual duty of answering on behalf of the Financial Secretary, who had no seat and was representing the Treasury in Washington. Soon afterwards he became Joint Financial Secretary to the Treasury, not only a junior minister but holder of the office traditionally regarded as the doyen of junior ministers, until the creation of the intermediate rank of ministers of State. He was forty-nine, old for a newly appointed junior minister.

He proved to be good at the dispatch box, and in difficult Treasury assignments, especially in relations with the Bank. Very soon, to his own surprise, he was regarded as a coming man. But he was still a junior minister.

At the end of the war, the coupon election returned what Keynes called the 'hard-faced men who looked as if they had done well out of the war'. So had Baldwins Ltd, which is perhaps one reason why he wrote to *The Times* saying he was devoting a fifth of his fortune, then about £500,000, to cancellation of war debt. He signed it 'FST', the initials by which the Financial Secretary has been known through many political and civil service generations. They are initials well known in a wide circle, and one can't help wondering whether he intended the gift to be attributed, especially as he went through a ceremonial burning of the bonds he bought. The transaction could have been more secret, and while his letter was designed to induce others to follow him, 'ABC' or 'XYZ' could have had the same result.

He had a surprising offer, through Law, to go to South Africa or Australia as High Commissioner and Governor-General. The suggestion has been made that this was Beaverbrook trying to remove someone close to Law. Law in fact persuaded Lloyd George to make Baldwin President of the Board of Trade. He carried through a moderately protectionist measure, the Safeguarding of Industries Bill, but was a very quiet participant in Cabinet.

But he was becoming increasingly obsessed with what he called 'the morally disintegrating effect of Lloyd George on all whom he had to deal with, whether MPs, Civil Servants, trade unionists or the public . . .' He was equally disgusted with Lloyd George's relations with the press barons. He regarded Northcliffe, Beaverbrook and Rothermere, it has been said, 'as a close conspiracy alien to the proprieties of Cabinet Government'. His aim was to 'restore and maintain the unity of the Party'. It was probably his long experience not as a minister, but as a back-bencher, which made him so determined.

Baldwin's intervention was, as has been seen, decisive in the Carlton Club meeting. Before Chanak, no one could have forecast that Baldwin would be Chancellor within weeks, or Prime Minister within about seven months. The most formidable politicians do not always look formidable.

This judgment must be applied to a question about Baldwin's short period at the Treasury. Subsequent commentators have almost all agreed to accuse him of naïveté on his public relations handling of his negotiations over the war debt settlement with the United States. He had secured authority to go to Washington to settle the quantum, the period of repayment and the rate of interest. That he accepted a very rough diktat from the Americans is not questioned: what one must ask is whether he had to accept it, or whether he could have adjourned the negotiations, or said he must go home to report in person. It is also highly arguable that he should not have committed Britain to a formidable annual charge on her balance of payments for decades to come until he had secured guarantees about German reparations and Allied war debts to Britain. But this is not the charge in the books. The charge relates to his naïve response to press questions when he came ashore from RMS *Olympic*.

The terms he had negotiated, still *ad referendum* Congress, as he made clear, had leaked and led to an outcry in Britain. Worse, it was highly doubtful whether the Cabinet would endorse them. Indeed, it was widely known that Bonar Law regarded them as unacceptable. To Baldwin he said: 'I should be the most cursed Prime Minister that ever held office in England if I accepted these terms.'

Law had joined the King in condemning both Baldwin's terms and the statement Baldwin had made when he disembarked. More, he had, it was widely believed, written an article for a newspaper denouncing the terms, unsigned, but no such literary effort escapes attribution. There can be very few precedents or parallels in history, if any at all.

What Baldwin had said, after making it clear that the terms required Congressional approval, was that they were the best that could be obtained in any circumstances: 'The debt can only be funded on such terms as can be got through Congress and the Senate and that is the root of difficulty with which we are now faced. . . .' The 'provisional settlement' would be considered very savage and even ungenerous by the British people. But it would be useless to put forward any further counter-proposals, since the Americans 'have gone to the limit of what they are likely to propose'.

Naïveté, ignorance of the fact that he was on the record, a rush of blood to the head? He must have known of the Cabinet's views; the telegraph service with Washington was well established. If he did not know, he should have sent someone home, or returned himself, to find out. It is inconceivable that there were no communications with Downing Street during the five or six days he was on board. Satisfactory shore–ship communications were sufficiently advanced in 1910 to ensure the arrest of Dr Crippen. The British press had printed the American leak of the details, and London's reaction was well published.

It is equally inconceivable that there had not been continuing discussion between Baldwin and his entourage on board ship, and indeed earlier. It happens every time a negotiating team comes back from America, even on a seven-hour flight. It happens throughout the negotiations. The leader and his team know what the Cabinet reaction would be; they would sit down over drinks as soon as the final terms are agreed and discuss them. But what outside

Opposite Stanley Baldwin and his wife on honeymoon, 1892.

commentators fail so often to realize is that negotiating teams abroad so often go native. They think London has gone mad, or perverse. London quickly forms a similar view of them. Telegrams would expressly say so, in very basic English. It is impossible to believe that in nearly a week's voyage, over meals, drinks or walks around the deck, the problem of what to say to the waiting press had not been discussed. Of course it had, and Baldwin had every word ready: the style of the speech as reported was too precise for it to have been off-the-cuff. The fact that it was uttered, with high risk of dismissal, suggests that it was calculated, even having regard to the other risk that was aired, the Prime Minister's own resignation. Bonar Law in fact told Cabinet that he would not remain if the terms were ratified. The meeting was adjourned to the next day, when the Prime Minister actually refused to attend. The majority of the Cabinet accepted the terms, and in the end so did Bonar Law. Churchill's 'most formidable politician' had won. He had a similar success in the House – a Parliamentary triumph indeed.

He scored again in his crushing reply to the Leader of the Opposition, Ramsay MacDonald, at the opening of the new session in February 1923.

Bonar Law, dying of cancer, resigned on 20 May 1923, and died in October. The Conservative leaders who had thrown in their lot with Lloyd George were out of the running. The choice lay between Baldwin and the Marquess of Curzon. The King, it is now known, supported Baldwin, not only because of the problem of appointing a Prime Minister in the Lords. Bonar Law's family informed the Household – the King's private secretary told Salisbury – that 'he would, if asked to advise the King, have been in favour of the Premiership remaining in the Commons.'

Curzon was sent for by the King to be told that he had not been chosen. He had interpreted the summons as indicating that he was to go to Downing Street. He was overcome with the bitterest disappointment, but nevertheless accepted Baldwin's invitation to continue as Foreign Secretary. Had he refused, Baldwin would have invited Austen Chamberlain.

Baldwin was a committed protectionist. He was also a very honest man. He could not see any solution of Britain's industrial and trade problems, except on the basis of what it had become fashionable to call the 'safeguarding' of British manufacturing industries, going far beyond the Safeguarding of Industries Act, with which he had been intimately concerned. As Prime Minister his intellectual conviction became a matter of dedication. He could not see any way through, except on the basis of further protectionist legislation. But as a proceduralist he was faced with Bonar Law's damaging bequest to him, the commitment that there would be no major fiscal change without an election. And Baldwin was an honourable man, but one who was intellectually converted to the doctrine of protection. It was an honourable, but politically foolhardy, decision to say that since he could see no way forward except through an extension of protection he must seek the judgment of the electorate, not because of any pledge he had given but because he was the leader of a majority party elected on the basis of the pledge given by Bonar Law.

The cynics of the Lloyd George era might feel such scruples to be the unrealistic convictions of a naïve and inexperienced politician, but they had to go to their constituencies, as he had, to seek to justify an historic policy-change, as compared with the pledge by his predecessor. Their judgment about his naïveté they would have felt was confirmed by the stalemate which followed

At the Imperial Conference at Chequers in 1923. Left to right: Smuts (South Africa), Warren (Newfoundland), Massey (New Zealand) and Baldwin

the counting of the votes. The Conservatives were still the leading party, with 257 seats, but since Labour had won 191 and the Liberals 158, the Government no longer had a majority. He had served them ill, and he faced the same attacks on his leadership as he had later to face after the 1929 election. Conservatives, red in tooth and claw, are always more ruthless than others in pursuit of their leader's head when he has led them to defeat. Witness 1929–30, 1964–6, 1974 – though not 1945 or 1950.

Baldwin placed his resignation at the disposal of the King. A constitutional point was involved. Since Disraeli's defeat in 1868, the custom had been to resign when a Government lost its Parliamentary majority, without waiting to face the House of Commons. But that was in a two-party age. The 1923 result produced a stalemate, in modern parlance a 'hung' election. Baldwin was convinced that he could not form a Government viable in Parliamentary terms, but the King virtually ordered him to continue in office – he led the party with the largest single Parliamentary following – unless and until he was defeated in Parliament. Baldwin unhappily agreed. In 1929, in a majority again, he respectfully asked to be excused from such a royal injunction, for in that year, though no party had an overall majority, he was no longer leader of the largest Parliamentary party.

Thanks to Asquith's decision to give Labour a chance on carefully sanitized terms, Baldwin was defeated on the King's Speech, and Labour came into office. Within a year, the Liberal amendment on the Campbell case had brought MacDonald down, and Baldwin won a great majority, with the virtual certainty of four or up to five years in office. He was master now.

The Government he formed was exciting. Neville Chamberlain was formally invited to resume his earlier tenure of the Treasury, but, to his credit, wanted to take Health, as he was bursting with proposals for local government reform, rating and housing measures. Perhaps on leaving the Cabinet room he was a little disconcerted to see Churchill, not technically a Conservative MP, waiting outside. Churchill became Chancellor, to general surprise: no one was more surprised or gratified than Winston himself. His fiscal policy, particularly on the crucial issue of the return to gold in 1925, and his Budgets showed a refreshing approach. But it is now generally agreed that he was wrong, on returning to gold, to keep sterling at the same exchange rate with the dollar as in 1914. He was living, it must be remembered, in the era of Montague Norman, who was vigorously pressing, on the basis of the then conventional wisdom, for the restoration of sterling's parity in the old rate, $4·88 in a world very different from 1914. The parity, Churchill felt, was overvalued, condemning Britain to an export slump and chronic balance of payments deficit, until six years later a so-called 'National' Government, formed to safeguard the pound, promptly devalued it and went off gold. Churchill fought hard against the Normanite hard-liners. He involved Keynes and other unorthodox economists against the Bank of England. He memorialized incessantly against a return to the 1914 rate, stressing that the high level of unemployment provided the case for a parity that would enable Britain to trade competitively. In the event, he succumbed. Both Baldwin and he should have pulled rank and overridden the powerful alternative Government in Threadneedle Street.

Baldwin was the antithesis of Lloyd George. His task as he saw it was to see that the Cabinet business went through, the work being done by the departmental ministers. He would conduct the orchestra, and not tire himself. No man can do two men's work at all well, and certainly not the work of three. So Churchill was given his head on finance, though for most of the Government's life Baldwin was consulting Churchill more than any other colleague on issues going far wider than finance. One of Baldwin's successes was an extension of Lloyd George's Irish agreement, settling a number of matters in dispute, particularly boundaries, left unresolved by Lloyd George. On this issue, Baldwin put Churchill in charge, and ratified the outcome with a handshake with the Irish leaders.

But another minister given solid backing and encouragement to put his ideas into practical effect was Neville Chamberlain. As will be seen he put through e greatest set of reforms ever seen in the field of housing, land planning and cal government, including health. He was incomparably the best housing and cal government minister in this century until Aneurin Bevan twenty years ter.

Baldwin himself was in the lead in the epic events of 1925–6 leading up to e miners' strike and the General Strike. The basic cause was the Govern-ent's return to gold on the wrong parity. Every export industry was hit – tton for example suffered as badly as coal – and, given the overvalued change rate, the only means of increasing exports was to cut costs to a level mpetitive at the Bank of England parity. The private colliery-owners – and harder-faced bunch of Gradgrinds never polluted British industry, with just e or two statesmanlike exceptions, including men who realized that costs uld be cut by modernization and new technological capital investment – were termined to bring down wages. This had been made clear in 1918–19 when Ir Justice Sankey (later Labour Lord Chancellor) presided over the oddest ommittee of Inquiry ever set up.

In addition to Sankey it had consisted of representatives of the colliery vners, other industrial leaders, the mineworkers and non-coal trade unions. produced five reports: the industrialists could not stomach the attitude of e coal-owners, and there were significant differences between the views of e miners and the independent, mainly left-wing economists.

Sankey recommended nationalization. (He was Welsh, and once told me at Jesus College debating society dinner that he had to telephone the gist of e report through to Lloyd George, who was at the peace talks in Paris. Every-ing in Paris leaked, so Sankey opened up in Welsh. The bewildered journal-ts called up language experts, one of the best-known for his scoops rapidly iring a linguist skilled in Serbo-Croat.)

Baldwin knew industrial workers better than any Prime Minister before him. e was anxious to avoid an industrial confrontation, and had a real sympathy r the miners' case. He and Churchill upset the orthodox by providing a tem-rary subsidy – 'bought off' the strike, to use his own words – to maintain nployment for a period long enough for a newly appointed Royal Commission nsisting of three 'independents' to report. It was headed by Sir Herbert amuel; the others were Sir Kenneth Lee (a cotton manufacturer) and Sir 'illiam Beveridge. They recommended the end of the subsidy, drastic re-ganization of the industry, including the nationalization of coal royalties arried through in 1938), the amalgamation of smaller undertakings and a re-uction in wages. The Miners' Federation, led by A.J. Cook, responded with e slogan 'Not a penny off the pay, not a minute on the day' in response to e two demands the owners were making.

The miners, instead of fighting on their own, skilfully delegated their auth-ity as a negotiating body to the General Council of the TUC, who promptly clared a General Strike, Britain's first and only such industrial conflict. Bald-in was sympathetic to the miners, but his highly developed constitutional inciples rejected any attempt to coerce Government and Parliament by such essures. Moreover, the sources open to him were reporting that Soviet money as being transmitted to the country to sustain the strike.

He and Churchill, working closely together, threw themselves into the fray. hey were firm, but both were seeking a way out, not only for the Government, it one which the TUC could accept without loss of face. Face-saving is as important in an industrial situation as in any international crisis, even involving autocratic rules, and Baldwin was a master in such a situation. Some later commentators have endeavoured to contrast Baldwin's statesmanship with what is regarded as Churchill's lust for battle. But the key phrase in Baldwin's emollient broadcast published in the *Gazette*, 'No door is closed,' followed almost identical words used by Churchill in his own conciliatory speech in Parliament five days earlier: 'The door is open ... I am hoping and working and praying for peace.' But Baldwin went on: 'I will not surrender the safety and the security of the British constitution.'

Though the General Strike ended, the miners stayed out through the summer and into the autumn, barely subsisting and, as the weather grew colder, scratching pitifully at the pit spoilheaps for dried slurry and barely combustible colliery duff. Their last two months, after their surrender on 'pay and day', was an honourable fight to maintain a national wages system instead of the 'district ascertainment' scheme on which the owners were determined, setting district against district and miners' union against union. It required the compulsions of the Second World War for the mines to revert to a national system.

It had been a cataclysmic experience, and, despite the collapse of the TUC, industrial relations generally were the poorest for a generation. New hope came in 1927, with the Mond–Turner talks. Sir Alfred Mond, later Lord Melchett, of the newly formed ICI, and Ben Turner of the wool textile workers came together unofficially and with no clear mandate from those they sought to represent, and succeeded in creating a new era in industrial relations. The press, and those affected, were enthusiastic. Few at the time knew that it was Baldwin who had inspired and masterminded the operation. Only Baldwin among Prime Ministers would have failed to take a bow when it succeeded. In a healing mission he was concerned not to imperil the results.

The remaining years of the 1924–9 Parliament were relatively uneventful – progress in Europe, stagnation at home. In August 1928, Neville Chamberlain wrote privately of Baldwin that he 'often vexes me by what seems to me timidity or lethargy when rapid or vigorous actions are needed.' Yet Baldwin's Government sought to break the stagnation by a wide-ranging, imaginative scheme – De-rating – aimed at liberating industry from the burden of rates, and raising production and employment, especially in the depressed areas. The whole scheme arose from a chance remark by a young Conservative MP, Harold Macmillan – whose constituency was in one of the depressed areas – and was taken up with vigour by Churchill and his Treasury advisers, backed by Baldwin at every stage: two years' hard work in the departments was involved. Baldwin's support was again from behind the scenes, yet again firm. 'The PM intervened quite decisively,' Churchill wrote to his wife, 'and declared that we must act,' and Baldwin later commented in a letter to Churchill: 'For a Tory Cabinet they have successfully and pretty contentedly swallowed a large morsel.'

In 1929 the election Baldwin called led to a serious defeat, with Labour the biggest single party but still in an overall minority. Baldwin resigned and MacDonald formed his second ministry. His arrival coincided with a sharp downturn in the trade cycle. Unemployment began to rise remorselessly to over two millions, ultimately reaching three millions in January 1933. The Government had no economic policy of any kind to deal with what must be said to have been an unprecedented situation, moreover one which engulfed the entire advanced industrial and trading world.

The Treasury was in the hands of Philip Snowden, whose dedicated *laissez faire* politics owed far more to Richard Cobden than to Keir Hardie. Indeed, in so far as there was a modicum of protection, as defined in terms of the post-world war Safeguarding of Industries Duties and the Dyestuffs Act, his reforming free trade zeal led to its repeal, increasing the numbers unemployed. The Dyestuffs Act had been introduced to defend the British industry from the hitherto all-powerful Germans at a time when they had no political influence following defeat. Philip Snowden, MP for the Colne Valley division of Yorkshire, hit one of his local industries hard.

Ramsay MacDonald at the head of Government was paralytic, seeking refuge in wandering speeches signifying nothing but the Government's paralysis and in a strange social life mirroring the Asquith age, though mainly concentrated on a duchess whose wealth had been and was based on Durham coal profits.

In 1931 there was a crisis of confidence in sterling. An international currency, as a new generation has learnt in the Sixties and Seventies, is subject to major assaults due to correct or incorrect assessment of the nation's domestic policies, often inspired by phobias and fetishes associated with the doctrines of some economist with a high public-relations rating. Such crises may have different origins, but the prescription is usually related to cuts in Government expenditure.

So it was in 1931. Keynes was teaching that in a great slump, with inflation contained by unemployment, indeed in this case one where deflation ruled, economic policy should be based on a great public deficit, through spending on public works, in order, by increasing demand, to get industry moving again. But in 1931 the high priests noted that an element in the British public spending was unemployment benefit, and sterling came under attack. MacDonald panicked and set up an inquiry packed mainly by the orthodox. The May Committee forecast a budget deficit of £120 millions (it turned out to be £170 millions), and proposed to save £67 millions by cutting the miserably inadequate unemployment insurance scales and civil service salaries.

The Labour Government refused to endorse what MacDonald and Snowden were urging, and MacDonald went to the King and was authorized to set up the 'National' Government. Baldwin had rushed back from his holiday in Aix, and arrived at Victoria facing a battery of cameras and carrying his trousers over his arm: he had clearly had no time, even on boat or train, to open his suitcase! He expected the King to give him the commission to form a Government, but the King had second thoughts, and invited MacDonald. MacDonald was joined by Snowden, Thomas and Sankey, while Neville Chamberlain, Hoare and Cunliffe-Lister joined the small Cabinet from the Tories, Samuel from the Liberals. Only fourteen Labour back-benchers followed MacDonald. Income tax was raised to five shillings in the pound – it should have been reduced – with ten per cent cuts in unemployment pay and in the salaries of the civil service and the armed forces, the latter provoking the Invergordon naval 'mutiny'.

Confidence was slowly re-established, and unemployment continued to rise, but less rapidly, and began to turn down in 1933. It was to fall cyclically in the Thirties until the pre-war rearmament brought it down to a low level in arms centres and the prosperous South, while remaining endemic in the 'distressed' and finally 'special' areas in the North, in Wales and in Scotland.

In September 1931, MacDonald called an election, Snowden's bitter tongue attacking Labour 'as the party that ran away' and predicting that if Labour won there would be 'Bolshevism run mad'. The Colne Valley was said to be running with tears, but the National Liberal won. Pro-Government MPs numbered 556, the combined Opposition 56, of which Labour held 46, losing nearly all the members of the previous Cabinet.

Baldwin was Lord President of the Council, the real power in the Cabinet because of his following, and as time passed he took over many major responsibilities. He carried through the historic Statute of Westminster, which laid down the sovereign equality of the self-governing Dominions, bound together only by a common allegiance to the Sovereign. He headed the delegation to the Ottawa Economic Conference which led to an Imperial Preference system, the realization of Joseph Chamberlain's dream of thirty years before. This produced a problem for the Liberals, or rather the 'wee frees', the Samuelite connection; the Simonites having no such scruples. In the event, the Parliamentary endorsement of Ottawa was marked by an 'agreement to differ', an account of which appears in an appendix to my book *The Governance of Britain*. But soon the 'wee frees' were out.

For five years, from 1930 to 1935, the issue of India dominated a considerable part of Baldwin's activities, first as Leader of the Opposition during the MacDonald Government, later as Lord President of the Council, leader of the 'National' Government Tories under MacDonald.

In the days of the 1929–31 Labour Government, under pressure from Irwin (later to be Lord Halifax) in India, his own ministers and party, MacDonald proposed far-reaching reforms in the governance of India. The Conservative Party was outraged, and Baldwin shocked them with a very mild speech when the proposals were debated, Labour MPs cheering him, Conservatives in a hostile silence. Churchill was among those who campaigned against the proposals and Neville Chamberlain regarded them as going too far and too fast. But Churchill refused to join in the hysterical Beaverbrook–Rothermere campaign: he would not join them, he told them, in destroying his party. It was in response to the extravagances of the press lords that Baldwin used his memorable phrase, said to have been coined by his cousin Rudyard Kipling: 'Power without responsibility – the prerogative of the harlot thoughout the ages.'

When the coalition Government was formed in 1931, Baldwin rightly or wrongly decided that something on the lines of Labour's proposals was essential to maintain the Government in being. Although its formation was originally intended to be for a short period, after which its members would return to their traditional loyalties, Baldwin maintained his support. The nearest parallel in our own time would be the 'social contract' between the Labour Government and the Trade Union Congress: matters of importance under that arrangement have been regarded by Government as essential to its maintenance. So did Baldwin view Indian policy, and he went to great lengths in its defence.

Baldwin set up a Joint Select Committee of both Houses while insisting that those proposals would never lead to Indian independence as such but were specifically designed to keep Indian reform in play in the hopes of blunting the intensity of Conservative criticism. The Manchester Chamber of Commerce had prepared evidence highly critical of certain aspects of the proposals, because of their fear about the effects on the cotton trade. This was highly embarrassing for Tory ministers, and efforts were made, through Lord Derby, to get the original draft changed. The original submission, although sent up

Opposite A drawing of Stanley Baldwin 'The Worcestershire Lad'. *Punch*, 12 May 1937.

EMPIRE
Bernard Partridge

to London, was withheld from the Committee. What was finally submitted in no way represented the considered views of the Chamber. This became known and the Committee of Privileges was asked to investigate allegations – not from Churchill – which, if substantiated, would amount to a contempt of the House. The ultimate Report of the Committee of Privileges was a white-washing document: evidence available since, but deliberately withheld from the Committee at the time, shows that the charges were well-based, and that ministers had in effect perjured themselves. There is little doubt that Baldwin was implicated – not the 'honest Stan' of legend, but the episode shows clearly how far he and, in particular, certain of his colleagues were prepared to go to keep the Government together. Churchill was right, though he suffered in reputation at the time from the 'disproving' of his allegations.

The greatest subject of controversy over Baldwin's ministerial conduct, both with MacDonald and after 1935 when he became Prime Minister, was the issue of rearmament and the response to the rise of the Hitler menace, including the accusation of appeasement, an accusation which rightly rose to a massive level after Chamberlain succeeded him.

First, it would be right to acquit him of one charge, that he had deliberately misled the electorate in 1935 by concealing from it his decision to rearm. The words which have been so often quoted against him were, in fact, used in Parliament: 'Supposing that I had gone to the country and said that Germany was rearming and that we must rearm, does anybody think that this pacific democracy would have rallied to that cry at that moment? I cannot think of anything that would have made the loss of the election from my point of view more certain.'

These twenty-one concluding words have been used as an admission that Baldwin put electoral considerations before those of national security. He was – as the context shows – talking not of the election which he called in November 1935 but of a hypothetical appeal to the country in 1933 or 1934. 'I am speaking', he said, 'of 1933 or 1934.' In fact, electoral considerations were never predominant. Disarmament was his considered, carefully worked-out policy on international grounds. Indeed, two days *before* the famous 'pacifist' by-election at East Fulham, when the National Government candidate was defeated because of the public desire for disarmament, the Cabinet had already decided – in secret of course – to seek 'the limitation and reduction of world armaments'. It was a decision reached despite the appeal from the service ministers in favour of immediate rearmament, and despite the Air Minister's firm declaration to Baldwin that 'a much more substantial increase' would command 'widespread support both in Parliament and in the country at large'. Baldwin ignored these appeals and assessments, denying the urgency of the danger, and putting a lower estimate on German air potential than did his service chiefs, and Churchill. Then to the amazement of those who followed Baldwin's lead in 1934 in belittling Churchill and denying his air forecasts, six months later Baldwin told the Commons that the Government had been 'completely wrong' in its previous estimate of German air strength.

By the time of the 1935 general election he had announced a programme of substantial rearmament, but it was not as large a programme as his service chiefs or advisers believed necessary. The real charge against him is not that he misled the electorate on rearmament, but that he never got on with the programme he announced. Indeed, Chamberlain was persistently at him to cut it ack. Chancellors have the duty of querying all spending programmes, not least efence. By the late Thirties, it is now clear, the Chancellor's arguments did ot even rest mainly on concern for the public purse. So far as Chamberlain nd his relations with Horace Wilson are concerned, it was rapidly acquiring e nature of a conspiracy, as will be seen in a later chapter.

Baldwin's own approach to rearmament was peculiarly convoluted. He made series of announcements about increased provision for defence expenditure, articularly on the Royal Air Force. But he combined them in his own mind, nd more elliptically in his public pronouncements, with a search for multi-teral disarmament. He wanted disarmament in order to avoid an arms race, ut on the basis that in any arms levels to be agreed, Britain would disarm ss than others, because of the need to 'catch up', to overtake the disparities hich had arisen in preceding years when other European nations had increased eir arms more rapidly than Britain. In any agreement, as he said, some ountries would have to come down, and others go up. It was, indeed, an even ore complicated argument: the 'catching up' process would be concentrated ore on the 'qualitative' value of the arms, than on sheer quantity, measured y millions of public expenditure, or the physical number of aircraft, tanks r guns.

In preceding years there had been an assumption for planning purposes that ere would be no major war for ten years ahead. This was abrogated, in the nse that at any time within the 'defence year' ahead it could be questioned. ut although the Committee of Imperial Defence recommended abrogation 1933, no action was taken for a year. Even then the decision, of which much as been made, was further complicated by the parallel search for disarmament, nd the 'qualitative' elaborations. But in 1933 Hitler withdrew from the Dis-mament Conference and the League of Nations; his mind in any event was ore directed to 'qualitative' questions than anyone, in his case, to qualitative armament. His pocket battleships threatened to revolutionize naval warfare nd render much of Britain's ageing fleet out of date. Even here disarmament as a problem: when Baldwin's Cabinet in 1928 had considered the naval pro-amme, the Admiralty pundits warned ministers that any decision to build arships competitive with Germany would be in default of the Washington aval Agreement setting out limits as between the US, Britain and Japan!

In 1933, while defining Japan as the immediate but lesser threat, Baldwin id: 'We take Germany as the ultimate potential enemy, against whom our long range" defence policy must be directed.' The 1934 Air Estimates were fact lower than those of the previous year. This was despite his famous warn-g of 1932: 'The bomber will always get through. The only defence is offence, hich means that you have to kill more women and children more quickly than e enemy if you want to save yourselves ...' This statement caused desperate guments and competing interpretations. Those pressing for rearmament who ok comfort from these words interpreted them as meaning that Baldwin in-nded to rearm against the bomber. But others were more concerned to inter-ret him as meaning that since the bomber would always get through, what as the purpose of rearmament? Churchill, who had been warning against the erman menace, was particularly concerned.

Perhaps Baldwin was confusing himself, as well as others, by his complicated fferential rearmament–disarmament theories. Perhaps he was just playing for ne. In fact he was *losing* time every year, and falling behind. From then on the Cabinet and its Defence Committee put as great an emphasis on presentation – how shall we set this out to Parliament? – as on the mechanics and quantity of arms orders.

The Disarmament Conference ploughed deeper and deeper into the sand. Churchill was the first to warn publicly about the secret rearmament on which Germany had embarked. For Hitler it was not only the reversal of Versailles. There were seven million unemployed when he became German Chancellor. On the 1934 Air Estimate, Baldwin warned:

> If all our efforts for an agreement fail, and if it is not possible to obtain equality in such matters as I have indicated, then any Government of this country – a National Government more than any and *this* Government – will see to it that in our strength and our power this country shall no longer be in a position inferior to any country within striking distance of our shores.

That meant Germany. But the Estimates he was presenting were lower than those of the previous year. Again, when the weakness of Britain's air strength was exposed, and his air-strength pledge was shown to be a sham, a new phrase, 'air power', led to the presentation of a new and mystical concept in which air power became something different from the number of aircraft available to the RAF. The new concept was in some esoteric sense transcendental, and as Germany's air strength rose above that of Britain, it was used more and more, though it signified nothing. By the time Germany had twice as many aircraft as Britain, the argument reached its apogee: Germany could not compete, they urged, in air power. It was a strange emphasis on 'air power' that led the Cabinet to close down one of the few RAF training stations.

Chamberlain, as will be seen in a later chapter, was budgeting for a much more stretched-out defence production programme. Why all this insistence on the obsessional date of 1939?

The 1923 programme of forty-one squadrons by 1933 had not been achieved. It was stretched for a further year while Germany was drawing rapidly ahead, to see whether disarmament would make progress. MacDonald submitted Britain's proposals to the Geneva Disarmament Conference in March, and pressed for a *reduction* from 694,000 to 400,000 in the French army, while the Conference was discussing an increase in that of Germany!

After the Silver Jubilee celebrations in May 1935, the sorry, shambling played-out figure of MacDonald left Downing Street. On 7 June, Baldwin formed his third administration.

Unfortunately, most of his Cabinet appointments were pathetic: Hoare to the Foreign Office – he was later to regret that, though it was certainly arguable at the time that any substitute for Simon could only be an improvement – and Cunliffe-Lister to Air, a competent and cultured politician, but not one to make the rearmament programme that was on paper into a programme of hardware on the ground and in the air, by mobilizing Britain's industrial resources.

Hoare did not last long. Mussolini had invaded Abyssinia, at the very time when the Peace Ballot in Britain had recorded an overwhelming verdict for collective security and the League of Nations. He used poison gas against unarmed tribesmen – 'The man,' said Baldwin, 'is a savage.'

Baldwin, while authorizing Eden to seek to buy off Mussolini with compensations elsewhere, plus some of the Abyssinian lowlands, compensating Abyssinia with tracts of land from British Somaliland, had earlier sent Hoare to Geneva tell the League that Britain stood under the Government for 'steady and llective resistance to all acts of unprovoked aggression'. He further sent a bstantial naval force to the Mediterranean, but his lead was not followed either France or, regrettably, the Dominions, and Baldwin had to disclaim y intention of 'taking isolated action in this dispute'. He was particularly arful of Italian retaliation in Malta or Alexandria.

Hoare went to the Continent at the end of the year. His remit was clear, it, without any authority, he drew up a pact with Laval, the French Foreign inister, proposing an Italian takeover on the basis of a lethal carve-up of Haile lassie's kingdom which conceded to Mussolini vast areas going beyond those s troops had captured. Eden, seeing the telegrams, expressed alarm. Baldwin first followed a Prime Minister's normal reaction – back your man, whatever ur doubts. The Cabinet, with Neville Chamberlain in the lead, were in a ood to dissociate; Cunliffe-Lister was in a state of resignation. Baldwin, as ime Ministers will, took Hoare gently by the arm, and the deed was done. len became Foreign Secretary. Vansittart, head of the Foreign Office, later be moved upstairs by Chamberlain who wanted none of his anti-Hitler ughness, had been a party to the Paris sellout; his judgment on the Hoare–aval pact was: 'The aggressor was getting more than he had, though less than would take.' This was true; Mussolini ended by taking the lot, and Haile lassie was a refugee in England until finally, during the war, a small British rce sent the Italians packing.

Even when Baldwin was uttering anti-Hitler warnings which could be selec-ely interpreted as bloodcurdling, he was refusing to set up a Ministry of pply. It was not only that, as in 1914–16, he was refusing to offer war con-acts to engineering companies outside the arms field; the established contrac-rs were underemployed. A programme of 'shadow' factories was announced. hey remained shadows for too long. Potential aircraft workers were not receiv-g their essential training.

Following Baldwin's rejection of the need for a Ministry of Supply, there is pressure for a Ministry of Defence. Churchill's name was inevitably entioned, not only because of his First World War experience but because s once discounted and indeed abused warnings were being recognized as justi-d. The Baldwin Establishment message was that you should hold the trump rd in reserve; alternatively that it would provoke Hitler. Baldwin decided play safe. He appointed a lawyer with no defence or production experience, r Thomas Inskip.

It was Baldwin's error to appoint safe men who could be expected to produce thing but reassurance. Inskip let him down. He had access to all the figures d to the urgent, desperate representations of the defence chiefs. He produced r the Cabinet a most devastating statement on Britain's inferiority in defence uipment right along the line, and undeniable evidence that the gap would ow in the years immediately ahead. Baldwin had another disappointment in s choice for Air Minister of Viscount Swinton, formerly Philip Lloyd-aeme, who had later changed his name after a bequest to Philip Cunliffe-ster. No man, surely, could be more safe or more amenable. But, contrary the reputation he had earned in the earlier Baldwin age, he went into the r Ministry, opened the books, and came into the Cabinet room with all guns azing.

The Defence White Paper of 1936 spoke of increasing the Air Force by 250 aircraft to an eventual total of 1750 first-line machines for home defences. But Swinton was reporting that German production would reach 1500 by April 1937, and 2000 later. That very week, Hitler ordered German troops to march into the Rhineland, forbidden to him by the Versailles Treaty. Baldwin's reaction was to warn his colleagues *against* any action in concert with France. The danger, he said, was that Germany could be crushed, 'but it would probably only result in Germany going Bolshevik'. Anthony Eden warned the Cabinet that unless Britain and France acted together, war with Germany would be a certainty in the near future, under far less favourable conditions. But despite Eden's warnings, Baldwin firmly and successfully resisted any joint Anglo–French action. There were also at the time several attempts by both Inskip and Swinton to bring about emergency powers in industry for arms production. Vansittart, for the Foreign Office, supported the Defence and Air Ministry views. But Sir Samuel Hoare and Neville Chamberlain warned of the great shock to the country and the 'grave financial consequences', and Baldwin sided with them. The result was that Britain fell two years behind in the arms race – with disastrous results in 1940, when all the deficiencies Baldwin had been warned of by his experts from years before were seen to have been both real and grave.

That Baldwin himself knew of these deficiencies is beyond doubt, for twice in 1936 he received a defence deputation of senior Conservative Privy Councillors, MPs and peers, led by Austen Chamberlain, who had been his Foreign Secretary for five years and was also a former Chancellor of the Exchequer. The first meetings were on 28 and 29 July, two whole days of intense discussion. The deputation expressed its 'grave anxiety and doubts' about the adequacy of Britain's defence programme, listing in great detail the relative air, army, navy and other defence weaknesses, and warning with great accuracy of Germany's military capability and of her intentions. Churchill, who was a member of the deputation, urged Baldwin to make contracts in the United States for aviation material. Lord Trenchard urged a higher standard of Air Force recruitment. Grave deficiencies in reserves of all sorts were pointed out. Churchill stressed that if Baldwin were to take the trade unions into his confidence, they too would respond to the emergency. Baldwin's answer was that Germany would not move west, but east. He then added: 'I should not break my heart' and he reiterated: 'I do not believe she wants to move west because west would be a difficult programme for her.' Baldwin then told the deputation (his words remained secret for the next thirty-five years):

> I am not going to get this country into a war with anybody for the League of Nations or anybody else or for anything else. There is one danger ... supposing the Russians and Germans got fighting and the French went in as allies of Russia ... you would not feel you were obliged to go and help France, would you? If there is any fighting in Europe to be done, I should like to see the Bolshies and the Nazis doing it.

Baldwin did not answer any of the specific points, nor did Inskip, the Minister for Coordination of Defence, who was present. But he sent the details to the Air Ministry and War Office, who in the main points upheld them. 'It is agreed,' replied the Air Ministry, 'that the potential war output of the British aircraft industry is not equal to that of the Germans.' No steps, they added, had yet been taken 'to deal with the question of *war* supply.' Yet when the eputation called again on Baldwin four months later, he continued to deprecate their warnings, having again refused – two weeks before – to set up a Ministry of Supply. As for his having told the first deputation that an earlier rearmament programme 'might have lost the general election when it came', Churchill answered that publicly:

> I have heard it said that the Government had no mandate for rearmament until the general election. Such a doctrine is wholly inadmissible. The responsibility of Ministers for the public safety is absolute, and requires no mandate. It is in fact the prime object for which Governments came into existence.
>
> The Prime Minister had the command of enormous majorities in both Houses of Parliament, ready to vote for any necessary measures of defence. The country has never yet failed to do its duty when the true facts have been put before it, and I cannot see where there is a defence for this delay.

The climax of Baldwin's neglect of the defence issue came in January and February 1937, when Lord Swinton with all the air figures in front of him pointed out how Baldwin's parity pledge had become quite obsolete, and that German air strength – in 1934 still below Britain's – would by 1939, on existing programmes, be far in excess. But Neville Chamberlain had the last word. 'Was it really necessary,' he asked, 'to stick rigidly to a date in 1939 [*sic*] for completion of our programme?' To this, Baldwin made no protest, and his Cabinet concurred in playing out even the existing air programme to 1941, despite the fact that this would give Germany four years of known air superiority in which to pursue her European ambitions undeterred by any fear of British ability to force her to call a halt. Right up to the end of the Baldwin ministry, after the Coronation in 1937, Baldwin was refusing to back Swinton in an adequate air programme.

But in the autumn of 1936, a different crisis hit the headlines, temporarily enhancing Baldwin's reputation, and diverting interests from defence. In the autumn of 1936, the crisis over the King's wish to marry Mrs Simpson was simmering, known to the cognoscenti and readers of certain low-circulation newsletters. It was blown wide open by Bishop Blunt of Bradford, who had not heard the rumours but whose sermon queried the King's poor record of church attendance. Understandably the press exploded: they all knew the story, and each feared that a competitor would use the Blunt sermon to trigger off the crisis.

Baldwin was concerned with two things: the reaction of Parliament and of the Dominions. He was firm, fatherly, and above all conscious of his constitutional duty. No one could have done it better, and the waters closed over the crisis as though it had never been.

After the Coronation of King George VI he resigned, full of honour. Few Prime Ministers have left in such a universal harmony of encomia. It was too early to blame him for having nursed Chamberlain as his unavoidable successor, and his record on rearmament was less well known to his party. In these days the major parties elect their leaders, in Government as well as in Opposition.

Baldwin could have ensured that Chamberlain was not the heir apparent. He should have nursed Eden, the young idol of a generation extending far beyond his own party. He departed at sixty-seven, the last Prime Minister to

Stanley Baldwin leaving Downing Street during the Abdication crisis of 1936.

go voluntarily – not defeated, humiliated in Parliament, rejected by the electorate, or ill – until 1976.

He left office with praise abounding round his ears. But as the drift to war continued, and the Chamberlainite policies were unfolded, the praise turned to blame. The succeeding years were unkind to the point of cruelty. He was reviled first as a secret appeaser, second as having sponsored a more self-admitted one. After his death in 1947 there was none to speak well of his memory until, in 1949, Churchill praised him. Baldwin had at least backed and encouraged Churchill when a Prime Minister's backing and encouragement was needed. The fact that on the rise of Hitler he failed to match the threat by an adequate and urgent defence programme was exactly measured and demonstrated by his failure to listen to the warnings of Churchill, and even of those of his ministers best fitted to assess the danger, and to act upon them.

8

Ramsay MacDonald

ASA BRIGGS, REVIEWING David Marquand's authoritative life of James Ramsay MacDonald in March 1977, refers to the tendency of writers to deal with Labour's first Prime Minister not so much as a man as a myth, or rather two myths:

> There seemed to be two MacDonalds, one the socialist pioneer, the other the prime minister of a – spurious – 'national' government. The drama like that of Henry IV had two parts, although the sequence was different. Socialist historians tended to ignore or at least to underplay MacDonald Part I; non-socialist historians were unimpressed by MacDonald Part II, some of them dismissing him, as Churchill once did, as a 'Boneless Wonder'.

There was no Socialist leader whose oratory and power of organization did more to create the Labour Party than MacDonald. Many had contributed – Keir Hardie's campaigning zeal above all, the leaders of the TUC at the turn of the century, but thousands of unknown figures as well, brought to the ideal of a new society, some by religious inspiration, some by the teachings of Socialist writers. They were of widely varying ideas and aims, equally of class and background, visionary Socialists or unideological LibLabs. But they were men and women dedicated to building somehow, sometime, but here in the Britain they knew, a 'loftier' society out of the evils, the ugliness, the squalor of nineteenth-century industrialism, to ending for ever the inequality, the exploitation, the grinding inhumanity of man to man which they saw all around them. They drew their inspiration from Merrie England or from dry statistics, they sang their widely differing battle-hymns. It was MacDonald who had to create, from the strains of Ebenezer Elliott's 'When wilt thou save the people' of Corn Law days, Edward Carpenter's 'England Arise', 'Jerusalem', the 'Internationale', the 'Red Flag', from 'These things shall be', a new harmony.

In 1906, when Ramsay led the celebrations at Queen's Hall of the election of twenty-nine Labour MPs to Westminster, he saw it as a new era:

> Up to now the Labour Party had always been subordinate in politics. The cottage had had to fight for the palace, and the palace had always been neglecting to legislate in the interests of the cottage. The cottage the previous month had said: 'I am going to fight for myself and I am going to work and legislate for myself, because my experience has been that if I don't do it nobody else will do it for me.'

The new Parliamentary Party would carry into the House of Commons the fight for the Right to Work Bill, social reform and the repeal of Victorian legislation limiting trade union activities, and it would campaign and proselytize for a new world order. The new Parliamentary apprentices, some of whom were to achieve Cabinet rank in wartime coalition years before any of the twenty-nine entered a Labour Cabinet, learnt their craft under the leadership of Keir Hardie, organized by MacDonald. They had to face the disillusion of the early years, the disappointment when their numbers fell, the new Jerusalem deferred. An even greater blow to MacDonald himself was the death in 1911 of Margaret MacDonald, his wife, a greatly-loved heroine of Labour people. I remember, as a small boy in the early Twenties, studying the Cooperative movement's wall calendar in the kitchen, with an entry for each day of a historic event from past years. One entry said 'Margaret MacDonald died, 1911'. My mother explained that she was a good woman, and everybody loved her.

Previous page Ramsay MacDonald.

But all the time MacDonald was planning, speaking all over the country, writing articles and draft programmes and manifestos, organizing, taking to heart Keir Hardie's words of years earlier: 'Look to the register.' When MacDonald became leader of the Party there was a ceremony at which Keir Hardie presented to him portraits of himself and Margaret.

> No words were required from any quarter to testify to the value in connection with the Labour Party. As was written in St Paul's Cathedral regarding Wren, 'If you want his monument, look around ...' Many are the influences which went to the building up of a great movement, but without the man to rally round, no movement recorded in history had ever found its way to success ... It would be sheer folly on his part to tell them of MacDonald's ability, of his past, of his energy, and of his voracity for hard work. He could hit hard, but he could work hard; and it was for the work he had done that they were paying him this tribute of their respect.

MacDonald was not one of those who believed that Lloyd George's social reforms, pensions and national insurance, would steal the clothes from the new Party, or that the new Britain could arise only out of insupportable misery:

> It is not a society unnerved with panic and distracted with hunger that advances towards socialism, but one in which a certain success in satisfying physical needs has awakened mental desires and made easy the exercise of the social instincts and consciousness of the individual ...

MacDonald suffered a severe reverse, in party terms, during the First World War. He was opposed to the war when Labour MPs were supporting it and furnishing members to the wartime Government. The Party was hopelessly split, and, right or wrong over the central issue, he showed great courage in sticking to his opinion. At no time did he join those who would have been content to see a German victory. He was in favour of a negotiated settlement of a war which he felt had been brought about by dynastic rivalries. But despite the Somme and Passchendaele, or because of them, he secured little popular support for his views, especially in the trade union movement. He lost his seat at Leicester, but was back in 1922 for Aberavon. The reaction of the Party to the post-war Lloyd George years soon provided a reconciliation, and MacDonald led the Party in the 1922 and 1923 general elections. In 1923, as we have seen, Labour was the second most powerful party in the House, and Asquith saw him into Downing Street, carefully safeguarded against adventurism by the ever-present threat of a Liberal veto.

Relations with Russia were re-established by MacDonald in his dual role of Prime Minister and Foreign Secretary, and it was relations with Russia, or a perversion of them in the Zinoviev incident, which compounded the Campbell case. There has been wonderment about MacDonald's refusal to accept the Liberal motion for an independent inquiry; the reason was almost certainly that the Prime Minister was fully involved in the Attorney-General's decision. Successive Prime Ministers have always quoted that case as a reason for leaving such decisions to the Law officers without political interference.

The Baldwin Government's four and a half years of office were a lean time for MacDonald. His main achievement was to keep his Party together, despite the ideological new Left, and the ILP's forays in search of 'Socialism in our time'. In 1929–31 he again led a minority Government, Labour now being the

biggest single Party in the House. He did not, this time, seek to combine the Foreign Office with the premiership, and appointed Henderson Foreign Secretary, to the intense annoyance of J.H. Thomas, who complained that he had been tricked. Relations between MacDonald and Henderson, we now know, were stormy, but Thomas would have been a disaster.

Two years later MacDonald was head, not of a coalition Government, but of a Government formed – on one interpretation – of a minor Labour defection of a few ministers and hardly any back-benchers. A more accurate interpretation of the facts is analysed below. MacDonald never intended such an outcome: almost to the end he assumed that his Party would follow him in what he believed – what financial pressures had forced him to believe – was necessary.

The previous chapter has attempted to describe relations between MacDonald and Baldwin. Though he felt himself let down by the Tory conduct of the 1931 election which he himself called, no Conservative minister attacked Labour with anything approaching the venom of Snowden, and MacDonald led the coalition for nearly four more years, until a premature political senility brought about his retirement. He still embodies a legend of betrayal to the Labour Party, without having secured a word of tribute from those who then and since have supported the formation of the coalition. Perhaps, just as it was his record which has besmirched Baldwin's reputation, so it was Baldwin's record in failing to react to the menace of Hitler's resurgent Germany which accorded to MacDonald a retrospective verdict of guilty by association. In fact it was the world depression which destroyed Labour's first Prime Minister, as it destroyed Governments throughout Europe, as well as Hoover in America.

MacDonald's achievement was to ensure that the Labour Party he did so much to create replaced the Liberals as the natural alternative to the Conservatives: in this the Lloyd George post-war years and the fatal split between Asquith and Lloyd George played an undeniable part.

Harold Macmillan, in his latest book *The Past Masters*, begins his chapter on Ramsay MacDonald with this judgment:

> Historians will regard the rise of the Labour Party in the first quarter of the twentieth century as the most dramatic change in the long history of party politics in England. Roundheads and Cavaliers, Whigs and Tories, Liberals and Conservatives ... until 1914 the two-party system seemed unshaken and unshakable. The Lib–Lab and Labour group members would be no different in their relationship with the Liberal Party than had been the old radicals, like Cobden and Bright towards Whigs such as Lord John Russell. They would grumble, bring pressure to bear, bargain, occasionally blackmail; but in the main they would see to it that a Liberal Government remained in power or that a Liberal Opposition was not broken up. Yet in 1923 a Labour Government was formed, which although in a minority in the House of Commons was still a true Labour Government, independent both of Conservatives and Liberals.

Since 1922, Labour has been, when not *in* Government, the *alternative* party of Government.

Ramsay MacDonald was born on 12 October 1866 in the humblest surroundings, in Lossiemouth, in the north of Scotland. No future Prime Minister, before or since, has come so far from such obscure beginnings.

After his school years he undertook some teaching, as an uncertificated pupil

Opposite Ramsay MacDonald on his twenty-first birthday in 1887, in the days when he was still a soap-box orator in Hyde Park.

Keir Hardie, the man whose campaigning zeal did more than anyone else to create the Labour Party.

teacher. When he was eighteen, he tried for a number of jobs all over Britain, and became assistant to a Bristol clergyman who was trying to set up a Boys' and Young Men's Guild at his church. He soon came under the influence of local Socialist groupings, beginning with the Social Democratic Federation, still dominated by Hyndman, and he became local SDF librarian. In 1885 the Federation ran three candidates in Nottingham, Hampstead and Kennington. They did badly, but the SDF was hit still harder by allegations that the candidates had been financed by 'Tory gold' to split the Liberal vote. MacDonald returned briefly to Lossiemouth, and then set out again for London. Tramping the streets for work, he got a job at ten shillings a week addressing envelopes for the National Cyclists' Union, and later a City job at 12s. 6d. He was active in various small Socialist groups, and witnessed Bloody Sunday in November

1887, when the troops and police broke up a free speech demonstration in Trafalgar Square. He went to Birkbeck College to study science, but had a serious breakdown in health. His next job was as private secretary to a tea merchant with radical commitments – who was in fact elected MP in a by-election in 1889. For a while MacDonald was involved in Scottish Home Rule at the same time as Lloyd George's involvement in Home Rule for Wales.

In the late 1880s he joined the Fabian Society, on one occasion standing in for George Bernard Shaw in a lecture series. He became secretary of an odd organization called the 'Fellowship of the New Life', and was being talked of as a possible secretary of the Fabian Society.

In 1886 the TUC, which throughout this period was pushing ahead more coherently than any of the competing Socialist movements, set up a Labour Electoral Committee aimed at pressing Labour candidates on Liberal Associations. Others on the left were urging Labour to set up a separate party, like the Irish, to put pressure on existing parties. None of these devices produced much result, and in 1893 the Independent Labour Party was set up in Bradford. MacDonald, after helping the ILP candidate in a by-election in Sheffield, joined the organization. In 1894 he was elected to the executive committee of the Fabian Society.

The emergent Socialist organizations were going through a period of stress, as new groupings entered into competition with one another. Fabians and others were in competition with the new Second International, whose conference was held in London.

MacDonald came out strongly against the Boer War, and resigned from the Fabian Society executive when they refused, by a majority, to issue a statement condemning the war. The Fabians followed the practice, then as now, of not issuing statements on issues of current affairs.

In 1898 the TUC carried a resolution moved by the ASRS (railwaymen), urging trade unions to support the working-class social parties, and elected a Parliamentary Committee. Soundings were taken and the proposal was ratified at the Plymouth Congress in 1899. In December meetings were held between representatives of the ILP, SDF, Fabians and the Parliamentary Committee. Two months later a conference was held at the Memorial Hall, Farringdon Street, attended by 129 delegates, representing 570,000 members, to establish the new organization which became the Labour Party. MacDonald was elected its secretary.

In the 1906 general election, the new Party returned twenty-nine MPs, MacDonald again being elected for Leicester, running in double harness with the Liberals. The Party sat on the Opposition side of the House, though not in any way making common cause with the Conservative Opposition. They supported the more radical Government measures, and sought in Committee, with varying success, to put more spunk into the Liberal legislation. MacDonald and his colleagues supported the Government in their Bill to end the, to them, odious denominational Education Act of 1902, but went beyond the Government in pressing for totally secular education.

With Hardie's leadership subject to widespread criticism by Snowden and others, MacDonald's star rose, but it was Henderson who became chairman (i.e. in effect leader) of the Parliamentary Party. MacDonald played a small part in the Budget, but made his name with the so-called 'right-to-work' Bill, though failing to carry the second reading.

He successfully won a running battle with Hardie and the ILP, after the latter had supported a SDP (as the SDF was now called) candidate against Labour at the Newcastle by-election. In the January 1910 election, Labour, now joined by the mining MPs, had forty members, and in the November election forty-two.

MacDonald was despondent, not only with the splits in the Party, and the launching of maverick Labour candidates, but also about the poor impact of the Party in Parliament. As an independent party, Labour had not established itself. Henderson again became leader. The convention was that the leader retired after two years; Henderson retired. For a moment it appeared probable that MacDonald would succeed; he was in fact announced as the choice in the *Daily Telegraph* and *Daily Chronicle*. He was himself very unwilling; after all he was secretary to the Party and felt that that position would be put in jeopardy if he accepted the Parliamentary leadership. His sponsors sought to reassure him on that point, but had to return to him to say that there was not enough support for him. George Barnes, later a member of the wartime Government, was chosen. But the Party recovered its élan following the Osborne judgment in December 1904. This was a House of Lords judicial decision ruling, in a case affecting the ASRS, that it was illegal for a trade union to spend any part of its funds for political purposes. The Parliamentary Party now had a rallying-cry.

In 1911, on Barnes's resignation, MacDonald became chairman of the Parliamentary Party and the effective leader. Throughout the Parliamentary Labour Party's history until 1970, there was no election of leader as such. He was chairman. But it was to the chairman, *de facto* leader, that the Sovereign was to turn in 1923 and in 1945. (It was only in 1970, after an election defeat, that I separated the PLP chairmanship from the leadership, and invited the PLP to elect a separate chairman. But in 1923, 1929, 1964 and 1974 it was the elected chairman who was sent for by the Palace to form an administration.)

The outbreak of the First World War presented a problem for the Party. MacDonald, though leader, was opposed to the war, and when the PLP by a majority decided to vote for the Asquith Government's war credits of £100 million, MacDonald immediately resigned. In political terms he had a bad war. While playing a part as a back-bencher, and in the Party in the country, he stood by while one Labour leader after another joined the Asquith and Lloyd George administrations.

The peace settlement, attacked by Keynes and the Liberal establishment, helped him to re-establish himself. At the end of the war he was out of Parliament, and as late as 1922 was writing that we have 'nothing to cherish but our memories'. In 1922 he was elected for Aberavon, to a Parliament where Labour was for the first time the second biggest party. Baldwin's quixotic election of 1923, to redeem the Bonar Law pledge on protection, produced the 1923 electoral stalemate, followed as we have seen by Asquith's decision to give Labour its head while binding its feet.

Asquith's decision to give Labour the opportunity of forming a Government in January 1924, and his vote on the King's Speech to dispatch Baldwin, meant that the first Labour Government was in leading strings. Had it headed a Parliamentary majority, the reaction of the Establishment at home, and Governments and financiers abroad, would have been to scream red revolution, if not a Bolshevik takeover. But every action they took was dependent on Asquith's

Opposite The widower: Ramsay MacDonald with two of his daughters in 1917.

endorsement: one false or wildly ideological move and he could withdraw their right to govern. This in fact happened on the Campbell case, as we have seen, when MacDonald rejected the Liberal amendment and was out of office for four and a half years.

The Labour Government was formed on 22 January 1924, and was to last a little over nine months. In many quarters there was more amusement at the sight of the Socialist ministers going to kiss hands, dressed in the most formal Court dress, than concern. Cartoonists and countesses were united in feeling that these men were safe and conformist.

In fact their record was not unimpressive. MacDonald insisted on taking the Foreign Office himself, and it is certainly arguable that this double burden might have made him less vigilant over the issue which finally brought him down. His conduct of foreign affairs demonstrated an interesting freshness of approach. He had to handle at once the difficult situation in the Ruhr, occupied by the French a year earlier when Germany defaulted on the terms of the reparations settlement. MacDonald succeeded in getting France and Germany to agree to a new settlement, drawn up by a transatlantic group of ministers headed by the American General Dawes, later in the year to be elected Vice-President of the US. It was widely accepted as an impressive act of independent conciliation, based on holding the balance between the quarrelling French and Germans. He was less fully committed than many of his idealistic supporters to the concept of the League of Nations, though he personally visited Geneva, the first British Prime Minister to do so. He made a great impression with his speech pressing for the Germans to be admitted, and played a considerable part in the creation of the 'Geneva Protocol', interpreting and partly rewriting the Covenant. The provisions for sanctions against an aggressor, capable of involving military action, for which he pressed, were anathema to some of his pacifist supporters, and the issue was still unresolved when Labour lost office.

He improved relations with the Soviet Union, but without any starry-eyed nonsense about 'Left speaking to Left'. His approach was based on hard-headed negotiations on trade – including the first Anglo–Soviet trade agreement – debts and loans. But any agreement with the Soviets aroused criticism on the right, which came to a head with the Campbell case.

On the domestic front the record was indifferent. Snowden as Chancellor was orthodox and safe. A committed free trader, he cut indirect taxes by £29 million and direct taxation by £14 million, claiming that his Budget was the 'greatest step ever taken towards the Radical idea of the free breakfast table'. But unemployment, though falling a little, was still obdurately high, and MacDonald and Snowden came under heavy pressure from the ILP and Labour back-benchers to take emergency action, including electrification of the railways, on which finally Government policy was announced, though not implemented. The greatest domestic success of the nine months was in housing. John Wheatley, the brilliant left-wing Clydesider, as Housing Minister, introduced a Bill to encourage local authorities, by substantial subsidies, to embark on imaginative programmes of building houses to rent. The building industry was called in, and encouraged to expand its capacity by the prospect of a long-term housing programme.

C.P. Trevelyan, the Minister of Education, also created a reputation. He withdrew the notorious Circular 1190, which the previous Government had

sued to force a reduction in local government expenditure. Local education ıthorities were now encouraged by Trevelyan to go ahead. His stated policy as that 'every child should have a full opportunity for a career in life'. More an that, he carved a reputation as a highly successful administrator, and added that reputation in the 1929–31 Government. Labour could, in fact, after l, govern.

The first Labour Government. From left to right: MacDonald, J. H. Thomas and Arthur Henderson leave Buckingham Palace after the meeting of the Privy Council, January 1924.

In the 1924 general election, the Conservatives made 155 gains and had 413 PS; Labour lost 40, cutting their total to 151; the Liberals lost 118, with only members in the House. But the Labour vote rose by a million to 5,400,000. The four and a half years in opposition provided a long and frustrating period for MacDonald. The ILP, becoming more a ginger group than the driving force of the Party, went off to campaign for 'Socialism in our time'. A period in opposition is difficult enough for the leader of any party. Its leader, and his Shadow Cabinet, have to spend each week being forced to say yes or no to a question he never wanted to hear put, a challenge embodying what for him is the wrong question to the answer. It is a question which the Government pose because they have decided the general direction of policy. In the words of the old saying, in response to the question 'Which is the way to Ballymena?' it is no use for the Opposition to reply: 'If I wanted to go to Ballymena, I wouldn't start from here.' The starting-point is determined by the Government's own policy and actions. The Opposition's policy might involve totally different geography, but Parliamentary debate, particularly on legislation, but also on the Government's executive actions, is on subjects dictated by the Government's strategic planning and tactical responses.

If this is the fate of any Opposition leader, that of a Labour leader is further complicated by the week by week and, at times, almost hour by hour requirement to keep his Party together and driving to the same goal. Parties of the left are more prone to split than those of the right. Even if the broad strategy of policy is agreed, there will be those who want to move more rapidly and others who will want to move more slowly to the desired objective. But in a party of the left there will be a still deeper division, between the ideologists and theologians who seek a fundamentalist approach, and the more moderate, pragmatic group, no less idealist but less prone to determine the reaction to any situation in terms of its relevance to some revealed truth, some ultimate state of society.

MacDonald was not a theorist, still less a fundamentalist. David Marquand has rightly described him as an 'evolutionary utopian': once you removed the fear and the want from the lives of men, there would be no wickedness and no class war. As Asa Briggs put it in his review of Marquand: 'His socialism was ultimately a socialism of faith not of works ...'

Guide thou my feet, I do not ask to see
The distant scene, one step enough for me.

In one of my two periods as Opposition Leader I described the Labour Party as a stagecoach: 'As long as you keep it rattling along at a quick pace, the occupants are either too exhilarated or too seasick to cause any trouble. It's when you stop at crossroads and everyone gets out and pores over the maps that you get trouble.'

That is why a Labour leader places more faith in the manifesto, or policy statement, than in discussion about the colour of the wallpaper in the ultimate Utopia, than is the case with parties of the right.

The Labour leader who took a different line was Hugh Gaitskell following Labour's third successive election defeat in 1959. The wake took place at a weekend Party conference in Blackpool. Hugh Gaitskell, opening the debate, sought to call the conference to look towards the future, with a noteworthy sociological analysis of what ordinary families were seeking in Harold Macmillan's 'you've never had it so good' Britain. He was seeking to move the Party from 'Clause IV', the famous statement of Party objectives of the 1918 Constitution, drafted by Sidney Webb – 'the nationalization of the means of production, distribution and exchange'. Only the fundamentalists had seen it as a

›licy declaration – more practical Party members as the Party's equivalent ˙ the detailed architectural passages of the Book of Revelations. Uproar fol-wed. Gaitskell was saved, so far as the conference was concerned, by Aneurin evan's reconciling speech – his last conference speech before his fatal illness.

But when Labour returned to London the National Executive Committee, en still dominated by the right wing, particularly right-wing unions, moved . It was the most traumatic period the Party had faced since the war. After battle which began in great bitterness and ended in a spirit of reconciliation, document was agreed by all the near-thirty membership of the NEC, except r Harry Nicholas. *Labour in the Sixties* embodied the Saint's prayer of 'Lord, ve me chastity, but not yet.' Clause IV was repeated as an ultimate objective, God's good time but not in ours. Meanwhile a completely practical set of oposals was agreed for the years ahead. *Labour in the Sixties* was moved at e 1960 conference by the present writer, and the debate was wound up by ugh Gaitskell. After three specific left-wing amendments had been rejected, e document was, to quote the chairman's summing up, and the official con-rence report, 'carried by acclamation'.

Labour was back on the doctrine of the practical manifesto, written in the rcumstances of the time, in advance of each general election: the doctrine at agreement on the manifesto, whether in Government or opposition, parti-larly in opposition, is always difficult to achieve, but once reached, each can sist on holding the other to strict compliance with it. What *Let us face the ture* of 1945 was for Attlee, or *Let us Work Together; Britain Will Win with abour* were during and after the two general elections of 1974 for a later genera-on, the hard-won compromise document *Labour and the Nation* was for Mac-onald, finally endorsed by the October 1928 Party conference at Birmingham. arquand's summary is worth quoting, not as the assessment of a document ly but as that of MacDonald and MacDonaldism:

> It consisted in essence of a high-minded, if sometimes prosy statement of the moral case for gradualist socialism, heavily flavoured with the scientific optimism of the day. With great skill, the Labour Party was portrayed as a movement of all classes, ranged against a small minority of property owners, and socialism as the creed, not only of the working class, but of all 'practical men and women' who wished to apply the 'resources of science to bring within the reach of all the conditions of a dignified and civilized existence'. Without haste and without rest, land, coal, power, transport and life insurance would be transferred to public ownership. Taxation would be 'scientifically adjusted' to the ability to pay, arms expenditure would be cut down; and the social services would be expanded. The ultimate goal was a 'Socialist Commonwealth' based on the conviction that cooperation was 'the Law of life'.

ı unemployment and the worsening economic position, *Labour and the ation* was virtually innocent of anything except platitudes.

The 1929 election did not only rob the Baldwin Government of its majority. nlike 1924, Labour, which was still in an overall minority in the House, were w the biggest single party. Baldwin resigned forthwith and MacDonald rmed his second administration.

He faced an unemployed total of a million, though internal economic pros-cts suggested a slow improvement. But a month before the November 1929 election, the United States had gone through the Stock Exchange crash, and the 'Great Depression' had begun. The US were so dominant that no country, advanced or developing, could escape the consequences. In the post-war world it has often been said that if America sneezes, the rest of the world catches pneumonia. 1931 was not a sneeze, or a cold, it was a convulsion which rapidly affected the economy of every other nation. Within a year the dole queues in Britain had doubled to two million, and were remorselessly set on course towards the three million figure.

No Government of any party which might have been formed would have been capable of dealing with this situation. None of the Government's advisers in the civil service, still less the dinosaurs of the Bank of England, had anything to contribute except a virulent insistence that what was a chronic deficiency of demand should be met by cutting demand still further, preferably in the most socially regressive way that could be devised. Outside Government service, Keynes, Kahn, Cole and Hobson were pressing for reflation and an unbalanced Budget. MacDonald in January 1930 set up the Economic Advisory Council, chaired by himself, with fifteen members including Keynes, R.H. Tawney and G.D.H. Cole, with H.D. Henderson on the secretariat, but, as Cole told me shortly afterwards, the reflationists were outnumbered by the orthodox and City voices. Lloyd George had fought the 1929 election on his New Deal programme, 'We Can Conquer Unemployment', and he had the utmost contempt for the official Treasury and City view, and for the MacDonald Government which seemed incapable of resisting it.

Inevitably, it was an unhappy Cabinet, and MacDonald tried one appointment after another to seek to devise an economic policy, with J.H. Thomas as Minister for Unemployment assisted by Tom Johnston, Sir Oswald Mosley and George Lansbury. Mosley, then a left-winger, was the only one to come forward with anything approaching an expansionist programme, including public control of industry, and of banking to ensure finance for development, and a boost to spending through increased pensions and allowances. He also advocated protection. But the Chancellor, Snowden, now totally embracing Cobdenism, not only opposed new protectionist measures but, as we have seen, was soon to be proposing the repeal of post-1918 legislation such as the Dyestuffs Act. The answer must be, Snowden insisted, *freer* trade and a balanced Budget. The effort to find an alternative policy was over; Mosley resigned (and his red shirt soon began to take on a blacker shade), and J.H. Thomas was sent to the Dominions Office. MacDonald announced that he was taking personal charge of the battle against unemployment, which speedily rose from 2 million to 2½ million. By this time, and despite the most rigid insistence on deflation, whose very irrelevance and perverse wrong-headedness ought of itself to have persuaded the markets of the soundness of the Government's policy, the pound sterling was under heavy pressure.

The 1929–31 Labour Government was dominated by the crisis. In this sense, at least, it died as it had lived. It is for this reason that so little attention was paid then, or since, to the Government's actions in other areas, particularly in the implementation of the positive proposals in *Labour and the Nation*. Plans were worked out for a massive roads programme to provide employment, but there were arguments about how much unemployed labour it could absorb, and, increasingly, fears about how the increased expenditure would sap foreign confidence in sterling. A great campaign for import boards and duties – 'registration fees' – on agricultural imports ran into the implacable opposition of Snowden and the free traders, and perished. Soon the emphasis was on international agreements to prevent tariffs from rising, as more and more countries turned to high tariffs and policies of self-sufficiency.

The preoccupation with the crisis gave MacDonald far less opportunity even than in the brief 1924 administration for developing his ideas in foreign policy. In 1929, unlike 1924, he was not his own Foreign Secretary. Arthur Henderson was appointed, and soon became the hero of a significant section of the Party and a wider area of the country for his internationalist views, his support of the League and his initiatives in disarmament.

Unfortunately he and MacDonald became more and more separated, active mutual hostility setting in. Time after time, Henderson was on the point of resignation, though he always held on, even though humiliated. There were abundant signs that MacDonald was briefing the press against his own Foreign Secretary. MacDonald insisted on taking charge of Anglo–American relations, and took personal control, too, of the negotiations at the London Naval Conference of 1930–1. The mutual limitation of naval armaments which was ultimately agreed was to be quoted by the relevant ministers in Baldwin's Cabinet against those who were pressing for rearmament against Hitler's naval plans.

One of the most important initiatives of the MacDonald ministry lay in progress to constitutional reform in India. Fostered mainly by the Viceroy, Lord Irwin (later Lord Halifax), and the India office, the plan was the first move to a substantial measure of self-government in the subcontinent. It was strongly opposed by most Conservatives, and as we have seen led to trouble for Baldwin in his own Party, not only in 1930–1 but in the subsequent 'National' Government.

Snowden was involved in a different area of international negotiations. A fresh round on reparations took place at the Hague. Snowden treated his European partners with brutality and contempt, refused to budge an inch, and returned a hero. He had a triumphant return, and the writer remembers the cheers which greeted him in his Colne Valley constituency as the man who had put all those foreigners in their place. The indefatigable Belgian secretary of the conference, M. Jaspar, was continually sent to the other finance ministers with the Iron Chancellor's repeated refusal of any concessions: 'You are doing first-rate, M. Jaspar, be not weary in well-doing.' But within a year, it was the Europeans who were saying that every million the stony Chancellor wrung out of his colleagues on that occasion cost Britain £10 million in the run on sterling that brought the Labour Government down and led to Snowden himself being shunted into a House of Lords appointment with more prestige than power.

Marquand's dramatic sixty-page account of the financial crises of 1931 which destroyed the Labour Government, split the Labour Party and ushered in the 'National' coalition Government is almost comparable in its inevitability with classical Greek tragedy – in inevitability but not in remoteness. Though it has been told many times before, the account, line by line, and shock by shock, reads almost like a trailer or dress rehearsal of the events of 1957–77. The same falling-off of confidence in sterling, the same reaction in the markets to each action of the Government, the same fetishism about Government expenditure, made even more articulate in 1931 than in the Seventies, by the market operators' insistence on a particular victim for expenditure cuts, the £1 per week

dole for the near three million unemployed. As the tragedy grew and the monetary operators moved in for the kill, it became increasingly clear that if the same amount of money could be saved by a cut in some other spending programme, it would not suffice: their target was no longer purely quantitative, subjective though even such quantitative targets invariably are – it had become qualitative and identified. The amount involved was £12½ million, saved by cutting the dole by ten per cent to eighteen shillings. By the time that the necessary credits were on offer, there could have been any combination of economies which would have failed to ensure their transfer to the vaults of the Bank of England.

MacDonald was the first Prime Minister to use an aeroplane. This photograph shows him leaving for London in response to an urgent summons.

The other fetish was the maintenance of gold payments on the basis of the parity fixed in 1925. The loss of gold had been so devastating that when the final demand was made and Britain's gold reserves were almost at vanishing point, the pound's gold backing could be held only if the credits were there within hours. It was for this that the Labour Government gave way to the coalition which, less than four weeks after its formation, went off gold, devalued the pound and introduced legislation to relieve the Bank of its statutory obligations under the Gold Standard Act of 1925.

The international currency crisis stemmed from the American Stock

Exchange crash. In May 1931 the powerful Austrian bank the Kreditanstalt failed. Germany's financial credit, already weak, could not withstand panic withdrawals of foreign funds. The German Chancellor, Bruning, and Foreign Secretary, visiting MacDonald, demanded the right to suspend reparation payments. On receiving a message from MacDonald, President Hoover proposed a year's moratorium on all such payments. Paris resisted, and a fortnight's negotiation began. In those two weeks, German reserves were drained dry, and on 13 July cash payments were stopped, and exchange controls introduced. MacDonald was warned that the backlash would fall on Britain, and on 15 July the Bank of England suffered heavy losses of a kind made painfully familiar in the 1950s, 60s and 70s.

By 1 August, a quarter of the Bank's reserves were gone. Urgent European consultations took place: MacDonald and Henderson visited Berlin; Henderson went to Paris. (This is the only divergence from modern practice: the Prime Minister would have been advised to be photographed on the golf course.) The Americans proposed a conference in London, mainly to bail out Germany. Things were not helped by growing strains between MacDonald and Henderson, who was playing his own hand in Paris, making somewhat illiterate proposals and telling MacDonald that they had come from the French, who were not all that averse to seeing Berlin further in the mire. A conference was arranged in London for 21 July, but the French refused to attend unless the Germans first agreed to wait on them in Paris. This occurred, but the Germans were told that the prospective French loan carried with it political obligations, namely the acceptance by the Germans of the terms of the peace settlement for ten years – i.e. until 1941. The French may not have realized that their activities were being welcomed by the entourage of an Austrian house-painter, one Schickelgrüber, who would himself be prancing in Paris before 1941 dawned.

MacDonald's London Conference was a failure. Britain had nothing to lend to Germany, nor could MacDonald move the French from their desire to grab political concessions from Germany as a condition for financial aid. He noted in his diary that France was to blame for the failure of the Hoover Plan: 'Again and again be it said: France is the enemy; we shall pay with our honour for that war.'

The first result of the breakdown of the London Conference was a further run on sterling. As Marquand says, 'What had begun as a liquidity crisis gradually turned into a confidence crisis.' Bank rate was raised (in the 1960s we learned that such action, instead of steadying the situation, was frequently regarded as a sign that the situation was more serious than had been feared). Speculators attacked sterling: they could not withdraw from Germany because of the freeze. The May Committee, consisting mainly of obsessive City ideologies, reported with a demand for action to close the Budget deficit partly caused – as in 1976 – by the cost of unemployment benefit at a time of high unemployment. Left-wing members of MacDonald's Economic Advisory Committee, such as Keynes and Cole, advised the Prime Minister to reject the May Report.

At a time of unprecedented deflation, the bankers and pundits were concerned with the dangers of inflation, since if not they, at least their mothers, had been frightened by past inflationary excesses. On 6 August the chairman of the London clearing banks issued a remonstrance to MacDonald demanding a restoration of confidence. The Bank lost another £60 million, and had little to rely on except the hope of French and American credits. MacDonald formally rejected Keynes's advice. What Britain faced was a classical run on sterling, with MacDonald showing neither the nerve nor the expertise to resist baleful advice. At such times the pressures indeed are strong.

Whereas the May Committee had forecast a Budget deficit of £120 million, Snowden told the 'economy' committee of the Cabinet that the latest figures indicated that it would be £170 million. The Prime Minister told the press that the Government was 'of one mind' in its determination to balance the Budget. It was not. Splits began to develop. Some proposed increased taxes rather than expenditure cuts. Snowden on 17 August demanded £90 million from increased taxation and a cut of £99 million in expenditure, £67 million of this from unemployment insurance – a twenty per cent cut in the standard rate of unemployment benefit, an increase in contributions from those at work and their employers, and a cut in the transitional benefit. It was Snowden's proposals which laid down the parameters of the next ten days' discussions of a now deeply divided Cabinet.

The Cabinet was in almost constant session. It soon became clear that the majority was against MacDonald and Snowden, and that Henderson was clearly with the majority. Snowden dug his heels in. He knew, and they knew, that his resignation would hit confidence more than all that had happened in previous weeks.

The Prime Minister and Snowden met the Opposition leaders and put them very fully in the picture. Meanwhile Henderson was consulting with the Parliamentary Labour Party's consultative committee – MacDonald should have done this himself, not left it to a colleague near to the point of dissociation.

He met the TUC. An always formidable Citrine – he was brutally ordering Attlee's ministers about fifteen years later – told MacDonald that the TUC could not 'acquiesce in new burdens on the unemployed'. Yet these were not only integral to the arithmetic, they were the King Charles's head of the Establishment. Bevin, never backward in forceful language, supported Citrine. MacDonald should have been warned. He was now buffeted about by the TUC in one direction, the City and industry in the other, by the majority of his Cabinet, backed by the Parliamentary Party, and by Snowden and other intransigents as well as a Conservative Party speaking in moving national terms, but with its political tail up. The Tory Party were now fully committed to dole cuts, and when in an economic crisis a Conservative Opposition so commits itself, there is little delay in the reaction of the markets. The image presented to the financial world was of indecision, dithering, delay, politicking, a divided administration: the image did not differ from the reality. Sterling came under fresh attack, and the bankers pressed still harder.

It was now only a question of time, but monetary movements were rationing the time. It was clear that the choice lay between insurance cuts and a fall, perhaps a collapse, in the value of sterling.

MacDonald was by now unequivocally pledged to staying on gold and holding sterling. The TUC had, if possible, to be educated; if not, to be fought. Fight it was. With a disintegrating Cabinet, MacDonald faced still stiffer demands from Sir Ernest Harvey, Deputy Governor of the Bank – Montagu Norman was ill – and those of his colleagues who were responsible for mobilizing US credit. The brokers' men were in.

Ramsay MacDonald in court dress.

Not only the brokers' men of Threadneedle Street, but the Americans too took a hand. The last hours of the Government were at pistol-point. A démarche, more in the form of an ultimatum, reached Downing Street. It was from the Federal Reserve Bank. The proposals for a public loan were not now practicable: all that could be made available was a short-term credit of between $100 million and $160 million. That could not be guaranteed until the next day, and then only if the French offered a similar credit. Although this was a direct communication from an American federal banker to the Prime Minister, it went on offensively and contumaciously to press the Government further. It would not be enough for the Government to make its expenditure proposals clear. MacDonald had to give an assurance that the Government's suggestions would have the 'sincere approval and support of the Bank of England and the City generally', for the FRB's ability to help would depend on the public's response to the Government's measures. It is arguable that, after the fall of France, Hitler's cavortings in the railway carriage at Compiègne, after the capitulation, showed more consideration for a defeated enemy than the Federal Reserve Bank showed for a British Government. The phrase 'banker's ramp' used by left-wingers after 1931 I have always regarded as overdrawn; Harrison of the FRB did his best to earn it, and all for a short-term conditional credit of £30–40 million.

MacDonald had made up his mind. Let those of his Cabinet colleagues who were with him stand up and be counted. He knew that if he made a fight of it, this could only be on the basis of a Government whose membership transcended party lines.

It became a matter of hours. The reserves were low. Even the mobilization of credits was becoming problematical. What was not in doubt was the stringent terms for the Budget and for unemployment benefit; that would be a condition of credits, if credits were to be available at all. The inevitable consequence for a man of MacDonald's convictions was a coalition Government. The only doubt was whether a Labour leader or a Conservative would head it. MacDonald could not know how many of his Cabinet would follow him, though clearly they would be a minority; had that not been so he could have carried the Labour Cabinet, despite resignations. Still less could he forecast how many back-benchers would support him. This must have been a problem for the King, who at one point considered inviting Baldwin to head the new Government, and Baldwin on his arrival thought that he would indeed be offered the commission to form a Government. But the King, possibly concerned with the repercussions within industry, settled for MacDonald, under whom Baldwin and his colleagues agreed to serve.

Where MacDonald had gone wrong was in his first political assessment, that once the Labour Cabinet realized the implications they would back him. He was not, until very late in the day, expecting a majority to refuse to accept the terms which he and Snowden regarded as essential. When he was disillusioned on that, he envisaged, it would seem, a very short-term coalition to put through the painful terms, after which normal party Government would resume. This again was unrealistic. Although Henderson showed a certain degree of cowardice, he could not resign against the terms, leaving MacDonald to do the dirty work, and return to share the burden. It is almost certain that, even so, MacDonald when the 'National' Government was formed, did not expect to be fighting a general election against the mass of his old Party. This as probably still his view after the split. But the pressures were too strong: erling was still vulnerable, and political uncertainty of any kind was danger-s. Perhaps too the strong reaction of his own colleagues, the cries of 'traitor' om the Party in the country, and the magisterial rebuke from his own constitu-ncy party caused him to grit his teeth.

The formation of the 'National' Government produced a short-term swing monetary movements, though the position remained highly vulnerable for onths. Given the objective facts of Britain's balance of payments, a Conserva-ve Government possesses, on any figure for that balance, a more favourable reign reaction. Twenty years ago the writer told the then Deputy Governor the Bank of England that at a rough guess the Conservatives would carry nfidence some £300 million better on international monetary movements an a Labour Government with the same objective import–export situation. onversely, in terms of internal inflation, a Labour Government is likely to ve a corresponding advantage in terms of trade union cooperation. So it has oved over the years. MacDonald as a Labour Prime Minister had to endure ery insult from the purveyors of credit; as head of a predominantly Conserva-ve Government he could get away with anything, even, as it proved, defection om the gold standard.

That it was a Conservative Government could not be disguised. Sankey, a iling and embittered Snowden, Jowitt, Aitchison, the Scottish Lord Advo-te, made up the cream of the ministerial team; fourteen back-benchers came 'National Labour'. The Liberals with Samuel, Simon, Sinclair and aac Foot were stronger in quality. MacDonald was a prisoner.

His hopes that the arrangements would be temporary and that the next elec-n would be fought on traditional party lines proved illusory. The legend the traitor MacDonald was already established in the industrial and mining eas. It persists today, still an effective charge against any Labour MP who thought to be treating with the enemy. He was wounded by the resolution ssed against him by his Seaham constituency party. Even his son Malcolm, e of the two greatest proconsuls in the post-war Commonwealth – the other as Lord Caradon, son of Isaac Foot – approached me with the greatest diffi-nce when asking me to speak at the lunch arranged by his family to celebrate e centenary of MacDonald's birth, making it clear that it would be understood any reference to 1931 and later years were to be condemnatory. At the end this chapter is to be found the exchange of letters, sad rather than bitter, tween Jim Middleton, secretary of the Labour Party, and MacDonald, read t at that lunch.

Although Baldwin behaved with great tact in the new coalition Government, fusing to take any post except Lord President, there was never any doubt at it was a Conservative Government. Only on India, as recorded above, was e Conservative leadership prepared to stand up to the Tory back-benchers a concession to help MacDonald and his colleagues. What is virtually in-plicable is MacDonald's decision to dissolve and seek a new mandate for e coalition. His Government had overwhelming Parliamentary backing: any ection must be bitter and result in a massacre of his own colleagues. After lling the election he complained of the tone adopted by his Conservative col-agues. In fact the most violent attack on Labour came from the venom of ilip Snowden, accusing his former Cabinet colleagues of running away, and terms forecasting 'red revolution' should Labour be returned. In the event,

Ramsay MacDonald with Queen Mary – at Balmoral.

discredited, he resigned over the free trade issue, when the real nature of the Conservative Government he had done so much to create became clear.

The result of the election was the greatest landslide in history. The Government candidates polled 14,500,000 votes against Labour's 6,600,000. In Parliament, MacDonald's National Labour group had thirteen members, the Conservatives 471, the Samuelite Liberals thirty-three, the Simonites thirty-five. Labour had forty-six, the now separate ILP six, and the Lloyd George Liberals four. The Government majority was 500 over all other parties. All the leading Labour front-benchers were defeated except Lansbury, Attlee and Cripps. In the next few years, MacDonald acted – some would say postured – as Prime Minister, though the suavely considerate Baldwin held the power. He travelled extensively abroad, where he secured an acceptance as head of the Government which he shrank from asserting at home.

The last MacDonald years were the first of those which history recognizes as being those the locusts had eaten, as became clearer in a tired Baldwin's last administration and that of Neville Chamberlain, the heir to the 1931 Conservative triumph. MacDonald was ageing and gradually becoming a pathetic figure, tired, ill, rambling and taking refuge in virtually meaningless and almost unending phrases. The great orator of emergent Socialism was dead long before MacDonald himself was put to rest – he died in November 1937 on a sea voyage.

The party he had created, and succeeded in directing on pragmatic British lines, was virtually destroyed. Had it not been for the war, it could well have been out of office for a generation. In fact, nine years after 1931 Labour's leader was virtually Deputy Prime Minister, and ratified as such two years later. Fourteen years after 1931, Labour's predominance in Parliament challenged comparison with any party victory in history, even 1906.

That Labour would become a potential party of Government if only in a minority situation, was MacDonald's achievement above all others. That it could become established as a natural party of Government, and occupy the Treasury bench for almost half of the thirty-two years since 1945, was the achievement of Clement Attlee.

Correspondence between Jim Middleton, the General Secretary of the Labour Party, and the Prime Minister, the Rt Hon. J. Ramsay MacDonald, on the formation of the National Government, August 1931.

27 Aug 1931

My dear J.R.M.,

I am too full and puzzled to write at length. There is much I feel, that is 'greatly dark'. But all I wrote a few weeks ago still stands. On the merits of the situation, like practically everyone of your political friends I feel strongly and instinctively unconvinced. As to your own stand – one simply witnesses it with the awe the heroic is bound to command, mingled with almost the deepest sadness I have ever known.

I am glad you are back at Lossiemouth this week-end. Amid all the worries and unhappiness of these last days – those much unhappier days of twenty years ago return so very often to my mind.

I feel so surely that beneath and back of all that is now happening your own fount of strength remains now as it has for all these years a source of comfort and quiet serenity.

That remains for you amid all the dust and clamour and for some of us in the outer court of the shrine it keeps the soul sweet too and gives a sense of the verities of things beyond the day to day duties we fulfil.

Yours,

J.M.

The Hillocks,
Lossiemouth.

29 Aug. 1931

My dear Middleton,

I am so glad you wrote though no good purpose can be served in discussing details at present. I know I have done the right thing for both the country and the Party, and I am much encouraged by the support I am having from the older friends in the Socialist Movement. So soon as I am freed from my day to day burdens, I shall turn my attention to Party opinion without in any way dividing the organization or making strife. I hate the kind of praise I am getting for the moment and place no value upon it. What saddens me much at this time is the loss of our unfinished work, but I strive hard to maintain it. At any rate, I have saved the Party from having been kicked out ignominiously in a week. Others will use that good result, for by this sacrifice of mine they will have a chance of sending out such manifestoes as that of yesterday and allow time to bring them back. I am sore at heart to lose such support as yours, but when excommunication takes place I suppose I must be thorough. It looks as though we have saved the country from a general Act of Moratorium, though that is not quite certain, and, as we survey the road we may be compelled to go, it threatens to be longer than I hoped it would be. I have put my hand to the plough and, be the consequences what they may, I shall not turn back till the end of the furrow. You speak of twenty years ago. Today I am no more happy than I was then and far more burdened and lonely. But now as then I am standing on principle and with a clear idea of what is required.

Of you I shall never think otherwise than I do now and have done since you first came to work for me. Believe me to be

Yours always sincerely,
J. Ramsay MacDonald.

P.S. My great comfort now is Malcolm and Ishbel, both of whom, on their own initiative, are prepared to stand by me. Malcolm is to help me in the Government on the strong request of my colleagues who know of his fine work.

J.R.M.

9

Neville Chamberlain

In any list of Britain's Prime Ministers, Neville Chamberlain is the odd man out, history's greatest misfit – which indeed he looked – the most improbable Prime Minister of all. He was improbable in the sense that he did not even become a member of Parliament until he was in his fiftieth year, though he was Chancellor of the Exchequer within four years. No British Prime Minister in modern times has entered Parliament so late in life. Yet in the vitally important years from May 1937, when he became Prime Minister, to the outbreak of war, he had the full support of the Commons, the Parliamentary products of the decadence of the Thirties.

Of the three Chamberlains, Joseph and his two sons, Austen and Neville, he was the least probable candidate for Downing Street. Joseph might have been Gladstone's successor had he not led the revolt of the Liberal Unionists over Irish policy which led to the defeat of the Irish Home Rule Bill in 1886 and virtually condemned the Liberals to the best part of thirty years in the wilderness. Equally he could have been a candidate for the Conservative leadership had he not, in turn, split the Unionists over the protection issue, and in so doing contributed so massively to the Liberal landslide of 1906. Austen was Chancellor of the Exchequer in 1903, fifteen years before Neville entered Parliament, and might well have succeeded Balfour as Conservative leader in 1911, when he stood down to give Bonar Law a clear run. But, as the cynical Birkenhead said of him: 'Austen always played the game and he always lost it.'

Neville himself might never have considered going into Parliament but for Lloyd George's treatment of him as Director-General of National Service, failing to give him a place in the administration, and leaving the defence of his policies in Parliament to an assortment of ministers. He was happy in his municipal role as Lord Mayor of Birmingham when Lloyd George brought him to Whitehall, one of the greatest municipal administrators and innovators in the history of local government – a record which was to be reflected in his years as Minister of Health under Baldwin. Entering Parliament in 1918 he could have had no hope of ministerial advancement while Lloyd George was in charge – 'Not a bad Lord Mayor of Birmingham in a lean year,' Lloyd George was to say of him. On any then reasonable expectation he would have been likely to have been nearer sixty than fifty before Lloyd George disappeared from the scene.

Yet, in Baldwin's Cabinet of 1924 to 1929, he was to carry through the most significant reforms in housing and local government seen in this century, at any rate until Aneurin Bevan. In MacDonald's 'National' Government from 1931 to 1935 he was to exert an irresistible influence, which became even greater when an ageing Baldwin took over from MacDonald in 1935. There was no conceivable challenge to him as Baldwin's successor, and no doubt of his utter control of his undistinguished Cabinet when he took over. Throughout the years of appeasement there was no successful challenge to him round the Cabinet table, despite much dissatisfaction, at any rate after he had made it impossible for Eden to continue as Foreign Secretary. Churchill might fulminate on the back-benches, and the younger Tories, Macmillan, Boothby and their soulmates, protest, but Chamberlain dominated his Cabinet, not like a Lord Mayor, but like a city boss, with a hardly wider conception of the issues he had to face. In Birmingham his majority had been such that he had had few problems about carrying through his policies, enlightened and pathbreaking as they were. The mettle of most of his Conservative back-benchers

Previous page Neville Chamberlain at his desk.

ovided no more challenge to him. Another distinguished municipal leader, erbert Morrison, even more distinguished in the local government field d with a far longer experience in Parliament, was to find that the mother of rliaments demanded more than the political management of County Hall.

It was Britain's tragedy, indeed that of a wider world, that Chamberlain in ose crucial years was in charge of the response to Hitler. Municipal experience d not disqualified him from national management, but it provided no guide the greatest international challenge Britain and her allies had to face in the ven centuries since Simon de Montfort summoned the first Parliament to nvene. It was not only that he was totally inadequate: many are and some t by. What was tragic was that he was totally opinionated, totally certain was right. A greater man might have paused and consulted; he picked a tally inadequate crony, Sir Horace Wilson, experienced in nothing more than e conciliation and arbitration procedures of the then very non-interventionist inistry of Labour. That the two were adequate in flattering each other's nity and certainty at such a time would have been bad enough, but, even on e facts of the situation falsified by their limited perceptions, they began to nspire to withhold essential facts from the Cabinet and Parliament, even to lsify the information they made available.

More than that, Parliamentary critics were not treated simply as ill-formed: Churchill, Attlee and the official Opposition, and a growing number MPs, some with service or diplomatic experience, were treated as scare-ongers, or even as actively disloyal. The Establishment press – except the *aily Telegraph* and indeed the *Yorkshire Post* – supported Chamberlain rough every crisis Hitler provoked: neither did they nor the solid rump of e Conservative back-benchers challenge the man-for-man inadequacy of the hamberlain Cabinet. Compared with the quality of the Asquith Cabinet hich took Britain into the war against the Kaiser in 1914, Chamberlain's was rdly comparable with a Birmingham City Council in a worse than lean year. e inherited a poor team, and almost every subsequent change seemed to be rected to raising the average level of the back-benchers.

Yet throughout the years leading up to 3 September 1939 and the nine onths which followed, the Government back-benchers failed to exert y significant pressure. It took Norway, the acceptance of the need for a nuinely national Government, and the Labour Party's refusal to serve under hamberlain, to force his resignation and bring Churchill into office.

eville Chamberlain was born in Edgbaston, Birmingham on 18 March 1869, ring Gladstone's first administration. He was educated at a small prep school ar Southport, and at Rugby. He was destined for a business career, and udied accountancy. In 1890 he went with his father to the West Indies, where ey became interested in the growing of sisal. They chose a site in the Bahamas, here Neville stayed for seven years, on his own, running the Andros Fibre ompany, a sisal estate of 20,000 acres. It was a failure, and some of his tra-ucers have made more than a little capital out of that failure. It was, in fact, ot so much mismanagement on his part, more the choice of the wrong site. is father lost £50,000 on the venture and Neville returned to Birmingham, coming chairman of a firm called Elliot, specializing in the manufacture of pper, brass and yellow metal, also running an engineering firm, Hoskins & ons, producing metal fabrications, mainly for the Merchant Navy and the

Neville Chamberlain with his mother.

Royal Navy. He thus became, together with Baldwin, Bonar Law and Macmillan, one of the very few future Prime Ministers with experience in manufacturing industry, all operating about the same time. A Sunday School teacher, an active member of the Chamber of Commerce, secretary of the city Liberal Unionist Association, he answered the call to municipal politics. There was nothing in his record, or probably in his mind, to suggest that he would ever wish to stride the national political stage. He played a prominent local part in the 1906 election, working for his father, identifying himself in particular with the Chamberlainite policy of protection with an Empire slant.

In 1911 he was elected to the Birmingham City Council, a growth area, for its boundaries had been extended by decree of Parliament. It was now the second city in the Empire; his mission in the years ahead was to make it the centre of municipal innovation. 'Municipal socialism' was already the cry of the Labour Party, still deprived of any major role in national government. It would be argued that, while they orated, he was the pioneer. In 1914 he became an Alderman, and the following year, with unusual rapidity, Lord Mayor. (It similarly took him hardly any longer between entering Parliament and taking over the Treasury.) He founded the Birmingham City Orchestra, the first of its kind in the country, and Birmingham's Municipal Savings Bank – in the face of great opposition from the banking world.

Chamberlain as a young man.

While still Lord Mayor he was summoned to Downing Street by the Prime Minister, who offered him the post of Director-General of National Service, a new post for mobilizing the nation's manpower. It was a cruel appointment Lloyd George was offering. The terms of reference were vague; more important he was not given ministerial status, as his successor Sir Auckland Geddes was. It was a hot seat, subject to close Parliamentary scrutiny, and the responding ministers were an odd assortment coming from different departments. An Irish member, John Dillon, said: 'If Mr Chamberlain were an archangel, or if he was Hindenburg and Bismarck and all the great men of the world rolled into one, his task would be wholly beyond his powers.' After seven months, Chamberlain resigned. He took it very badly, writing at the end of the year: 'If the Government had accepted my suggestions . . . we should have had some hundreds of thousands more men in the field. What would Haig have done with them. Would he have been able to win Ostend and Zeebrugge?'

His Whitehall experience had taught him the importance of Parliament. The loss of his cousin Norman, killed in France – 'the most intimate friend I had' – led him to edit his cousin's letters. One made a particularly deep impression:

> Nothing but immeasurable improvements will ever justify all the damnable waste and unfairness of this war – I only hope those who are left will *never*, *never* forget at what sacrifices those improvements have been won.

Chamberlain decided to seek a nomination to Parliament, and was selected for the Ladywood division of Birmingham. At the same time he declined a GBE for his Whitehall service. In 1918, nearly fifty, he was a member of Parliament. Yet he noted in his diary: 'My career is broken. How can a man of nearly 50, entering the House with this stigma, hope to achieve anything?'

His maiden speech was on an amendment to the Rent Restriction Act, a subject he could have debated in his sleep. His proposal was accepted by the Attorney-General. A week later he was up again, on canals and waterways, and shortly afterwards carried an amendment to the Electricity Bill. All these were then municipal subjects.

The Lloyd George coalition was coming under strain. Bonar Law resigned because of ill health. Brother Austen became leader of the Unionist Party. It was only a matter of weeks before the Carlton Club meeting was to destroy the coalition. Chamberlain was away in North America. On his return he became Postmaster-General in Bonar Law's Government, not an easy appointment to accept, since Austen had voted in the Carlton Club minority. Within months Neville was in the Cabinet as Minister of Health. When Baldwin took over, he went to the Treasury, but only for a few weeks because Baldwin called the 1923 election on the protection commitment. Chamberlain never introduced a Budget.

The election was heralded by a meeting at Plymouth addressed by both Baldwin and Chamberlain. This was the occasion when Baldwin first hinted at his decision to seek freedom from Bonar Law's commitment. Chamberlain was more specific, saying that if the unemployment situation were to be dealt with adequately the following winter, it would be necessary 'that we should ask to be released from that pledge'. *The Times* interpreted this as:

> A definite decision on the part of the Cabinet to go to the country on the question of tariff reform, and it is already obvious that there is to be a great struggle between those who want an early election and those who believe that the appeal to the country should be deferred until as late as possible next year.

Quite true: the die was cast. The main issue was the timing, and Baldwin decided on an immediate election. This brought the indecisive result which left Asquith and his Liberals with the casting vote – the vote which produced MacDonald's first Government.

Baldwin faced considerable criticism as an innocent abroad, worse as a man who put Britain's natural ruling party at risk because of scruples about his predecessor's pledge. He strengthened his Shadow Cabinet by bringing Austen Chamberlain back out of the shades. He was also toying with the idea of making an honest Tory of Winston Churchill. A year later, after the Campbell case and the 'Zinoviev Letter', Baldwin was back, with Austen Chamberlain – after some pressure from the King – at the Foreign Office.

The King was told also that Winston Churchill would be invited to join the Government, and we have seen the events when he and Neville Chamberlain were in attendance at Baldwin's room in Central Office together, when Chamberlain, after being asked about the Treasury, asked for Health, and saw Churchill in the ante-room.

Opposite Chamberlain in his robes as Chancellor of the Exchequer.

The next five years were for Chamberlain the consummation of a lifetime's training. His remit covered housing and local government, and Harold

Macmillan in *The Past Masters* refers to him as having:

> ... proved himself as one of the great reformers – not in words or promises, but in deeds and performance. Those who today only think of Neville Chamberlain in connection with Munich and the tragic years of his premiership, should not, in justice, forget this splendid period of solid achievement.

Within a month of going to his department, he had given instructions for the drafting of no fewer than twenty-five Bills covering every area of housing and local government, rating and valuation, local government reform, council housing, housing for rent and for owner-occupation, land planning and local government boundaries. Almost all, twenty-one in fact, became law and dominated the local government scene for a generation and more ahead, some of them surviving to the present day the efforts of later Governments. Chamberlain must go down in history as one of the greatest social reformers in the sphere of housing and local government of his own or any other age. Aneurin Bevan, the creator of the National Health Service, as well as a great innovator in housing and local government, remains the only one who could challenge his record. But in terms of personal contact with the back-benchers, Chamberlain was already showing an arid self-confidence. His Rating and Valuation Act moved local government forward half a century: it transferred rating powers from the poor law guardians to what he called 'the real living bodies of today', the county, borough and district councils. He established a single basis of valuation – based on income tax – instead of the chaos he inherited. He standardized assessments and established a system of quinquennial valuation to keep valuation for rating up to date. Twelve thousand parish overseers, responsible to no one, gave way to 648 new elected rating authorities; six hundred Victorian poor law guardians gave way to 343 new assessment areas.

Basically what Chamberlain created has lasted to the present day: few social reformers could make such a claim. By revivifying local government on an elected basis, he created a new system of local democracy and what today would be called 'participation'. His critics were found not in the ranks of the Labour Opposition, which included many with local government experience: criticism came from his own Party, some of whom protested that the Bill 'nationalized local government and seriously affected the liberties of our English country people'. The truth is that his reforms used national power to transfer real authority to ensure democratic local control.

On the eve of the 1929 general election, which Baldwin, an inaccurate forecaster of election results, did not expect to lose, he asked Chamberlain whether in the new Government he would prefer to go to the Colonies or to take the Exchequer. Chamberlain, loyal to his dynasty, chose the opportunity of building on what his father had sought to achieve as Colonial Secretary. But the election was lost, and the Conservatives were not even the leading party in an indecisive election. Baldwin was once again under attack, and Chamberlain in his private correspondence was one of his critics. But in the period of backbiting which usually follows a lost election, Chamberlain had an alibi: he went on a tour of East Africa, where his speeches advocated indigenous local reform and his father's concept of 'trusteeship for the backward races and development of undeveloped estates'.

On his return he became chairman of the Conservative Party, a not uncongenial post, and one which helped to confirm him as Baldwin's successor.

Chamberlain and his wife go to the polls during the 1929 General Election.

In the Conservative Party the post was and is the leader's gift: was Baldwin simply confirming Chamberlain's ultimate right to the succession, and mobilizing his undoubted local government grass-roots influence, or was he buying him off as a potential troublemaker? In fact he proved a tower of strength when Baldwin was under fire from the Beaverbrook–Rothermere cabal. When Baldwin was under the fiercest attack during the 'power without responsibility' period, Chamberlain resisted all who might have put the knife in to make Chamberlain leader. But over Baldwin's decision to support MacDonald's India policy, Chamberlain was totally reserved, even hostile.

The events leading to MacDonald's formation of the 'National' Government have been described in preceding chapters. The formation of the new Government meant that while Baldwin held a convenient watching brief, Chamberlain had the undoubted power of the Treasury behind him. An impartial commentator, the Liberal leader, Herbert Samuel, has assessed their relative contribution to the new Government. On Baldwin:

> Reticent in Cabinet, one might almost say taciturn, Baldwin rarely, if ever, initiated a proposal; but often, when a discussion was taking an awkward turn, he would intervene at the end with some brief observation, full of common sense, that helped us to an agreement.

That was Baldwin, the finely tuned manipulator of the steering wheel: direction without engine-power, the prerogative of the bosun throughout the ages.

Chamberlain was in the engine-room. Again to quote Samuel:

Neville Chamberlain, on the other hand, was always ready to take the lead, particularly on economic questions which then held the field, and which had always been his special province. His ideas were positive and clear-cut; he was tenacious in pursuit of them, whether in the Cabinet itself, or its Committees, or in the conversations that, as in all governments, were continually proceeding among its members. Courteous and agreeable in manner, Chamberlain was always willing to listen to arguments with a friendly spirit – but a closed mind.

Chamberlain was a member of the delegation at the Lausanne negotiations, which brought German reparations to an end. He wrote to his sister:

> The P.M. is I think going to rely on my help very much. He had a good deal of difficulty in following the more technical side and he doesn't understand French, so he likes to have me about and in fact he won't now conduct any conversation with the other delegations without having me there too. I get on very well with the French – the Wigrams declare that Herriot 'adores' me, and also with the Germans, though I must say the latter, especially von Papen, are incredibly stupid.

After Lausanne, Chamberlain accompanied Baldwin to the Ottawa Imperial Preference Conference. Perhaps his finest hour, certainly in family terms, was when he introduced into Parliament the schedule of import duties from which the Dominions were exempt. This was the issue on which Joseph Chamberlain had destroyed Balfour's Government and created the Liberal landslide of 1906. Now, speaking for a Parliamentary majority far exceeding even that of a quarter of a century earlier, emotion took charge, with a voice almost breaking, in a passage of filial piety:

> There can have been few occasions in all our long political history when to the son of a man who counted for something in his day and generation has been vouchsafed the privilege of setting the seal on the work which the father began but had perforce to leave unfinished. Nearly 20 years have passed since Joseph Chamberlain entered upon his great campaign in favour of Imperial Preference and Tariff Reform. More than 17 years have gone by since he died, without having seen the fulfilment of his aims and yet convinced that, if not exactly in his way, yet in some modified form his version would eventually take shape. *His work was not in vain.* Time and the misfortunes of the country have brought conviction to many who did not feel that they could agree with him then. I believe he would have found consolation for the bitterness of his disappointment if he could have foreseen that these proposals, which are the direct and legitimate descendants of his own conception, would be laid before the House of Commons, which he loved, in the presence of one and by the lips of the other of the two immediate successors to his name and blood.

Austen Chamberlain came down from his back-bench seat and silently shook Neville's hand. It was just eighty-six years since Peel had carried the destruction of the Corn Law system, with Lord George Bentinck, Disraeli and the massive rump of his party vilifying him. It was no longer true that protection was 'not only dead, but damned'. Now a different Conservative Party, far more representative of industry and finance, but not entirely excluding the rural landlords, was cheering the new protectionist era.

Chamberlain earned credit by his further financial measures, the conversion of £2000 millions of 5 per cent War Loan to 3½ per cent; the creation of the Exchequer Equalization Fund.

It was a Chancellor's job to cut back spending, but in his case his approach went beyond normal Treasury considerations; it was doctrinaire.

In June 1934 Baldwin suggested a Defence Loan, but Chamberlain opposed this measure, calling it 'the broad road that led to destruction'. A month later, in answer to the Chief of the Air Staff, who was asking for just £10 million, he suggested that the Air Force should 'dispense with reserves'. In February 1936 he opposed his brother Austen's view that Churchill should be made Minister of Defence, preferring Sir Thomas Inskip, of whom he wrote in his diary: 'He would excite no enthusiasm but he would involve us in no fresh perplexities.' But a month later, when Inskip himself urged the Government to accelerate the rearmament programme and take emergency powers, Chamberlain, going far beyond his Treasury brief, was the decisive voice in opposition. Germany's 'next forward step,' he said, 'might not necessarily lead us into war.'

From 1933 to 1937, and under two Prime Ministers, Chamberlain dominated the defence policy of the Government, thus forcing all three senior ministers to reduce even what they believed was minimum possible spending on defence. He was dominating the Cabinet: Baldwin, now Prime Minister on MacDonald's resignation, was leaving everything to him. He was clearly to be Baldwin's successor.

A tired Baldwin resigned after George VI's Coronation. Chamberlain succeeded on 28 May 1937. He was to be Prime Minister for a few days under three years, of which the last eight months were in wartime. Practically the whole of his premiership up to the outbreak of war on 3 September 1939 was dominated by the twin themes of rearmament and appeasement. For a Prime Minister with such a departmental record as a thrusting reformer, it is surprising how little was achieved in domestic reform.

The biographies of Chamberlain can hardly find any space to record progress on the home front. Iain Macleod devoted ninety-three pages to his premiership; hardly a line refers to domestic legislation and executive decisions. There is no reference whatsoever in Francis Williams's *A Pattern of Rulers*. Sir Keith Feiling devotes 138 of his 450-odd pages to his premiership, but only four pages to his domestic legislative record. He carried through a measure introduced during Baldwin's administration on National Insurance, in favour of 'black-coat' workers, a consolidation of the Factory Laws, and his own Physical Training Act. He played a big part in drafting a White Paper on milk, recalling his earlier social reform days, but now falling foul of the farmers' lobby. Right up to Munich he was taking time off to prepare for a central authority, in the shape of an information bureau to help the location of industry, and to act as 'a central body for the country as a whole', including adequate provision for agriculture. The Coal Bill was passed, nationalizing royalties – as recommended to Baldwin in 1926 – and permitting compulsory amalgamation of privately owned colliery companies. A Housing Bill concentrated subsidies on slum clearance and over-crowding. Sir Samuel Hoare, as Home Secretary, carried a Criminal Justice Bill. His Government negotiated the Anglo–American and Anglo–Canadian trade treaties, which went beyond, or on certain issues resiled from the Ottawa agreements, in that they eased duties on American wheat in return for concessions on the American tariff on British manufacture. But it was an uninspiring record of achievement for over two and a half years at No. 10, with a Prime Minister dominating his Cabinet more than most twentieth-century Premiers. As Francis Williams has put it:

> Although energetic in the conduct of Cabinet business he regarded his ministers not as joint architects of policy but as executive officers called together from time to time to report what they were doing and receive their instructions. He expected them to have ideas on administration but to accept simply his authority on general policy, and he had the obstinacy and egotism which is to be found in many men who have controlled successful private businesses and have been used to working with subordinates whose economic dependence makes them unlikely to criticize the policy decision of the man who controls the purse-strings.

Harold Macmillan, in *The Past Masters*, recorded this judgment on the basis of intimate knowledge:

> In his earlier days his undoubted intellectual arrogance was partly concealed. After he became Prime Minister, and especially after Munich, it developed almost to a form of mania. Yet at all times he was a difficult man to argue with. Thus in debate he was seldom conciliatory and generally unyielding. He knew he was right on every question. Baldwin was never quite sure that anybody was right, especially himself. Baldwin's approach to problems was largely one of temperament and feeling. Chamberlain brought to them a clear, logical and sometimes ruthless mind. Nor did he take any trouble to make himself agreeable even to his supporters, still less to his opponents. He seldom if ever came into the Smoking Room or joined in the camaraderie of the House of Commons. He was in Dr Johnson's phrase, an 'unclubbable' man.

Macmillan is right to draw attention to this feature. In the last fifty years, perhaps for many years before that, the successful Prime Ministers have on the whole been those who spent hours each day in the smoke-room, tea-room or members' dining-room. Churchill, Attlee, Macmillan, and others of us; Douglas-Home and Heath much less.

The modern working of the British constitution depends on the doctrine that while the Prime Minister is more important than any member of the Cabinet, he is not more powerful than his Cabinet as a whole. Chamberlain set out to be more powerful than all his colleagues taken together. Each of them counted for one, Chamberlain for more than them all – and his Rasputin, Horace Wilson, for more than any two or three. Horace Wilson might have been regarded as an acceptable, if autocratic, permanent secretary to the Ministry of Labour in a lean generation. His influence on foreign affairs in the Chamberlain–Wilson alliance – at times an alliance against both Cabinet and Parliament – was greater than that of the Foreign Secretary. Compared with Eden's profound knowledge of foreign affairs, Horace Wilson was an ignoramus, but unlike Eden he was a yes-man to Chamberlain. Had he not as an industrial mediator brought employers and trade unionists together? What then was the difficulty in the industrial dispute with Italy or Germany, or the third dimension of the Soviet Union, which Horace Wilson probably garded as a tiresome Communist infiltrator into a factory dispute? Chamber-n equally felt there was no real difference between negotiating with a German natic with almost overwhelming armed forces at his disposal, and the type deals he had done with Birmingham businessmen or civic chiefs. Attlee, in interview, once remarked: 'Who was it said, Lloyd George or Churchill, at Chamberlain always looked at foreign affairs through the wrong end of a unicipal sewage-pipe?' It was in fact Lloyd George.

We have seen in a previous chapter that the Chiefs of Staff had recom-ended, in March 1932, abandonment of the Ten Year Rule on the likelihood war. Yet no steps were taken towards making up the deficiencies which had uilt up over the previous eight years. The Japanese attack on northern China rced the Cabinet to re-examine the defence situation in February 1933, and e First Lord, the War Secretary and the Air Minister tabled strong warnings. hamberlain knew better:

> Today financial and economic risks are by far the most serious and urgent that the country has to face, and ... other risks have to be run until the country has had time and opportunity to recuperate and our financial situa-tion to improve.

MacDonald, as Prime Minister, agreed with him: 'In the financial conditions scribed by the Chancellor of the Exchequer the Cabinet would have to take sponsibility, as they had done before, for the deficiencies of the Defence De-rtments.'

On 14 July of the same year, Sir Robert Vansittart of the Foreign Office rculated secret information about Germany's rearmament. Chamberlain told abinet: 'France ought not to be pushed by us into a position of weakness.' abinet decided simply to express official concern 'at the indication of German armament'.

On 14 March 1934, the question was reviewed again. Sir John Simon, reign Secretary, steered the discussion on to disarmament, proposing further ncessions to Germany to prevent a breakdown of the Disarmament Con-rence. 'A German menace, if it developed, was more likely to be in the east d south than the west. Austria, Danzig, Memel, appeared to be principally enaced.' Chamberlain felt that 'when confronted by an expenditure of over 70,000,000 in five years' the Cabinet were 'bound to consider whether there as no alternative'. On 25 June, on a firm demand for the means to finance programme already decided, he said: 'It is necessary to cut our coat according our cloth' and flatly rejected a proposal from Baldwin for a Defence Loan 'the broad road that led to destruction'.

Apart from a limited priority programme for the Air Force, which was in-easingly being left behind by Germany's rearmament, Chamberlain main-ined his veto. His self-esteem was not growing less. He wrote to his sister:

> As you will see I have become a sort of Acting P.M. – only without the actual power of the P.M. I have to say 'Have you thought' or 'What would you say' when it would be quicker to say 'This is what you must do'.

In April 1935, the Cabinet faced the crisis which Chamberlain's two years cutbacks of defence spending had made inevitable. Lord Londonderry in-rmed them that their firm decision, publicly announced, to achieve and maintain parity with the German Air Force had no hope of realization: on all existing plans the gap would widen. The Cabinet were told that within two years the Germans would have twice as many aircraft as Britain. Chamberlain was quite calm, and persuaded the Cabinet to rest themselves on Baldwin's semantic suggestion that we should use a different formula: our Air Force would not be 'inferior'. Chamberlain further proposed that we should stop giving the figures to Parliament and the country, but 'deal with the matter in terms of air power and air strength'.

In June 1935, Londonderry went and Swinton was appointed to the Air Ministry. The situation continued to worsen, and pressure for Churchill to be called into the Cabinet was growing. So was opposition in the Cabinet to Winston's appointment: his presence there might affect the choice of Baldwin's successor – obviously, if all went according to plan, Chamberlain. By late 1936 some members of the Cabinet, including Eden, Swinton and Duff Cooper, were reacting against complacency. Chamberlain continued to warn against increasing arms programmes.

Chamberlain succeeded the ageing Baldwin on 28 May 1937. Though one of the oldest to succeed to the premiership, and less than two years younger than Baldwin, he himself was not tiring. He was now in a position, recalling his letters to his sister, to give the orders. Halifax visited Hitler and was largely taken in by his professions of peace; in the subsequent debate in the House, Chamberlain showed his annoyance that Parliament should presume to debate these matters. The widening aircraft gap was discussed in a pre-Christmas Cabinet. Chamberlain discounted the idea of parity with Germany – in any case: 'No pledge can last for ever.'

He was by this time controlling foreign policy. Eden might as well have been a PPS. He, unlike Chamberlain, had a contempt for Mussolini and resented Chamberlain's overtures, conducted on a purely direct personal basis with Grandi, the Italian Ambassador. He systematically and obviously deliberately bypassed Eden and the Foreign Office machine. They clashed on two major issues, both related to the responsibility of the Foreign Office for foreign affairs. President Roosevelt had taken an initiative proposing international discussion on the increasingly dangerous situation. Eden wanted to take this up, but Chamberlain had already rejected it out of hand. He had planned his own talks with the dictators, and he would not have brooked American intervention if as Minister of Health he had been discussing rate support with local authorities. Eden wrote in his diary (18 January 1938):

> I fear that fundamentally the difficulty is that Neville believes that he is a man with a mission to come to terms with the dictators. Indeed one of his chief objections to Roosevelt's initiative was that with its strong reference to International Law it would greatly irritate the dictator powers.

The other issue was relations with Italy. Chamberlain's own diary says all that need be said:

> In July I had a meeting with Grandi *in the course of which* (sic) I wrote a letter to Mussolini in friendly terms and this was followed by a very cordial reply from him in which he declared his readiness to open conversations with a view to the removal of all points of difference. I did not show my letter to the Foreign Secretary for I had the feeling that he would object to it.

In February 1938, the Prime Minister told Eden that he wanted to open conversations with Italy, without first insisting that Italian forces be withdrawn from Spain, where a bloody civil war had been turned into an undeclared Nazi–Fascist invasion. Eden records the dialogue:

> N.C. made it clear that he knew exactly what he wanted to do. He wanted to . . . open conversations at once . . . I demurred, pointing out that we had still made very little progress in the Spanish affair . . . N.C. became more vehement, more vehement than I have ever seen him, and strode up and down the room saying with great emphasis, 'Anthony you have missed chance after chance. You simply cannot go on like this.'

This was clearly dismissive, clearly the statement of a man who had decided to get rid of his Foreign Secretary. But Eden went on, according to his own account: 'Your methods are right if you have faith in the man you are negotiating with.' Chamberlain replied: 'I have.'

Chamberlain commented in another letter to his sister: 'I have gradually arrived at the conclusion that at bottom Anthony did not want to talk with Hitler or Mussolini, and as I did, he was right to go.' In fact he was pushed out. As Harold Macmillan has written of Chamberlain: 'He . . . drove Eden to resignation by acts of disloyalty which are hardly believable . . . The tragic story then unfolds, Italy, with all the inevitability of a Greek drama.' So if Palmerston was sacked by Queen Victoria for ignoring her demand that she should see FO telegrams before they were dispatched, Eden was sacked because, as Foreign Secretary, he wanted to see Downing Street telegrams which he and the Foreign Office had neither drafted nor seen.

In April, Chamberlain was speaking at Birmingham about the 'good prospect of restoring those old friendly relations' (with Italy), attacking the Labour and Liberal critics of his policy and saying he would eat his hat if he were wrong. But the signs of revolt were beginning. The Foreign Affairs Committee of the Conservative Party sided with Eden. In the resulting debate, when Churchill spoke with great effect, one Conservative only voted against the Government but twenty-one abstained, the small beginning of the much larger army which was to end Chamberlain's premiership although more than two years of disaster had first to elapse.

In March Chamberlain secured Cabinet support in rejecting a demand for an inquiry into air defence. A week later the Foreign Policy Committee of the Cabinet, a close and mainly loyal combination, started to hedge over the imminent German threat to Czechoslovakia – 'a modern and very artificial creation with no roots in the past,' said Simon. (Like King Wenceslas?) Chamberlain had told the Commons that the Government would review defence spending: the House took this as meaning that the nation's defences would be strengthened. The Cabinet minutes of 22 March recorded:

> The Cabinet were reminded that at the present time the Defence Services were working under instructions to cut down estimates, and it was suggested that this was hardly consistent with an announcement that we were accelerating our armaments.

Two days later, with Cabinet approval, Chamberlain announced that armaments were being increased: 'Acceleration of existing plans has become essential.' He mentioned in particular the RAF and anti-aircraft defences.

In April he announced an agreement with Mussolini ratifying the conquest

f Abyssinia: Italy agreed to reduce her garrison in Libya, Britain to refrain om further fortification on the coast of Palestine. 'I believe,' Chamberlain old the House, 'we may look forward to a friendship with the new Italy .. firmly based, as that by which we were bound to the old.' Churchill warned Chamberlain and his Cabinet: 'You are casting away real and important means f security and survival for vain shadows and ease.'

Chamberlain's attitude to rearmament was partly conditioned by his desire o restrain expenditure, but his basic attitude sprang from a driving belief that e could negotiate with the dictators: that and his attitude to rearmament were mply two faces of a single coin. Swinton decided to go.

The story of Munich, which requires a book in itself, has been told in umerous histories, by Churchill, in Martin Gilbert's Churchill volumes, and y the more Chamberlainite Sir Keith Feiling. Iain Macleod's elegant study, hich on the whole is sympathetic to Chamberlain, seeks more to explain an to defend him.

Chamberlain had been confident that the crisis over Hitler's next chosen arget, Czechoslovakia, could be averted. The retired National Liberal minister ord Runciman was sent to Prague. Chamberlain swung from a broadcast bout 'a faraway country about which we know nothing' to acute concern and n unprecedented degree of personal intervention, including his visits to Bad Godesberg and Munich. Whether he genuinely believed that the personal relationships he thought he had established with the dictators might lead to his uccessful mediation, or whether he felt that his two years of dedicated appeasement would be discredited, has been much debated. But his private letters and he Cabinet minutes show that in fact he had an obsessive belief that he and e alone could deal with the dictators.

The three German visits – that to Godesberg was the first time this nearseptuagenarian had ever flown – amount, through the eyes of history, to a total umiliation. But that was not the universal, or even the majority view of the me. Effete establishment newspapers – not, again, the *Daily Telegraph* or he *Yorkshire Post* – supported him, and almost certainly the majority of the eneral public felt a great sense of relief that war had been averted. Chamberlain as in no doubt. Waving aloft the Munich declaration – 'the desire of our two eoples never to go to war with one another again' – he claimed to have brought ack 'Peace with Honour', to that extent devaluing Disraeli's much more justifed claim on returning from the Congress of Berlin.

Chamberlain had found the Cabinet less united than a competent managing irector might have expected of his departmental heads, though he had already xperienced a growing opposition on rearmament. Halifax expressed doubts; is own objective, he made clear, was the destruction of Nazism. Lord Hailham (Senior) could not trust Hitler's words. Duff Cooper, who was to resign ver the deal, challenged the whole Munich concept and urged that the Navy hould at once be put on a war footing. Hore-Belisha, the War Secretary, and he old stalwart Walter Elliot supported him. Inskip, Kingsley Wood, Stanhope nd Malcolm MacDonald – sole survivor in the coalition of the pre-1931 Labour Party – supported the Prime Minister.

Chamberlain must have found this irksome. He told his Cabinet colleagues, he minutes record:

> Ever since he had been Chancellor of the Exchequer, he had been oppressed

Opposite Neville Chamberlain with Adolf Hitler.

with the sense that the burden of armaments might break our backs. This had been one of the factors which had led him to the view that it was necessary to try and resolve the causes which were responsible for the armaments race.

He thought that we were now in a more hopeful position, and that the contacts which had been established with the Dictator Powers opened up the possibility that we might be able to reach some agreement with them which would stop the armaments race. It was clear, however, that it would be madness to stop rearming until we were convinced that other countries would act the same way. For the time being, therefore, we should relax no particle of our effort until our deficiencies have been made good. That, however,

Mr and Mrs Chamberlain appearing at the window of Number 10 after the signing of the Munich Agreement.

was not the same thing as to say that as a thank-offering for the present detente we should at once embark on a great increase in our armaments programme.

He spoke in very similar terms in the House. But leading figures in the Commons were more disturbed. Attlee said: 'We have felt that we are in the midst of a tragedy. We have felt humiliation. This has not been a victory for reason and humanity. It has been a victory for brute force.' Sir Archibald Sinclair, the Liberal leader, warned: 'A policy which imposes injustice on a small and weak nation and tyranny on free men and women can never be the foundation of lasting peace.' Eden warned that successive surrenders bring only successive humiliation, and they, in their turn, more humiliating demands.

The lumpen Tory back-benchers supported Chamberlain, as the country did. But Bonar Law's son Richard proved an independent hard-liner. Chamberlain, himself proofed against criticism, wrote to his sister:

> I tried occasionally to take an antidote to the poison gas by reading a few of the countless letters and telegrams which continued to pour in expressing the writers' heartfelt relief and gratitude. All the world seemed to be full of my praises except the House of Commons, but of course that was where I happened to be myself, so naturally its voice speaks loudest in my ear.

It is when a Prime Minister evaluates his postbag as an offset to Parliament that democracy is in danger. But Chamberlain had, in fact, had an easy ride in Parliament.

The Munich debate over, the Cabinet had to resume its work; every man to his oar. Those who read the crisis in terms of Britain's weakness pressed for speedier rearmament, Chamberlain still pressing the Treasury view. But the Cabinet's voice counted little with Chamberlain: better packed than Parliament could be, it was not, at a crunch, a problem for him. But no member of the Cabinet, none of his creatures – nor the Cabinet as a whole – had as much influence as Horace Wilson. They at least had reached their positions by having been elected to Parliament. Horace Wilson had not. Yet his influence was such that he, not the Prime Minister, took it upon himself to explain to Kingsley Wood, the Air Minister – more under pressure than any of his colleagues in Parliament – that the proposed increase in aircraft production capacity 'to a level equal to the estimated German capacity' was unacceptable because Germany would 'take it as a signal that we had decided at once to sabotage the Munich agreement'. If there had been doubts that Munich was a surrender, that argument, in November 1939, had it been publicly known, would have confuted them. 'Germany,' he went on, 'was extremely unlikely to violate the neutrality of Belgium'; the Maginot Line was 'probably the strongest system of fortification that has ever been constructed'. This was ten months before the outbreak of war, seventeen months before the fall of France.

Influential members of the Cabinet were pressing for full preparedness. Halifax told the Foreign Policy Committee that Hitler had been reported as saying:

> If I were Chamberlain I would not delay for a minute to prepare my country in the most drastic 'total' war and I would thoroughly organize it. If the English have not got universal conscription by the spring of 1939 they may consider their world empire as lost. It is astounding how easy the democracies make it for us to reach our goal.

War production was still on a peacetime basis. Those, mostly outside Government, who had mobilized Britain for war under Lloyd George, could not understand the Government's lassitude. Industry itself was pressing for an all-out production effort based on a three-shift system. Not so Chamberlain: he was convinced that he could persuade the dictators, and wrote in those terms to his sister. He was cultivating better relations with the Spanish dictator Franco, who he thought might help to improve British relations with Italy. But: 'I repeat once more that I believe we have at last got on top of the dictators ... if they had asked nicely after I appeared on the scene they might already

A weekend house party in 1938 at the country home of Chamberlain's young PPS, Alec Douglas-Home.

have got some satisfaction . . .' As late as March 1939 he was writing to his sister that all was well: everywhere he went, 'and along the route', he was cheered.

Poland was now under threat. Parliament – including many members who had voted for Munich – was moving to regard this as the test case. But to his sister he was writing that Britain's concern was not with the boundaries of States, but attacks on their independence. 'But it is we who will judge whether their independence is threatened or not.' The Poles should have realized, after Czechoslovakia, that this criterion represented no idle threat.

At home even the industrialists were demanding that he should at long last set up a Ministry of Supply. He gave way; it was created and set up under a Liberal National lawyer called Burgin. I worked there for a short time in early 1940: despite the experience that could have been culled from the First War's Ministry of Munitions, its organization under Burgin's ministerial direction would not have been capable of running a chip-shop.

Relations with Russia became an issue. If Chamberlain had had any sense of history – as every Prime Minister must have – he would have given them top priority. A Continental power does not make war on two fronts: four years later we were to see Hitler plough disastrously into the Russian snows as had another dictator in 1812. Chamberlain, faced with a world-scale opportunity, showed the smallness of his municipal mind. To his sister again he wrote: 'I am so sceptical of the value of Russian help that I should not feel that our position was greatly worsened if we could do without them.'

In the event it was Stalingrad, Leningrad and Moscow itself, long before American intervention in the West and the final confrontation in France, that destroyed Hitler. More than that, a different reaction by Chamberlain in 1939 would have immensely eased the task of Churchill in the final war years, and of the Western powers in the post-war settlement.

A final crisis arose over Danzig. Chamberlain had seen the destruction of Austria, following that of Czechoslovakia. Mussolini had cynically attacked Albania. The balance-sheet of appeasement was by this time recording dividends which would have been considered derisory by the Birmingham businessman Chamberlain had once been. Disillusioned, losing control of his Cabinet, he gave assurances to Poland and Romania which on purely geographical grounds could not be made good in military terms.

Hitler demanded the Danzig corridor linking Germany with East Prussia. Chamberlain still hoped, but nearly hopelessly, that an appeal from him would reawaken the glories of Bad Godesberg and Munich. Hitler invaded Poland on 1 September. Although the Cabinet the next day demanded that an ultimatum should be sent expiring at midnight, there were still hesitations. Chamberlain and more particularly Horace Wilson still hoped to persuade Hitler to withdraw and agree to negotiation. Chamberlain went to the House, which now almost to a man expected a robust ultimatum followed by a declaration of war, if Hitler refused to comply. Chamberlain, incredibly, spoke of further negotiations, though his conditions now required a German withdrawal:

> If the German Government should agree to withdraw their forces, then His Majesty's Government would be willing to regard the position as being the same as it was before the German forces crossed the German frontier.

If the troops withdrew, 'the way would be open to discussion' between Germany and Poland, and Britain would be willing 'to be associated' with these discussions. The reaction of the House was totally hostile. In the words of Leo Amery, 'The House was aghast.' The Chief Whip, the loyal Captain Margesson, feared physical violence in the Chamber. The Cabinet, after the firm decision they had taken on an ultimatum, were demoralized. Attlee was away ill. Greenwood rose to deliver the *coup de grâce.* Amery adjured him: 'Speak for England.' Greenwood demanded that when the House met at noon on the Sunday, a decision must be announced: 'Every minute's delay now means the loss of life, imperilling national interests . . . the very foundations of our national honour.'

The Cabinet was in revolt. Simon, Hore-Belisha, Sir John Anderson, Walter Elliot and Earl de la Warr went to Chamberlain's room, demanding an ultimatum. Chamberlain met Halifax for dinner – an incredibly leisurely proceeding – and the Simon group sent a letter demanding action. The Italians, on whom Chamberlain was depending, said they did not 'feel it possible' to ask the Germans to accept a conference: they would not agree to withdrawal. At 10 pm Chamberlain telephoned Daladier, the French Premier. There could be no question, after the scene in Parliament, of a forty-eight-hour ultimatum. It had to be now. At 11 pm the Cabinet met and agreed to an ultimatum closing at midday on the Sunday.

The ultimatum expired, and at 11 am Britain was at war. The right response should have been a genuinely National Government, but Chamberlain stood in the way. It was, therefore, a Conservative Government which took Britain into the war and endured until the following May. But it was a War Cabinet overpopulated with 'former members of the Chamberlain Government', with one difference: 'Winston is back', as the Admiralty signalled the Fleet, announcing the appointment of their new First Lord.

The next few months were the period of the 'phoney war', conjuring up illusion in the civil population and encouraging Chamberlain to feel that the end would come not by defeat of the enemy but by early negotiations. Nothing had changed. Writing to his sister he said:

> I have a hunch that the war will be over before the spring. It won't be by defeat in the field but by German realization that they can't win and that it isn't worth their while getting thinner and poorer when they might have instant relief and perhaps not have to give up anything they really care about. My belief is that a great many Germans are near that position now and that their number, in the absence of any striking military success, will go on growing with increasing rapidity.

His illusions remained, but his authority was gone. No longer could he dictate terms to a Cabinet. He had been proved wrong in peace. It was a War Cabinet now, and one that included Churchill. Relations between Chamberlain and Churchill were formal, correct, almost friendly, but it was a Cabinet no longer dictated by a single man; a Cabinet where the terms of reference were no longer dictated by Treasury economics, still less by the theology of appeasement; a Cabinet whose every action, whose every decision, whose every word almost was relevant only if it was directed to winning the war – a phoney war at first, which must have rejoiced Chamberlain's heart. Poland was overrun of course, but Britain was not bombed.

Nor was Germany, except with leaflets. One set consisted of extracts of Hitler's past speeches, showing with superb Foreign Office pedantry that there were certain semantic contradictions therein. Another set contained extracts from Chamberlain's speeches. Unfortunately one bundle failed to open, and a civilian was killed, the first victim of British aerial bombardment.

There were naval encounters in the South Atlantic, air-raid warnings unrelated to air-raids. The production of the munitions of war began to be taken seriously, though the administration of that production was unsatisfactory. Could this not go on for years?

The answer came in Norway, and shortly afterwards in France, though Chamberlain had decided to resign on the very eve of the attack in Western Europe. Norway was a disaster: it had not been adequately foreseen by Intelligence, the strategy and tactics were wrong as the RAF had no bases to enable them to protect ground troops from bombing and strafing; but the inadequacy of the response was itself, through shortages of equipment of all kinds, an indictment of the Chamberlain years.

The debate in Parliament was decisive. Some MPs, particularly on the Conservative side, had fought in Norway; others had returned in uniform from other theatres of war. Dominating them all, in full Admiral's uniform, was Sir Roger Keyes, hero of Zeebrugge. The debate was bitter. Amery, a scrupulously honest statesman, but no doubt also harbouring memories of warnings rejected, went back to the words of Oliver Cromwell when discussing the Long Parliament and challenged Chamberlain: 'You have sat too long here for any good you have been doing. Depart, I say, and let us have done with you. In the name of God, go.'

Attlee had opened the debate for the Opposition. Speaking on the second day Morrison announced that Labour would force a vote. Chamberlain's answer was tragic: he appealed to 'his friends' to support the Government in the division lobby. This is a perfectly normal Parliamentary expression: a Minister, or an Opposition spokesman, always refers to members of his own party as 'my Honourable' – or Honourable and Gallant, or Honourable and Learned, or Right Honourable – friends. Chamberlain may have meant no more than that, but it was at least infelicitous. He was appealing to cronies, to party ties and tribal loyalties. Critical senior Tories tried to draw a distinction between Chamberlain, who bore the years of responsibility, and Churchill. Churchill rose to accept full governmental responsibility for the naval conduct of the Norwegian campaign. Lloyd George, in his last decisive action in Parliament, recalled the glories of his past with a quiet admonition to Churchill not 'to be converted into an air-raid shelter to keep the splinters from hitting his colleagues'. Referring to Chamberlain's appeal for sacrifice, he charged him to make the first, the sacrifice of the seals of office.

The Government's majority was 81, against a normal 240, measured on party alliances. Thirty-three Conservatives voted against the Government, including senior Privy Councillors. Some young members, in uniform or not, went into the lobby in tears. Some sixty Government supporters abstained or were away. It was a devastating result. There were cries of 'Resign, Resign!' and the Prime Minister went out past the Speaker's Chair, 'No crowds,' as 'Chips' Channon recorded in his famous Diary, 'to cheer him as there were before and after Munich, only a solitary little man, who had done his best for England.'

Churchill in his greatness advised Chamberlain to soldier on. He had himself put the case for the Government over Norway. But the vote was not about Norway. It was about Chamberlain, and 1934, and the years that the locusts had eaten. It was about leadership, and a Parliament so recently sycophantic for Chamberlain had turned against him. There had to be a new leader. There had to be a national coalition, embracing Labour and the Liberals. For Labour the very concept of coalition carried with it memories of MacDonald and 1931. But, by sheer coincidence, the Labour Party conference was in session in Bournemouth. Chamberlain had invited Attlee and his colleagues to join a coalition the previous March, and they had refused. Now Chamberlain met Attlee. The discussion centred on two questions. Would Labour join a coalition under Chamberlain? If not, would they join a coalition under a different Prime Minister? The Labour leaders insisted on their duty to discuss the matter with the Shadow Cabinet in Bournemouth, and ultimately to seek a decision of conference. But Attlee, making clear that he was speaking only for himself said, 'Mr Prime Minister, the fact is our Party won't come in under you. Our Party won't have you and I think I am right in saying that the country won't have you either.'

At dawn, before the question had ever been put before the Labour conference, the peace of Europe was roughly broken by the Nazi invasion of the Low Countries and France. The urgency of getting a new Prime Minister into command was even greater. Attlee sent the reply to the two questions. To joining a coalition under Chamberlain the answer was 'No'; to joining a coalition under another leader, 'Yes'. It had to be Churchill. There was no one else. Halifax had been mentioned, but he was not only unacceptable as a national leader, he was in the House of Lords.

Chamberlain was shocked and broken, but he had the generosity to accept Churchill's invitation to join the new Government, as Lord President of the Council. He was one of the War Cabinet of only five: the departmental ministers for the most part were outside, summoned when needed to the Cabinet's discussions. There were some of us at the time who saw a poetic justice in the exclusion of the Chancellor of the Exchequer, a mordant judgment on the Treasury's powers in the years when Britain failed to prepare herself, not necessarily *for* war, but to *deter* war.

Chamberlain survived for only a few months. Doctors have written that cancer can be brought on by shock or heartbreak. He became seriously ill in the summer and he died on 9 November in that tragic year of 1940.

The years when he was in command bequeath to later generations questions that can be debated but never answered. Could Churchill, had he become Prime Minister in, say, 1937, have stopped the drift and mobilized the resources of the country? Could he have done it in time? Certainly a growing proportion of Chamberlain's Cabinet felt that the drift to war could have been halted. But more, he would no longer have been a voice crying in the wilderness. He would have been speaking for the nation, to the nation.

Speculation about Hitler is not an exact science: it is not in the realm of political philosophy or guesswork about a political response to any hypothetical situation. It is rather within the province of the alienist, the specialist in paranoia.

But one factor that cannot be ignored is that the Cabinet was not functioning as a Cabinet. It was a packed Cabinet. Richard Crossman believed that all Cabinets were so appointed. Had he wanted a case to quote – there are few others – it would have been Chamberlain's. He regularly refused to appoint the best man available in his party, or to promote the young back-benchers. Chamberlain's Cabinet was, to use a more modern phrase, almost 'programmed' to give the answers he sought to the questions he himself insisted on formulating. No post-war Prime Minister would seek to appoint a Cabinet of like-minded men. A Parliamentary party covers a wide arc, at least 180 degrees of national politics. It is a prescription for disaster to concentrate upon a small and necessarily unrepresentative sector.

But that was not all. The tragedy of 1939 and the devastation and loss of life of the succeeding years were due not only to an aberration in the conduct of Cabinet government. They have to be ascribed also to the fact that Parliament itself abdicated its responsibilities. Perhaps this was due to the events of 1931 and the virtual breakdown of party government. It was due to the complacency and lack of urgency of many in the Conservative majority, due possibly too to the decimation of the Labour Opposition, and the irrelevance of some of those who remained. One has to go back to the eighteenth century to find a Parliament as subservient, lazy and irrelevant as that led by Chamberlain – and there are few to record even in that age. It would not happen now. A modern Government is more broadly representative of the country: it is – and this applies to all relevant parties – more competent, more expert, more dedicated, more irreverent, above all more speedy in its reactions, as indeed is the press, which deals even more than MPs in instant reactions. This may be inimical to strategic thinking and relaxed decisions, but it is infinitely to be preferred to the glacier-like seeming immobility of the Chamberlain years.

No post-war Government, Conservative or Labour, could have adopted so fainéant an attitude. They would not have tried. Had they tried they would have been swept from office by their own people.

The demolition of party government in 1931 had something to do with it. After that the majority party did not have to look over its shoulder, or consult the people. To that extent Chamberlain was a unique product of a unique political and Parliamentary situation. But others of that generation would have reacted differently. Churchill was already a product of forty years of political experience, even excluding heredity. Chamberlain arrived late, the political ugly duckling of his family. The discovery that he could nevertheless quickly master the task of legislator and administrator went to his head. He was a vain man, certain that his every instinct was right. He could have been, though he was not, the inspiration of the phrase, 'I wish I was sure of anything as much as he is sure of everything.' It was his vanity that debauched the quality of government, it was the fault of his party that allowed him and them to debauch the House.

But on the major crisis of 1938, his crisis, Britain's crisis, the world's crisis, it is harder to make a judgment. It depends on how far back one goes, how far Munich was the product of those earlier years. If one takes the whole period when Chamberlain's influence was decisive, he must bear full responsibility. The one thing that could be said, even by those who opposed Munich, was that he had gone to such lengths in search of a negotiated peace that if even those efforts could not set Hitler on a new path, then the war-guilt was clear, and there could be no longer any division in the country about Britain's attitude to the Nazi threat. Thus it was that Winston Churchill paid tribute to him in the House on his death:

> It fell to Neville Chamberlain in one of the supreme crises of the world to be contradicted by events, to be disappointed in his hopes, and to be deceived and cheated by a wicked man. But what were these hopes in which he was disappointed? What were those wishes in which he was frustrated? What was that faith that was abused? They were surely among the most noble and benevolent instincts of the human heart – the love of peace, the toil for peace, the strife for peace, the pursuit of peace even at great peril and certainly to the bitter disdain of popularity or clamour. Whatever else history may or may not say about these terrible, tremendous years, we can be sure that Neville Chamberlain acted with perfect sincerity according to his lights and strove to the utmost of his capacity and authority, which were powerful, to save the world from the awful, devastating struggle in which we are now engaged. This alone will stand him in good stead for what is called the verdict of history is concerned.
>
> But it is also a help to our country and to our whole Empire, and to our decent, faithful way of living that, however long the struggle may last, or however dark may be the clouds which overhang our path, no future generation of English-speaking folk – for that is the tribunal to which we appeal – will doubt that, even at a great cost to ourselves in technical preparation, we were guiltless of the bloodshed, terror and misery which have engulfed so many lands and peoples, and yet seek new victims still. Herr Hitler protests with frantic words and gestures that he has only desired peace. What do these ravings and outpourings count before the silence of Neville Chamberlain's tomb?

10

Winston Churchill

WINSTON LEONARD SPENCER-CHURCHILL'S Parliamentary life spanned sixty-five years, apart from the two years between losing Dundee in October 1922 and being elected for Epping in October 1924. Though he lost sixteen years' seniority by his defeat at Dundee, nevertheless in his post-1924 years he achieved the dignity of Father of the House.

He was a minister for over twenty-five of those years, Prime Minister for eight years, eight months – three days less than Asquith, longest-serving Prime Minister in war and peace this century. He served in the Cabinets of Asquith, Lloyd George and Baldwin, and in Neville Chamberlain's war administration from September 1939, holding most of the principal offices of State – Trade, the Home Office, Admiralty, Munitions, War, Air, Colonies, and the Treasury, though not the Foreign Office. He was in Cabinets with every leading statesman of the century from Campbell-Bannerman and Asquith to Attlee, Eden, Macmillan and Heath.

He was above all the great Parliamentarian. As one who had twice crossed the floor of the House, from Conservative to Liberal and back again, he was to emphasize the political discipline of a rectangular Chamber in putting before Parliament, in October 1943, his views on plans for rebuilding the Chamber in the same style as the one Hitler's bombers had destroyed:

> We shape our buildings and afterwards our buildings shape us ... There are two main characteristics of the House of Commons which will command the approval and the support of reflective and experienced Members. They will, I have no doubt, sound odd to foreign ears. The first is that its shape should be oblong and not semicircular ... The semicircular assembly, which appeals to political theorists, enables every individual or every group to move round the centre, adopting various shades of pink according as the weather changes. I am a convinced supporter of the party system in preference to the group system. I have seen many earnest and ardent Parliaments destroyed by the group system. The party system is much favoured by the oblong form of Chamber. It is easy for an individual to move through those insensible gradations from Left to Right, but the act of crossing the Floor is one which requires serious consideration. I am well informed on this matter, for I have accomplished that difficult process, not only once but twice ...

(His second 'characteristic' enabled him to oppose members having desks, and banging lids at times of stress.)

In the First War, he carried the awesome responsibilities of First Lord of the Admiralty: at the height of the Dardenelles campaign he found himself a controversial, defeated, discredited ex-minister who sought a new duty in command of a battalion in Flanders. Between the wars, he held the strings of Treasury power as Chancellor – a few years later he was a political outcast, condemned by the Establishment and by an obsequious Establishment press because he warned, in Baldwin's and Chamberlain's times, of the dangers that Britain and the free world faced as the shadow of the jackboot menaced European civilization. In September 1939, when his warnings became a reality and he was recalled, four or five years late, to the administration, every man serving in every ship in the far-flung if inadequately prepared Royal Navy, already deployed in its wartime posture, was electrified by the three-word signal from the Board of Admiralty: 'Winston is back.'

Previous page Winston Churchill, MP for Oldham.

He became Prime Minister in May 1940, after the failure of the Norway campaign, and on the day of the German invasion of Belgium, Holland and France. He led a united team – ministers of all parties, commanders and fighting men, the men and women workers in the aircraft and ammunition factories, and those who maintained the essential home services. Each of them was willing to submerge his own identity and interest in a great cause under Churchill's lead; it was his leadership and his response which saved Britain by his exertions, and at a critical time saved Europe by his example.

Vigorously though he had warned, weak though Britain was because those warnings had gone unheeded, in his war memoirs he tells of his 'profound sense of relief' when in the midst of the disaster of the battle of France he became Prime Minister. 'I felt,' he said, 'as if I were walking with destiny, and that my past life had been but a preparation for this hour and for this trial . . . Therefore, although impatient for the morning, I slept soundly and had no need for cheering dreams.'

The morning, and all the mornings, provided the proof. Those five years brought forth all the qualities born in him, the qualities that half a century of war and peace had nurtured.

As a leader of the nation in the Second World War he ranks with Chatham, the younger Pitt and Lloyd George. He forged the great transatlantic alliance with Roosevelt, as Allied forces challenged the Germans and Japanese in France and the Low Countries, in the Mediterranean and North Africa, in Scandinavia and the Middle East and in the Far Eastern theatre. In the telegraphic exchanges with Roosevelt he signed himself 'Former Naval Person' – Roosevelt had been Assistant Secretary of the Navy during part of that time when Churchill was First Lord.

His qualities were transcendent. First, there was the quality of indomitable courage. Never in the hour of greatest peril doubting ultimate victory, he could at once rebuke and inspire fainter hearts than his own. That inner certainty which enabled him to stand almost alone in seeing and warning of the danger, that certainty became an unshakeable rock when it was Britain and the Commonwealth who stood alone.

Second, there was his power to evoke response. Winston Churchill had through his power over words, but still more through his power over the hearts of men, that rare ability to call out from those who heard him the sense that they were a necessary part of something greater than themselves; the ability to make each one feel just that much greater than he had been; the ability which runs like a golden thread through our national history to inspire a slumbering nation so that it can call up those inner reserves of effort and of character which have never failed us when our very survival has been at stake.

Third, there was his great quality of humanity. The man who could move armies and navies and embrace the world in one strategic sweep could himself be moved to uncontrollable and unashamed tears at the sight of an old soul's cheerfulness in a shelter, or of a street of devastated houses, at the thought of the human realities which lay behind the war communiqués.

It was his courage, his humanity, the response he evoked in our people that wrote in those wartime years that imperishable chapter in our history which will always bear the title he gave to one part of that chapter: 'Our finest hour'. For overriding and sustaining those qualities which marked his years of leadership was his great sense of history, of, in his own words, 'walking with destiny' – thinking there not so much perhaps of himself but of his country and of the

Blenheim Palace,
a most splendid birthplace
for any Prime Minister.

Lord Randolph Churchill.

Commonwealth. 'I was not the lion,' he said, 'but it fell to me to give the lion's roar.'

He was born on 30 November 1874, the son of Lord Randolph Churchill, briefly Chancellor of the Exchequer. Winston worshipped his father, who was perhaps not altogether worthy of his devotion. The young schoolboy was an individualist – 'General conduct, very truthful, but a regular "pickle" in many ways,' said his school report. He received, on entering Sandhurst, a savage letter of criticism about his qualities, or lack of them, from his father, dated 9 August 1893. Winston did not know that his father was dying of syphilis.

Churchill was well known long before he entered Parliament. As an intrepid soldier, charging under Kitchener at Omdurman, he regarded all this – including his later escape from a Boer prisoner-of-war camp – as an apprenticeship for a political career. He would take over in his twenties the career his father ended at forty-six. In a letter to his mother in 1895 he said: 'The more I see of soldiering the more I like it, but the more I feel convinced it is not my métier.'

All the time he was studying the politics of his age, reading the Annual :egister for the past twenty years. When he was twenty-one, he annotated a eport on Stafford Northcote's 1876 Budget with a detailed fiscal commentary f his own, even urging taxation on unearned income. In 1897, from Bangalore, e sent his mother a comprehensive personal political manifesto, covering elec- oral reform, India, imperialism, Europe – isolation for Britain in defence, the olonies; including significant extension of compulsory education and the fran- hise.

He resigned his Army commission in 1898 to free himself for politics, and hat same day made a political speech at Bradford, launching his political career. bout this first speech he was self-critical, but felt that 'with practice I shall btain great power on a public platform. My impediment [his inability clearly o pronounce the letter 's'] is no hindrance.' He, like Aneurin Bevan, had to truggle with his impediment.

But on his defeat in a by-election at Oldham he used his new-found freedom o go to South Africa to report the Boer War, where he was to find himself nder fire on forty separate operations. He was one of the first few to ride into liberated Ladysmith, and was a vigorous critic of Kitchener – the man whose eservations were fifteen years later to destroy Churchill's preparations and opes for the attack on the Dardanelles. His criticisms were of what he regarded s Kitchener's inhuman neglect of the wounded enemy.

Elected Conservative MP for Oldham in 1900, when he was twenty-six, he uickly made his mark, never speaking unless he had fully mastered his case. Ie was not afraid to be unpopular, but above all he was concerned for Parlia- nent, and to maintain the status of Parliament. In his maiden speech, despite or because of – his experiences, he said: 'If I were a Boer I hope I should e fighting in the field.'

As one who at twenty-six had seen more of war than most of his generation, e warned his own front bench, and Parliament, against those who spoke com- lacently and 'glibly', his own phrase, about a future European war. But he vas also turning his attention to home affairs, to *Poverty, a Study of Town ife*, by Seebohm Rowntree. This book about York, not a deprived area by he standards of those times, had almost as devastating an effect on a twenty- even-year-old Churchill as East End conditions six or seven years later were o have on a twenty-five-year-old Attlee.

He was beginning to question established party loyalties. He wrote to Rose- ery, condemning the 'sordid selfishness and callousness of Toryism' equally vith the 'blind appetites of the Radical masses'. He was talking of a coalition: "Tory Liberal" is a much better name than "Tory Democrat" or "Liberal mperialist". Should the tariff issue come to the forefront, that would be it.'

Joseph Chamberlain brought the issue to the forefront with 'Tariff Reform', nd the abandonment of free trade led to Winston's first crossing of the floor f the House. On so doing he made his famous attack on Conservatism – quoted y every Labour candidate against the Tories when Churchill had returned o them and came to lead them:

> ... a party of great vested interests, bonded together in a formidable con- federation, corruption at home, aggression to cover it up abroad, the trickery of tariff juggles, the tyranny of a party machine; sentiment by the basketful, patriotism by the imperial pint, the open hand at the Exchequer, the open

Winston Churchill as a schoolboy with his mother and brother.

door at the public house, dear food for the millions, cheap labour for the millionaire.

In 1906 he was elected as Liberal member for North-West Manchester, having already become Under-Secretary for the Colonies in the Liberal Government, in charge of complex legislation in the Commons as his chief was in the Lords. In 1908 he became President of the Board of Trade, succeeding Lloyd George: these two were the first of five Presidents who became Prime Minister in the next two generations.

In the Liberal Government he began to make his mark. As Under-Secretary for the Colonies he was a notable conciliator with South Africa; as President of the Board of Trade he played a leading part on social insurance – what in an important memorandum to Asquith he portrayed as the 'Minimum Standard' – and on the establishment of Labour Exchanges. Now in his new department he was again successful in piloting complicated and particularly controversial measures through the House: he led the fight against sweated industries with the Trade Boards Bill; when this was enacted the young Attlee was to become one of its administrators and propagandists. In 1908 Churchill set out his programme to Asquith:

1. Labour Exchanges and Unemployment Insurance;

The actor Simon Ward playing the part of Winston, the young reporter during the Boer War. Churchill and Disraeli are the only Prime Ministers to be the subject of a major film.

> 2. National Infirmity Insurance, etc;
> 3. Special Expansive State Industries – Afforestation – Roads;
> 4. Modernized Poor Law, i.e., classification;
> 5. Railway Amalgamation with State control and guarantee;
> 6. Education Compulsory Bill 17 . . .
>
> I say – thrust a big slice of Bismarckianism over the whole underside of our industrial system, and await the consequences whatsoever they may be with a good conscience.

('Underside' was clearly a trailer for his wartime 'Soft under-belly of the Axis'.)

Inevitably, Churchill and his party were receiving the full treatment of which the hostile press is capable. At Birmingham he responded: 'Boldly and earnestly occupied, the platform will always beat the press.' His attacks on appeasement against an almost uniquely hostile – personally hostile – Conservative press were to prove him too optimistic, though after 1940 there was a change.

He had become an egalitarian. He fought the battle over social insurance. 'If I had my way I would write the word "Insure" over the door of every cottage, and upon the blotting-book of every public man':

> The greatest damage to the British Empire and the British people is not to be found among the enormous fleets and armies of the European continent,

Clementine Hosier at the time of her marriage to Churchill in 1908.

nor in the solemn problems of Hindustan: it is not the Yellow peril nor the Black peril. No, it is here in our midst, close at home, close at hand in the vast growing cities of England and Scotland, and in the dwindling and cramped villages of our denuded countryside. It is there you will find the seeds of Imperial ruin and decay – the unnatural gap between rich and poor, the divorce of the people from the land, the want of proper discipline and training in our youth, the exploitation of our boy labour, the physical degeneration which seems to follow so swiftly on our civilized poverty, the awful jumbles of an obsolete Poor Law, the horrid havoc of the liquor traffic, the consequent insecurity in the means of subsistence and employment which breaks the heart of many a sober, hard-working man, the absence of any established minimum standard of life and comfort among the workers, and at the other end, the swift increase of vulgar, joyless luxury – here are the enemies of Britain. Beware lest they shatter the foundations of her power.

In 1910, after the first general election of that year, Churchill became Home Secretary. The stage was set for his incredible visit to Sydney Street, heavily guarded, as the police and troops shot it out with embattled desperadoes. He was in fact there because someone had to give the orders both to the fire brigade, if fire should spread, and to the police. Less spectacular, more socially significant, were his wide-ranging prison reforms. But with the Labour and trade union movements his name became a legend for many years to come when he was believed to have sent the troops into the Rhondda to deal with the coal-miners of Tonypandy. In fact it was the Chief Constable, but Churchill ordered the troops to detrain at Swindon. In answer to Tory criticisms in Parliament for calling off the troops he said: 'There can be no question of the military forces of the Crown intervening in a labour dispute.'

In the clash between the Commons and the Lords over Lloyd George's Budget, Churchill was a militant. He minuted Asquith in favour of the creation not of Asquith's projected 250 peers, but of 500. But once the constitutional clash was over, he urged that the Government should follow a policy of political appeasement on policy issues, combined with a generous list of honours for leading Opposition members in the Coronation Honours List.

In 1911 serious anxieties developed over Germany's aggressive policies. Churchill and Lloyd George were quick to see the danger, especially of the German navy. Churchill, still Home Secretary, pressed for speedy naval re-armament: he was to become First Lord in October. Before that appointment, he was proposing a triple alliance to provide guarantees to Belgium, Holland and Denmark. As First Lord he pursued the policy of alliance and guarantees with great vigour.

When war came, Churchill became at once a member of Asquith's *inner* War Council. Asquith relied heavily on him, as did junior ministers and young officers, to seek his sponsorship of new ideas, such as the tank, when the War Office was still fighting the Boer War.

Churchill resigned over the Dardanelles, referred to earlier. The previous assessment holds: Kitchener never gave it the necessary backing, despite his assurances and the strategy adopted at top level. Churchill's strategy was probably right, as indeed Attlee, who fought there, always argued. It could have meant a decisive breakthrough which would have relieved pressure on the bloody and unproductive Western Front. 'How much longer,' he appealed to Asquith in January 1915, 'have we to chew barbed wire in Flanders?' Historians will continue to argue. What was incredible, in a war where continuous failure led only to piling more expensive offensives on top of one another in France and Belgium, was that Churchill seemed irremediably disgraced, at the instance of Tory ministers, and had to resign. He took over a colonel's command in France, and shared with his men the grim reality of war in the front line. He expressed his frustrations to his wife:

> ... I can't help longing for the power to give those wide directions which occupied my Admiralty days. There seems such want of drive and fresh thought in the military world. As for the Navy, it has dozed off under that old Tabby [Balfour]...

And again:

> Whenever my mind is not occupied by work, I feel deeply the injustice with

> which my work at the Admiralty has been treated. I cannot help it – tho' I try. Then the damnable mismanagement which has ruined the Dardanelles enterprise and squandered so much life and opportunity cries aloud for retribution: and if I survive, the day will come when I will claim it publicly.

In fact official obscurantism prevented him from so doing in his lifetime. Even though I relaxed the fifty-year rule to thirty, the Dardanelles documents did not become available until a year after his death.

The day had to await his epic history of the First World War.

He returned to Parliament to pour out his heart against all he had seen in France, the 'glibness' and the futile and costly offensives. In May 1916, he said in the House:

> I say to myself every day, what is going on while we are here, while we go away to dinner, or home to bed? Nearly 1,000 men – Englishmen, Britishers, men of our own race – are knocked into bundles of bloody rags every twenty-four hours, and carried away to hasty graves or to field ambulances, and the money of which the Prime Minister has spoken so clearly is flowing away in its broad stream ...

To his brother he wrote even more bitterly:

> Is it not damnable that I should be denied all real scope to serve this country, in this tremendous hour? Though my life is full of comfort, pleasure and prosperity, I writhe hourly not to be able to get my teeth effectively into the Boche ... Jack my dear I am learning to hate ...

In 1917 Lloyd George brought him back to get his teeth into the Boche: he was made Minister of Munitions. It was the department for which Lloyd George himself had left the Treasury. Churchill showed the same qualities as Lloyd George had shown, the more determined by all he had seen in France. His conciliation endeavours with the work force, the vigour he put forward with the supplying contractors, the speeches he made up and down the country, reflected the urgency of 1917, the year of the U-boat, the year when shells were being fired on the Front to little effect except running down the ammunition stockpiles. He devoted his energies particularly at the inter-Allied level, and especially in coordinating Britain's efforts with those of France, Italy – and of the United States, now in the war.

In the crucial spring months of 1918, when Lloyd George kept his head when all around him were losing theirs and blaming it on him, the Prime Minister turned to Churchill for sustenance, not in vain. In that decisive March, Churchill wrote to Lloyd George:

> Violent counsels and measures must rule, seek the truth in the hour of need with disdain of other things, courage and a clear plan will enable you to keep command of the Nation. But if you fall below the level of the crisis, your role is exhausted.

Lloyd George sent Churchill to France on a secret mission and used his daily telegraphic reports from the front-line positions to convince the Cabinet that the war was not lost.

Within weeks, days almost, the virulence of the German offensive had exhausted itself, and the German onrush was halted. More than half a year

Churchill as Secretary of State for War in 1918.

of retreat and internal collapse were needed before the flags went up and the streets were filled to cheer the Armistice. Two months later, Churchill went to the War Office. His political views led him to support Lloyd George's insistent aid to those Russians who were fighting against the Bolsheviks, but eventually the British Forces were evacuated without loss and without success; Churchill said, 'it must be by Russian manhood and courage'.

In 1921 he went to the Colonial Office where with the aid, among others, of Lawrence of Arabia he established the two Arab kingdoms of Iraq and Transjordan and created the conditions necessary for the Jews to establish their national home in Palestine, of which he was a lifelong supporter.

He was no less successful when entrusted by Lloyd George with negotiations to end the Irish Civil War. The Irish leader, Michael Collins, expressed his judgment of the negotiations both before and after the Treaty of 1922: 'Tell Winston we would never have done anything without him.'

Churchill's role in the Chanak operations has been described in a previous chapter. In the 1922 Carlton Club destruction of the Lloyd George Government, he not only went out of office with Lloyd George; shortly afterwards he lost his seat in Dundee. But all the time he was warning, seeking to open up the future. In January 1924 he forecast the nuclear revolution and guided weapons:

> Have we reached the end? ... May there not be methods of using energy more intense than anything heretofore discovered? Might not a bomb no bigger than an orange be found to possess a secret power to destroy a whole block of buildings – nay, to concentrate the force of a thousand tons of cordite and blast a township at a stroke? Could not explosives even of the existing type be guided automatically in flying machines by wireless or other ways, without a human pilot, in ceaseless procession upon a hostile city, arsenal, camp or dockyard?

Baldwin encouraged Churchill's return to the Tory fold. He did not insist on Churchill's taking a Tory oath of loyalty in the 1924 election. He accepted his return, on leaving the Liberals, as a 'Constitutional' candidate and surprised the Westminster scene, as has been described, by appointing him Chancellor of the Exchequer. Churchill's first reaction to the offer was: 'Would a bloody duck swim?'

His concern was with social reform, a true son of Asquith's pre-war Cabinet. He had expected, and indeed hoped for a social service ministry, but on being sent to the Exchequer used it as a base for his attack on poverty. There was no task he enjoyed more in his whole ministerial career. He wrote to Neville Chamberlain, Minister of Health, on 20 March 1925:

> It is clearly contrary to public policy to allow the present condition to continue under which the dependent and often helpless children of a widow are deprived of the care and attention they ought to have because the mother is compelled to work long hours and laboriously to provide a bare maintenance for them. This then is the foundation on which our treatment of the uncovenanted should be built ...

On 22 March he wrote to his wife: 'I have been working all day [Sunday] and am very tired.' After meeting a deputation of old age pensioners he instructed his officials:

> It is when misfortune comes upon the household, when prolonged unemployment, or old age, or sickness, or the death of the breadwinner comes upon this household, that you see how narrow was the margin on which it was apparently living so prosperously, and in a few months the result of the thrift of years may be swept away, and the house broken up.

His cry was: 'Insure, insure.' He asked the Government Actuary to calculate what the insurance contribution would have to be. All pensions were to begin at sixty-five, and widows provided for from the outset. Men over sixty-five would pay £1 a year for three years, as a contribution to their £25 pension, to avoid 'pauperization and the stigma of dole: it will promote each man's self-respect and make him value his pension the more when he gets it.'

In a letter to the King he explained his keenness for this reform in his Board of Trade days nearly twenty years before: 'The immense opportunities which the state gift of pensions at 70 offered for a contributory Insurance Scheme for pension at 65 ...' Nationwide insurance was a 'miracle' which gave 'millions of people a stake in the country which they will have created largely by their own contributory efforts'. He explained the scheme in his Budget speech on

28 April, setting out the pension for widows, and their children up to fourteen and a half, and the general pension for all at sixty-five.

Churchill in fact introduced five Budgets. The first embodied the pension proposals. That of 1926 imposed a betting tax of five per cent on all bets, as an incentive to 'thrift and economy'. In 1927 he increased tobacco taxes to come largely 'from the profits of the Imperial Tobacco Company', but rejected a demand from his own party to reduce death duties: he would not, he said, benefit the landowning classes unless 'other classes of taxpayer' were also helped. In 1928 he reduced the size of the civil service, imposed a tax on all imported fuel oil, and a duty on cigarette lighters (to prevent avoidance of the match duty), increased child allowances, and introduced the industrial de-rating scheme originally suggested to him by the young Harold Macmillan. Finally, in 1929, he remitted the tea duty, and provided Treasury funds to extend the provision of rural post offices.

His Budget speeches were notable for both their broad perspectives and his mastery of detail, and also for his humour. Neville Chamberlain said his 1929 speech was 'one of the best he had made and kept the House fascinated and enthralled by its wit, audacity and grace'. Only four previous Chancellors had introduced five formal (annual) Budgets, Walpole, Pitt, Peel and Gladstone, and each was at the time, or was to become, Prime Minister.

His non-legislative record at the Treasury has been described, including his conciliatory handling of the coal industry dispute and his vigorous fight against the Threadneedle Street establishment over the parity of the pound. Churchill was right, his surrender wrong, though it was not until 1931 that the full account was rendered, with Churchill out of office, apparently without hope of return. The battles over Indian constitutional reform, and the vindictiveness of successive Conservative administrations, were to ensure that he played no part in the government of Britain throughout the eight years from the 1931 election until the outbreak of war in 1939. For Churchill they were the years of warning and warning and warning.

His warnings were based on a meticulous sorting of the facts. High-ranking serving officers and civil servants, particularly in the Whitehall departments, felt, however unconstitutionally, that the smooth dismissal of their warnings by Downing Street and the Cabinet justified their alerting Parliament and the nation through Churchill. All his instincts were repelled by the Government's concealment and misrepresentation of the facts, and their refusal to act. He disdained the attacks made on him as, with total persistence, he pressed his question and his utterly fearless speeches. From the start he was urging a more active defence policy, with heavy emphasis on the Royal Air Force, and an effective system of alliances, especially with France. He supported his attacks with speeches, articles and books. For this, Lord Beaverbrook's *Evening Standard* sacked him from its list of regular contributors, but the *Daily Telegraph* welcomed him with open arms.

From the rise of Hitler onwards, he was warning not only about weapons but also about Hitler's persecution of minorities. In answer to the MacDonald Government's attempt to rearm Germany as a prelude to disarmament, Churchill said in the House as early as May 1932:

> I should very much regret to see any approximation in military strength between Germany and France . . . I would say to those who would like to

> see Germany and France on an equal footing in armaments, 'Do you wish for war?'

And in November he told the House:

> If Geneva fails let the National Government propose to Parliament measures necessary to place our air force in such a condition of power and efficiency that it will not be worth anyone's while to come here and kill our women and children in the hope that they may blackmail us into surrender.

In March 1933:

> In the present temper of Europe can you ever expect that France would halve her air force and then reduce the residue by one third? Would you advise her to do so? If she took your advice and did it, stand by her side and make good the injury? . . .
>
> You talk of secret diplomacy, but let me tell you that there is a worse kind of secret diplomacy, and it is the diplomacy which spreads out hope and soothing-syrup for the good, while all the time winks are being exchanged between the people who know actually what is going on.

He was shocked to hear a minister admit that Britain was only the fifth air power. By May 1935, Churchill had penetrated the Government's obscurantism and discovered that the Cabinet had now fallen two years behind Germany in arms and also in the capacity to produce arms.

> When the situation was manageable it was neglected, and now that it is thoroughly out of hand we apply too late the remedies which then might have effected a cure.
>
> There is nothing new in the story. It is as old as the sibylline books. It falls into that long, dismal catalogue of the fruitlessness of experience and confirmed unteachability of mankind.

He pointed out to the House that the Air Minister's statement in March 1935 – that Germany's air strength was only half that of Britain in November 1934 and that Britain would still have superiority by the end of the year – was false, and challenged any member of the Government to say we should have the superiority they had claimed: 'No, Sir. The whole of these assertions made in the most sweeping manner and on the highest authority, are now admitted to be entirely wrong.'

In August he was warning the new Air Secretary, Lord Swinton, with a wealth of detailed briefing, that we should be falling further and further behind air parity and industrial capacity for arms production. In November he was advising the country to read *Mein Kampf* and see what was threatening: once again he raised the question of the persecution of the Jews.

By April 1936, Sir Robert Vansittart, Permanent Under-Secretary at the Foreign Office, secretly sent a senior FO diplomat to see Churchill and enlist his support against the Government's complacency, asking him to bring together all who were concerned about the German danger and threat to democracy. Churchill was not backward in his responses, approaching even trade union leaders.

The Establishment, whose daily voice was *The Times*, continued to press the thesis that the ostrich was the most intelligent of God's creatures. Its editor

In the early thirties Churchill became known for his 'die hard' attitude towards Indian Independence.

warned against prematurely abandoning the hope, 'supported by so many authoritative pronouncements on the German side, that Germany is prepared to reach a general understanding and settlement with the British Empire'. The 'Thunderer' bleated the hope that Churchill would guard against making any appeal for Anglo-French collaboration that might lead to 'misunderstanding and controversy'.

In September 1936, responding to secret encouragement from the Foreign Office, he made a great speech in Paris appealing for Anglo-French cooperation to meet the common danger in defence of democracy. For the first time, press comments began to respond, even to demand that Churchill be taken into the Government. There was another secret approach: Robert Watson-Watt, the inventor of radar, was being driven frantic by Air Ministry delays in developing and testing radar. Following his personal appeal, Churchill took up the matter at once and wrote to Swinton in the strongest terms.

Churchill and Lindemann were serving on a Committee of Imperial Defence on air defence research, and soon began to feel, and to tell Swinton, that he could have done more by agitation and public attacks. Churchill had an uneasy feeling that his membership on the Committee gagged him publicly without increasing his influence on the inside. He took up deficiencies in tank production as well, and in his speech in the House made his long-remembered comment on the Government: 'So they go on in strange paradox, decided, only to be undecided, resolved – to be irresolute, adamant – for drift, solid – for fluidity, all-powerful – to be impotent.'

The warnings continued. Rearmament had begun in a measured way. Yet Chamberlain still could not understand the reference to 1939, of all years, as a year of particular danger. Despite the 'party' pledge, on 'security' grounds no figures of air defences were published. In fact the number of aircraft fell further and further behind.

On 4 February 1938, Churchill warned again about Nazi intentions to subjugate Central Europe. Twelve days later, Hitler demanded the inclusion of

Austrian Nazis in the Austrian Government. For Vienna now it could only be a matter of weeks. On 14 March, Churchill struck a yet more resonant note of urgency:

> Europe is confronted with a programme of aggression, nicely calculated and timed, unfolding stage by stage, and there is only one choice open, not only to us but to other countries, either to submit like Austria, or else take effective measures while time remains to ward off the danger, and if it cannot be warded off to cope with it ... If we go on waiting upon events, how much shall we throw away of resources now available for our security and the maintenance of peace? How many friends will be alienated, how many potential allies shall we see go one by one down the grisly gulf? How many times will bluff succeed until behind bluff ever gathering forces have accumulated reality?... Where are we going to be two years hence, for instance, when the German Army will certainly be much larger than the French Army, and when all the small nations will have fled from Geneva to pay homage to the ever waxing powers of the Nazi system, and to make the best terms that they can for themselves?

Even after Munich, Chamberlain rejected Churchill's demands for a Ministry of Supply. In a Parliamentary debate Churchill went over the arguments, his warnings and demands over the years. He was appealing now, not to the Government, but to Tory back-benchers:

> ... hon. Gentlemen above the gangway – pledged, loyal, faithful supporters on all occasions of His Majesty's Government – must not imagine that they can throw the burden wholly on the Ministers of the Crown. Much power has been vested with them. One healthy growl from those benches three years ago – and how different today would be the whole lay-out of our armaments production! Alas, that service was not forthcoming ...
>
> I put it as bluntly as I possibly can. If only fifty Members of the Conservative Party went into the Lobby tonight to vote for this Amendment, it would not affect the life of the Government, but it would make them act. It would make a forward movement of real energy. We should get our Ministry of Supply, no doubt, but much more than that we should get a feeling of renewed strength and a prestige outside this country which would be of real service and value ...
>
> This is no party question. It has nothing to do with party. It is entirely an issue affecting the broad safety of the nation...

He did not get fifty Conservative MPs in the Lobby. Apart from himself there were only Brendan Bracken and Harold Macmillan.

As late as 9 December 1938, Chamberlain was attacking Churchill for his 'lack of judgment'. By the spring of 1939, he was throwing out guarantees to Poland and Romania, regardless of the power he had thrown away which would have been necessary to honour them. Less than nine months later Britain was at war in the cause of honouring one of them, Poland. With the outbreak of war, Winston was back at the Admiralty, the post he had first held twenty-eight years earlier. He worked loyally with Chamberlain, though always conscious of a decade of lost opportunities. On 4 April 1940, Chamberlain appointed him chairman of a Committee consisting of the three service ministers and the heads of the three fighting services. A Parliament previously dominated by the complacent adherents of appeasement voted decisively on Norway. It was a tribute to Churchill's sense of collective Cabinet responsibility that, setting aside nearly a decade as a vilified Cassandra, he accepted full responsibility for his part in the Norway operations, in fact being shouted down by some of those who for so many years had traduced him. It was Lloyd George and Amery, as we have seen, who sheltered him from the splinters, and it was Parliament, including the Labour Opposition, which called him to the premiership.

Churchill's conduct of the war is in many ways more distinguished than that of Lloyd George in the First World War. For one thing, he was in control – though at a more advanced age – for a far longer time. Lloyd George was wartime Prime Minister for less than three years; Churchill for five. Churchill had to face two new dimensions: first the complete subjugation of Europe by the enemy, who for four years controlled Europe's coastline, including the Channel ports; and, second, air attack. Had it not been for that last squadron which routed the Luftwaffe in the Battle of Britain in September 1940, Britain's war factories, docks and lines of communication would have been destroyed. A still further dimension was created by the aerial attack on the civil population.

In 1940 there was a call for a quality of war leadership such as never existed in the First War. Tens of thousands were huddled in wartime shelters and London Underground stations as Hitler's bombers rained devastation first on London, then on the Midland and Northern cities, in an attempt to terrorize the civilian population into surrender. Churchill's wartime leadership was at its greatest in those months. For, after the surrender of France, Britain stood alone, apart from the Commonwealth. The United States was friendly and cooperative, but non-belligerent. Those were the months of Churchill's greatest speeches, relayed to the people, and the shelters, not by the two-dimensional press, valuable though that was, but by the vibrant medium of the radio, which brought through to the nation the full Churchill message, and pronunciation. Never could Nazi have sounded so detestable as in Churchill's anglicized, almost guttural, 'NARZI'. It might be for years, or it might be for ever, but there would be no surrender.

Those of us who saw the Top Secret assessment of our defence strength, including coast-defence and anti-aircraft equipment, in the summer of 1940 could have believed in nothing but for the emotive leadership Britain was given. As an official of Churchill's Cabinet office in those lonely months I learned of one example. A colleague of mine was duty officer when a 2 am call came in from President Roosevelt, no doubt forgetting the five-hour timelag, who wanted to speak to Churchill. It was no easy matter to awaken the Prime Minister, but my colleague woke the Cabinet Secretary, Sir Edward Bridges, who decided to rouse a grumpy Churchill. Britain had asked the US to lease to us fifty over-age destroyers no longer required by the American Navy. The President told the Prime Minister that he would make the destroyers available in return for a lease of West Indian bases for ninety-nine years. But he must ask for a clear assurance: the Prime Minister must give his personal word that if the Germans successfully invaded Britain, the destroyers would be at once ordered to the US or Canada. It is not always easy to be at one's most articulate if awakened at 2 am: Winston was equal to the challenge. 'Yes,' he said, 'I will certainly give that assurance, but that is a fate more likely to befall the Nazi fleet than the British.'

Churchill had one great advantage over Lloyd George; he had the loyal adherence of Clem Attlee and his Labour colleagues in the coalition. Lloyd George was himself partly to blame: he relied heavily on Balfour, who had resigned the Conservative leadership in 1911, rather than on Bonar Law, the acknowledged Tory leader. In his later years he had dealt mainly with an odd assortment of Conservative ministers, and virtually ignored the principal Liberals. Churchill had won increasing Labour support before war broke out. In 1939, even Stafford Cripps appealed to Churchill to come out against Chamberlain.

Churchill enjoyed the total loyalty of Attlee, who was the effective No. 2 throughout the wartime administration, and officially recognized as Deputy Prime Minister later in the war. With Churchill taking charge of military decisions as Minister of Defence, Attlee virtually took charge of the administration. For long periods Churchill was absent – at wartime summits, his tours of the war theatres and also in North Africa, recuperating from his long illness. Attlee was in charge of the Cabinet, and also represented the Prime Minister in Parliament. Not only Attlee but other Labour ministers: Herbert Morrison was appointed Minister of Supply when the National Government was formed, but when the bombing began in the autumn of 1940 he was made Minister of Home Security. Morrison, the virtual creator of modern London government, had been the greatest municipal administrator in the free world; he was responsible for Civil Defence and morale in the shelters. No less – probably more – significant was the appointment of Ernest Bevin as Minister of Labour. Churchill had faced him eyeball to eyeball in 1926, and respected him. It is a mark of a great man that he can appoint a formidable opponent, instead of resenting him.

The Conservative ministers he appointed were of equally high quality. He made great use of Eden, and brought in Lyttelton and Woolton from business. Kingsley Wood was Chancellor, but outside the Cabinet in the early years, no doubt Churchill's response to the baleful influence of the Treasury in Chamberlain's time.

Churchill was well served too by his private secretariat under Professor Lindemann, later Lord Cherwell, though at the cost of causing resentment on the part of colleagues. This team had been appointed while Churchill was still First Lord, and it moved into No. 10 with Churchill. Lindemann, who manifested a ruthless, some would say German, efficiency and dedication, had serviced Churchill on defence and scientific questions in the lonely Thirties, and with Churchill had been more often right than wrong, in contrast with the Prime Ministers and their advisers of those years. Lindemann's team included men of great distinction such as Donald (later Sir Donald) MacDougall, but they were much resented in Whitehall, which remembered, or had read legends of, Lloyd George's secretariat in the 'Garden Suburb' of No. 10. The Lindemann staff tended to telephone saying that 'the Prime Minister wanted' this or that information, when it was the staff who were taking an initiative.

Churchill took office on the eve of the Battle of Britain. By a miracle, and the organization of the little boats, the Expeditionary Force was rescued from Dunkirk. Invasion was expected almost daily, air bombardment hourly. Churchill, while belatedly whipping up a Whitehall team to meet the challenge, was untiring in inspecting air defences, coast defences and military installations. When the Battle of Britain began he was at fighter headquarters, or visiting bombed sites, cigar between his lips, his V-sign extended.

What Churchill sought to bring to the war leadership was, first, action against the spirit of defeatism which was inevitable when France fell and Italy entered the war. He saw his task as rallying public morale and lifting the people's eyes towards ultimate victory. His main executive task was to reorganize the whole machinery of the war, and the respective chains of command, both for fighting the war and for procuring the munitions of war. His main international preoccupation was to build up the closest possible relationship with the United States, first, and successfully, with its President, Franklin Roosevelt, and soon afterwards, with equal success, with Congress. He had also, despite his limited contacts, to inspire loyalists inside occupied Europe to hold on, and ultimately to cooperate with the invasion troops in expelling the occupiers.

He was no less punctilious in maintaining relations with the various 'Governments in exile' in London. Among refugee leaders, the one who presented him with the most difficulty was General de Gaulle, particularly as the United States maintained diplomatic contacts with Nazi-occupied Vichy France. Only a fraction of the stories told about Churchill are true, and this is not important. What is important is the fact that the best of them ring true. It was said that he was on record as saying: 'The only cross I have to bear is the Cross of Lorraine.' The problem, de Gaulle's personality apart, was that the two men had entirely different conceptions of the General's role in London. For de Gaulle it was quite simple: he was the legitimate head of the French people, albeit in enforced exile. To Churchill, de Gaulle was a leading French general who was commander of those of the French fighting services who had escaped from France or North Africa and come to London, waiting and training to take their part in the invasion of Nazi-occupied France, though Churchill worked to get him accepted by the British people.

One of the main arguments between them related to the French gold owned by the Banque de France and held on 'customer's account' in the vaults of the Bank of England. The Bank of England is always punctilious about the deposits it holds on behalf of customers, and will not submit to any Government direction about it. (In early November 1965, just before the Rhodesian unilateral declaration of 'independence', for instance, the Bank resisted all Government pressure to refuse to allow the then legitimate Rhodesian Government to withdraw its holdings.) So with de Gaulle; the Bank held their French gold and foreign exchange on behalf of their customer (not the French Government) whoever that might be. After repeated representations, de Gaulle asked to see Churchill to seek a Government direction, to which, the story has it, Churchill replied in his impeccable but not inimitable Churchillian French: 'Mon cher Général, quand je me trouve en face da la Vieille Dame de Threadneedle Street, je suis tout à fait impotent.' He should no doubt have said 'impuissant', but that is how the story goes.

Churchill's control of the war did not derive entirely from his position as Prime Minister: he took a second appointment, as Minister of Defence. The service departments were among the 'ministers of Cabinet rank', but outside the War Cabinet, attending as required.

He spent more of his time than is realized at Chequers, except when required in Parliament, or for Cabinets and the principal committees of Cabinet. He worked to a punishing schedule, examining every detail. He regularly had one or more of the Chiefs of Staff there, and frequently kept them up very late, yarning, reminiscing, more often working, or arguing about some brilliant new war-winning idea he had thrown at them, or they at him. Some of these ideas proved after detailed scrutiny to be utterly impracticable, and he showed no animosity when they made that clear. At weekends there were, often after midnight, films in the then chill and cheerless Hawtrey room; Churchill is said to have seen *Lady Hamilton* five times, not for the charms of Miss Vivien Leigh, but because of the reproduction of the Battle of Trafalgar, in fact using model ships.

There is a good but authoritative story about one of Churchill's post-midnight activities. In the Great Hall of Chequers is a large painting of the Aesop fable in which a lion caught in the toils of a net is rescued by a mouse nibbling at the rope which binds the net to a tree, attributed to Rubens. Churchill, in the small hours, decided: 'can't see the mouse', and immediately demanded that his paints, brushes and a ladder be produced. He painted in the mouse – though later Prime Ministers telling the story to their visitors still had some difficulty in 'seeing the mouse'. It takes a confident and authoritative Prime Minister to decide to touch up a Rubens. The sequel is a little unhappy. The Churchill £1,000,000 fund-raising effort to get money for Churchill College, asked the Chequers trustees to agree to loaning the picture for three months to the Churchill exhibition in London. It was decided to clean the canvas of its centuries of varnish and stains. This was successfully accomplished, but of course Churchill's adornment had been over the varnish and his artistic effort went with the varnish.

Almost surrounded by hills, Chequers is not easy to find from the air, but at times of full moon – 'bombers' moon' – Churchill used to go to Dytchley. Aerial attack was not the only problem. Years of neglect in organizing arms production, and the supporting equipment and materials, were exercising their toll. He and the Defence Committee had to issue priority directives. Immediately after the fall of France he made his determinations. At the top of the list was coast defence, followed by the naval construction programme, and the construction of fighters for the Battle of Britain – indeed, the task of making up deficiencies in aircraft production as a whole.

The operation originally was botched. The naval programme held 1.AA (the top) priority. Aluminium was the material in shortest supply. The Admiralty invoked their priorities: priorities are by definition overriding. *Any* Admiralty use, however inessential, took ordinal priority over all other demands: their Lordships of the Admiralty, in accordance with peacetime specification, had allocated aluminium for washbasins. On the priority schedule these must take precedence over fighters for the air war. After a series of complaints, Churchill intervened: 'priorities' gave way to allocations, quantitative figures for each use, *related* to priorities, but to none could go absolute priorities, regardless of essentiality.

With the troops safely home from Dunkirk, once the battle for total air superiority over Britain's airspace had been weathered, and the odds against a naval invasion reduced, Churchill for the first time was able to concentrate on longer-term strategy, including the political strategy of alliances. In this Hitler created a new situation by his invasion of Russia in June 1941.

Churchill had had an inveterate hatred for Soviet tyranny since the Revolution. He had played an important part in the intervention in 1919, though as Hitler continued his record of aggression Churchill and Eden in May 1939

Churchill with General de Gaulle.

had the courage to propose a formal treaty of alliance with the Soviet Union. It was greatly to his credit, and to his sense of first things first, that his immediate reaction was one of solidarity. Co-belligerents, if not allies, was the theme. Whom Hitler attacks, with them Britain makes common cause. He was not going to 'unsay' a word of a generation's condemnation of Soviet Communism, but:

> We have but one aim and one single irrevocable purpose. We are resolved to destroy Hitler and every vestige of the Nazi régime. From this nothing will deter us – nothing. We will never parley, we will never negotiate with Hitler or any of his gang. We shall fight him by land, we shall fight him by sea, we shall fight him in the air, until with God's help we have rid the earth of his shadow and liberated its peoples from his yoke. Any man or

Churchill landing in Normandy during a visit to the landing beaches, where he was met by General Montgomery.

> state who fights against Nazidom will have our aid. Any man or state who marches with Hitler is our foe . . . that is our policy and our declaration. The Russian danger . . . is our danger . . . we shall give whatever help we can to Russia and the Russian people.

Churchill was true to the eighteenth-century principle: whom Britain's enemy attacks is our ally, regardless of other considerations. As a historian too, perhaps he recalled the error which destroyed Napoleon. Hitler's attack was in June, but the snows would not be deferred indefinitely. The concept of the Grand Alliance was in Churchill's thoughts, but the decisive grand alliance would be with the United States.

It was not Germany but Japan, with the attack on Pearl Harbor, which created the alliance that won the war. President Roosevelt, with a significant part of his Pacific Fleet destroyed, did not waste time on procedural formalities. The United States was at war with Japan and Hitler declared war on America. Hitler's Italian lackey of course joined in. Churchill went straight away to Washington: the strategy was recounted, and at Roosevelt's insistence the war objectives were agreed, to be tightened and promulgated as the Atlantic Charter when they met again on an American warship. The strategy was: victory in

Europe first, then in the Far East. A total command structure was agreed for the main theatres, Europe, the Far East, the Middle East, North Africa.

Though the war would be long and hard, Churchill, from the moment he heard the news of Pearl Harbor, said: 'I knew the United States was in the war . . . there was no more doubt about the end.' Only time, only negotiations about the allocation of duties, only priorities and the timing of operations.

During the years of waiting, Cabinet committees were hard at work on planning the transition from war to peace, and seeking coalition agreements on issues which had traditionally divided the parties. The results, to say the least, were mixed.

On social security the Beveridge Report paved the way. Beveridge was hated in Whitehall. Many now senior civil servants had served under him, and he had been very imperious. In 1940 he was called into one short-term job after another by ministers: Whitehall feared he might get a war job which lasted, and were happy to recommend that he left them to run the war while he spent the next few years preparing a one-man report on social security. He worked more rapidly than they expected, and reported in 1943: the Government substantially accepted his recommendations.

An internal document on full employment policies for the post-war world was hacked about in ministerial committees, published and debated. It reflected a good deal of the new conventional Keynesian wisdom, but on issues in dispute between the political parties it represented a somewhat low common denominator of compromise. On such issues as the future of the coal industry, gas, electricity, transport, there was no agreement: the various representatives of the principal parties, in the wartime phrase, retired to previously prepared positions. Although Duncan Sandys and others were working vigorously on post-war housing, progress was hampered by lack of any Cabinet decision on land planning, compulsory acquisition powers, and the valuation of land used for public building programmes. Churchill appointed W.S. Morrison as Minister of Town and Country Planning, no doubt hoping that would be the last he would hear of it. Three expert reports had been laboriously produced – Scott, Uthwatt and Barlow. A Cabinet committee had sat for months and produced an agreed report, avoiding many of the controversial issues. It required Cabinet ratification.

The story of the Prime Minister's summing up, told to me within an hour by a minister who had been present, became a legend in Whitehall. A recent check on the somewhat uninformative Cabinet minutes casts doubt on some of the details, but it illustrates the difference between Churchill's decisiveness on matters affecting the war and his lack of interest in some of the boring pre-occupations of the post-war world. It was the last item on the agenda. Winston had already closed his Cabinet folder and was lighting another cigar. The Cabinet Secretary drew his attention to the last item and Churchill said: 'Ah yes, all this stuff about planning and compensation and betterment. Broad vistas and city centres and all that. But give to me the eighteenth-century alley, where footpads lurked and the harlot plied her trade, and none of this new-fangled planning doctrine.'

If Morrison had been wise he would have said that he fully agreed with the Prime Minister; that he could see that the Prime Minister had read his paper, which he clearly had not; that he assumed the Prime Minister in the words he had used was approving his paper, that he assumed the Cabinet agreed, and that in all his planning he would take care to make full provision for narrower vistas and alleys for appropriate activities such as those mentioned. Winston would have said: 'Quite right, my boy, you go ahead.' Instead, Morrison stammered out: 'I take it then, Prime Minister, you want me to take it back and think again.' Winston replied: 'Quite right, my boy.'

Questions about post-war Britain were not all handled in this way; the Churchill of the social reform period of the 1920s and earlier was to tell the British Medical Association that there would have to be, in some form, a national health service. The difference between his treatment of questions which interested him and those which did not has been commented on by Sir David Hunt, who was private secretary to both Attlee and Churchill in the periods just before and just after the general election of October 1951:

> While Attlee had a great power of decision, Winston Churchill, on subjects in which he took little interest, affected horror when his advisers pressed for a decision; they were confusing him with a dictator, and he said, 'This is a democratic government. These matters must be decided by the Cabinet as a whole; I cannot possibly settle them on my own authority.'

Hunt, who with the other three private secretaries took his turn at Chequers one weekend in four, eating with the family, has made an interesting comment on these different styles of Churchill and Attlee:

> Many people have expressed surprise to me when I mentioned this as a point of contrast between Attlee and Churchill. It goes completely contrary to the popular idea of both these men. Attlee is usually thought of as good-natured, a compromiser, but not a strong character and it is always supposed that Churchill was one of those determined men who made up their minds in a flash. To assert that the opposite was true might make it seem that I was disparaging Churchill.

Montgomery broke through in Alamein and sped along the North African coastal strip to link up with the Americans. The next decision was where the attack on Southern Europe should take place; where was, in Churchill's growling phrase, 'the soft underbelly of the Axis'? Sicily and Italy were attacked and conquered, then Southern France. Yugoslavia under Tito, with the help of distinguished British officers, was moving to regain its independence. Churchill was concerned that the attacks on Europe were too confined to Western Europe: the victorious Russians were not only driving the defeated Germans through Poland back to Berlin, they were enveloping most of Eastern Europe, Bulgaria, Hungary, Romania, Czechoslovakia as well as Poland. In the event they did not relax their grip on the part of Germany, now the German 'Democratic' Republic, which they occupied. Austria's destiny was in doubt: it was in the event neutralized. All these questions involved Churchill in prodigious travels: Moscow, Washington, Canada, Teheran, Malta – even Greece on Christmas Day 1944.

The war in Europe ended with Germany's surrender on 7 May 1945. The war with Japan, the second priority in the Allied strategy, was still to be won. Few expected an immediate collapse. This raised problems for Churchill and Attlee in Britain. Churchill asked Attlee whether the Labour ministers would remain in the coalition until the war with Japan was over. Fortuitously, as in 1940, the Labour Party's annual conference was due to convene. The answer o Churchill was that the coalition was at an end. A purely Conservative Government was formed, a caretaker Government as it proved. Churchill's esponse was that an election would take place in July. This he was perfectly ntitled to decide: Britain was still governed by a Parliament elected in 1935, he longest Parliament since Stuart times. Not many Labour leaders expected Labour victory, despite what some subsequently wrote in their memoirs. Dalon in his autobiography expressed his total retrospective confidence in the outome of the election: in fact, in the train on the way back from Blackpool he old a number of us that Labour would win 290 seats, giving a viable majority o the Conservatives.

The votes cast in the election of 5 July were not counted for three weeks, o allow time for the overseas service votes to be returned to Britain. Meanwhile Churchill was in Potsdam negotiating with Roosevelt and Stalin. He returned or the count. It was a Labour landslide with 393 seats, including many who never for one moment expected to be elected. When, after Parliament had been ummoned and the Government formed, Attlee, with Bevin, the Foreign Secreary, went to Potsdam, the Soviet representatives expressed total incredulity.

The Conservatives were in opposition, led by Churchill. It was a humiliating xperience for one who had led Britain in the war and since June was more ualified than any man to speak for Europe. His stature in Europe and the Jnited States was greater than that of any living statesman, and he began to leploy himself increasingly in speaking to mass audiences abroad. His speech f 5 March 1946, in Fulton, Missouri, called on the US and Britain to be the guardians of the peace, and warned against Soviet policies: this was the 'iron urtain' speech. It was not an original phrase, but Churchill made it echo hroughout the free world. Six months later came his Zurich speech calling n the free nations of Europe to form a new Council of Europe, which duly ame into being. Churchill can fairly be regarded as one of the principal ounders of the modern European Movement.

Attlee's Government, as has been seen, took over the task of governing a Britain shattered by the war, facing world shortages of food and raw materials, nd confronted with financial disaster by the cancellation of Lend-Lease when he war with Japan was brutally ended by the atomic bombs on Nagasaki and Hiroshima. The 1950 election gave Labour a narrow majority. Wrong timing, n the wrong advice, led Attlee to go to the country in October 1951. An election n the spring of 1952, when the economic situation had significantly changed, might well have confirmed him in office.

Churchill was back in power, with only a small majority, it is true, but it vas he who had coined the phrase: 'One is enough.' He stayed there for nearly hree and a half years. It was something of a derogation from his wartime tature, and from the European and world status he had the right to claim, hat he should have to make little party speeches about the merits of the decision o end the wartime nationalization of the Liverpool raw cotton market. As he erceptibly aged, it was pathetic to see him baited by Labour back-benchers uch as Emrys Hughes and Sydney Silverman. He was increasingly becoming misfit in the rapidly changing Britain of the post-war world, and in the postvar world itself. But he more than deserved the glory of the Queen's Coronation nd the award of the Garter on the morning of the ceremony, itself illuminated y the arrival of the news that a British team had been the first to conquer Mount Everest.

Above VE Day.

Opposite The war leaders leave St Margaret's, Westminster, after Parliament's thanksgiving on VJ Day. Churchill was now Leader of the Opposition and Attlee was Prime Minister.

The world was changing. The nuclear developments which had ended the Japanese war did not stop there. Devastating though Nagasaki and Hiroshima had been – as was also Britain's own atomic capability, developed under the Attlee Government – all these were dwarfed by the thermonuclear weapon the United States had created. This was detonated over Bikini, in the Pacific. There were stories of clouds of noxious fumes capable of being blown five thousand miles and threatening life over a wide area. The House of Commons debated the issue. An ageing Churchill replied in terms uncharacteristic of a lifetime in the House of Commons, no doubt reflecting an unimaginative Foreign Office brief but taken by the House as showing insensitivity. The reception to which he was then subjected totally unnerved him, and those of us sitting on the Opposition front bench close to the Speaker's Chair saw him go out whimpering, on the arm of the Chief Government Whip. It was time to go, and within six months the pressures of his Party Establishment, combining unimaginable public sympathy with the utter ruthlessness always shown to one who has served his turn, saw him off the scene. To any Parliamentarian – and there

is no camaraderie, irrespective of party, to compare with that of Parliamentarians – it was a tragic period. At least it could be said that in those days before the Conservative Party adopted elections for choosing its leader, Winston Churchill had left an unchallengeable successor in Anthony Eden. The tragedy was that Baldwin had not so contrived matters that Eden had been his successor eighteen years earlier. Had he done so, perhaps the Second World War might never have occurred – with the paranoiac Hitler one cannot be dogmatic. But the Eden of 1955 was a different Eden: rightly obsessed with the dictators of the Thirties he saw another dictator in Nasser, hence the Suez operation which led to his downfall.

Winston Churchill was, above all things, a Parliamentarian. He loved the House, he had dominated it over the years. In its most degenerate days it had refused to listen to his warnings and had treated him with disdain and hostility. His loyalty to Parliament, and his obeisance to the courtesies of an almost forgotten age, caused him to take personal initiatives which the world of today might find it hard to understand. When Aneurin Bevan and I resigned from the Attlee Government in April 1951, because we could not accept the unrealistic arms policy forced on the Government – and in Bevan's case its consequences for the National Health Service – Winston came up to us. He expressed sympathy with us: we were facing a situation which had been much familiar to him, though, as he pointed out, we would never be obsecrated as he had been. We had gone out with honour, but, he added with a twinkle in his eye, he and his party would make the most of the situation which resulted.

That evening Brendan Bracken sought me out. He had been charged, he said, 'by the greatest living statesman, for that is what Mr Churchill is' to give me a message to convey to my wife. First, Mr Churchill wanted me to know, he had been 'presented' to my wife, otherwise he would not presume to send her a message. The message was that whereas I, as an experienced politician, had taken a step of which he felt free to take such party advantage as was appropriate, his concern was with my wife, an innocent party in these affairs, who would undoubtedly suffer in consequence; he recalled the number of occasions his wife had suffered as a result of his own political decisions. Would I therefore convey to her his personal sympathy and understanding? Thanking Bracken, I went home – about 1 am, we had a narrow majority – and conveyed the message, which was greeted with gratitude and tears. I was enjoined to express her personal thanks. On leaving home the next morning I was again enjoined to see 'the old boy' and make sure I delivered the message.

In the early evening I saw Winston in the smoke-room and went up to him and told him I had a message from my wife. He interrupted me to point out that he had on one occasion been presented to her, otherwise he would not have presumed, etc. I acknowledged this undoubted fact, and expressed her thanks. Immediately – and with Winston this was not a rare event – tears flooded down his face, as he expatiated on the way that wives had to suffer for their husbands' political actions, going on to recall a number of instances over a long life.

When I reached home – it was 2 am, but she was awake – I was asked if I had seen the old boy and thanked him. I had, and recounted the interview. She burst into tears, and I was moved to say that whereas two days earlier I had been a minister of the Crown, red box and all, now I was reduced to the position of a messenger between her and Winston Churchill, each of whom burst into tears on receipt of a message from the other. Of such is the essence of Parliament, or at least of bygone Parliaments, but this was the essential Winston Churchill.

There were many opportunities in the succeeding years for intimate chats with him. In 1954 I was due to visit the Soviet Union, where I expected to meet Soviet leaders. He called me across the smoking-room for a drink. Anthony Eden was ill, and Churchill had taken over the Foreign Office for the duration: he was eighty. 'What we want,' he said, 'you tell them – is *easement*. We may not settle all our problems: we want EAZHEMENT.' Then the old statesman told me what to look for: consumer goods. If they were allocating more materials for the production of consumer goods, he went on, it was a sign that they were looking to a peaceful solution; it might mean, it did not necessarily mean, that they were having to take more notice of the aspirations of ordinary people. 1954 was the first post-war year that foreigners were free to take photographs. I was able to take for him a picture of a mother carrying home what in the West would be called a fairy-cycle. Unfortunately I photo-

Opposite above The drawing-room at No. 10 Downing Street in Lady Baldwin's time, *below* Chequers.

April 1955. The Queen and the Duke of Edinburgh attended a dinner party at Number 10 Downing Street as the guests of Prime Minister Winston Churchill.

raphed her outside the Lubyanka (security) Prison, and had to spend an unappy hour under arrest by one of the less endearing members of the MVD, ater KGB. The camera and photograph survived. In the same discussion we vere concerned about an attempt I was making, with his backing, to get a British businessman out of jail in Hungary after being wrongly arrested for lleged spying. Cheerful telegrams pursued me through both Moscow and Budapest embassies until the mission was accomplished.

Much has been written about Churchill's fading powers in his last months. My meetings with him in 1954 showed no sign of this. It has been said that e had a stroke later in the year, and his communicative doctor has written bout these things. Certainly by early 1955 some of his closest colleagues felt hat the time had come for a retirement, and with the consummate terminal xpertise of the Conservative Party, the desired end-result was achieved.

Churchill was working and scheming for a summit conference. He had ecured Eisenhower's interest and support, but the Russians were being diffiult. It was to be his final achievement, but when he heard from them that he decision was 'Yes – but not yet', he resigned. A statesman who had been naking headlines for more than half a century resigned almost in silence, during Fleet Street strike. Only the then *Manchester Guardian* and the rest of the provincial press, as well as radio and television, were able to record his going.

On Churchill's ninetieth birthday, the House of Commons paid tribute to im. As Leader of the Opposition I proposed that the official speeches made n that occasion be bound in traditional Parliamentary green leather, and that he party leaders and the most senior back-benchers, should attend on him

Opposite Winston Churchill by Sir William Orpen.

at his home to present it. When we saw him we were a little shocked: he did not seem to be with us. But when Shinwell, a contemporary of the early 1920s and 1930s spoke, he was animated, fully recalling all the incidents through which, in retrospect, Shinwell led him.

In January 1965, as Prime Minister, I called on him again at Hyde Park Gate, but he was past recognizing anyone. On 24 January he died. He lay in state in Westminster Hall, and hundreds of thousands filed past the catafalque.

It is difficult to sum up in a few paragraphs what Churchill, as politician, statesman and Prime Minister has contributed to his country and the world. The following words are those of a tribute the then Prime Minister addressed to the House of Commons the day after his death, in moving in the presence of Lady Churchill and members of her family a resolution in reply to the Queen's message to the Commons on his death, and proposing that the House should adjourn for a week until his funeral service at St Paul's, and his interment.

The House was crowded. I had given instructions that the seat he had occupied for so many years after his retirement – next to the gangway alongside the Treasury Bench – should be left vacant. It was a House of Commons occasion. So was the vigil which was kept around his coffin in Westminster Hall the night before his funeral, by Mr Speaker and three of Winston's successors at No. 10 who relieved the guard kept by members of the three services. I had to present, at the Bar of the House, the Queen's Gracious Message to the Commons. I said:

> I beg to move, that an humble Address be presented to Her Majesty humbly to thank Her Majesty for having directed for the body of the Rt Hon. Sir Winston Churchill, K.G., to lie in state in Westminster Hall and for the funeral service to be held in the Cathedral Church of St Paul and assuring Her Majesty of our cordial and concurrence in these measures for expressing the affection and admiration in which the memory of this great man is held by this House and all Her Majesty's faithful subjects.
>
> This House, and, by virtue of its representation in this House, the nation, collectively and reverently will be paying its tribute to a great statesman, a great Parliamentarian, a great leader of this country.
>
> The world today is ringing with tributes to a man who, in those fateful years, bestrode the life of nations – tributes from the Commonwealth, from our wartime allies, from our present partners in Europe and the wider alliance, from all those who value the freedom for which he fought, who still share the desire for the just peace to which all his endeavours were turned. Winston Churchill, and the legend Winston Churchill had become long before his death and which now lives on, are the possession not of England, or Britain, but of the world, not of our time only but of the ages.
>
> But we, Sir, in this House, have a special reason for the tribute for which Her Majesty has asked in her Gracious Message. For today we honour not a world statesman only, but a great Parliamentarian, one of ourselves.
>
> The colour and design of his greatest achievements became alive, on the Parliamentary canvas, here in this Chamber. Sir Winston, following the steps of the most honoured of his predecessors, derived his greatness from and through this House and from and through his actions here. And by those actions, and those imperishable phrases which will last as long as the English

Churchill makes a speech after the presentation of a portrait of himself by Graham Sutherland on the occasion of his eightieth birthday.

language is read or spoken, he in turn added his unique contribution to the greatness of our centuries-old Parliamentary institution.

He was in a very real sense a child of this House and a product of it, and equally, in every sense, its father. He took from it and he gave to it.

The span of sixty-four years from his first entry as its youngest Member to the sad occasion of his departure last year, covers the lives and memories of all but the oldest of us. In a Parliamentary sense, as in a national sense, his passing from our midst is the end of an era.

He entered this House at twenty-five – already a national and controversial figure. He had fought in war, and he had written of war, he had charged at Omdurman, he had been one of the first to enter Ladysmith, an eye-witness of the thickest fighting in Cuba, a prisoner of a Boer commando – though not for as long as his captors intended.

And he brought his own tempestuous qualities to the conduct of our Parliamentary life. Where the fighting was hottest he was in it, sparing none – nor asking for quarter. The creature and possession of no one party, he has probably been the target of more concentrated Parliamentary invective from, in turn, each of the three major parties than any other Member of any Parliamentary age, and against each in turn he turned the full force of his own oratory. If we on this side of the House still quote as a classic, words he uttered over half a century ago, about the party he later came to lead, hon. Members opposite have an equally rich treasure-house of quotations about us, to say nothing of right hon. and hon. Gentlemen below the gangway.

When more than forty years after his first entry as a young MP he was called on to move the appointment of a Select Committee about the rebuilding of this Chamber, he proclaimed and gloried in the effect of our Parliamentary architecture on the clarity and decisiveness of party conflict; he recalled, with that impish quality which never deserted him, the memories of battles long past, of his own actions in crossing the Floor of this House, not once in fact, but twice.

For those who think that bitter party controversy is a recent invention and one to be deplored, he could have had nothing but pitying contempt. As he sat there, in the seat which I think by general wish of the House should be left vacant this afternoon, in those last years of the last Parliament, silently surveying battles which may have seemed lively to us, could we not sense the old man's mind going back to the great conflicts of a great career and thinking perhaps how tame and puny our efforts have become?

A great Parliamentarian, but never a tame one – they misjudge him who could even begin to think of him as a party operator, or a manipulator, or a trimmer, or a party hack. He was a warrior, and party debate was war; it mattered, and he brought to that war the conquering weapon of words fashioned for their purpose; to wound, never to kill; to influence, never to destroy.

As Parliament succeeded Parliament he stood at this Box, at one time or another holding almost every one of the great Offices of State. He stood at the Box opposite, thundering his denunciation of Government after Government. He sat on the bench opposite below the Gangway, disregarded, seemingly impotent, finished. His first Cabinet post – the Board of Trade – made him one of the architects of the revolution in humane administration of this country. He piloted through the labour exchanges; he laid the first faltering steps in social insurance.

The Home Office and then the more congenial tenure of the Admiralty – Ministerial triumph and Ministerial disaster in the First War. Colonies, War, the Treasury: the pinnacle of power, and then years in the wilderness. The urgent years, warning the nation and the world, as the shadow of the jackboot spread across an unheeding Europe. And then came his finest hour. Truly the history of Parliament over a tempestuous half century could be written around the triumphs and frustrations of Winston Churchill.

But, Sir, it will be for those war years that his name will be remembered for as long as history is written and history is read. A man who could make the past live in Marlborough, in his dutiful biography of Lord Randolph, who could bring new colour to the oft-told tale of the history of the English-Speaking Peoples, for five of the most fateful years in world history was himself called on to make history. And he made history because he could see the events he was shaping through the eye of history. He has told us of his deep emotions when from the disaster of the Battle of France, he was called on to lead this nation.

'I felt,' he said, 'as if I were walking with destiny, and that all my past life had been but a preparation for this hour and for this trial. Ten years in the political wilderness had freed me from ordinary party antagonisms. My warnings over the last six years had been so numerous, so detailed, and were now so terribly vindicated, that no one could gainsay me. I could not be reproached either for making the war or with want of preparation for it. I thought I knew a good deal about it all, and I was sure I should not fail. Therefore, although impatient for the morning, I slept soundly and had no need for cheering dreams. Facts are better than dreams.'

His record of leadership in those five years speaks for itself beyond the power of any words of any of us to enhance or even to assess. This was his finest hour, Britain's finest hour. He had the united and unswerving support of the leaders of all parties, of the fighting services, of the men and women in munitions and in the nation's industries, without regard to faction or self-interest. In whatever role, men and women felt themselves inspired to assert qualities they themselves did not know they possessed. Everyone became just those few inches taller, every back just that much broader.

To this task he brought the inspiration of his superlative courage, at the hour of greatest peril. Personal courage such as he had always shown, and indeed which needed a direct order from his Sovereign to cause him to desist from landing on the Normandy beaches on D-Day. Moral courage, the courage he had shown in warning the nation when he stood alone, now inspired the nation when Britain and the Commonwealth stood alone. There was his eloquence and inspiration, his passionate desire for freedom and his ability to inspire others with that same desire. There was his humanity. There was his humour. But above all, he brought that power which, whenever Britain has faced supreme mortal danger, has been asserted to awaken a nation which others were prepared to write off as decadent and impotent, and to make every man, every woman, a part of that national purpose.

To achieve that purpose, he drew on all that was greatest in our national heritage. He turned to Byron – 'blood, tears and sweat'. The words which he immortalized from Tennyson's 'Ode on the Death of the Duke of Wellington' might well be a nation's epitaph on Sir Winston himself:

> Not once or twice in our rough island-story,
> The path of duty was the way to glory;
> He that walks it, only thirsting
> For the right, and learns to deaden
> Love of Self, before his journey closes,
> He shall find the stubborn thistle bursting
> Into glossy purples, which outredden
> All voluptuous garden-roses.

The greatest biographer of Abraham Lincoln said in one of his concluding chapters: 'A Tree is best measured when it is down.' So it will prove of Winston Churchill, and there can be no doubt of the massive, oaken stature that history will accord to him. But this is not the time.

We meet today in this moment of tribute, of spontaneous sympathy this House feels for Lady Churchill and all the members of his family. We are conscious only that the tempestuous years are over; the years of appraisal are yet to come. It is a moment for the heartfelt tribute that this House, of all places, desires to pay in an atmosphere of quiet.

For now the noise of hooves thundering across the veldt; the clamour of the hustings in a score of contests; the shots in Sydney Street, the angry guns of Gallipoli, Flanders, Coronel and the Falkland Islands; the sullen feet of marching men in Tonypandy; the urgent warnings of the Nazi threat; the whine of the sirens and the dawn bombardment of the Normandy beaches; all these now are silent. There is a stillness. And in that stillness, echoes and memories. To each whose life has been touched by Winston Churchill, to each his memory. And as those memories are told and retold, as the world pours in its tributes, as world leaders announce their intention, in this jet age, of coming to join in this vast assembly to pay honour and respect to his memory, we in this House treasure one thought, and it was a thought some of us felt it right to express in the Parliamentary tributes on his retirement. Each one of us recalls some little incident – many of us, as in my own case, a kind action, graced with the courtesy of a past generation and going far beyond the normal calls of Parliamentary comradeship. Each of us has his own memory, for in the tumultuous diapason of a world's tributes, all of us here at least know the epitaph he would have chosen for himself: 'He was a good House of Commons man.'

11

Clement Attlee

CLEMENT RICHARD ATTLEE can be described as the most reluctant Prime Minister. No one, least of all himself, would have expected him to achieve the post, and he would never have sought it. He had no ambition. Yet in a tenure of office of six and a quarter years he had a record of achievement which would challenge that of any of his predecessors in peacetime, and this came directly after more than five years' intense preoccupations as Deputy Prime Minister – *de facto* from May 1940, and formally holding the title from 1942 – in the most dangerous war Britain has ever fought.

Attlee proved that Labour could govern. Labour was no longer the provider of short interim minority Governments such as those of 1923–4 and 1929–31. From Attlee's time Labour was *a* natural – if not *the* natural – 'party of Government'.

He carried through the transition from total war conditions to those of peace, in sharp contrast to the failures and unconcern of 1918 to 1922. Unlike the post First World War transition, there was virtually no unemployment. Attlee and his ministers linked the returning servicemen and displaced munitions and aircraft workers to the jobs that had to be done, not only to repair the ravages of war and the tasks postponed by the war, but to make up for the years of pre-war neglect in housing and education. This was, of course, in part, the result of Ernest Bevin's wartime planning for the post-war period; Attlee's too, as he had been chairman of the relevant Cabinet committee. In house-building, leaving out of account the temporary 'prefab' programme inherited from the wartime Government, his ministers were responsible for the completion of 400,000 permanent houses, in three years after the end of the war, compared with 75,000 in a comparable period after the First World War. The 240,000 'pre-fabs' were in addition.

He presided over the introduction of the 'Welfare State', the revolution in the social services carried through by Jim Griffiths as minister, and the creation of the National Health Service by Aneurin Bevan. But Attlee, with a record of experience in social and local government questions to which no other Prime Minister except Chamberlain could lay claim, took the closest interest in the details, and above all in the administration. Moreover as Prime Minister he, very quietly, dictated the priorities in public expenditure and Parliamentary time which made the revolution possible.

Attlee exercised a Prime Minister's right to move the second reading of the National Insurance Bill. He spoke nostalgically of the East End, and of Labour aspirations of forty years earlier, but, drawing on his East End experience, he could not deny himself the opportunity of airing a pet scheme he had always cherished, though it was in no sense Cabinet policy; the nationalization or municipalization of funeral services. He spoke for thirty-five minutes, one of his longest-ever speeches.

In a world setting, his achievement was historic: it was he who initiated the peaceful transition from Empire to Commonwealth, taking personal charge of the entire operation. Most difficult of all was the achievement of independence and self-government for India, Pakistan, Ceylon and Burma. This was not an inheritance from the wartime coalition: Churchill had agreed to no such proposals, and his Secretary of State for India was totally opposed to them. Beginning the process in July 1945, Attlee ensured that it was completed in just a few days over two years, due as we shall see to his fixing a timetable for withdrawal of British sovereignty, and, no less, to his appointment of Earl

Previous page Attlee with King George VI in 1945 after submitting the list of members of the new Labour Government.

Mountbatten as Viceroy with plenipotentiary powers. Successive Governments, Conservative and Labour, have continued the process almost to completion; there have been Parliamentary arguments, but from Attlee onwards they have been only about timing and method, and the protection of minorities.

Clement Attlee is the undisputed founder of the modern Commonwealth.

The Commonwealth at the time of writing is made up of thirty-five nations linked in close association one to another, and by the acceptance by each of the Queen as Head of the Commonwealth: a reality in world affairs, ever since his time, now covering one quarter of the individual member States of the United Nations, and one quarter of the population of the world. One of his proudest moments was the ceremony in Westminster Hall when the King formally opened the rebuilt House of Commons on 31 October 1950. Following the Lord Chancellor and Mr Speaker, presiding officers of the Lords and the Commons, was a great assembly of Speakers of the Commonwealth, black, white, yellow and brown, many wearing the traditional Westminster robes and wigs, others the colourful robes of their countries. Among the Cabinet that day there were few dry eyes.

If there is one phrase that describes his whole life it is that he had 'a sense of duty'. He felt the call of duty when as a young man he first went to a boys' settlement in the East End and came into contact with social conditions he had not dreamed existed; when war unexpectedly broke out in 1914 and he joined up at once; when on his return he was chosen Mayor of Stepney though he was not an elected councillor; when his East End friends drafted him to run for Parliament; when, after the 1931 election left Labour with only a small group of members in the House, he accepted what he and others thought to be the position of temporary leader. When more important figures returned to Parliament it became clear that the well-loved Arthur Greenwood could not win a majority, and that Greenwood's supporters could not accept Herbert Morrison, so Attlee was elected to the leadership. It was the same when he took the post of Deputy Prime Minister under the often mercurial Winston Churchill in the wartime coalition, and when, to his and the nation's surprise, there was a Labour landslide in the 1945 election. He took it calmly: 'Job to do,' one can imagine him saying. Similarly, when he narrowly lost the 1951 election he remained leader for another four years, until he was nearly seventy-three – long enough to ensure that Morrison had no hope of election, and to get a new and younger team working together.

Richard Rose in a recent essay rightly says that Attlee's education was 'for service, not leadership'. Haileybury was above all a school turning out boys for the nation's service, a high proportion of whom went to rule the Empire, or joined the armed forces of the Crown. He was the product of a solid, comfortably off, London professional family. His father was a successful City solicitor; the family lived in a pleasant house in Putney, then much more of a village separate from London. His sisters had the same governess as Winston Churchill. At Oxford, where he earned no high academic honours, he took no interest in politics. He joined but did not speak at the Union, and spoke once at his college debating society, in favour of a variant of Chamberlainite limited protection. He read history with a view to a career at the Bar.

When he left Oxford he began reading for the Bar, but never practised. His first fee was for drafting a bill for the Licensed Victuallers' Association. He

Above A contemporary photograph of two compartments in a dormitory at Haileybury at the time Attlee was a pupil.

applied for two legal posts in the civil service, one with the Church Commission, one with the Charity Commissioners. He did not get either post. Had he done so he would probably have settled down to a lifetime of quiet legal work.

One night he went with an old schoolfriend to Haileybury House, a boys' club run by old Haileyburians in Stepney. He felt a call to attend regularly and, in 1907, at the age of twenty-four, became the club manager, leaving home to move in there. He and his brother Tom, who worked at a club in Hoxton, were appalled at the economic and social conditions, the sweatshops and the outwork, the piece-rate jobs done in the workers' homes. As he recalled forty-seven years afterwards, women working at trouser-finishing were 'paid a penny-farthing a pair, out of which they had to buy their own thread', grossing about five shillings a week.

But side by side with his sense of outrage at the conditions in which millions of people were forced to live was a sense of admiration for the comradeship he found there. In his characteristically brief autobiography, *As It Happened*, he says: 'Thrift, so dear to middle classes, was not esteemed so highly as generosity. The Christian virue of charity was practised, not preached.' What impressed him is the quality that has impressed so many who have come to know conditions in a depressed mining area of Wales, Scotland or the North-East. However poor a miner might be he has always something to spare for

Opposite Attlee (left corner) with his parents and brothers and sisters.

a colleague or a family who, perhaps because of injury, or a death in the pit, is still poorer.

Clem and his brother began to ask each other what was wrong with an economic system that produced such depressed conditions – sweated incomes, unemployment, appalling housing conditions, infant and maternal mortality, only the barest provision for health treatment or for education. They flirted with co-partnership, even syndicalism, then a fashionable rostrum; it did not add up. They turned to politics. The Marxist Social Democratic Federation founded by Hyndman was too doctrinaire. Clem attended a meeting, addressed by Aylmer Maude, William Sanders, Sidney Webb and Bernard Shaw – 'They all seemed pretty formidable to a neophyte.' The Fabians seemed too intellectual and remote. The two brothers joined Keir Hardie's Independent Labour Party, which so far as many of its members were concerned was inspired by a religious and ethical approach.

He became a propagandist. He was greatly impressed by the Minority Report of the Royal Commission on the Poor Law written by the Webbs and Beveridge, and became an ill-paid campaign speaker, addressing meetings on the Report in different parts of the country. He became resident secretary of Toynbee Hall for nine months in 1909–10, and then sought a precarious living researching into and lecturing for the organization set up under the 1909 Trade Boards Act to deal with the sweatshop system, and later for various other Government campaigns, such as that to explain Lloyd George's National Insurance Act of 1911. With all this he combined a great deal of political speaking and organization. Attlee was never a theoretical Socialist and had something of a contempt for those who were. He first attended a Labour Party conference in 1908. Looking back on those years in his memoirs, he writes: 'It will be seen that during those years from 1907 to 1914 I served my apprenticeship in the Labour and Socialist movement; I was a rank and file member with no special ambitions.' His comment on the Labour group of members elected in 1906 is revealing. 'It was not rigidly dogmatic. It was inclusive rather than exclusive and it preached a socialism which owed far more to the Bible than to Karl Marx . . . a way of life rather than an economic dogma . . .'

For a time he had no work at all, but thanks to the Webbs he became a lecturer at the London School of Economics in the department of Social Science and Public Administration. He later said that this was not on the score of academic qualifications but 'because I was considered to have good practical knowledge of social conditions'. One story of those days he liked to tell. 'Met a barefoot girl who asked me where I was going: "Oh, I'm going home for tea – Oh, I'm going home to see whether there is any tea."'

He went to see the Sidney Street siege, helped emergency feeding in the London dock strike and joined in the campaign for women's suffrage.

When war broke out in 1914, he became an officer in the South Lancashire Regiment, and served at Gallipoli and in Mesopotamia, where he was wounded. Invalided from there to Malta, he missed an operation where his division suffered between 6000 and 7000 casualties. He served in France, joined the tanks, and was in the battle at Passchendaele. He was known as Major Attlee to many rank-and-file members right up to and even after the 1939–45 war.

His war service had a profound effect on him. He always retained a soft spot for Lancashire men. But his analytical mind was directed by all he had seen in the ordering of the war into studying all aspects of defence, and he became

Stepney Borough Labour Council. Alderman Attlee is in the front row, fourth from the left.

one of Labour's leading authorities in debates, and in government, during and after the war.

This was not the only effect of his wartime experience. In lunch or dinner conversations at the Cabinet table in the Commons Members' dining-room, he repeatedly entertained his colleagues with clipped comments on the proclivities of certain European countries some of whose nationals he had met and served with in the war – he was particularly waspish about the Italians (though in more measured language than Dalton) and the French, critical in an entirely different way about the Germans. But for the Commonwealth soldier he had nothing but praise. It is probable that his unremitting opposition to the European Common Market from the Fifties until his death – expressed in language unusually strong for him – owes a great deal to his war years.

On returning to London from the war, he was co-opted in 1919 as Mayor of Stepney: his pre-war efforts to be elected to the Council and to the Board of Guardians had failed. His period on the Council gave him practical experience of social problems such as housing, rating and valuation that was going to be of value to him in his early Parliamentary years. He was chairman of the municipal electricity authority, which enabled him to speak on the Conservative

Above Attlee (front row, second right) with the South Lancashire Regiment during the First World War.

Opposite Attlee as deputy leader of the Opposition in 1931 with George Lansbury.

Government's measures to unify electricity generation. It was also relevant when he supervised the preparation of the post-1945 measure to nationalize the electricity industry. He was selected as candidate for Limehouse and won the October 1922 election against a 'Conservative–Liberal' candidate by 9688 votes to 7789. Soon after entering the House he became PPS to Ramsay MacDonald. In the elections of 1923 and 1924 he had a two-to-one majority over the Conservative, as he did again in 1929. He was soon speaking regularly on the Army Estimates, and was a member of the Committee on Rating and Valuation. In the first Labour Government from 1923 to 1924 he was Under-Secretary for War.

In the late Twenties he accepted nomination to the Indian Statutory Commission, and spent a long time away from the House taking evidence in India. Because of his Commission work he did not take office in 1929, but when the Duchy of Lancaster became vacant in May 1930 he was appointed there, and ten months later became Postmaster-General, the highest post he held until he joined Churchill's national coalition in 1940. It was perhaps because he had so little experience of departmental ministries that he gave his ministers their heads – and sacked them if they proved inadequate.

The Government fell with MacDonald's resignation and the formation of the Conservative-dominated 'National' Government. The 1931 landslide left fewer than fifty Labour members in the House, and Attlee, one of the few

survivors with ministerial experience, became Deputy Leader to George Lansbury. Lansbury was much-loved, a dedicated pacifist, but totally unsuited to such responsibilities. When he had to spend months in hospital following an accident, in 1934, Attlee had to take complete charge.

Throughout that Parliament Attlee, despite his traditional taciturnity, filled more columns of Hansard than any other member, speaking, as he records, often three or four times a week. These speeches were not only in major debates – he was in constant demand on legislation and statutory orders, because he was one of the few Opposition MPs whose training enabled him to construe Bills and motions. Because, Stafford Cripps apart, there was no one to whom he could delegate, he was working longer hours than he was later to work as Prime Minister.

Just before the 1935 general election, Lansbury resigned after a cruel hatchet-job by Bevin and other union leaders at the 1935 Labour conference. Bevin charged him with 'hawking his conscience around from conference to conference'. Union leaders, though not yet Attlee or the Parliamentary Labour Party, were beginning to move towards support of rearmament. Attlee was elected leader. Few thought that this would be more than a temporary appointment, because a number of former Cabinet ministers who had lost their seats in 1931 were likely to return as soon as Baldwin called a general election.

The 1935 election returned a Parliamentary party of nearly 150. The candidates for the leadership were Greenwood, Morrison and Attlee. On the first ballot Attlee won fifty-eight votes out of 135, against Morrison's forty-four. Greenwood, who received thirty-two votes, dropped out, and in the runoff between Morrison and Attlee virtually all of those who had voted for Greenwood swung to Attlee. There was no love lost between Greenwood and Morrison, and very little between their respective followers. Attlee won by eighty-eight to forty-four.

He was soon educating the Party on defence. In the debates on Abyssinia he advocated collective security. His arguments were more and more moving towards a qualified support of rearmament in face of the threats of Hitler and Mussolini, but on the assumption that they would be used as part of collective action, preferably through the League of Nations, to deter or destroy aggressor nations. He called for oil sanctions against Italy.

In 1937 came the resignations of Eden and Salisbury: the Chamberlain–Horace Wilson axis was in total control.

Attlee had a difficult furrow to plough. A substantial number of his party were pacifists; others were not against war but not in favour of a 'capitalist' war. The big unions were moving steadily in favour of the rearmament programme and, with their block votes, had swung the 1936 Party conference at Edinburgh in that direction. Conference endorsed overwhelmingly a formal leadership statement on policy and defence, supporting collective security, and declaring that 'the armed strength of the countries loyal to the League must be conditioned by the armed strength of the aggressors.'

Attlee, with many of his party, would have supported rearmament to meet the Hitler menace, but he had no confidence that Chamberlain would think of either defence or foreign policy against a background of collective security. In spite of past clashes, he would probably have found it easier to support a Baldwin rearmament programme, particularly if the foreign and defence policies had been run by a Baldwin–Eden partnership. Despite the backing

Opposite Clement Attlee.

of conference and the unions, Attlee, while supporting rearmament, could only feel that Eden's resignation confirmed his doubts.

In a debate in November 1937, he asked pointedly about the Government's plans for defence, air raid precautions (ARP), evacuation, anti-aircraft defences, the building up of the Royal Air Force, and the location of industry for protection against air raids. He had, even before the Edinburgh conference, qualified his concern with the anxious remark that he felt little satisfaction with the Government about their preparations on these matters, 'which, as I have told the House, were the creation of their inept foreign policy'.

When Chamberlain flew to meet Hitler at Munich, Attlee and he met before Chamberlain set off: this would now be normal practice between the Prime Minister and the Leader of the Opposition at a time of crisis, indeed in much less cataclysmic situations. Attlee's own account was: 'I told him that I had little faith in the venture.'

Attlee was in hospital at the outbreak of war, as described in a previous chapter. He was soon back and, as we have seen, played a decisive part, *the* decisive part indeed, in the dispatch of Chamberlain's Government.

When Churchill formed his Government, Attlee became Lord Privy Seal, a title that could have meant a great deal or nothing. In fact it meant a great deal. Churchill, playing an active part in the conduct of the war, not only as Prime Minister but as Minister of Defence, taking decisions by day and long into the night, was more than content to let Attlee look after a great part of the administrative side of government, the home front, and in the later years the economic direction of the administration. When a Britain which had stood alone became a relatively junior but essential part of a great alliance, Churchill was abroad for long periods at a time – bilateral meetings with Roosevelt or Stalin, and a succession of tripartite summit conferences of the alliance.

Churchill's illness in North Africa also caused a prolonged absence. All this meant that Attlee, operating from 1940 onwards from 11 Downing Street, in addition to his administrative duties was more and more responsible for accounting for Government to Parliament. The incredible thing is that he carried these burdens virtually alone and never sought to set up a team of sympathetic advisers, if only to counter the influence of Churchill's equivalent of the Lloyd George 'Garden Suburb', under Professor Lindemann, later Lord Cherwell.

He was totally loyal to Churchill, despite his impatience at some of the Prime Minister's posturings. Not for him the conspiracies of certain of the Conservative members of Asquith's Cabinet. But then Churchill was not an Asquith; still less was Attlee a Bonar Law, a Balfour or a Carson. It is not even profitable to speculate on how loyal Attlee would have been if he had been a member of a coalition under Chamberlain: it was Attlee who ensured that Chamberlain went. He was probably surprised at Churchill's vigour. In the early days of the war he had regarded a Churchill Government as inconceivable. The first time I met Attlee was in October 1939. A group clustered round him and asked who, in his view, would take over from Chamberlain. I asked 'Churchill?' Attlee replied: 'Not Churchill. Sixty-five. Old for a Churchill.' He was wrong – Churchill did not rely for his longevity on any inheritance from his father. Attlee lived to be glad that he was wrong.

But he found Churchill very difficult on at least certain matters affecting the post-war world. The wartime coalition was able to agree on some plans to

Opposite Harold Macmillan.

The Deputy Prime Minister.

which all parties were committed – the Beveridge programme for social security, for example. The agreed White Paper on full employment represented little more than agreement on the lowest common denominators. We have seen the fate of the work done by the coalition on town and country planning. The same was true of discussions in 1943 and 1944 on the future ownership – national or private – of the coalmines, the railways, and gas and electricity undertakings.

The causes of the break-up of the wartime all-party Government have been recorded. Labour would not give the assurance that the coalition would last until the end of the war with Japan, which few expected would follow the end of the war in Europe so quickly. Even fewer foresaw the result of the election Churchill called. It was anything but a 1918 coupon election. The service vote and the wives of servicemen produced a Labour landslide. Attlee certainly did not expect it, despite the calm way he had fought the election against Churchill, who allowed his own political judgment to be overborne by Beaverbrook and Bracken to the point where he was making incredible hysterical accusations against the Labour leaders who had worked so closely with him.

Attlee had to deal with an intervention, pedantic and unhelpful, by Professor Laski, who was promptly told: 'A period of silence on your part would be advantageous.'

Attlee celebrated the declaration of the poll on 26 July 1945, with a quiet tea with Vi his wife at Paddington station hotel, before being summoned to the Palace. There were celebrations at the London Labour Party social that evening, but Morrison and Laski were at work. Attlee was already forming his Government; he had to leave for the Potsdam Conference of the Allies within hours: Churchill had been negotiating there and had returned to London for what he assumed was the formality of an election count. Roosevelt and Stalin were waiting.

Constitutionally, Morrison and Laski argued, Attlee had been the Leader of the Parliamentary Labour Party for the previous Parliament. Now there was a new Parliament. The Chief Whip, William Whiteley, Ernest Bevin and others moved in. Every Labour MP elected or re-elected that week was summoned to a meeting of the PLP at Beaver Hall in the City. Nearly four hundred turned up; most of the new members were surprised at the general election result, having modestly calculated as favourable signs of victory had developed in their own constituencies, that this was a purely personal vote.

Morrison's manoeuvre was crushed by sheer bulk. The Chief Whip, in the chair, simply called on 'the Foreign Secretary'. A couple of hundred new members thrilled at the thought that one of their own held that historic post. Ernest Bevin rose to his feet. He formally moved that Clem Attlee be confirmed as leader of the Parliamentary Party. It was accepted with acclamation; no one could possibly have tried to move an amendment. Attlee completed the formation of his Government and left for Potsdam.

Attlee's strength in Cabinet was due in part to his businesslike control of its proceedings and his utterly clear capacity for summing up its decisions. The recent publication – under the thirty-year rule for disclosure of Cabinet documents – of the Cabinet Conclusions for 1946, have led commentators to express surprise at Attlee's domination of the proceedings. The writer did not enter the Cabinet until 1947, but if 1946 was like 1947 and the succeeding years it is not at all surprising.

What Attlee did was to preside over a team of five headstrong horses, Ernest Bevin, Herbert Morrison, Hugh Dalton, Stafford Cripps and Aneurin Bevan.

Bevin was his lock-forward, packing more weight than any two others. Morrison was not so much disloyal as watching for a favourable opportunity to be disloyal. He had the right to be Lord President and Leader of the House, but he was foolish to take the post. When I was a very junior minister I was told by Aneurin Bevan that Morrison, having no department but only a small – mainly personal – staff, would lose out in the long run. He did, until, pulling rank, he insisted on the Foreign Office, on Bevin's breakdown, and proceeded to destroy himself. Cripps was a brilliant lawyer, with strong support on the left, but not seriously regarded by Attlee, who said to me at a time of crisis in 1949: 'Stafford, political goose.' Dalton, apart from his loud voice, had little to commend him. He crumpled in the 1947 crisis, Attlee simply pressing his Cut Golden Bar the deeper into his pipe as the Chancellor outlined his excuses. In his more confident periods, Dalton had an infinite capacity for meeting himself coming back.

The Prime Minister's crispness in Cabinet reflected his greatest quality, courage. In six years of war, bread had not been rationed, but in 1947 world wheat supplies were inadequate to meet demand, indeed to avert starvation. Once the figures were brought before Cabinet, Attlee was in no doubt what had to be done: bread rationing was announced.

The same courage had been shown in 1945, when Lend-Lease suddenly ceased. Lend-Lease was once described by Churchill as 'the most unsordid act in history'. So in one sense it was: Britain did not have to count or meet the cost of the supplies of food and raw materials crossing the Atlantic to British ports as a result of a vote of Congress. But at a price: as part of the Lend-Lease arrangements Britain voluntarily surrendered some of her distant markets, such as those in Latin America, to American exporters. There could be no complaint in wartime; it saved shipping. But markets once lost are difficult to regain, and so it proved.

Lend-Lease involved Britain's surrender of her rights and royalties in a series of British technological achievements. Although the British performance in industrial technique in the inter-war years had marked a period of more general decline, the achievements of our scientists and technologists had equalled the most remarkable eras of British industrial greatness. Radar, antibiotics, jet aircraft, British advances in nuclear research – these have created an industrial revolution all over the developed world. Under Lend-Lease these inventions were surrendered as part of the inter-Allied war effort, free of any royalty or other payments from the United States. Had Churchill been able to insist on adequate royalties for these inventions, both our wartime and our post-war balance of payments would have been very different.

The Attlee Government had to face the consequences of this surrender of our technological patrimony. But there was worse to come. Congress had voted Lend-Lease until the end of the war with Germany and Japan, and no longer. When the war with Germany ended most people expected the war with Japan to last for a year or more longer. The nuclear bombs on Nagasaki and Hiroshima ended that assumption. Three months after the war in Europe ended, the Japanese sued for peace. Almost within the hour, President Truman, unwillingly no doubt but without any choice in the matter, notified Attlee that Lend-Lease was cut off. At that time our essential exports were being financed as to £2000 millions a year, in 1945 prices, by Lend-Lease. There was no possible means of increasing our exports to the United States. Britain was in pawn, at the very time that Attlee was fighting to exert some influence on the post-war European settlement, as well as in bilateral issues. One of these related to sea transport: the US had taken over the Cunarders to repatriate from Europe and Asia US servicemen whose period in the ranks was much less than that of their British counterparts. The 'Queens' were taking Americans home, while British soldiers with up to six years' service were sweating it out. Attlee demanded our rights in the vessels and won.

The end of Lend-Lease meant the negotiation of an American loan, the repayments and servicing of which placed a burden on Britain's balance of payments right into the twenty-first century. It was not even a straight loan: the economic theologians who then 'infested' – Keynes's phrase – the State Department and the US Treasury attached conditions to the loan, such as the acceptance by Britain of total convertibility of sterling by the summer of 1947. Because Cripps was ill, I had to stand in for him at No. 11 in the consequences of that condition, when a world hungry for dollars, including a broken-backed Europe, exchanged every penny it possessed, or could earn, in Britain into dollars. Whatever judgments one makes on the original offer of Lend-Lease, on its ending, and the conditions of the loan which financed its withdrawal, one can hardly avoid questioning the phrase 'the most unsordid act in history'.

This was Attlee's view. But he did not complain. The consequences for Britain were ascribed by a less-than-totally pro-Government press to the excesses of Socialism. Attlee got on with the job: not only Britain's problems, but those of Europe and the wider world.

The Russian alliance with the West was breaking up. Some of the Americans, notably Byrnes, the Secretary of State at a critical time, were notably relaxed on Soviet demands, unlike their Pentagon colleagues. Bevin, in Moscow, at the meeting of the Council of Allied Foreign Ministers which signalled the end of wartime cooperation, had to ask the American Chiefs of Staff to a breakfast briefing to warn them of the sellout he thought Byrnes was content to offer. As Secretary for Overseas Trade at that time, I was sent by Attlee at Bevin's request to join Bevin for the final week's talks, and was fully briefed by a very sick man – Bevin had had a near fatal heart attack in Moscow a fortnight before – on the issues at stake.

In response to Soviet expansionism, Attlee and Bevin played a leading part in the creation of NATO. At the twenty-fifth anniversary celebrations in 1975, I put this question: 'Who in 1948 would have had any confidence that not only Italy but France would not have surrendered to the Communist embrace if NATO had not been created? Not only NATO but the "Marshall Plan"?'

General Marshall, the Secretary of State, had made a speech at Harvard in

Attlee with his wife and children.

June 1947, half-hinting, but no more, that if the bankrupt European nations would prepare four-year plans for recovery the US might be prepared to provide the foreign exchange needed. We may never know whether it was a firm proposal, but Attlee and Bevin decided to act as though it was. They accepted an offer which had not been made, and called a conference in Paris which worked throughout the summer of 1947. In the event the 'Marshall Plan' was decisive in saving Europe, whose nations accepted, country by country, a degree of Socialist planning – at private enterprise America's request and expense – without which they could not have survived. In private discussions it appealed to Attlee's not inconsiderable sense of humour and irony; in public his comments were characteristically laconic.

But this was the very period when Attlee was planning a much grander conception, the end of British rule in India. In 1946 he sent out a mission of three Cabinet ministers – Pethick-Lawrence, Cripps and A.V. Alexander – to tour India and discuss the problems with every local administration and the principal religious communities. On receipt of their report, he decided to act. He had the benefit of his experience on the Simon Commission. If India was asked to negotiate, agreement would be deferred for years. Attlee was one, one of the first indeed, to recognize the magic of the timetable. Fix a date, he decided, on which the British Raj would withdraw. It was for the Indians – including those who were to become known as Pakistanis and Bengalis – to produce a definitive constitutional settlement for the subcontinent. Not only this, Attlee decided to appoint a Viceroy, Lord Louis Mountbatten, who as allied Commander-in-Chief for the Asian War had commanded the Indian troops and received the unconditional surrender of the Japanese. Lord Louis accepted, on the basis that he had plenipotentiary powers. To his surprise, Attlee said that that was just the proposition: Attlee was simply laying down the timetable. As far as Mountbatten was concerned, that was the only thing that was not negotiable, not within his plenary powers. Mountbatten would find that the withdrawal timetable was his strongest card.

(Lord Mountbatten tells another story about that interview, characteristic of Attlee. Before the meeting ended, Mountbatten told Attlee that there was great concern among the service chiefs that 'X' had been decided on as chief of the (Army) General Staff. The right choice, he felt, would be Sir William Slim. To his surprise, Attlee agreed: Slim was the man he wanted. His Lordship pointed out that 'X' had been told that the choice had fallen on him. 'Untell him,' said Attlee.)

Lord Mountbatten combined great tact and charm with a strict insistence on the doctrine of the timetable. His relations with Nehru and Liaquat Ali Khan, who were to become first Prime Ministers of the two countries of the divided subcontinent, India and Pakistan, were intimate and proved decisive. In July 1947, Attlee introduced the Indian Independence Bill into the House. It passed without a division, and on 15 August, India and Pakistan became free and equal members of the British Commonwealth of Nations. And with Conservative back-benchers grumbling, Winston Churchill, the great critic of devolution of a lesser responsibility in 1929–31, and later, in characteristically generous Parliamentary comment, simply paid tribute to Mountbatten for his achievement, and to the Prime Minister who had had the imagination to appoint him.

Burma and Ceylon soon achieved their own independence, though Burma did not opt for membership of the Commonwealth.

Later that year Attlee was faced with a ministerial resignation. Dalton resigned, having carelessly given a journalist a preview on his Budget proposals just before announcing them to the House. Dalton assumed that there would be no pre-publication, but copies of the *Evening Standard* with the details of the Budget were passing from hand to hand on the Opposition front bench while he was still speaking.

That was the only time that I ever saw Attlee rattled. Sir Victor Raikes gave notice the following day of a private notice question to Dalton about the disclosure. In those days, because of the bombing of the Commons Chamber during the war, the House met in the Lords' Chamber, 250 yards from the Prime Minister's room which is only a few strides from the traditional Commons Chamber. I saw Attlee rushing along, in a very agitated state, for the question. Dalton took full responsibility and apologized to the House. Winston Churchill accepted his words magnanimously, and expressed sympathy with him. But later in the evening, probably following a meeting of the Shadow Cabinet, Churchill, Eden, Sir John Anderson and Clement Davies, the Liberal leader, tabled a motion for a Select Committee of the House to inquire into the leak. Dalton resigned and was succeeded by Cripps.

Normally Attlee was in full control, of himself, his Cabinet and the House. His answers in Parliament were concise and clear, with a tight little sense of humour. In the first debate of the 1945 Parliament, referring to Churchill as his 'Right Honourable Friend', he paid an unstinted tribute to his predecessor's war leadership. Later in the session, as Churchill was attacking the Government, Attlee recalled the general election, referring to a nationwide poster with Churchill's portrait and 'Vote For . . . (the local Conservative candidate of the area)'. In Oxford, where Quintin Hogg was candidate, a humorist had written: 'Love me, love my Hogg.' On another occasion, when Attlee was dealing with a particular problem, Churchill intervened to say that that issue had been brought up several times in the wartime Cabinet. Attlee replied: 'I must remind the Right Honourable Gentleman that a monologue is not a decision.'

His speeches in Parliament were usually very short – members of his Cabinet summoned to brief him, or calling on some other issue, would find him upstairs in the flat picking out his text with two fingers on a non-standard keyboard, probably going back to Stepney days. He could bring a Cabinet discussion to a brisk close, before producing a clear summing-up, with a very few words.

Once, when Winston had rushed in with an attack on some Government announcement without thinking things through, and then found himself committed to an untenable proposition, Attlee told Cabinet: 'Trouble with Winston: nails his trousers to the mast and he can't climb down.' In a Cabinet warning to ministers about industrial contacts and press attacks: 'A Tory minister can sleep in ten different women's beds in a week. A Labour minister gets it in the neck if he looks at his neighbour's wife over the garden fence.'

My wife was once asked by Mrs Attlee to go to Wimbledon with her, and first went to lunch at No. 10. Clem had two main subjects of conversation, cricket and history. He asked Mary whom she liked in history. She said, knowing that he would not approve: 'The romantic ones, Charles II, Rupert of the Rhine, Byron.' His reply was: 'Bad history, wrong people.'

There is a little-known story about John Strachey, at that time Minister of Food. A Cabinet rule in the manual 'Questions of Procedure for Ministers' forbids any minister from publishing written work such as a book or a press article without the specific authority of the Prime Minister (this is not usually withheld for a literary or historical work, such as Iain Macleod's *Neville Chamberlain*). Strachey telephoned the Prime Minister – he should have gone to see him. 'Oh, Prime Minister,' he said, 'I see that under the rules I have to get your permission to publish a book. Well I have written a small book of poems – there is nothing political or controversial in them. I take it you will agree to my publishing them.' Attlee replied: 'Better send them to me.' A fortnight later, Strachey had not heard from him, which was unusual, since Attlee normally completed his boxes every night, and never deferred any tasks. So Strachey phoned again: 'Oh, Clem, I take it you've no objection to letting me go ahead and publishing those poems I sent you.' 'Can't publish,' said Attlee, and when Strachey asked for his reason: 'Don't rhyme, don't scan.'

When Clem sacked a minister, he was equally brief. One asked him why his resignation had been asked for. 'Not up to the job,' said Attlee. To older friends and colleagues he would say: 'Well, you had a good innings. Time to put your bat up in the pavilion.'

Despite his sense of history, or possibly because of it, great events failed to move him. After his premiership, but while still party leader, he was chairing a Parliamentary Party meeting which assembled in a mood of great anxiety owing to the exploding of the first American thermonuclear bomb in the Pacific. There was great concern at the risks of possible nuclear fallout, even thousands of miles away. Labour MPs expressed their very deep concern – there was no motion before the meeting – and as one pacifist ended an impassioned speech, Attlee picked up his papers, saying: 'Agree, we've got to watch it,' and adjourned the meeting.

He was calmer than anyone I have known at times of crisis. In early 1951, towards the end of the Labour Government, he had to face an extremely serious two-day debate in the House on the grave international situation, amid anxieties that the war in Korea would escalate into a world confrontation. On the afternoon of the second day, the Press Association tickertape in the House carried a story that President Truman had said in Washington that General MacArthur, supreme commander in Korea, had delegated authority to use the nuclear weapon there without reference to the White House. There was uproar in Parliament, where Attlee was due to wind up the debate at 9.30 pm. Early in the evening he called a Cabinet in his room at the House. He referred calmly to the report, and said that he had concluded that he must fly to Washington – not then a routine operation – and see the President. In other circumstances he would have asked the Foreign Secretary to go, but Bevin's health ruled that out, and a sea voyage would take too long. He would try to contact the President on the transatlantic telephone, a very uncertain means of communication in those days, especially if the President were away from the White House. He would hope to receive confirmation of his planned visit before he wound up the debate. The Cabinet concurred. At 7 pm he came into the dining-room and sat at the table reserved for ministers. Those of us in the Cabinet clearly would not raise the Washington issue in the presence of ministers not in the Cabinet. But none felt like raising any other issue, which with his preoccupations, including the wind-up speech, might have appeared frivolous. He broke the silence, turning to me, and said: 'Just been reading Philip Guedalla. Tell me, which of the popular historians do you prefer, Guedalla or Arthur Bryant?'

To the answer, 'Bryant', he concurred, and for half an hour the conversation was centred on the Peninsular War. At 9 pm the President's agreement came through, and Attlee's speech steadied the Parliamentary atmosphere.

Cabinet business was carried through with brevity and discussion kept firmly to the point. Professor Mackintosh has described Attlee's conduct of a Cabinet perfectly:

> At Cabinet, Mr Attlee's great objective was to stop talk. There is evidence that two ministers rightly talked themselves out of the Cabinet. Discussion was limited by the Premier's habit of putting his questions in the negative. A non-Cabinet Minister with an item on the agenda would be called in at the appropriate point, simply bursting to make a speech. Mr Attlee would begin: 'Mr X, your memo says all that could be said – I don't suppose you have anything to add to it?' It was hard to say anything but 'No.' Then: 'Does any member of the Cabinet oppose this?' Someone would indicate a desire to contribute, and say: 'An interesting case occurred in 1929 which was very similar to this, and I remember then that we...' 'Do you oppose this?' 'Er...No?' 'Very good, that is settled...'

In one of the interviews with Francis Williams which make up the book *A Prime Minister Remembers*, Attlee summarized his style:

> A Prime Minister has to know when to ask for an opinion. He can't always stop some ministers offering theirs, you always have some people who'll talk on everything. But he can make sure to extract the opinion of those he wants when he needs them. The job of the Prime Minister is to get the general feeling – collect the voices. And then, when everything reasonable has been said, to get on with the job and say 'Well, I think the decision of the Cabinet is this, that or the other. Any objections?' Usually there aren't.

The devaluation crisis of 1949 inevitably centred on No. 10, because Cripps was ill and in a sanatorium in Zurich. Attlee was tone-deaf as far as all economic questions were concerned, unless they involved the kind of people he knew – trade unionists, miners, dockers. In Cripps's absence, I was standing in at the Treasury and had to provide the briefing, later joined by Hugh Gaitskell and Douglas Jay. A unanimous recommendation for devaluation in September was agreed by early August, and Attlee accepted. All recognized that this would be extremely difficult for Cripps, who had repeatedly forsworn devaluation as an answer to Britain's problems. As a minister of impeccable integrity, there was a real fear he would feel compelled to resign. I was due to go to Annecy, near Geneva, for the GATT conference. It was decided that a letter drafted by the three, for Attlee to sign, would be taken by the principal private secretary at the Board of Trade to Switzerland and handed to the President, who would deliver it personally to Cripps at the Bircher-Benner clinic. This was done, Cripps agreed, and devaluation took place the following month. Attlee's comment on Cripps's reply has been recorded.

In 1950, the Korean War added a new dimension to the Government's difficulties. British troops were committed to defence of the South, and panic speculative purchases of raw materials forced up the price – raw wool for example going up to twelve times the pre-war level. This generated a wave of inflationary price-rises, and gravely aggravated the balance of payments.

It also drove the White House into an apocalyptic anti-Russian attitude. A vast rearmament programme was announced and America's allies were pressed to follow suit. Attlee came more under the influence of Gaitskell, now Chancellor, whose financial policy was more and more dictated by his strong views on the international situation. Gaitskell was passionately pro-American, and as Ernest Bevin's powers declined he even went into the Foreign Office and took meetings on the confrontation with the Communist powers and the increased arms programme the Americans were pressing upon us. In the face of rising prices for raw materials, he wanted me as President of the Board of Trade to buy up the whole Australian, New Zealand and South African wool clips for three years ahead at the then inflated prices, plus five per cent. At a conservative estimate, this would have cost the Treasury £500 million. I refused. In the event the speculative market, which had over-reacted, brought the wool price down to a third within a month.

The argument which led to the resignation of Aneurin Bevan, myself and John Freeman was over two issues. We rejected the proposed arms programme, not on the question of whether it was needed, but on its practical feasibility. Aneurin Bevan in particular rejected its financing, which Hugh Gaitskell almost obsessively wanted to fund in part by reducing the National Health Service vote by imposing health charges.

In a debate on 15 February, Aneurin Bevan, by this time Minister of Labour, made a superb speech in support of Government policy, on which Chutter Ede, Home Secretary, said in the lobby that he had heard Lloyd George at his best, and this speech was at least equal to Lloyd George. But the Budget was approaching. When it was found to contain 'health charges', resignations appeared inevitable. The Morrison–Gaitskell axis forced the issue, Dalton panicked and approached Gaitskell without success, but Attlee appointed Bevin, now Lord Privy Seal, to mediate and if necessary arbitrate on the health service proposals. In a meeting at Bevin's home on Tuesday, 10 April, the very sick Bevin told Nye Bevan and myself that he was going to report in our favour: he clearly suspected Morrisonian machinations.

On the following Saturday, 14 April, with nothing on paper on the issue, he died. Morrison by this time had become Foreign Secretary, where he proved disastrous – it is now known that Attlee was considering James Griffiths, Colonial Secretary, but was not in a position to resist Morrison's demand. The resignations were submitted at the end of the month, Aneurin Bevan's on health charges, mine and John Freeman's on the arms programme. It is more than arguable that if Attlee had not been in hospital – with Morrison in charge – and certainly if Bevin had not died they would not have taken place.

The health charges were imposed, the inflated arms programme was endorsed. When Winston Churchill became Prime Minister after the election of October 1951, he moved quickly to cut the extended arms programme by a third, the exact figure which the resigning ministers were proposing.

Attlee called the election for October 1951. It was an unwise decision, but was urged upon him by Gaitskell, who as Chancellor feared still more serious economic difficulties. Morrison, who was in Canada and had more experience of these matters, would have advised against the timing. He was right. Britain's economic burdens, including the high level of prices, eased by the following year. Raw material prices collapsed. It was the Conservatives who reaped the advantage.

A factor influencing Attlee was his small majority. He was to say later that

I celebrate with Attlee at Transport House after the General Election of 1964.

› Government could survive with a majority of less than ten; he was disproved ʼ the fact that three of the four Labour Governments elected between 1964 ıd October 1974 had smaller majorities.

When the general election returned the Conservatives with a majority of fif-en, Attlee remained as leader, and fought the 1955 election, when the Con-rvative majority over Labour rose to sixty-eight, Liberals and others account-g for eight. The Conservatives were in office, in fact, for thirteen years, until ıe election of 1964.

After 1951, the arguments continued to rage over the arms programme. But :w problems were taking the centre of the stage: at home the Conservatives' ove to more orthodox Treasury policies, abroad the rift between NATO and e Comintern, and the political impact of thermonuclear technology. Britain as moving further and further from wartime austerity; rationing was abol-hed in favour of rationing by the purse. We were moving into the days of 'ou've never had it so good.'

Attlee remained leader of the Party until after the 1955 election defeat. He as intent on blocking the claims of Morrison, and hoping to see the younger ›ntestants of 1951 working together. In the 1955 Party conference at Margate – ›e last held at Whitsun, before the move to October – rumours of his forth-›ming resignation led Barbara Castle and others of the Left to plead with him stay.

Morrison had a mini-triumph in his conference speech which led a leading

Attlee and other statesmen at the funeral of Winston Churchill.

journalist to tell me that this had clinched his bid for the leadership. 'Not on,' I told him. 'He won't get forty votes when the PLP chooses its leader.' My forecast was wrong. He got exactly forty votes.

In October the Conservative Chancellor, R.A. Butler, who had taken 6d. off income tax in the pre-election Budget, introduced an autumn Budget which restored the loss to the Treasury with a long list of purchase tax increases on household equipment and other items. The fight over the subsequent Finance Bill was a classic, directed by Gaitskell and myself. After two all-night sittings, after studying Erskine May at 4.0 am, I moved at 8.0 am a procedural amendment, which was unwisely accepted by the Tory Leader of the House, and killed the Finance Bill, which had to be reintroduced. When Attlee came into the Chamber that Thursday afternoon for the business questions, he shook hands with me, and the Chief Whip then told those concerned that Attlee had said: 'Now those two are working together, I can go, leaving the party in safe hands.'

He resigned in December 1955, and was succeeded by Gaitskell. James Griffiths was elected deputy leader, followed in 1960 by Aneurin Bevan.

Attlee, an honoured elder statesman, went to the Lords. His great campaign in the years of retirement was against the Common Market. Attlee, the creator of the modern Commonwealth, feared for its future with Britain inside the EEC. Perhaps also it was Attlee the Major of the First World War, with his never-disguised contempt for certain of our European partners, who felt doubts about Britain's future in such a grouping. It was certain that Attlee, the defender and guardian of the constitution, had the gravest doubts about placing Britain under a written constitution, indeed a constitution whose writers were not in fact British, or aware of the thousand years of history which had produced British Parliamentary institutions.

He died on 8 October 1967, honoured and revered by his contemporaries in Britain, and in the wider world, above all in the Commonwealth.

No peacetime Prime Minister this century has achieved more in his years of office. With his profound sense of history, he carried Britain out of the imperial age into that of the Commonwealth; he played a major part in forging the links of NATO and the transatlantic partnership. He revolutionized the system of care for those in need, and the organization of Britain's basic industries. In the age of the common man he, looking and sounding like its prototype spokesman, elevated the role of ordinary human beings. One has only to compare the social and political attitudes of the sterile pre-war days with those of 1945 and beyond to see his achievement.

To carry forward the British people a generation and more from those days into the second half of the twentieth century enables him to rank with Peel and the very select group of those other past Prime Ministers who built on the cherished traditions of the past to carry Britain forward into the future.

But in a wider world setting, Attlee's achievement, measured *sub specie historiae*, is even greater. For none will deny that he was the statesman who transformed, irrevocably, the British Empire into the Commonwealth of Nations, linked together in common allegiance to the Sovereign as Head of the Commonwealth.

A Little Too Late 1955–1957

Anthony Eden was one of the great gentlemen of British politics, and one of the great tragedies. A tragedy because he came to the supreme power in political terms at the very time when Britain's position in the world was changed in ten days by Suez. A tragedy because he was already ill. That this was so was no less a tragedy for Britain.

It had been at the time of the Hitler challenge that Britain needed him most. Eden had assessed the danger correctly. Two turns of history, or bad premiership, led to a world tragedy. One, as we have seen, was Baldwin's failure to groom Eden as his successor; the second was Chamberlain's obsessive desire to get rid of him. Baldwin should have seen that it was a time for youth. Britain had languished under a succession of sexagenarians. Bonar Law's brief premiership was in his middle sixties. Baldwin in his last premiership was in his very late sixties, and tired. MacDonald went on to sixty-nine, though his dotage had set in earlier. Chamberlain was sixty-eight when he went to No. 10. Britain was entitled to a young Prime Minister, one in his prime.

With a paranoiac Hitler, would Eden's succession in 1937 have prevented war? One cannot be certain, but Eden, as a product, like Macmillan, of the First World War, at least would have rejected appeasement, as he tried to resist Chamberlain's pathetic approaches to Mussolini. He would have insisted on rearmament, when there was still just time for it to be effective, instead of leaving it, as did Baldwin and Chamberlain, to the last minute of the last hour.

Eden's period at the Foreign Office under Chamberlain ended when Chamberlain rejected Roosevelt's initiative without even consulting Eden, and when Chamberlain insisted on communicating direct with Mussolini, bypassing the Foreign Secretary and the Foreign Office on the ground that he knew that Eden would have disapproved.

Eden had the courage with Churchill to call, in the last desperate months after Munich, for a preventive alliance with Russia.

He was called back into the ministry by Chamberlain as Dominions Secretary in the 'phoney war' period; then under Churchill he had what looked like being a key post as War Secretary in wartime. But in no time he was Foreign Secretary, and held that position from 1940 to 1945. From 1942, despite his lack of seniority in a Parliamentary sense, he was also Leader of the House of Commons. Churchill at least was grooming him for the succession to the premiership, though of course from 1945 to 1951 Labour was in Government.

He again became Churchill's Foreign Minister for three and a half years in 1951–5, and Churchill, since this was peacetime, was prepared to leave more to his discretion than either Chamberlain before Churchill, or Macmillan after him would have been prepared to do. He had already been ill at the time of the election, and illness dogged him through much of his last period at the Foreign Office. He had his serious bile-duct operation in 1953, from which he never seemed fully to recover. Indeed Churchill, who was senior by twenty-three years, began to have doubts about Eden's physical staying-power. This was a further tragedy. Churchill had begun the grooming process nearly twenty years after Baldwin should have begun it. Nevertheless Churchill still wanted Eden. Churchill might himself have gone in 1953, when he was himself seriously ill, but waited, giving Eden time to complete his recovery.

Eden had a jealous temperament. In some circumstances this can be the mark of the second-rate man seeking to assert himself. Not so Eden. With him it was, rather, concern for the job and for protecting the rights of that job. That was what had been at stake in his break with Chamberlain. So it was now.

Eden was probably oversensitive to a press attack on his attitude to the Middle East. Accused of softness to the Egyptians, he perhaps overreacted. But he was ill. When, for some reason, King Hussein of Jordan dismissed Glubb Pasha, British mastermind of the Arab Legion, Eden reacted strongly again. Seeing Nasser, rightly, as a man who was trying to coalesce the Arab

States against the West, he began to equate him almost with Hitler. The tragedy was that he had not been given his head against Hitler. It was a matter for regret, too, that he never had the opportunity to show what he could do on the home front. He had never been given the Treasury, or Labour or Housing. He was pitched into the top job at a time when he and Macmillan, neither of them holding the Foreign Office, were jostling for the post of *de facto* Foreign Secretary and hammer of the Egyptians. He was in charge of Suez, not the mastermind. He was its scapegoat. But by that time illness was taking its toll.

The pity was not only that he did not serve the rounds of the home departments, but that he never had time to enjoy Parliament, though his period as Leader of the House in the war showed his Parliamentary potentialities. He had so little time to meet his fellows, of all parties, in smoke-room or tea-room.

In his retirement there were many of all parties who had reason to be grateful for his friendship and courtesy. I for one, shall not forget that in 1976, though he was desperately ill and forbidden by his doctor to go to Windsor for the annual Garter ceremony, he wrote to me that though he could not be there all day and would have to miss the Investiture ceremony, he would be there for lunch, and for the Installation in St George's Chapel.

He deserves a more serious biography than he has so far had. His own autobiography, *Full Circle*, covers only his post-war period at the Foreign Office and his premiership. Whatever its length it will not be more perceptive than Lord Blake's obituary tribute in the *Sunday Times*, which expressed the quality of classical tragedy which was Anthony Eden's life and final years:

> If Aristotle was right in describing the tragic hero as the man who 'in enjoyment of great reputation and prosperity' brings disaster 'not by vice and depravity but by some great error', then surely Eden was a hero in Greek tragedy if ever there was one in real life. Whatever his health, he could not long have politically survived this débâcle. It was left to Macmillan to achieve the silent transition from grandeur, masking, by a display of political legerdemain unequalled since Disraeli, a process which would have been insufferable if transacted in the naked light of day. When he quitted the scene six years later we had moved into a different world. Suez was almost as remote as Crimea.

Anthony Eden in 1935.

12

Harold Macmillan

DURING THE 1956 CONSERVATIVE CONFERENCE a Conservative newspaper began its review of the economic debate, addressed by the Chancellor of the Exchequer, by saying that we then heard Harold Macmillan doing an impersonation of an elder statesman, or rather Harold Macmillan doing an impersonation of an actor doing an elder statesman.

That he is a poseur cannot be denied, indeed he would be the last to do so. No Prime Minister can compete with him in this regard, except Disraeli, who had largely ended his posing before he became Prime Minister. In my *Times* review of the sixth and final volume of Macmillan's memoirs, I said:

> Those of us were wrong who regarded him as a 'Premier Ministre fainéant'. He was utterly hard-working, even discounting the long hours he must have spent recording the events of each day for posterity and the time he spent on detailed and perceptive letters to Buckingham Palace. As I wrote two years ago, Macmillan's role as a poseur was itself a pose.

A patrician in a non-patrician age, a dedicated professional who gave the impression of effortless government, one of the most articulate of Britain's Premiers, he was one who regarded the premiership as a source of continuous enjoyment.

He was a Disraelian, perhaps the last Disraelian Prime Minister Britain will see. It is a fact that on the relatively few occasions during his premiership that he visited Chequers for relaxation, as opposed to the convening of an international conference – he preferred Birch Grove – he would be driven out to Hughenden, to refresh himself, to seek inspiration and communion.

He would not disagree with this assessment. When the question of his successor came up he records: 'I personally favoured either Hailsham or Macleod, preferably the former, for I felt that these two were the men of real genius in the Party, who were the true inheritors of the Disraeli tradition of Tory radicalism . . .' Macleod, certainly: he was of a later political generation, post-war, the young Tory Central Office entrants recruited by R.A. Butler after the election defeat of 1945, of whom Macleod, Maudling and Powell were to become members of the Cabinets of the 1950s. Hailsham, if a Disraelian, belonged to a somewhat older generation, one steeped in the legends of the older Hailsham generation, and nurtured at the Bar.

Macmillan had what Disraeli had, a profound sense of history. It is not impossible, but it is difficult for a Prime Minister to fulfil his duties without that sense. This was Macmillan's strength, even if it became perverted over Suez.

Macmillan's reference to 'Tory radicalism' struck a chord in the history of his party. Most of the great Tory Prime Ministers were radicals, apart from Salisbury: Peel, Disraeli himself, Churchill and Macmillan. Heath was a radical certainly, but in a modern management sense. Macmillan could have used the phrase 'Tory democrat', for such he was; we have seen the young Churchill's search for a phrase which would identify Toryism with a liberal approach. But whereas Disraeli, and Churchill, sought for an alliance between the old Toryism of the shires and the newly emergent radical manufacturers, Macmillan's Tory democracy was based on those he came to know and love in Stockton, the workers – and, in the years he represented Stockton, the unemployed. Like Disraeli he sought allies in the workers.

Descended from a successful Scottish emigrant who set up a thriving publishing empire in London, he was nevertheless Whig by tradition. In his

Opposite Under Macmillan's leadership the Conservative Party still retained its 'grouse moor' image.

Harold Macmillan at the age of eleven.

last book, *The Past Masters*, he has a nostalgic chapter on 'The Whig Tradition'. Immediately after his war service in the trenches of the First World War, he was appointed ADC to the Governor-General of Canada, the Duke of Devonshire, whose daughter, Lady Dorothy, he married. Not a Whig by birth, he became one of the Hartington dynasty which had broken with Gladstone on Home Rule for Ireland. Before acceding to the dukedom, Macmillan reminds us, Hartington was to stand for West Derbyshire as a 'Liberal anti-Gladstonian'; his younger brother standing as a Liberal candidate in 1906. In *The Past Masters* Macmillan emphasizes the importance of the old Whig families in the Cabinets of the 1870s and 1880s. In Gladstone's first Cabinet of fifteen members, he points out, there were Hatherley, de Grey (Later Ripon), Kimberley, Clarendon, Granville, Argyll and Hartington, 'Whigs, and grand Whigs' – the only radical was Bright. Gladstone's 1880 Cabinet included Argyll, Spencer, Harcourt, Granville, Kimberley and Hartington, the only radicals being Bright and Chamberlain. It was the 'Hawarden kite', he recalled, Herbert Gladstone's leak of his father's conversion to Home Rule, which offended 'the graver Whigs': 'The announcement was like a flash of lightning, over went the Whigs as it might have split an ancient oak in one of their great parks.'

This was Macmillan writing in 1975; it is quoted to show his links with the patrician past. He remained at least a Whig manqué throughout his career; his speeches even in the Fifties and Sixties still held out the elegant charms of the last enchantments of the nineteenth century, even on occasion of the eighteenth.

Yet the young Macmillan came into politics as a rebel. His searing First World War experience, where so many of his generation had been destroyed, and his reaction against the post-war politicians who had condemned his Stockton constituents to unemployment, made him a new latterday Tory democrat, one of a small new generation dismissed by the hard-faced members of his Party as 'the YMCA'. His earlier experiences could well have led him to cross the floor of the House, as Churchill did, twice, had he not looked across that great divide at the Parliamentary Labour Party of those days, and decided there was nowhere to cross to.

In the 1930s he was one of the very few who identified himself with Churchill when on any calculation of early political advantage this was totally unprofitable. In 1936 he was a lone Tory in the Lobby opposing the ending of sanctions which had been imposed against Mussolini's rape of Italy. He supported the Master of Balliol, A.D. Lindsay, in the Oxford by-election against the official Tory candidate, Quintin Hogg, and resigned the Conservative Whip. As we have seen he and Bracken were the only Conservatives to go into the Lobby with Churchill in the debate on the rape of Austria.

But for 1940, and Churchill's accession, he would probably have remained a rebellious misfit to the end of his days. But Churchill gave him Cabinet rank (without being a member of the War Cabinet) was Minister–Resident in North Africa, at the time of Eisenhower's military occupation, preparatory to the invasion of Italy and Hitler's soft underbelly in Southern Europe. Losing Stockton in 1945, he was soon back for Bromley, and was in Churchill's 1955 Cabinet as Minister of Housing, achieving the Churchill election target of 300,000 houses in a year. He was speedily to do the rounds of Defence, Foreign Affairs and the Treasury, at the time of Suez, when his record was summarized by me at the time as 'First in, first out'. On Eden's resignation he became Prime Minister

Harold Macmillan was born in London on 10 February 1894, a month before the end of Gladstone's last administration. His father was heir to the successful publishing business founded by Daniel Macmillan; his mother, like Winston Churchill's, was an American, thus providing material, in both cases, for those speeches to Congress: 'If instead of my mother, my father had been an American, I should perhaps...'

His first name – passed on to his son, also a Cabinet Minister and Privy Counsellor – was Maurice, after the Rev. F.D. Maurice, the Christian Socialist, one of Daniel's great friends. Harold Macmillan was never to know poverty. He was educated at an Oxford prep school, at Eton and Balliol. He went straight from Oxford to the King's Royal Rifle Corps in France, and was wounded at Loos in 1915 and at the Somme in 1916, spending a great part of the rest of the war in hospital. He has not to this day forgotten those of his comrades who never returned.

After his service in Ottawa, he entered Parliament in 1923. His maiden speech was on Churchill's Budget in 1925. His YMCA period with Robert Boothby and others was spent mainly in attempting to find a solution for the country's economic stagnation, and the group produced a whole succession of publications, including Macmillan's own *Industry and the State* – and, a still more significant book, *The Middle Way*, in 1928. This was the work, quoted for forty years by radicals of all parties, which described the Stock Exchange as 'a casino'.

Meanwhile he was earning his living in the family business, one of those few Prime Ministers who had a long industrial experience before becoming a senior minister. Publishing is not normally regarded as a manufacturing industry, but there are few industries where the difference between success and bankruptcy so depends on saying 'Yes' or 'No' to one individual venture after another. Among his successful projects was Keynes's *General Theory of Employment, Interest and Money*. The 1936 generation of economic students noticed that, against Macmillan's charge of thirty shillings for each of the two volumes of *Treatise on Money*, of which he was not only publisher but a committed adherent, Macmillan invoked the theory of elasticity of demand by charging only five shillings for the *General Theory*, taking only the smallest profit on a large scale, the doctrine of SPQR – small profits, quick returns.

In the 1930s the emphasis, with Macmillan increasingly under the lonely influence of Churchill, was on foreign affairs, defence, the Hitler threat. As a good Disraelian, Macmillan almost automatically adopted Disraeli's maximum in *Endymion*, which as we have seen praised the mythical Lord Roehampton, who did not care a rap whether the revenue increased or declined, but thought of 'real politics: foreign affairs...' So did Macmillan. In the dangerous Thirties there was little alternative for a serious politician.

As long as the protracted Baldwin–Chamberlain régime persisted, Macmillan had no chance of office, neither did he seek it. Nor, one feels with confidence, would he have accepted office if it had meant accepting the prevailing equivocations on rearmament and appeasement. But it was a lonely role.

He was forty-six when, in wartime, Churchill gave him his first appointment, Parliamentary Secretary to the newly-created Ministry of Supply. He was chairman of the Industrial Capacity Committee – this was where he met Sir Percy Mills, later and unsuccessfully to join his Cabinet. (Conservative ministers, not all of whom know much about engineering and the hard-nosed industries, frequently fall for the first industrialist they meet. Churchill was the same with F.J. Leathers, who became one of the least successful of his ministers – Winston had been, at a time when money was hard to come by, a director of Leathers's firm in South Wales.) In February 1942 Macmillan was still an under-secretary under Salisbury at the Colonial Office. In December of that year he secured promotion to the post in North Africa, which he was to hold until 1945. He was an exile from Westminster, but he had a unique opportunity to work with the future United States President, General Eisenhower, in his capacity as 'virtual Viceroy of the Mediterranean'. He was the political mastermind of the freeing of Greece from both Nazis and Communists. His relations with Eisenhower were to be of historic importance, not least at the time when Macmillan was playing a leading part in the Suez conspiracy after it failed – as it turned out, not to the lasting detriment of Macmillan's political ambitions.

In Churchill's caretaker administration after Labour left the wartime coalition, Macmillan was Secretary of State for Air, but the Government was routed in the 1945 general election, when Stockton went Labour. The following month, Macmillan returned to the House as member for Bromley, which he retained until his retirement from the House in the 1964 election.

He played little part in national politics in the Labour years from 1945 to 1951, though he was close to Churchill in the political regeneration of Europe. Then in 1951 the Conservatives returned to office. Churchill saw in Macmillan the qualities so valuable to any Prime Minister: his adaptability was such that he could play in any position in the field. He became Minister of Housing. The 300,000 houses target was achieved, at great cost to educational and other social development. For six months he was Minister of Defence under an ageing and sick Churchill. On Eden's succession in April 1955, he became Foreign Secretary, and then after a short tenure of the Foreign Office moved to the Treasury in December. 'After a few months learning geography,' he said to me in the smoking-room, 'now I've got to learn arithmetic.' Hugh Gaitskell appointed me 'Shadow' Chancellor the following month, and from that time until Macmillan went to No. 10 in 1957 there was never a dull moment. It was an exciting period. Internal economic problems were compounded by Suez, for which the Chancellor, regardless of his departmental interest in quiet times, had a heavy responsibility. The economic situation was already critical in terms of financial burden on the country. Suez, according to the Shadow Chancellor, was Pelion upon Ossa.

In a strange way it was a happy and stimulating relationship between the Chancellor and his shadow. In those days, even on the Committee stage of the Finance Bill, the House would fill up when the respective party gladiators came to sum up. Today, it is rare to get more than a dozen or so members involved in even key debates on the Committee stage, so busy are MPs on Select Committees and other meetings. (Recently, Macmillan told me that in his view there should be a total ban on all meetings in the Palace of Westminster when Parliament is in session.) After a gladiatorial exchange, each of us illuminating economic problems in personal terms, the Chancellor would pass me a note, usually suggesting a drink in the smoking-room, occasionally congratulating me on my attack on him, sometimes asking a question about how the speech was prepared – 'Do you have a discard box?' – a reference, I discovered, to his custom on preparing a speech, when a favoured idea or phrase seemed inappropriate, of putting the rejected item in a box for use on a subsequent occasion.

Harold Macmillan at his wedding to Lady Dorothy Cavendish, daughter of the Duke of Devonshire in April 1920.

Of such is the camaraderie of the House of Commons at its best: it does not mean a betrayal on either side of deeply held principles, but it does mean that their expression need not destroy personal friendship. Would that this spirit still animated our Parliamentary debates! Even during the debates on Suez, when feelings ran high, the exchanges, deeply sincere on both sides, did not reach the point where Parliament became unworkable.

In July 1956, President Nasser of Egypt announced the nationalization of the Suez Canal, which had been controlled by an international consortium since long before Disraeli's purchase of the Khedive's minority shareholding ninety years earlier. For Eden, already more sick than was generally recognized, this was a challenge. He had been frustrated by the complacent régimes of Baldwin and Chamberlain when Hitler rose to power unchallenged. To him Nasser was a Middle Eastern Hitler. Appease him and disaster would follow. Up to a point he was right, but his response was ill-considered. Backed by Macmillan, he sought for means to destroy Nasser. He could not get the American backing he needed to frustrate the nationalization process. It did not help that the convoluted John Foster Dulles was Secretary of State, and that it was the year of the presidential election.

Macmillan's cool judgment might well have led him to counsel restraint. His sense of history, which included a deep understanding of nationalism, deserted him. He and Eden feared the emergence of an alliance of Arab states, under Nasser's leadership. In Volume IV of his memoirs, published fifteen years later, Macmillan says:

> The unanimous view of my colleagues was in favour of strong and resolute action... it was clear that Nasser was determined to throw his weight in favour of revolution and Arab expansion with the help of Communist intrigue and supported by Communist money and arms. With a jealous eye on the oil-bearing countries, he was determined to pursue an aggressive policy on lines of which we had only too recent and too painful experience.

Hugh Gaitskell was a committed friend of Israel, as were others of us in the Shadow Cabinet. His deputy-leader, George Brown, was an equally committed pro-Arab. It was only after long private discussions between them that Gaitskell told us that George had finally, with reluctance, come to accept the existence of Israel as a sovereign State. He was clearly unhappy about Gaitskell's pronouncement, but when it was Israel which attacked in the Canal Zone three months later, he claimed the right to insist that his leader should, despite his pro-Israeli views, condemn the aggression. This Gaitskell did with commendable resolution, leading the Party in the nationwide 'Law not War' campaign against the Conservative Government.

The Government's attack on nationalization of the Canal was fought on two fronts. The minor campaign sought to maintain that without the experienced pilots employed by the Suez Canal Company, every vessel would be piled up on the shore. This proved quite untrue. The major campaign was based on the destruction of Nasser.

A senior Conservative MP of great experience and close Government contacts mentioned to me when we were appearing on a Brains Trust that the Cabinet was seeking grounds, unrelated to the seizure of the Canal, to intervene and destroy Nasser. What they were determined to achieve was a pretext to get rid of him. Macmillan, it was understood, was chairman of the 'Pretext Committee' of the Cabinet. A further Nasserite adventure might have provided the excuse. As he unhelpfully failed so to act, another ploy must be invoked. The Foreign Office Establishment, in common with the Tory Cabinet, was hardly pro-Israeli. But Israel was the enemy of Egypt, and threatened by Nasser: one must not be too squeamish.

On the use of the Canal, Britain took the lead in seeking to unite the maritime nations, ultimately producing the somewhat ludicrous Suez Canal Users' Association (SCUA), a kind of international seafaring consumers' cooperative society, which it soon became clear was not going to pay any divi. The Egyptians refused to have any truck with it. Menzies, Prime Minister of Australia, gave full support to Eden's Government, but President Eisenhower – in the last weeks before the campaign for his re-election to the White House – was noticeably cool. On 4 September he made clear that America would not join those who were seeking a solution by force:

> For ourselves, we are determined to exhaust every possible, every feasible method of peaceful settlement... and we believe it can be done, and I am not going to comment on what other people are doing. I am very hopeful that this particular proposal [the maritime cooperative] will be accepted but, in any event, not to give up, even if we do run into other obstacles.
>
> We are committed to a peaceful settlement of this dispute, *nothing else* [Macmillan's italics].

Picking up a remark of Menzies, that American statesmen are often fond of answering an awkward question by 'no comment', Macmillan records that that would have been enough. No doors would have been closed; Nasser would have been kept guessing.

Selwyn Lloyd, the Foreign Secretary, pushed on with SCUA, but he was an operator, not a principal, in the war planning masterminded by Macmillan and Eden. The French, whose Government was unusually led by a Socialist, Guy Mollet, were fully committed to the same approach as the British, and he and his Foreign Minister, Pineau, were in the whole of the plotting, up to the neck. Macmillan asked Mollet to use his influence to bring Gaitskell into line; Mollet agreed to try but told Macmillan that it was the Conservatives in Britain who were the real Socialists, Labour were old-fashioned Liberals.

There was a sequel, nine years afterwards. Mollet and Pineau attended a Socialist leaders' conference at Chequers. New revelations had appeared in London about the real facts of the Suez invasion, and I got into a constructive discussion with Pineau, to see how much he would reveal. Mollet saw us together, took his colleague by the arm and firmly led him away. But Chequers was to provide further evidence. When Anthony Nutting, who had been a Foreign Office Minister at the time and resigned, produced his own book on Suez, he described the Villacoublay meeting, and a subsequent visit to Chequers by a high-ranking Israeli officer. Checking the entries in the Chequers guestbook, going back fifty years, there appeared to have been interference with one of the signatures. In the Long Gallery there is a powerful electrically-lit magnifier for visitors to use when examining a ring worn for years by Queen Elizabeth I, and taken by a courier – who became the first Earl of Home for his services – to prove to James VI of Scotland that she was really dead and he could come to claim the throne. This instrument showed clearly that a name had been excised, probably by a razor blade.

Macmillan's own account of the events, in which he was one of the prime movers, which led to the Anglo-French invasion of Egypt is blandly disingenuous and unrevealing. There is no reference to 'Operation Musketeer', which was the code-name adopted by the plotting powers. Eden and he, and a much more reluctant Selwyn Lloyd, with Mollet and Pineau, were engaged in a total conspiracy to create a situation where the two powers could attack Egypt and destroy Nasser, a conspiracy, too, to mislead America and, no less, the House of Commons. In the end, as we now know from General Dayan's *Story of my Life* (1976), they deceived Israel and forced them into a humiliating withdrawal. Dayan put the seal on revelations set out in an authoritative book by Professor Hugh Thomas, *The Suez Affair*, published in 1966, and Anthony Nutting's blow-by-blow account, *No End of a Lesson*, published in 1967.

The Israelis were taken for a ride. Britain and France were not intervening as their allies, not even as co-belligerents. In September the plans for 'Operation Musketeer', later 'Operation Musketeer Revised', later 'Operation Musketeer Revised A', were drawn up. In October, D-Day was put back from the 8th to the 20th, and again deferred. Macmillan had been to the United States, where his hopes of moving the administration were disappointed: his meeting with Humphrey, the Secretary for the Treasury, was a disappointment – Humphrey only wanted to discuss finance with the Chancellor. On his return, it is said, worried by the temporizing, Macmillan threatened to resign if, assuming the UN failed to accept the British demands, force was not used. Eden was ill, and his bile trouble flared up, creating a temperature of 105–106 degrees. The Defence Minister, Walter Monckton, resigned, ostensibly on health grounds but really because he disagreed with the invasion plans. Selwyn Lloyd was trying to find a peaceful solution, encouraging Pineau to negotiate with the Egyptian Foreign Minister, Fawzi. Throughout October, the plans were developed and refined.

Advancing the agreed date, Eden and Lloyd went to Paris to meet the French. Eden accepted Mollet's pressure, Lloyd was desperately worried. 'Musketeer Revised A' became 'Musketeer Revised B'. D-Day was fixed for early November. American Intelligence knew all about the plans, but hoped that at least the British and French would have the courtesy to wait until after the presidential election. Mollet and Ben Gurion, the Israeli Prime Minister, met at Sèvres. They were joined by the 'responsible British minister', identity not disclosed, but said to be an 'old-fashioned family lawyer'. It was, in fact, a still unhappy Selwyn Lloyd. The plan was for Israel to attack Egypt, and then for Britain and France to appeal for a ceasefire and intervene in the Isthmus. (All present swore that they would not in their lifetimes reveal what had happened at Sèvres. History caught up with them.)

Dayan's memoirs have revealed the duplicity. At the meeting in France on 1 October, there was still doubt whether Britain would join in; yet her bombers, a component in which France was deficient, were essential for the operation. A second meeting took place in Paris on 21 October. The proposal put to the Israelis was that Britain and France would demand that both Egypt and Israel should withdraw from the Canal area; if either refused Britain and France would intervene to keep the Canal open. Selwyn Lloyd arrived later. The proposal put forward was that Israel should attack the Canal Zone, Britain and France would go as policemen, demanding Israel's and Egypt's withdrawal, and would then take over the Canal. It was one of the most cynical international scenarios in history, nor was it revealed to Parliament even after hostilities had begun. An Israeli proposal for a sortie was rejected by Britain. A small-scale encounter would be no good: it must be 'a real act of war' (real enough for Britain to condemn). In the succeeding days the plans were worked out to the day, the hour, the minute.

The Israeli invasion took place on 29 October. The French and British bombed Egyptian airfields on 31 October, aircraft having been moved up over a period of several weeks.

There was a slight miscalculation about the arrival of British troops. In an earlier chapter I recalled how Disraeli's preoccupation with the Isthmus of Suez led to his obtaining Cyprus for use as a base in possible Middle Eastern fighting, particularly if the safety of the Canal was in question. British planning for the Suez War involved the use of Cyprus as a launching pad. Unfortunately the water was not deep enough. The depth, in a virtually tideless sea, had been known to hydrographers for eighty years, since the Congress of Berlin, indeed before. Lord Blake, in his comments on Disraeli's acquisition, says of the Suez operation: 'Because someone had forgotten to make Cyprus a deep water port, British invasion troops had to travel from Malta, 1000 miles and five days away.'

When the fighting began, the House, normally in adjournment for the eve of the Queen's Speech, met in a crisis atmosphere. Gaitskell hammered the Government, though the key issue proved not to be so much a clash between the two front benches and the main parties, as a legal question from a back-bench lawyer, Sydney Silverman, which caused the adjournment of the House. Were we at war? Would the troops have the protection conferred by the Geneva Convention and other international instruments by virtue of being at war? The Foreign Office, the Law Officers of the Crown, had no answer. No, we were not at war: it was a police action; it was 'armed conflict', not war. But the absence of any answer to Silverman added to the feeling of perfidy, illegality, and conspiracy, and fostered the concept of a Government which would not deal honestly with the House.

The national debate proceeded mainly on party lines. Not that all the arguments that could be mounted against the Government were popular in the country. Three months before, while strongly supporting resistance to any use of military force, I had warned the Shadow Cabinet that our stand would not be popular in the country. We should be in a 'pro-Boer' situation, 'pro-Wog this time': I hoped, I told them, that it would not fall to my lot to be smuggled out of Birmingham Town Hall, as Lloyd George had been in the Boer War, disguised as a policeman. In fact, in the 'Law not War' campaign I was allocated the Birmingham Town Hall, but the only problem was the overflow meeting and that of addressing the enthusiastic crowd outside. My view about the rallying of support for the war, however, was confirmed by the by-election at Chester. After a run of pre-Suez by-election reverses for the Government, Chester recorded a more than tolerable result for the Conservatives.

The pro-Arab Foreign Office Minister of State, Anthony Nutting, resigned. There was a scene at No. 10. Macmillan wanted the Press Secretary to inspire attacks on the defecting Nutting. He refused: this was the occasion when a desperately ill Eden, goaded beyond endurance, is said to have thrown an inkwell across the Cabinet table at the Press Secretary. It missed.

The military action ended in humiliation. Britain and France rejected the UN Secretary Dr Hammarskjold's demand for a ceasefire, then gave way to the Canadian Premier Lester Pearson's successful proposal to the UN Assembly that an international force should be sent to ensure an end to the fighting. Israel and Egypt accepted, leaving Britain and France as the only belligerents. Britain's 'pretext' had gone: they could no longer remain there in order to protect the Canal from the belligerent Israelis whom they had set up in the first place.

But pressure was coming also from the United States. From the start Eisenhower had made it clear that as far as military intervention in Suez was concerned, the US were total abstainers. Of all the laws of politics, one which had never been previously questioned is that nothing provocative must be allowed to occur in an allied country in the year leading up to an American presidential election: the law as I enunciated it takes effect from the September Labour Day in the presidential election year minus one. Indeed, in the Sixties and Seventies it was also becoming necessary to lay down a 'safe period' of up to a year preceding the mid-term Congressional elections. The Macmillan–Eden challenge was at its height in election week. Even the tolerant Eisenhower could not forgive that, especially as he had made his position clear from the outset. Still more, the tolerant Eisenhower had an intolerant and internationally dictatorial John Foster Dulles as Secretary of State. Eisenhower won the election, even though the massive Jewish vote had been put at risk. Now even that vote was hostile to Britain, for Israel felt let down. They had been put in the role not of ally, but of one who had been asked to play the role of a burglar so that the British and French policemen could go in and arrest him in order to 'hit the Egyptians over the head in the process'. The bitter comments of Dayan on his treatment by his 'allies' are a measure of his reaction, and that of Israel. Israel were the war criminals: the fellow-conspirators were concerned with American reprisals. Nearly twenty years afterwards, Dayan has made it clear that he and his country were totally let down by Britain and France.

An angry Eisenhower played the financial card. Sterling came under pressure, and sterling was vulnerable. Eden, totally innocent of these arcane financial matters, was shattered. The Chancellor, who had played so major a role in Suez, minuted him, meanwhile preserving a benign neutrality over sterling problems. They were weeks of humiliation, with Eden increasingly ill.

I remember the story of the visit of one of America's most distinguished journalists. He put in a request for an interview with the Prime Minister, not expecting even a reply. He was surprised to receive an invitation to come at once. More than that, the Prime Minister greeted him effusively at the front door. Downing Street rules are strict – the Prime Minister receives a Head of State, a Head of Government, only rarely a Foreign Minister, not even Dr Kissinger. Eden gave the journalist Head of Government status, took him inside and talked of nothing but the need for American finance to stem the run on sterling. The journalist was so taken aback that he asked me to go round to see him – he was staying with a friend of mine – so that he could unburden his surprise. In subsequent years we have had our problems, including OPEC and the IMF, but nothing so humiliating as this.

Eden's illness became worse. It was endemic, but must have been aggravated by what he had been through. He went for a holiday to (James Bond) Ian Fleming's villa in Jamaica. He returned to resign.

The choice of his successor lay between R.A. Butler, senior contender in every sense, and Macmillan. But Butler did not have the killer instinct required to succeed. He was a gentleman to the last. Kingsley Martin, editor of the *New Statesman*, put it well when he said that the Tory Party had been on a binge: in such cases, the next morning, with aching heads and mouths feeling like the bottom of a parrot's cage, the tendency was to turn, not against those who had taken them on the outing, but on the man who had gone along with them and drunk nothing but tomato juice. This was Rab. In the days before the Conservatives, in 1965, adopted a system of electing their leader, the choice was determined by 'consultations' – a system later described by Iain Macleod, after the choice of Alec Douglas-Home, as the 'magic circle'. In this case the rbiters were 'Bobbity' Salisbury, Leader of the Lords, and Kilmuir, Lord :hancellor, who as members of the Upper House were ruled out as candidates. 'he official version is that when the Cabinet met, Salisbury and Kilmuir inter- iewed each minister in turn, and that Salisbury consulted the Party machine the country. If he did, it was a most perfunctory consultation. In fact, Salis- ury had told Macmillan, in advance even of the Cabinet consultation, that he iought it was in the bag for him. Strangely, within weeks of his appointment, Iacmillan felt strong enough to drop Salisbury. Not a dog barked, and Mac- iillan could on that occasion, had he wished, have used the phrase he later sed on the resignation of the entire Treasury team of Thorneycroft, Powell nd Birch – 'a little local difficulty'.

Macmillan, who, as much as anyone, had masterminded Suez, had profited om it by seeing Eden off under the post-Suez financial pressures, had ecured for himself the inheritance. Now he invited the country to rally round) deal with those pressures. As Prime Minister, he never lost control of the 'reasury, which he saw as the means of creating a favourable financial system or winning elections. Had the trade cycle never existed, he would have invented and used it for his electoral purposes. As Chancellor under Churchill, Butler ad begun it. Sixpence off income tax before the election, an emergency Budget fterwards to ward off the resultant crisis by increased indirect taxes to claw ie money back. But whereas Butler was the apprentice, Macmillan was the raftsman. As Chancellor and Prime Minister he played the cycle. In 1958–9, ast tax remissions to stimulate the economy in time for the 'You've never ad it so good' election of 1959. He was right, he had played the cycle, and iw, even ahead of Gaitskell, the further electoral significance of an economic tuation based, not in a cyclical but a secular sense, on the sudden impact f the virtual first introduction to Britain of hire-purchase. He was still at it 1 1962–3. 1961–2 were years of acute depression. On 5 November 1962 – the eve f a number of significant by-elections – the Chancellor, Reggie Maudling, mbarked on a reflationary boom. It was only because of illness that Macmillan 'as not the presiding deity at the election of October 1964.

Macmillan's premiership could almost qualify for the title of Sir Arthur Bry- nt's book *The Age of Elegance*, had the author not used it to describe an earlier eriod of history. He was something of a classical Prime Minister with a strong mphasis on foreign and Commonwealth affairs.

Britain's role in the world had totally changed in the weeks before he went) No. 10. Her last imperial adventure had humiliatingly failed. Britain could ot go it on her own, or even for that matter in alliance with France. She could ot withstand the censure of the United Nations, with a Canadian Prime Iinister in the lead. Still less could she withstand a scowling US President, riefed by an obsessive and complicated Secretary of State, and if she tried isenhower could, almost anonymously, mount financial sanctions which could ring sterling to peril point. The only thing to argue about was how far Suez ontributed to Britain's changed position, how far it registered a decline which ad already occurred. That Britain could no longer impose her will on lesser reeds without the law was manifest, to the world, to a growing number of eople in this country, but to none more than Macmillan. It is to his credit iat he did more than anyone to adjust Britain's role to her circumstances,) seek to change things by influence rather than force. He recognized – and iis is still as true today – that Britain's strength lies above all in the wealth of experience still residing in a race of statesmen, administrators, industrialists, craftsmen, diplomats, traders, exporters and shipowners, and in the vast accumulated knowledge and expertise of the City. None embodied these qualities more than Macmillan himself.

He was quick to read the message from the shambles he had inherited and to a great extent caused. Our task was to restore relations with the United States and Canada, and to share in the destinies of the new Europe which had been created by the Treaty of Rome. As our strength began to recover, as our own confidence, and that of others in us, began to revive, we could, he hoped, take the lead in improving relations between East and West, perhaps be able to revive that Anglo–Soviet conference for which Churchill had postponed his retirement. A lot had happened, including the Soviet Union's own brutal enslavement of Hungary. Time and patience would be required. East–West relations would not be left wholly, or as Macmillan thought mainly, in the hands of the White House and John Foster Dulles. He had the time, the patience, above all the flair and the style. The style was that of the showman, but what would count would be the script – which he would be writing.

In Volume IV of his autobiography he sets out the six problems as he saw them on going as Prime Minister into the Cabinet room.

> The first need was to restore the confidence of the people in their Government and in themselves. The events of the last few months had been a grievous shock both to those who approved and to those who were opposed to the last Government's action. The fact that France and Britain, even acting together, could no longer impose their will was alarming. Never before in history had Western Europe proved so weak. The fact that they had been met by an unnatural combination between Russia and America was almost a portent...
>
> Secondly, there was all the aftermath of Suez. The clearing of the Canal, the indignities which would, no doubt, be imposed on us and which we must struggle to resist. There was the problem of oil and the dangers of fresh interruptions in the flow, and the question of whether, when the Canal was ready for use, the Egyptian authorities would accept sterling in payment or try to demand gold or dollars...
>
> Thirdly, how were we to treat the United States, and to re-establish that alliance which I knew to be essential in the modern world? Nor would it be worth arguing whose fault it was. Somehow, without loss of dignity and as rapidly as possible, our relationships must be restored...
>
> Fourthly, there was the economic situation in getting help from the United States, and the position had unexpectedly improved in other ways. Nevertheless, as I knew from my year in the Treasury and was to learn for the rest of my active life in politics, to maintain the British economy at the right level, between inflation and deflation, balancing correctly between too much and too little growth, was a delicate exercise... It was not a subject to be solved by mathematical formulae, or exact calculation. It was bicycling along a tightrope...
>
> Fifthly, defence. There were lessons to learn from the Suez expedition. The true value of Cyprus had to be re-examined. Still more important, as I knew from my short months as Minister of Defence, a reappraisal of the relative importance of conventional and unconventional weapons had to be made...

Opposite A photograph of Macmillan with Lady Dorothy in Number 10 Downing Street shortly after he had succeeded Sir Anthony Eden as Prime Minister in 1957.

> Finally, there was the future of the Commonwealth. In the Suez crisis, so far as I could judge, the old Commonwealth countries had stood splendidly firm with loyalty and understanding. India, in spite of her natural dislike of force as an instrument of policy, had shown sympathy and good sense. So had Pakistan and Ceylon. There would have to be a meeting of Commonwealth Prime Ministers in the next few months, and it would need careful handling. But what of the future?...

Referring to the impending independence of Ghana and Malaya, with others to follow he mused:

> This process was bound to continue. Could it be resisted? Or should it be guided as far as possible with fruitful channels? Was I destined to be the remodeller or the liquidator of Empire?

Or was he to take a hand in the remodelling of Europe?

The most immediate problem, as Macmillan had said, was the oil crisis, the closure of the Canal, and the consequence for the balance of payments. The Canal was cleared with surprising speed, and re-opened for traffic in April. But Britain's industry had had serious anxieties about shortages of fuel and feed-stock, and the crisis was surmounted only by recourse to a strict system of petrol rationing, the first in peacetime.

The main problem in diplomacy was to restore relations with the United States. In this, Macmillan personally and speedily succeeded, thanks in part to his personal association with Eisenhower during the North Africa campaign. On Eisenhower's suggestion there was a meeting in Bermuda, only nine weeks after Macmillan became Premier. One of the agreements reached there was that the United States should supply Britain with nuclear missiles. As we shall see this led to a series of heartaches and Parliamentary embarrassments for Macmillan.

Few on either side of the House, recalling the President's anger in the autumn of 1956, could have foreseen Macmillan's success in persuading Eisenhower to come over for an official visit on the eve of the 1959 election, and parade him round London as a prize exhibit to help in the winning of that election, with an increased Parliamentary majority.

Neither could anyone have bettered his establishment of close relations with President Kennedy, after his election in November 1960. Macmillan was quick to establish personal contact, meeting him in March 1961, at Key West, Florida. There were some who wondered what impression would be made on the young, vital President by this example of an older generation, whispering the last distinguished enchantments of the inter-war world. The urgent crisis in Laos played a big part in their first meeting, and confidence was quickly established. Macmillan cleverly built on this by his speedy and inspired appointment as Ambassador to Washington of one of his ministers, Lord Harlech, a long-standing friend of the Kennedys, and a near-contemporary. David Harlech was almost at Kennedy's elbow throughout the Cuba crisis, when the Soviets and the Americans were eyeball to eyeball, and war between the superpowers was nearer than it had been at any time since the war, not excluding the period of the Berlin airlift. It was through David Harlech that Macmillan was able to play a considerable part in advising the President during the most dangerous hours of the crisis, keeping in close contact by telegram and hot-line telephone

Macmillan with Kruschev.

with the White House. Macmillan's memoirs contain no less than forty pages almost exclusively quoting, verbatim, the telegrams exchanged and the transatlantic telephone dialogue.

The close links with the United States led also to the realization of another of Macmillan's cherished objectives, the Nuclear Test Ban treaty, signed on 10 October 1963, two days after he entered hospital as a result of the attack which led to his retirement eight days later.

Macmillan had had a well-published visit to the Soviet Union in February 1959, which went well. It led to the summit meeting in Paris in May 1960, which was broken off when an American U2 spy-plane flew over Soviet soil.

He also took a close interest in Commonwealth relations, one of the challenges he had listed on taking office. He chaired four Commonwealth conferences, in 1957, 1960, 1961 – during the last of which South Africa, facing expulsion for her racial practices, withdrew from the Commonwealth – and 1962. No Prime Minister during his period of office has visited more Commonwealth countries. In early 1958 he visited India, Pakistan, Ceylon, Australia and New Zealand; in 1960, Ghana, Nigeria, Rhodesia and South Africa. On the second tour he immortalized the phrase 'wind of change' (though he did not invent it). When he used it in Ghana it attracted no attention; repeated, appropriately, in South Africa – after his visit to Rhodesia – it was widely taken up.

It was in Macmillan's period of office that the ill-thought-out Federation of Rhodesia and Nyasaland disintegrated. The strains brought about by Dr Banda's election in Nyasaland led to the setting up of the Monckton Commission to review the future of the Federation, which in fact had to be disbanded. It was one of Macmillan's few churlish actions that he refused to accept Gaitskell's nomination of James Callaghan, then Shadow Colonial Secretary, as the Opposition representative, finally excluding him by insisting that all the Commission's members should be Privy Councillors.

In Volume II of *The Prime Ministers*, Duncan Crow sardonically comments: '... in place of a Colonial Empire overseas the British got the Empire in their back garden through immigration.' The big surge in Commonwealth immigration, then legally unrestricted, led to the introduction by the Government of the Commonwealth Immigration Bill, which was fought bitterly in the House, notably by Gaitskell. Macmillan, almost certainly regretting the necessity, gave a lot of his time to this, as he has recorded: any attempt to resist it would have led to a serious clash with his back-benchers.

Defence policy, particularly the question of the independent British nuclear deterrent, another issue he had listed on taking office, presented him with some of his greatest problems, both in overseas negotiations and in Parliament. The Conservative Government, in its decision to go nuclear with its own British deterrent, decided on the Blue Streak Missile. At the time of Macmillan's Moscow visit, no doubt to strengthen his claim to a hearing, evening newspaper headlines ran: 'Blue Streak wins. Britain rejects US Rocket. Now Macmillan will talk from strength.' The US rocket was in fact Polaris, shortly to resurface again. 'Blue Streak is in,' said *The Times*. 'Polaris is out.'

Four years, three defence ministers and £6000 millions later, Polaris was in, after a series of costly reversals of policy. Blue Streak had proved an expensive failure, and was dropped. Harold Watkinson had put his faith and still more defence millions on Skybolt. When I innocently asked in 1962 whether we should get Skybolt, doubts were indignantly repudiated, and the US Government were sent messages asking them to confirm the repudiation. The silence from Washington was deafening. In January 1963, an embarrassed Kennedy told Macmillan that Skybolt was out, and he must have Polaris after all. Labour – George Brown and myself – in a debate on the cancellation of Blue Streak during Gaitskell's absence in Israel, had queried whether Britain would have or could have, an 'independent nuclear deterrent'. George, ever unpredictable, and without warning to his front-bench colleagues, had gone further and said that the cancellation had meant that Britain was now out of the nuclear race, to the great embarrassment of Gaitskell. On no policy issue was Macmillan to be so politically embarrassed, and the Skybolt cancellation occurred when he received three blows within a single month, in January 1963. The second was de Gaulle's veto on British entry into Europe, the third a fresh economic crisis.

Macmillan had answered the question about the Commonwealth versus Europe by manfully seeking to make a reality of the Commonwealth, while soon deciding to apply for entry to the European Common Market, after its formation by the Treaty of Rome in 1957.

His Government approached the question with great thoroughness and a great deal of critical examination. His memoirs, quoting copious extracts from his diary, written at the time, set out the whole record of ministerial and inter-departmental in-fighting, concluding with his decision to put Reginald Maudıg in charge of the negotiations. (His diary, as page after page of his six ·lumes demonstrate, was voluminous; and its verbatim publication in the emoirs reveals a regard for the thirty-year rule and the preservation of ɔnfidentiality between colleagues' equalled only by Crossman, except that .acmillans' was much less subjective and much more accurate. To be fair Macmillan, whether by accident or design, the date of publication of each ·lume, while in each case reducing the period between the event and the velation, unlike Crossman, always exceeds ten years, which perhaps – until ɔrd Radcliffe's Committee in 1975 recommended fifteen years – might have ·en regarded as reasonable.)

Macmillan was right to take the issue seriously and slowly. His Party, the ırty of the Chamberlains and the 1922 general election, included a large pro-ɔrtion of Empire Free Traders, and the powerful agricultural element had ·ep and justified anxieties about what European farm planning might mean. here was an equally strong political feeling about sovereignty and about Euro-ɛan entanglements; many Conservatives would echo Hugh Gaitskell's speech the Labour Party conference at Brighton in October 1962, about 'a thousand ·ars of history'. On the other hand there were many younger Conservative .embers, idealistic, managerial or public relations types, organized industry ıd the City, turning more and more to Europe. Macmillan, here with the ıpport of leading members of the Labour front bench, sought to avoid the ·tificial division of non-Soviet Europe, and in particular to avert what was · become the split between the EEC and the European Free Trade Association, ·TA. 'Plan G', to which he devoted, and in his memoirs devotes, a great deal ˙ attention, was aimed at British association with the new developments in urope. After the shocks of Suez, Europe became more appealing, but Macmil-n was averse to being 'bullied' by the Six, particularly if it meant a parting ˙ the ways with other Western or Northern European associates. He decided · appoint a ministerial coordinator. In a minute to colleagues he wrote:

> One of [the] important duties would be to travel between now and the beginning of the great negotiation. It would be very important to travel both among the Six and among the Eleven. On the whole, it is important to hold firm the Eleven as it is to break into the Six. He should therefore be something of a St Paul: not merely the Jews should be his care.
>
> Now I come to who this Apostolic figure should be . . . I propose Maudling.

Negotiations proved extremely difficult. The Six were not only cohesive, they ·ere doctrinally pure, and refused to join with a wider European Free Trade rea including those less pure. The French, now headed by de Gaulle, after ıe Corsican rising, rejected in terms the kind of loose free trade area which ·ritain and others were proposing.

Finally, in the summer of 1959, the doctrine of the European Trade Associa-ɔn, on lines proposed by Sweden, was accepted by Her Majesty's Govern-ıent, and EFTA (the 'Seven') was agreed in November 1959. Europe was ıvided, but Macmillan was still working, though with less hope, for reconcilia-ɔn, or at least 'harmonization'.

EFTA did not solve the problem. Europe was divided by tariff barriers, and y an almost theological difference between the EEC, which was seeking eco-ɔmic and industrial integration over the whole of their territory, and EFTA, hich very much wanted to remain an 'Association' of States. The United

States, on grounds of broad foreign policy, wanted to see Europe unite, and in particular wanted to see Britain in the EEC. Kennedy pressed this on Macmillan: it would be easier for the US to deal with one group than two; moreover, the pragmatic British would be likely to prevent the EEC becoming too doctrinaire, not only in trade and industrial questions, but on foreign policy.

By July 1961 it was becoming clear that the Government was facing a choice. There was going to be little give and take between the Six and EFTA. The Six would be disciminating more and more against our trade, and against that of the Commonwealth. Macmillan, in a ministerial reshuffle, made Edward Heath Lord Privy Seal, with a special responsibility for European questions. Duncan Sandys, the Commonwealth Secretary, was a founder-member of the European Movement. Macmillan asked him to study, particularly, the effects of British entry on the Commonwealth.

Macmillan begins page 1 of his sixth and final volume with these words:

> On 27 July 1961, the Cabinet agreed that the British Government should make a formal application to accede to the Treaty of Rome. This was a necessary step in order to initiate negotiation for meeting the special needs of the United Kingdom, of the Commonwealth countries and of the other members of the European Free Trade Area. Should these prove successful it was our hope that the Community of the Six could be enlarged to include all, or almost all, the countries of Western Europe.

Sixteen years later the Community includes just two other members of the original EFTA in addition to Britain.

Macmillan's application for EEC membership was very similar to that of the Labour Government rather more than six years later: only by formally entering into negotiations could the terms be known, and then accepted or rejected. He was saying, as Labour was to say in the late Sixties, and again in the period of renegotiations from 1974 to 1975, 'it all depends on the terms', and in all three periods the interests of the Commonwealth were put high on the list. (In May 1975, after the Government had recommended entry, and the national referendum was being organized, the Commonwealth Conference at Jamaica, on its own initiative, surprised Britain by tabling a paragraph to the communiqué, expressing the hope that Britain would be in, on the terms newly renegotiated.)

Macmillan in 1961 put the Commonwealth case very forcibly:

> The maintenance of unrestricted and duty-free entry of New Zealand's products into the United Kingdom was absolutely vital... the possible damage that might be inflicted on British agriculture and Commonwealth trade was a question of vital importance. Much would therefore depend upon the issue of any negotiations...
>
> We must persuade the Six of the value of the Commonwealth to the Free World, and the meeting (of Commonwealth Leaders) concurred in the belief that neither the Commonwealth countries nor British public opinion would accept that Commonwealth interests should only be safeguarded during the transitional period...

It should be noted that the terms negotiated in 1972 did not approach anywhere near these conditions, though some improvement was reached in the renegotiations of 1974–5, de Gaulle having gone.

A year later, the negotiations were going badly. Five members of the EEC wanted Britain in; France did not. De Gaulle put every conceivable difficulty in Britain's way. In December 1962, Macmillan visited him at the Elysée. As always he was courteous, punctilious, but yielding nothing. He just stressed the difficulties without pronouncing a final verdict.

That verdict came, as did a similar one five years later, at a presidential press conference on 14 January 1963, with his pronouncement against any enlargement. Angry with Britain for her nuclear deal with the United States, he expressed his fear that Europe would be dominated by an Atlantic community led by America, though had there been no nuclear agreement his decision would almost certainly have been the same. The real reason was trailed by the French Minister of Agriculture in a conversation with Christopher Soames:

> *Mon cher. C'est tres simple. Maintenant, avec les six, il y a cinq poules et un coq. Si vous joignez (avec autres pays) il y aura peut-être sept ou huit poules. Mais il y aura deux coqs. Alors – ce n'est pas aussi agréable.*

So within a few days Macmillan had suffered the Skybolt blow, and now the veto. At the same time he was facing a censure motion on the rise in unemployment.

He had to face three bitter debates in January and early February. Hugh Gaitskell had died, and the Shadow Cabinet agreed that the three candidates for the leadership of the Labour Party, George Brown, James Callaghan and myself, should each lead in one of the debates.

The economic debate, where James Callaghan, then Shadow Chancellor, spoke, was a sad reflection on Macmillan's hopes for an improvement in the economic situation. Unemployment was almost at the highest level since the

Macmillan addressing a meeting in Clapham during his campaign for the 1959 General Election.

war (apart from a few weeks during the fuel crisis of 1947), though not so high as at the time of writing.

Macmillan had rightly underlined the problem of finding the right path between unemployment and inflation. The economic picture Britain presented was a curious one. There was undoubtedly growing debility and lack of competitiveness. Investment in the key sectors of manufacturing industry, especially for export, was languishing, and the movements in the trade cycle were growing shorter. Each period of expansion ended in a shuddering halt, as a combination of inflation and capacity shortage led to increased imports and falling exports.

Yet living standards were rising. Cyclical revival apart, the hire-purchase boom was bringing new products, refrigerators, TV sets, washing machines, cars, motorcycles, into more and more homes. Macmillan capitalized on it with his cynical phrase 'You've never had it so good.' He was criticized for it, though it had a ring of truth. That people *believed* it was why he so resoundingly won the 1959 general election. When he was later elected, to his great delight, Chancellor of the University of Oxford, it was a pleasure, in the Parliamentary setting, for one to congratulate him with the words '*Nunquam id habuisti tam bonum*'.

By 1961, the election boom had produced a worsening slump and growing disenchantment. The country was going through one of its periodic periods of strongly pressed wage demands. In September, the Cabinet decided to stand firm on pay claims by the civil service. A pay-pause policy was introduced. Selwyn Lloyd, Chancellor of the Exchequer, set up the National Economic Development Council ('NEDDY'), consisting of Government and both sides of industry. It has lasted to this day, and year by year under successive Governments has increased in influence and authority.

By the late months of 1961, party disenchantment and criticism caused Macmillan to move Macleod, who had been a distinguished Colonial Secretary, to the chairmanship of the Conservative Party, a post within the Leader's gift.

By-elections continued to go badly, particularly Orpington, where a traditionally safe Conservative seat swung violently to the Liberals. The Conservatives lost their deposit in West Lothian. Then came the North-East Leicester by-election, on 12 July 1962, with a calamitous result for the Conservatives. There was also dissatisfaction with Selwyn Lloyd's conduct of affairs at the Treasury. Macmillan panicked, and dropped a third of his Cabinet – 'the wrong third' we used to say in subsequent elections. Selwyn Lloyd, Kilmuir, Watkinson, Mills, Maclay and Charles Hill all went: Eccles resigned, refusing a move to the Board of Trade. Reginald Maudling became Chancellor.

On 5 November, in a week of by-elections which again went badly for the Government, he announced a spectacular list of tax reductions, hire-purchase easements, accelerated depreciation allowances, following upon a programme of repayment of 'post-war credits', a wartime compulsory saving levy. Clearly the way was being prepared once again for the general election which would have to come in less than two years at the outside. The appointment of Lord Hailsham as 'Minister for the North-East' was widely regarded as a gimmick, particularly when he toured his new province in a cloth cap.

Chapter 13 of Macmillan's last volume is called 'Security and Scandal'. It is an unhappy story, from 1961 to 1963, of 'security' crises, the 'Portland' case, involving espionage at the highly secret Underwater Weapons Establishment; George Blake, a member of the security services had been regularly shopping colleagues to the Soviets. A top-level inquiry was set up under a Law Lord, Lord Radcliffe. In September 1962 the Vassall case broke; a Judicial Tribunal was set up under the 1921 Act to inquire into further and unfounded allegations. A journalist was imprisoned for refusing to disclose his source. Macmillan blames the sensationalism by the press about the Profumo case on their anger at the journalist's committal to prison in the Vassall case. The defection of Philby – who had tipped off Burgess and Maclean – then followed. In the spring of 1963, the Profumo case hit the headlines, after being raised in the House by George Wigg and Barbara Castle. Its main press interest was an affair between a minister and a call girl, but there were strong suggestions of security overtones. The surprising thing was that Macmillan had known nothing about it when there had been talk for months. In no time, he came to be seen as distant, remote, uncaring, almost a fuddy-duddy. An inquiry was set up under Lord Denning, which dismissed most of the wild rumours of other scandals, but which was critical of the judgment of the group of ministers who had been asked to interview Profumo. It was an unhappy summer, most of all for Macmillan. Worst of all was to hear a former Secretary of State, Nigel Birch, who had resigned with two other Treasury ministers over Government expenditure, quote Browning in relation to Macmillan: 'It will never be confident glad morning again.'

Nor was it.

There was growing pressure for Macmillan to resign. He was nearing sixty-nine, and had had one of the hardest stints a Prime Minister could have. He had had great success, then his luck had turned. Was the old maestro losing his grip? Parliament is a cruel place.

Macmillan has told us the full story of his resignation. He had decided that he would either go quickly in the autumn of 1963, or stay and see the Party through the election, perhaps a year later. He was to meet the Cabinet, which was then about to leave for Blackpool for the Party conference. The previous evening he took a clear decision to stay on. There was to be no question of a postponed departure in the New Year. That very night, before Cabinet the following day, he was taken seriously ill. After treatment he attended Cabinet, and at noon stopped discussion on the items on the agenda. He announced his plan to continue and then left the Cabinet to discuss the question freely in his absence. The Chief Whip told him that the Cabinet had endorsed his staying on, with only one dissenter. Meanwhile, specialist medical examination led to his being sent to hospital for an operation to remove a tumour, which he was told might or might not be malignant. A message was sent to Blackpool saying that while he had previously decided to stay on and fight the election, he now had to resign.

The Conservative Party at that time had no machinery for electing a leader. The new man had to emerge – and the process began at Blackpool, in the full glare of press and television publicity, not only on the platform but in the fringe meetings, the corridors of the Imperial Hotel, and outside the bedrooms of the principal candidates and kingmakers. In the event it was Lord Home who 'emerged', relinquishing his peerage (under a procedure for which he had to thank Lord Stansgate, Anthony Wedgwood Benn). Iain Macleod, who refused to serve under him, wrote his famous *Spectator* article on the 'magic circle', and William Rees-Mogg wrote in the *Sunday Times* that the Conservatives had 'ceased to be gentlemen without becoming democrats'.

The long Macmillan tenure of 10 Downing Street had been a fascinating premiership. His opponents enjoyed his consummate style as much as did his friends. But behind that public nonchalance was the real professional.

The Times headed my review of his final volume 'Edwardian grandeur and a sense of history'. He brought the style of the Edwardian Age – but of other ages, too, including that of the great Whig families – to the study of nuclear technology and nuclear disarmament. He was a consummate Parliamentarian, with a great sense of timing. Whenever he was about to bring about a telling remark he kicked the front of the table below the dispatch-box. If he was winding up a controversial, perhaps noisy debate, he would spend twenty or twenty-five minutes of the final half-hour making serious points, sometimes consciously boring the House. A few minutes before 10 o'clock he would looked pained and say that he had not expected the Leader of the Opposition to treat so serious a subject in a controversial, indeed, he might say, partisan manner, but since he had done so, it was necessary to reply. He would then take out of his left-hand jacket pocket a carefully typed speech, probably composed the night before.

Few Prime Ministers have worked so hard, and even fewer derived so much enjoyment from it. Few have had so wide-ranging a grip on every aspect of government, or so clear – or so easy – a command over their colleagues. Few rivalled his sense of history, few felt as identified as he was with that history, and of those who did, even fewer savoured the challenges, the tasks and the protocol as much as he did.

POSTSCRIPT

Since Harold Macmillan's retirement, up to the time of writing there have been four Prime Ministers. They are too close to the present day, and as one who has been much involved in the controversies of their premierships I feel it unfitting to assess them, nor can they adequately be assessed until the miasma of day-to-day Parliamentary conflict itself passes into history.

For the record they are:

Alec Douglas-Home 18 October 1963 to 16 October 1964
Harold Wilson 16 October 1964 to 18 June 1970 and 3 March 1974 to 5 April 1976
Edward Heath 18 June 1970 to 3 March 1974
James Callaghan from 5 April 1976.

Acknowledgements

Photographs and illustrations were supplied by or are reproduced by kind permission of the following:

The pictures on pages 39, 63, 210 are reproduced by Gracious Permission of HM the Queen; 242 by kind permission of the Duke of Marlborough; 31 by kind permission of the Earl Mountbatten; 281, 283, 284, 285 by kind permission of the Earl Attlee; 53 by kind permission of the Earl Peel; 145 by kind permission of W. R. P. George; 114, 115, by kind permission of Sir William Gladstone; 139, 140, 165, 166, 169, 170, 173, 175, 188, 255, 269/2 The Baldwin Trust; 288 Elly Beintema; 181 Bewdley Museum; 65, 78–9, 82, 83 The Broadlands Archives; 270 Broadwater Collection; 261, 262, 266, 267, 251, 306, 309, 317 Camera Press; 213, 216, 217, 219, 221, 228, 233 Chamberlain Archives, Birmingham University; 121 Christchurch, Oxford; 17 Controller of Her Majesty's Stationery Office; 36 The Frick Collection, New York; endpapers Guildhall Library, City of London, 280 Haileybury College; 105, 158–9, 161 *Illustrated London News*; 267, 271, 273, 277, 290, 293, 299, 300, 323 Keystone Press Agency; 6–7, 11, 24–5, 31, 34, 41, 43, 44, 60, 64, 69, 74, 99, 102, 107, 118 Mansell Collection; 56, 85, 90–1, 125 Mary Evans Picture Library; 118 Merchant Taylors Company; 19, 21, 48 National Library of Ireland; 12, 14, 28, 33, 35, 39, 61, 287 National Portrait Gallery; 94–5, 96 The National Trust; 127, 130, 131, 132, 133, 142, 146, 149, 153, 189, 192, 194, 197, 199, 204–5, 208, 230–1, 239, 244, 246, 248, 303 Radio Times Hulton Picture Library; 50 Staffordshire County Library; 304 Syndication International. Picture research by Barbara Twigg.

Index